POPULATIONS OF THE MIDDLE EAST AND NORTH AFRICA

POPULATIONS OF THE MIDDLE EAST AND NORTH AFRICA
A Geographical Approach

Edited by
J I Clarke and W B Fisher

Professors of Geography to the University of Durham

APC Africana Publishing Corporation · New York

Published in the United States of America 1972
by Africana Publishing Corporation
101 Fifth Avenue
New York, N.Y. 10003

Library of Congress Catalog Card No. 72-80410

ISBN 0 8419 0125 2

Printed in Great Britain

PREFACE

This volume results partly from a prolonged interest of the editors in population study and in the geography of the Middle East and North Africa, and partly from close contact with many academic colleagues working in these fields, particularly within the University of Durham where there is a flourishing Centre of Middle Eastern and Islamic Studies. The authors of the various chapters, nearly all geographers specializing in different aspects and countries of the region, have been asked to consider the populations of individual countries from a geographical viewpoint, highlighting particular themes such as population distribution, urban patterns, ethnic divisions or pressure on resources. In this way the demographic significance of political units is stressed, as well as the diversity of population patterns and processes within this part of the developing world where there are, nevertheless, many elements of unity.

It is necessary to stress that the quantity and quality of population data vary greatly from country to country; while in some countries censuses were held during the last century, in others no census has ever been held. Inevitably, the availability of data has affected the approaches of authors.

Authors and editors are happy to acknowledge their debt to the skills of cartographers in the Department of Geography, the University of Durham, particularly Mr George Brown and Mr Arthur Corner, and also to Mrs Suzanne Eckford for her careful typing of the text. Thanks are also due to Mr J. W. Murray for preparation of the index.

LIST OF CONTRIBUTORS

G H BLAKE	Lecturer in Geography, University of Durham
B D CLARK	Senior Lecturer in Geography, University of Aberdeen
J I CLARKE	Professor of Geography, University of Durham
J C DEWDNEY	Reader in Geography, University of Durham
M P DRURY	Lecturer in Geography, University of Durham
W B FISHER	Professor of Geography and Principal of the Graduate Society, University of Durham
R G HARTLEY	Imperial Chemical Industries, formerly Demonstrator in Geography, University of Durham
A G HILL	Lecturer in Geography, University of Aberdeen
R I LAWLESS	Documentation Officer, Centre of Middle Eastern and Islamic Studies, University of Durham
R MCGREGOR	Formerly Senior Visiting Fellow, Department of Geography, University of Durham
A B MOUNTJOY	Reader in Geography, Bedford College, University of London
K SUTTON	Lecturer in Geography, University of Manchester

CONTENTS

Preface

Chapter 1
Introduction
J I Clarke

The region under consideration in this volume stretches over 75° of longitude from the shores of the Atlantic in the west to the borders of Pakistan and Afghanistan in the east, and nearly 30° of latitude from the shores of the Black Sea in the north to the Gulf of Aden in the south. It therefore includes some 22 countries of North Africa and South-West Asia, with an estimated total population of 164 million in 1968. The region has no single name, although at one time or another much of it has been termed the Middle East, but as few such definitions have included the whole of North Africa we have called the region 'the Middle East and North Africa'.

The aim of this volume is to depict the patterns of population distribution, migrations, composition and growth within this region and to relate them to the nature of places. This approach to population study is geographical, with an emphasis on area and space. Obviously it is only one way of looking at the populations of the region, and workers in other disciplines would certainly choose other approaches. Nevertheless, they would probably also be conscious of the elements of unity and diversity within the region, and their relevance to developing countries in general. Certainly, the authors of the various chapters in this volume are well aware of these issues.

Problems of data

Unfortunately, population data for the region are far from comprehensive and statistics available often have a low level of reliability (El Badry, 1965). While all the countries of North Africa have a long history of population censuses dating back in the case of Egypt, Algeria and Tunisia to the nineteenth century, and the more northerly countries of South-West Asia have all held censuses since the Second World War, there remain a number of countries in the southern zone of South-West Asia which have never taken a complete census: Lebanon, Yemen, Southern Yemen and Muscat and Oman (Table 1.1). Consequently, in these countries it is not easy to make reasonable estimates of population totals; the total for Yemen, for example, has long been estimated at 5 million with no concession to increase. Moreover, although a census was taken in the former colony of Aden in 1955, no census has been made of the entire country of Southern Yemen. A census has been held recently in the small state of Qatar, but its results have not yet appeared. As for Saudi Arabia, it held a census in 1962–3, but repudiated and refused to publish the results as the number enumerated (3,297,000) was only half the total estimated by the government. In general, the countries with a long record of censuses are those which have experienced European colonization or profound external impact, while those which have never held censuses, or have held them for the first time only recently, are poorer, more isolated and more backward. Lebanon, however, is an obvious exception to this generalization, for there the relative numbers of Christians and Moslems are a sensitive issue which has discouraged enumeration.

TABLE 1.1   POPULATION CENSUSES OF COUNTRIES OF THE MIDDLE EAST
AND NORTH AFRICA SINCE 1945

North Africa	
Egypt (UAR)	1947, 1960, 1966
Morocco	1950 (French), 1950 (Spanish), 1960
Algeria	1948, 1954, 1966
Tunisia	1946, 1956, 1966
Libya	1954, 1964
Spanish North Africa	1950, 1960
South-West Asia	
Turkey	1950, 1955, 1960, 1965
Iran	1956, 1966
Iraq	1947, 1957, 1965
Saudi Arabia	1962–3 (unpublished)
Syria	1952, 1960
Yemen	None
Israel	1948, 1960
Lebanon	None
Jordan	1952, 1961
Southern Yemen	None (but census of Aden colony in 1955)
Cyprus	1946, 1960
Muscat and Oman	None
Kuwait	1957, 1961, 1965
Bahrain	1950, 1959, 1965
Trucial States	1968
Qatar	1970

Enumeration has been particularly defective or absent in countries or districts where nomadic populations are preponderant or large, for apart from the logistic difficulties of taking a census, the fear and suspicion of enumerations is strong, and relevant factors are the prevailing illiteracy, the low status of women, the past imposition of taxes and the existence at

16

times of conscription. Deficiencies in population data are not confined to mere numbers: age and sex data, for example, are usually very irregular, an indication of their inaccuracy, and they must always be checked before analysis. Many other aspects of population structure similarly lack precise enumeration, even in states reasonably well provided with statistics. And for vital statistics the situation is usually worse, because registration of births and deaths is so deficient. Registration is becoming more efficient in some countries, as bureaucratic machinery improves and educational facilities expand, but in general reliable rates cannot be extrapolated from existing registration data, except for Israel.

In these circumstances it might be felt that there are insufficient reliable data for a survey of the populations of the Middle East and North Africa, but in fact by use of a wide variety of sources it is possible to build up a picture of the general features of the populations of the region—their youthfulness, high fertility, high but declining mortality, patchy distribution, increasing urbanization, patterns of migration and so on—as well as to examine the striking diversity from one part of the region to another and from one country to another.

Unity and diversity

Although not a populous region by world standards—it has less than one-quarter as many people as China, less than one-third as many as India, and less than either the United States or the Soviet Union—it offers considerable interest to students of populations, for there are many common elements of unity as well as much diversity (Fisher, 1971). Thus, although the region lies almost entirely within the Moslem World, non-Moslem communities are preponderant in Israel, Lebanon and Cyprus (and religious minorities occur elsewhere), with striking effects upon population dynamics and structure. Moreover, while the region covers much of the Arab World, these three small countries are largely non-Arab, as are the two big northern countries of Turkey and Iran. Similarly, although most of the region experiences the pervasive imprint of aridity, greatly affecting modes of life, especially pastoral nomadism, and reducing levels of population density, there are restricted areas of higher water availability, as in the coastlands of the Black, Caspian and Mediterranean Seas and along the Nile valley, where much more intensive agriculture and denser populations are possible. Another major element of diversity has been the localized impact of modern economy, in particular the oil industry which has brought immense wealth to a few pockets, areally and individually, with striking effects upon migration and natural increase. The traditional areal and social disparities between desert and sown, between nomad and cultivator and between town and country have been supplemented by sharp disparities in economic development within a complex political framework, with states ranging from 30 sq. km. to 1,760,000, from 80,000 inhabitants to 34 million, and from $70 *per capita* GNP to $3,500.

The fragmented political structure of the region is responsible for many of the vivid contrasts, as between Kuwait and Yemen, Israel and Jordan, Egypt and Libya. Although many political boundaries were only conceived and created after the two world wars, their superimposition upon the region has played an increasing role in population dynamics affecting both migration and natural increase. Indeed, they are fast becoming demographic divides. Just as the region offers a veritable laboratory for the comparative study of political modernization, so it also presents a wide variety of demographic conditions. Some countries are emigrant, like Cyprus, Lebanon and Southern Yemen, and some are immigrant, like Israel, Libya and Kuwait, but in general it is becoming more difficult to migrate internationally within the region, so that intra-national migration is more voluminous. It is also evident that wealthier oil-rich states, apart from attracting migrants, are able to effect rapid declines in mortality resulting in higher natural increase. As long as the oil gushes the population problems of these states are few, but it does produce anomalies and jealousies: while sparsely inhabited Libya, benefiting from an oil fever, is able to give family allowances and encourage population growth, neighbouring Tunisia with far more people but only a modicum of petroleum has to favour family planning.

It seems, therefore, that countries are progressing towards an increasing measure of demographic individuality, and it is also evident that, in view of rising nationalism, such demographic problems as occur are likely to find solutions only at a national level. It was with these points in mind that the editors decided on a country-by-country survey rather than a more thematic approach, and authors have been invited to concentrate on themes of particular importance to the countries concerned. In this way it is hoped that both the unity and diversity will be emphasized.

Micro-states and macro-states

Reference has already been made to the immense size variation among states. The five largest states, in terms of population—Turkey, Egypt, Iran, Morocco and Algeria—contain nearly three-quarters of the total population of the Middle East and North Africa, while at the other end of the scale there are a number of micro-states or enclaves like Ifni (returned to Morocco in 1968), Spanish North Africa (known as the *Plazas de Soberanía*), Qatar, Trucial States, Bahrain, Kuwait, Muscat and Oman and Cyprus, each with fewer than one million inhabitants, while several other states (Southern Yemen, Jordan, Lebanon, Israel, Libya and Tunisia) have between one million and five million inhabitants (Table 1.2). This range of state sizes is very important from the point of view of population dynamics, because of the growing influence of political factors upon both migrations and natural increase.

TABLE I.2 POPULATION SIZE, DENSITY AND GROWTH OF THE COUNTRIES OF THE MIDDLE EAST AND NORTH AFRICA

	Estimated population 1968 (thousands)	*Last census*		*Annual increase rate 1963–8*	*Area (thousand sq. km.)*	*Density (per sq. km.)*
		Date	*Population (thousands)*			
North Africa						
Egypt (UAR)	31,680	1966	30,076	2.5	1,001	32
Morocco	14,580	1960	11,626	2.9	445	33
Algeria	12,943	1966	11,833	2.9	2,382	5
Tunisia	4,730	1966	4,533	2.2	164	28
Libya	1,803	1964	1,564	3.7	1,760	1
Spanish N. Africa	162	1960	153	0.9	0.03	5,078
Ifni	54	1960	50	1.1	1.5	36
South-West Asia						
Turkey	33,531	1965	31,391	2.5	781	43
Iran	26,985	1966	25,785	3.0	1,648	16
Iraq	8,634	1965	8,262	2.4	435	20
Saudi Arabia	7,100	1962–3	—	1.7	2,150	3
Syria	5,738	1960	4,565	2.9	185	31
Yemen	5,000	—	—	—	195	26
Israel	2,745	1961	2,183	2.9	21	133
Lebanon	2,580	—	—	2.5	10	248
Jordan	2,102	1961	1,706	3.3	98	22
Southern Yemen	1,195	—	—	2.2	288	4
Cyprus	622	1960	578	1.1	9	67
Muscat and Oman	565	—	—	—	212	3
Kuwait	540	1965	467	6.8	16	34
Bahrain	200	1965	182	3.3	0.6	334
Trucial States	180	1968	180	—	84	2
Qatar	80	1970	—	7.8	22	4

Source: UN Demographic Yearbook, 1968, Table 2.

Small states tend to experience much greater demographic instability than large states although the causes and character of this instability may differ from one country to another. This is a matter of general import as it is associated with a scale-linkage problem, in which conclusions derived from analysis at one scale may not apply at other scales. In these circumstances we should experience quite different demographic conditions in micro-states and macro-states.

In general, large states are relatively little affected by international migration while small states are greatly affected. Essentially this is because the volume of migration to or from a place appears to vary inversely with distance. All of the small countries are known as sources of emigrants or attractions for immigrants. Emigration has long been a relief to population pressure in the Lebanon, which has provided a major emigration stream since 1860, so that people of Lebanese origin abroad now exceed 1½ million and their remittances have helped Lebanon to enjoy a higher *per capita* income than most countries of the Middle East and North Africa. Emigration has also played an important role in Cyprus, Oman, Yemen and Southern Yemen. In contrast, some small states attract powerful immigration streams, particularly the oil-rich Gulf states which are magnets for migrants from all over the Middle East, especially from Palestine and Iran as well as Pakistan. The populations of Kuwait, Bahrain, Qatar and some of the Trucial States have been utterly transformed by immigration, especially as male immigrants greatly outnumber females. Immigrants into Kuwait now outnumber Kuwaitis raising the total population from 206,000 in 1957 to 491,000 in 1966, an annual increase of more than 10 per cent. Moreover, Libya, once a source of emigrants, now attracts many migrants because of its oil riches. However, petroleum is not the only cause of immigration into small states: religion has been the main reason for immigration into Israel and for the exodus of refugees into Jordan, Syria, Lebanon and other states. After the June war of 1967 their number was estimated to have reached about 1.6 million, more people than there are in Southern Yemen and almost as many as in Libya, and a human problem of enormous dimensions which in Arab eyes cannot be solved without a return to Palestine and compensation. Jordan has been torn asunder by the conflict between Jordanians and Palestinians, the latter more numerous than the former.

The smaller states, especially the wealthy ones, are also able to effect more rapid reductions in mortality (Table 1.3), owing to the provision of better medical facilities, improved sanitation and rising standards of living which enable better nutrition and housing. In these circumstances youthful population structures enable very low death rates, which are below seven per thousand in Cyprus, Israel, Kuwait and Spanish North Africa. Further dramatic declines in mortality may be expected in Saudi Arabia, the Gulf states and Libya where oil royalties are available to provide free medical and health services. In larger states, where there are usually more complex ecological systems, cultures and infrastructural problems, the tasks of mortality and morbidity reduction are more difficult.

The situation as regards fertility is different, for here state size seems largely irrelevant, although it so happens that the only countries without high fertility are those where non-Moslem communities are preponderant —Spanish North Africa, Cyprus, Israel and Lebanon—and they are all small. Elsewhere birth rates are of the order of 43–50 per thousand and gross reproduction rates 2.8–3.4, with little sign of fertility decline, although Turkey has adopted a family planning programme—in marked contrast to its earlier policies designed to increase population size.

It follows from the above fertility and mortality conditions that mortality is the main influence upon natural increase, and consequently Moslem micro-states with high fertility and low mortality have the most rapid rates of natural increase, the best example being Kuwait, which has one of the

TABLE 1.3   SOME VITAL RATES OF COUNTRIES OF THE MIDDLE EAST AND
NORTH AFRICA

	Percentage of population under 15	*Birth rate (‰)*	*Death rate (‰)*	*Infant mortality rate (‰)*	*Current percentage rate of population growth*	*Projected population 1985 (millions)*
North Africa						
Egypt (UAR)	43	43	15	117	2.8	52.3
Morocco	46	46	15	149	3.3	26.2
Algeria	47	44	14	—	3.2	23.9
Tunisia	44	45	16	—	3.0	8.3
Libya	44	—	—	—	3.1	3.1
Spanish N. Africa	—	15	6	36	0.9	—
Ifni	—	36	12	53	1.1	—
South-West Asia						
Turkey	44	43	16	155	2.7	52.8
Iran	46	48	18	—	3.0	45.0
Iraq	45	48	15	—	3.4	16.7
Saudi Arabia	—	—	—	—	2.8	12.2
Syria	46	47	15	—	3.3	10.5
Yemen	—	—	—	—	2.8	9.1
Israel	33	26	7	26	2.4	4.0
Lebanon	—	—	—	—	3.0	4.3
Jordan	46	47	16	—	3.3	3.9
Southern Yemen	—	—	—	—	2.8	2.0
Cyprus	35	25	7	28	0.9	0.7
Kuwait	38	47	6	31	8.3	2.4

Source: Population Reference Bureau, Inc., *1970 World Population Data Sheet.*

highest natural increase rates in the world, while non-Moslem micro-states with low fertility and low mortality have much slower rates of natural increase, examples being Spanish North Africa, Israel and Cyprus.

Another important point concerning state size is that small states like Kuwait, Qatar, Bahrain, Trucial States, Israel, Lebanon, Jordan and Spanish North Africa tend to have the highest percentages of urban population, rather than larger countries like Turkey, Iran, Syria and Morocco, which have long traditions of urban life. Of course, some are mere city-states with almost entirely urban populations, and are therefore more comparable with other cities than with other countries: Kuwait offers more demographic comparisons with Riyadh than with Saudi Arabia.

It is therefore extremely important to remember the scale of political units we are considering and our dependency upon population data by political units: only six countries have more people than Greater London, which has, for example, about as many people as Israel, Lebanon and Jordan put together. And Cairo has more inhabitants than the majority of countries in the region. At the other extreme, Turkey, Iran and Egypt are large complex populations occupying substantial areas which have been occupied by man for millennia.

Past instability

One should not give the impression that demographic change is something new to the Middle East and North Africa. In fact, quite the reverse. The position of South-West Asia as a link between Asia, Africa and Europe and the position of North Africa between the Sahara Desert and the Mediterranean Sea have favoured the passage of many peoples bringing ethnic diversity, which has been further supplemented by the rise of Christianity, Judaism, Islam and many lesser religions and sects. The diversity of religious communities within the broad frame of the Moslem World has been encouraged by the social isolation perpetuated by linguistic and cultural barriers as well as by the physical fragmentation of the region, especially in the northern states, and this has fostered particularism and even separatism. One example of such particularism is the mountain-refuge (Planhol, 1962), where heretical or unorthodox peoples sheltered from the Arab Moslem majority. The Lebanese mountains, which were formerly forested, provided shelter for Druzes and Maronites, the Jebel Ansariya in Syria did the same for the Alawi and Ismaili, while in the Maghreb many Berber groups found refuge in mountains. Today mountain-refuges are generally experiencing downhill migration, like Kabylie in Algeria, although the rate of migration depends to some extent on the degree of religious tolerance. While at times in the past religious minorities have enjoyed considerable social and economic freedom in the heart of the Islamic world, their present status is not so fortunate, for religious differences have been intensified by the growth of nationalism. Of course, religious persecutions are not new to the Middle East, as Armenians, Assyrians and Jews will bear witness, but the situation has been further complicated at the present time by the introduction of the concepts of state and territory, concepts alien to Islamic doctrine which has held that Moslem territory was indivisible and inherently expansive. In these circumstances the Jewish state of Israel has been regarded as a particular threat, but religious divisions have also caused severe problems in Cyprus and Lebanon.

Another prominent cause of both political and demographic instability in the region has been the widespread distribution of pastoral nomadism. Existing in many forms from horizontal desert movements to long-range seasonal nomadism and transhumance in the mountains, it is clearly adapted to local conditions of aridity and ecological zonation with altitude, but its distribution also owes much to the medieval movements of Turkish and Arab nomads. Turkish bactrian camels were much more adapted to mountainous conditions than Arab dromedaries, and this fact had a very important influence upon the distribution of Turkish nomads who were consequently attracted to mountains, uplands and cold steppes, in contrast to Arab nomads who came to be localized in plains and hot deserts.

Nomads now constitute small minorities of most states, although their enumeration is usually inferior to that of sedentary peoples. Most nomadic peoples have lost their political power and are undergoing a process of sedentarization (Awad, 1959 and 1962; Barth, 1962; Capot-Rey, 1962), which has a variety of causes including increase in motor transport, decline of caravan traffic, political division of pastures, prohibition of raiding, attraction of work opportunities in industries and towns, and the success of central governments in their age-old struggles with nomadic tribes. It is, of course, in the interest of central governments to encourage sedentarization of nomadic tribes in order to impose a bureaucratic system (which is usually too inflexible to cope with them, because schools, dispensaries, police posts, law courts and so on are easier to establish as fixed rather than mobile phenomena) and to reduce their political danger to the state. So throughout the Middle East and North Africa governments encourage the settlement of tribes, although their policies have differed substantially in degree of authoritarianism: the policy of *fixation au sol* in Tunisia offers a sharp contrast with the Iranian Government's struggles with the Qashqai or the Iraqi Government's treatment of the Kurds.

Some sedentarization is spontaneous, and in the past was partly explicable by the more favourable demographic conditions, especially lower mortality, among nomadic tribes, so that surplus population moved from a nomadic to a settled life—from areas of low population density to areas of high density. However, the relative favourability of demographic conditions has swung in recent years to the settled communities, many of which are enjoying much lower mortality than before, but usually sedentary populations are more capable than nomadic ones of extending their economy to cater for higher natural increase rates. Nomadic peoples still move into villages and towns, but too often only at the lowest levels of sedentary society, so that the sedentarization of nomadic peoples may result in impoverishment and shanty-town dwellings on the fringe of large cities.

Few countries of the region are exempt from the problem of nomadism and its relations with modern society. Whilst relations between nomadic and settled communities were formerly sometimes happy and involved reciprocal trading arrangements, the development of modern states and modern economies has had severe effects upon nomadism, which has all too frequently been regarded as an anachronism for which there can be little or no place. Fortunately, most governments are now making conscious efforts to overcome these difficulties.

Tradition and modernity

The uneasy relations between tradition and modernity are seen everywhere in the developing world, although categorization of the differences as dualistic is often too simple, for generally the introduction of modern elements into a society has a profound impact upon the traditional elements, many of which undergo a rapid transition. In sum, a simplistic division into ancient and modern does not always fit the facts.

Exemplifying the traditions of the Middle East and North Africa is Islam, whose role is extremely pervasive because for most inhabitants of the region it is a way of life (Planhol, 1957). It has provided a code of behaviour for all aspects of life, and, for instance, profoundly influences human fertility. Moslem populations invariably experience higher fertility than neighbouring communities of other religious persuasions (Kirk, 1966), owing to pro-natalist social forces common to the Moslem World, in which marriage of women is early and universal and their subordination general, and matrimony and fecundity are fundamental virtues of the family. Moreover, sexuality is emphasized rather than criticized, while celibacy is abnormal and rare. Some have also considered polygamy a pro-natalist factor in Moslem societies, but there are contrary views, and in any case there is little doubt that polygamy is declining in most countries of the region.

Islamic resistance to family-planning is strong, but this is an aspect of the conservative cultural background which has impeded the diffusion of birth-control in Moslem countries despite the close contacts with Europe. Knowledge of modern methods of birth-control is confined to educated urban minorities, and the practice of birth-control is limited, but there is now evidence from a number of countries to suggest real concern about family size and a desire for its limitation. Faced by rapid population growth and conscious of growing population pressure, the three governments of Egypt, Tunisia and Turkey have encouraged family-planning programmes, which are interpreted particularly in terms of maternal and child health. It is true that the success of these programmes is as yet limited, and that they are dependent upon the success of the spread of education, the prohibition of child labour and the emancipation of women, but the programmes are indicative of changing attitudes and augur more rapid adoption of family-planning in the future (Kirk, 1966).

While the fertility levels of Moslem countries remain traditionally high, and urban fertility differs little from rural fertility, mortality levels are much more expressive of the impact of modernity. Traditionally, mortality was high. Endemic diseases such as malaria, bilharziasis and ankylostomiasis took a persistent toll, while epidemics of cholera, plague, smallpox, typhoid and other diseases ravaged populations from time to time. In addition, periodic droughts and famines, and a long history of warfare, piracy and raiding kept mortality levels high and natural increase low. Fortunately, the twentieth century has brought dramatic changes in the provision of medical and health facilities and considerable improvements in sanitation and standards of living with the result that death rates have been substantially lowered, especially in cities. While cities were formerly the great foci of diseases, their populations now tend to be healthier than rural populations, who enjoy far fewer medical provisions.

One significant result is that, because the urban-rural fertility differential is low and the mortality differential is high, urban centres tend to experience higher natural increase rates than rural areas, and these rates probably generally exceed 3 per cent per annum. As most cities of this region are old rather than recent creations, natural increase accounts for an important part of urban growth. Obviously its importance is less than migration in cities like Amman and Kuwait City, which have undergone rapid growth during the last few decades, but in general natural increase plays a greater role in urban growth than it does in tropical Africa. It also follows that except in cities like Amman and Kuwait City, the sex ratio imbalance is much less blatant, because high proportions of males are usually found in cities experiencing relatively large influxes of young adult migrants.

European impact

The impact of modernity in the Middle East and North Africa has been very much related to the degree of Western influence and penetration, which has been much greater in countries like Morocco, Egypt and Lebanon than in Yemen, Saudi Arabia or Muscat and Oman. Western influence has been greatest in those countries of the Maghreb colonized in large numbers by Europeans. It may be recalled that Algeria was under European rule from 1830 to 1962, Tunisia from 1881 to 1956, Morocco from 1912 to 1956 and Libya from 1911 to 1951, and during this time European colonization effected massive transformations in the Maghreb. Initially, European conquests caused much loss of life, especially in Algeria and Libya, but subsequently European rule introduced medical facilities, enabled a reduction in inter-tribal conflicts and brought about a gradual decline in mortality among the Moslem populations. By the 1950's not only were nearly two million Europeans settled in these four countries of North Africa, as well as considerable armies, but they also occupied substantial proportions of the cultivated land—two-fifths in Algeria, one-fifth in Tunisia, one-fifteenth in French Morocco and one-eighteenth in Libya—especially in the moister zone of Mediterranean climate. This caused regional disharmony within these countries, the steppe and desert zones being largely neglected except where maritime climatic conditions made them propitious for colonization. The steppe and desert zones were controlled rather than developed, and this had an adverse effect upon nomadism, particularly the summer migrations of nomads into the mountains of the Mediterranean zone. However, the European populations of the Maghreb were four-fifths urban and were mostly concentrated in large cities like Casablanca, Algiers, Tunis and Tripoli, where they engaged in service activities connected with the externally-oriented colonial economy.

This feature is much more marked in North Africa than in South-West Asia where Europeans have only colonized in Israel, and where, although the oil industry is externally oriented, agriculture was not transformed in the same way to the requirements of European markets. One result is that port cities are less notable on the map of city distribution (Fig. 1.1) in South-West Asia than in North Africa.

On the other hand, the Maghreb has undergone massive decolonization since the mid-century. During the period 1956–64 the numbers of Europeans in the Maghreb dropped from about 1,900,000 to 420,000 and since then numbers have continued to fall, though much less dramatically. Frenchmen, Italians, Spaniards and Jews have left in droves, leaving North Africans to rule their own countries and largely to run their own economies. The populations of the Maghreb are more homogeneous than ever before, especially as many have found it profitable to return to their own country; the return of Libyans to Libya is an example. Nevertheless, it will be a very long time before the colonial impact upon geographical patterns of the Maghreb is finally erased.

Urbanization

The process of urbanization is one of the most obvious features of the region, especially to the visitor from the West, but it is not easily quantifiable owing to variations in the definitions of urban status, the shortage of data on migration and natural increase, and occasionally the lack of published results of locality size. Definitions of urban status vary so much from country to country that international comparison of official levels of urban population (Table 1.4) has little value:

Definitions of urban population
(Source: *UN Demographic Yearbook*, 1968)

Algeria: Fifty-five most important communes having local self-government.

Bahrain: Towns of Manama, Muharraq (including Muharraq suburbs), Hidd, Jiddhafs, Sitra, Rifa'a and Awali.

Cyprus: Six district towns and Nicosia suburbs.

Iran: All shahrestan centres, regardless of size, and all places of 5,000 or more inhabitants.

Iraq: Resident population in the centre of cities and towns only. Excluding the suburbs whether or not these suburbs form a continuously built-up area with the centres of cities and towns.

Israel: All settlements of more than 2,000 inhabitants, except those where at least one-third of the heads of households, participating in the civilian labour force, earn their living from agriculture.

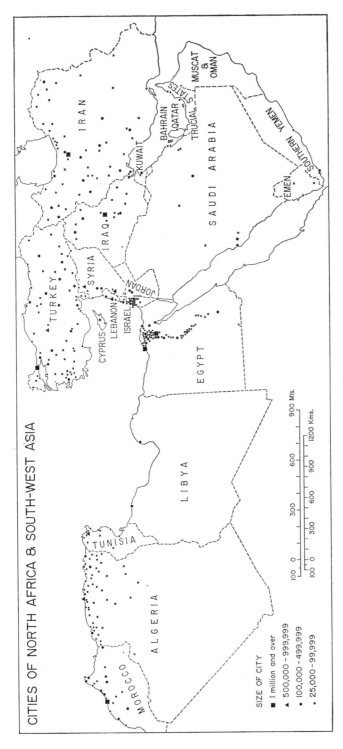

CITIES OF NORTH AFRICA & SOUTH-WEST ASIA

SIZE OF CITY

■ 1 million and over
▲ 500,000 - 999,999
● 100,000 - 499,999
· 25,000 - 99,999

FIGURE 1.1

27

Jordan: District headquarters; localities of 10,000 or more inhabitants (excluding Palestine refugee camps in rural areas) and those localities of 5,000–9,000 inhabitants and the suburbs of Amman and Jerusalem cities in which two-thirds or more of the economically active males are not engaged in agriculture.

Kuwait: Kuwait City (Dasman, Sharq/1, Sharq/2, Murgab, Salihia and Qibla) and Labourers City.

Libya: Total population of Tripoli and Benghazi plus the urban parts of Beida and Derna.

Morocco: 117 urban centres.

Syria: Cities, district (*Mohafaza*) centres and sub-district (*Mantika*) centres.

Tunisia: Population living in the communes.

Turkey: Population of the localities in the municipality limits of administrative centres of provinces and districts.

United Arab Republic: Governorates of Cairo, Alexandria, Port Said, Ismailia, Suez, frontier governorates and capitals of other governorates as well as district (*Markaz*) capitals.

Faced with such a variety of urban definitions, many of which are administrative, it is perhaps more appropriate to utilize locality size data, although mere size of settlement can never be an adequate criterion of urban status, and moreover there is the extra hazard that some censuses publish data of urban agglomerations while others give data only for administrative urban units. The contrast between the two may be striking in some instances: the respective totals for Istanbul in 1965 were 2,052,000 and 1,751,000 and those for Algiers in 1966 were 1,107,000 and 897,000.

Town life is of course very ancient throughout the region. Unlike most of Africa and Latin America, there are profound substrata of urbanism going back thousands of years, despite fluctuations in the numbers of town-dwellers and the occasional abandonment of city sites. The first urban revolution took place here, and the cities of Damascus and Aleppo claim to be the oldest continuously inhabited sites in the world. Most ancient cities were trading centres, the homes of traders who were often absentee landlords, and many were located at the coast or on desert margins (Fig. 1.1). In addition, there were strongholds and religious centres, bases for religious and military conquest. Surrounded by walls, cities tended to be alien elements in the life of the region. To some extent they were parasitic, draining revenues from rural areas, and as traditions of civic pride and responsibility were generally slight they were frequently filthy and fever-ridden.

During this century most cities have grown rapidly through both in-migration and natural increase, and their morphologies have been transformed. Modern suburbs with open layouts have been added, in sharp contrast to the old quarters, and they house the new urban educated *élites*

TABLE 1.4 PERCENTAGE OF POPULATION BY LOCALITY SIZE, MIDDLE EAST AND NORTH AFRICA, AT THE MOST RECENT CENSUS

| | Total population (thousands) | 1 million and over per cent | Locality size | | | | | | | | Urban population per cent |
| | | | 100,000-999,999 | | 50,000-99,000 | | 20,000-49,999 | | 10,000-19,999 | | |
			Per cent	Cum. per cent	Per cent	Cum. per cent	Per cent	Cum. per cent	Per cent	Cum. per cent	
North Africa											
Morocco (1960)	11,626	—	18.9	18.9	2.1	21.0	3.2	24.2	2.7	26.9	29.3
Algeria (1966)	11,833	—	14.3	14.3	8.0	22.3	14.6	36.9	3.0	39.9	33.3
Tunisia (1966)	4,457	—	10.3	10.3	4.0	14.3	9.2	23.5	6.7	30.2	40.1
Libya (1964)	1,564	—	25.5	25.5	—	25.5	1.6	27.1	7.7	34.8	24.6
Egypt (1960)	25,771	19.0	8.0	27.0	2.3	29.3	7.0	36.3	?	?	38.0
(1966)	30,083	20.0	9.2	29.2	2.1	31.3	6.1	37.4	?	?	41.1
S.W. Asia											
Turkey (1965)	31,391	5.6	9.4	15.0	4.0	19.0	6.9	25.9	3.9	29.8	34.4
Iran (1966)	25,078	10.8	11.8	22.6	4.3	26.9	5.3	32.2	2.7	34.9	39.1
Iraq (1965)	8,261	21.1	10.3	31.4	6.4	37.8	4.0	41.8	3.2	45.0	44.1
Syria (1960)	4,565	—	23.9	23.9	3.6	27.5	2.4	29.9	4.3	34.2	36.9
Jordan (1961)	1,706	—	14.4	14.4	9.2	23.6	12.5	36.1	4.3	40.4	43.9
Israel (1961)	2,183	—	33.9	33.9	6.6	40.5	21.5	62.0	8.1	70.1	77.9
Cyprus (1960)	578	—	—	—	16.5	16.5	13.6	30.1	3.4	38.5	35.7
Saudi Arabia (1962-3)	3,302	—	15.3	15.3	5.4	20.7	4.5	25.2	4.5	29.7	?
Kuwait (1965)	467	—	63.9	63.9	—	63.9	13.9	77.8	12.6	90.4	94.0
Trucial States (1968)	180	—	—	—	31.9	31.9	23.6	55.5	—	55.5	65.4
Bahrain (1965)	182	—	—	—	43.4	43.4	22.6	66.0	—	66.0	82.3

Note: Unfortunately incomplete data were available for Egypt, 1960 and 1966. Yemen, Southern Yemen, Muscat and Oman, Qatar and Lebanon are omitted through lack of censuses.

whose contacts with the countryside are much more tenuous than the old city-dwellers. At the same time, shanty-towns and slums have evolved, mostly housing migrants from rural areas who have become a new urban proletariat, often unemployed or underemployed and often disgruntled.

Urban growth is sometimes extremely rapid, especially in the larger cities (Fig. 1.2). Casablanca, for example, rose from a small town to a city of more than one million inhabitants in only 50 years; Baghdad grew from 1,056,000 inhabitants in 1957 to 1,745,000 in 1965; Tehran added 1,200,000 inhabitants between 1956 and 1966; Cairo and Alexandria both doubled in size between 1947 and 1966; and in 1966 Amman was more than ten times larger than during the 1930's. The examples could be multiplied, but it is difficult to calculate precise rates of growth and make reliable comparisons.

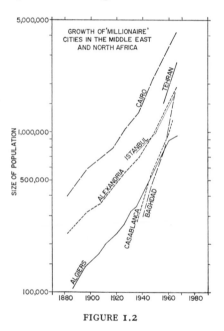

FIGURE 1.2

Analysis of the levels and growth of urban populations in the Middle East and North Africa reveals some striking facts (Table 1.4). First, most of the countries are more than one-third urban (by their own definitions or by using the threshold of 10,000 inhabitants as the lower limit of urban status), and they are therefore much more urbanized than most of the countries of South, South-East or East Asia or tropical Africa, although Afghanistan, Yemen, Muscat and Oman are feebly urbanized exceptions. As mentioned earlier, the percentages of urban populations tend to be inversely related to the size of the state, and they are also directly related to the importance of the modern sector. Certainly, traditions of urbanism appear to have little relationship to present levels of urban population.

Thus, Libya has now a higher proportion of urban population than either Morocco or Tunisia, which have much more profound traditions of urban life, and so does Algeria in which massive urban growth has been stimulated by the chaos and 'regroupings' of its war of independence (1954–62). Moreover, partly because of the influx of Palestinian refugees, Jordan has now a higher proportion of town-dwellers than Syria. It may also be surprising that countries like Morocco and Turkey have among the lowest proportions of town-dwellers, comparable say with Saudi Arabia. Despite relatively low proportions of urban population, these large countries have most of the town-dwellers and most of the large cities (with 100,000 inhabitants or more) in the region. By 1966 there were some 80 large cities within the region (Table 1.5), and two-thirds were located in four countries only: Egypt 17, Iran 14, Turkey 14 and Morocco 10. In Egypt, Kuwait, Iraq and Israel large cities contained over 30 per cent of the total population, and in Algeria, Libya, Iran and Syria between 20 and 30 per cent. Generally, the growth of large cities has been more rapid than that of smaller cities, but obviously not without exception. Particularly rapid growth has been experienced by ports and capitals, like Basra, Haifa, Beirut, Benghazi, Tripoli, Amman, Ankara and Riyadh.

TABLE 1.5   NUMBER OF LOCALITIES WITH 10,000 INHABITANTS OR MORE, MIDDLE EAST AND NORTH AFRICA, AT THE MOST RECENT CENSUS

	Locality size					*Total*
	1 million and over	*100,000– 999,999*	*50,000– 99,999*	*20,000– 49,999*	*10,000– 19,999*	
North Africa						
Morocco (1960)	—	8	3	12	22	45
Algeria (1966)	—	4	13	51	24	92
Tunisia (1966)	—	1	3	14	22	40
Libya (1964)	—	2	—	1	8	11
Egypt (1960)	2	12	8	63	?	?
(1966)	2	14	9	57	?	?
S.W. Asia						
Turkey (1965)	1	13	16	74	85	189
Iran (1966)	1	13	15	41	48	118
Iraq (1965)	1	4	7	10	19	41
Syria (1960)	—	3	2	4	14	23
Jordan (1961)	—	1	2	6	6	15
Israel (1961)	—	3	2	15	14	34
Cyprus (1960)	—	—	1	2	1	4
Saudi Arabia (1963)	—	3	3	5	12	23
Kuwait (1965)	—	1	—	3	4	8
Trucial States (1968)	—	—	1	2	—	3
Bahrain (1965)	—	—	1	1	—	2

Note: Unfortunately incomplete data were available for Egypt, 1960 and 1966. Southern Yemen, Muscat and Oman, Qatar and Lebanon are omitted through lack of censuses.

A very important tendency in each country is for the concentration of population in one or two large cities, so that there is sometimes a case for suggesting an overconcentration of population and urban amenities within primate cities. Certainly, the modernity and cosmopolitan atmosphere of cities like Tehran, Istanbul, Beirut, Cairo and Casablanca contrasts vividly with the torpor of many provincial towns. These are the great catalysts of change—parasitic, it is true, but also generative. With 4.2 million inhabitants in 1966, Cairo was the fifteenth largest city in the world and along with Alexandria contained more than one-fifth of the total population of Egypt. Moreover, Baghdad alone comprised 21 per cent of the total population of Iraq in 1965 (Jones, 1968), and with Casablanca and Algiers it refutes Cressey's (1960) contention that 'to develop a city with a population of over a million it appears necessary to have a country of 20 million people'.

Although large cities are growing quickly, the concept of urban primacy,

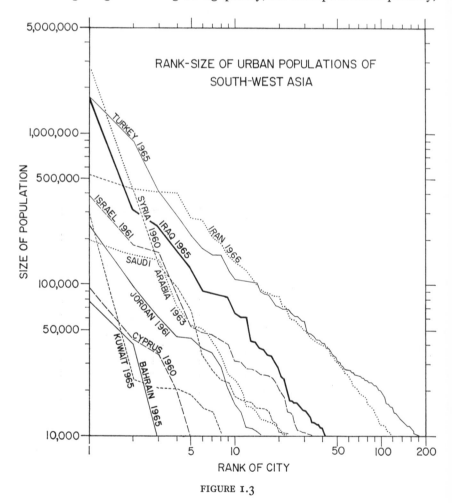

FIGURE I.3

in which the largest cities are many times larger than the second (and third and fourth) cities, does not find universal support. Urban primacy is most evident in Iran, Iraq, Tunisia and Kuwait, and to a lesser extent in Morocco, countries which have little in common in area, population size, location of primate city or type of economic development (Table 1.6). In Egypt, Libya, Turkey and Syria duality is more evident than primacy, and in Saudi Arabia there are three cities roughly similar in size.

Urban primacy is only concerned with the larger cities in city-size distributions (Figs. 1.3 and 1.4), and is indicated by steep or concave curves. The smoothness of rank-size curves is evidently influenced by the

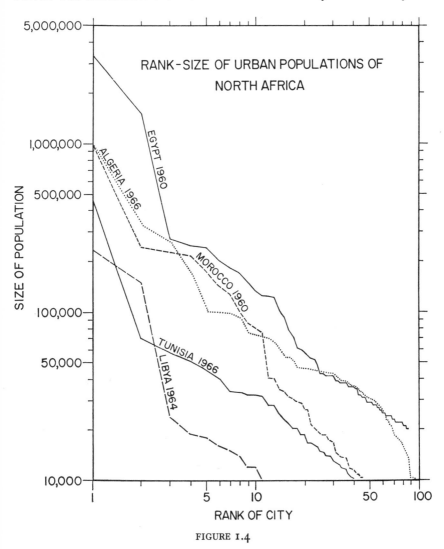

FIGURE 1.4

TABLE 1.6 URBAN PRIMACY IN THE MIDDLE EAST AND NORTH AFRICA, AT THE MOST RECENT CENSUS

	Population of largest city (thousands)	Percentage of total population in largest city	Percentage of total population in two largest cities	$\dfrac{P_1}{P_2}$	$\dfrac{P_1}{P_2+P_3+P_4}$
North Africa					
Morocco (1960)	965	8.3	10.4	3.97	1.41
Algeria (1966)	943	8.0	10.5	2.91	1.26
Tunisia (1966)	469	10.3	11.9	6.66	2.60
Libya (1964)	214	13.6	22.4	1.56	1.21
Egypt (1966)	4,220	14.0	20.0	2.34	1.59
S.W. Asia					
Turkey (1965)	1,751	5.6	8.5	1.94	1.09
Iran (1966)	2,720	10.8	12.5	6.42	2.20
Iraq (1965)	1,745	21.1	24.9	5.58	2.41
Syria (1960)	530	11.6	20.9	1.25	0.80
Jordan (1961)	246	14.4	20.1	2.57	1.22
Israel (1961)	387	17.7	26.2	2.12	0.88
Cyprus (1960)	96	16.5	24.1	2.19	0.97
Saudi Arabia (1962–3)	225	6.0	10.8	1.24	0.52
Kuwait (1965)	229	63.9	69.0	12.65	4.60
Bahrain (1965)	79	43.4	62.3	2.30	1.71

Note: (a) $\dfrac{P_1}{P_2}$ is a simple measure of urban primacy in which the population of the largest city is divided by that of the second largest.

(b) $\dfrac{P_1}{P_2+P_3+P_4}$ the population of the largest city divided by the next three, is known as the Four City Index and probably gives a better indication of urban primacy, because primacy is affected by the number of urban centres.

(c) No calculations have been made for Southern Yemen, Muscat and Oman, Qatar, Lebanon and Yemen, owing to lack of census data.

number of towns, and the curves of the three most populous countries, Turkey, Egypt and Iran, are remarkably similar except for their largest cities. Turkey and Jordan may be said to have log-normal rank-size distributions, but many of the other distributions are irregular and short. In some countries where provincialism is strong, like Libya, regional rank-size analyses are more pertinent, and it may also be noted that many large cities in this part of the world comprise socially and functionally segregated urban units which may be distinguished separately on the rank-size curve.

The question arises as to whether the speed of urbanization is too great. While there is a case for suggesting that there is sometimes over-concentration of population (Abu-Lughod, 1963) in primate and other major cities, especially when unemployment and housing conditions are deplorable, there is less evidence to suggest that over-urbanization is general (Sovani, 1964), although it is perhaps present in Syria, Iran and Morocco (Kamerschen, 1969). In Cyprus, on the other hand, it may be suggested that there is relative under-urbanization.

Growing concentration of population

Although population distribution in the Middle East and North Africa is extremely uneven, the present trend is toward increasing unevenness; in other words the nodes of denser population—cities or regions—are experiencing more rapid population growth than the areas of sparse population (Fig. 1.5). This is sometimes in spite of a conscious effort by governments, such as of the United Arab Republic, Israel and Tunisia, to offset this process of growing concentration of population by development of under-developed areas. It is, however, difficult for governments to reduce the 'islandic' nature of modern economic development which is particularly strong in so-called developing countries, as the 'islands' are attractive to migrants from rural areas and from small towns, and also usually enjoy lower mortality and higher natural increase.

With the exception of Turkey and a few small states such as Cyprus and Lebanon, each country of the Middle East and North Africa has a very patchy population distribution with the bulk of its population localized on a small proportion of its total area. In Israel, for example, three-fifths live on one-tenth of the area; in Iraq over one-half live on 15 per cent of the area; and in Egypt, the classic case of population concentration, 99 per cent inhabit only 3.5 per cent of the country. Nearly every country has a large uninhabited or sparsely inhabited area, which is only sporadically studded with oases or mining settlements, and for long posed great difficulties of communication and control. Many desert areas, however, have proved immensely valuable sources of petroleum, which has multiplied their resource potential, if not their population potential, but it would be wrong to imagine that these 'negative areas' will become much more

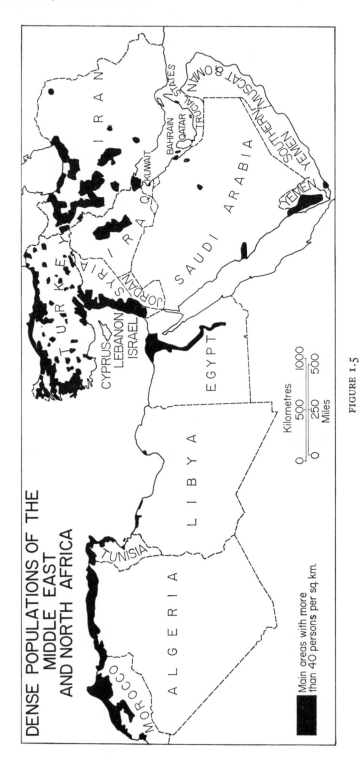

DENSE POPULATIONS OF THE
MIDDLE EAST
AND NORTH AFRICA

Main areas with more
than 40 persons per sq. km.

Kilometres
0   500   1000
0   250   500
Miles

FIGURE 1.5

populous because of their petroleum reserves; the oil industry has contributed to more urbanization outside the oilfields than within them. It is, of course, one of the great ironies of the region that several of the most populous countries of the region, such as Turkey and Morocco, possess little oil (while some small desert states have been entirely transformed by it); in these countries the process of population concentration has been less dramatic, although the drift from the land and the growth of cities is still important.

In our discussion of the process of urbanization and growing concentration of population it may have been forgotten that most people in the region still live in villages, which are the main nuclei of population distribution. Their location is greatly influenced by the availability of water and soil, but political insecurity and the need for a defensive site have also been influential. Still the stronghold of traditionalism, villages are changing, especially when connected to the outside world by a road. More and more are able to produce crops for remote markets, and more and more have public baths, schools, clinics, coffee bars and growing contacts with the outside world. In Egypt, for example, substantial progress has been made in improving village life.

Despite some land reforms, inequalities in landholding and the landlord–tenant relationship are still basic facts of most of the region, and progress in this field depends greatly upon the nature of the political regime and its own relationships with the landowning class. Enormous disparities between the wealth of landowners and the poverty of peasants may still be found, but in countries like Egypt, Iran and Algeria the disparities are being reduced.

Undoubtedly, one of the most powerful instruments of change within the region has been the movements toward universal primary education and expanded secondary and higher education, which have made immense strides in recent years, especially in the wealthier countries. The effects of educational improvements upon the modernization of agriculture, urbanization, the growth of the tertiary sector, the rise in the status of women and upon numerous other aspects of life in the Middle East and North Africa are already obvious, but they will augment rapidly as the process is diffused throughout the region.

In sum, there can be little doubt that the region is in the throes of political, social and economic flux, which is having considerable influence upon population distribution, composition and dynamics, so that predictions for the future can be made with little confidence. Who at mid-century could have foreseen clearly the rise of the oil industry and decolonization in the Maghreb, or the evolution of socialism in Egypt, Algeria and elsewhere? Who can confidently predict the future of Israel, Jordan or the Gulf states, or the trends of Moslem fertility? Whatever happens, there can be little doubt that political structures and events are likely to play a vital role in the demographic future of the region. Certainly governments will be much more conscious of their demographic situations with respect to economic and social development.

REFERENCES

AMIN, S. (1966) *L'Economie du Maghreb*, Paris.

AWAD, M. (1959) 'La sédentarisation des tribus nomades et semi-nomades au Moyen-Orient', *Revue Internationale du Travail*, pp. 27–60.

AWAD, M. (1962) 'Nomadism in the Arab lands of the Middle East', in UNESCO, *The Problems of the Arid Zone*, pp. 311–24.

BAER, G. (1964) *Population and Society in the Arab East*, London.

BARTH, F. (1962) 'Nomadism in the mountain and plateau areas of South-West Asia', in UNESCO, *The Problems of the Arid Zone*, p. 341.

BENYOUSSEF, A. (1967) *Populations du Maghreb et Communauté Economique à Quatre. Esquisse d'une Théorie Démographique de l'Intégration*, Paris.

BERGER, M. (1962) *The Arab World Today*, London.

BERGER, M. (Ed.) (1963) *The New Metropolis in the Arab World*, New Delhi.

BRICE, W. C. (1966) *South-west Asia*, London.

CAIRO DEMOGRAPHIC CENTRE (1969) *Demographic Measures for Arab Countries of North Africa and South-west Asia*, Cairo.

CAPOT-REY, R. (1962) 'The present state of nomadism in the Sahara' in UNESCO, *The Problems of the Arid Zone*, pp. 301–10.

CHEVALIER, L. (1947) *Le Problème Démographique Nord-Africain*, Paris.

CLARKE, J. I. (1964) 'Rural landscapes and settlement in the Maghreb' in J. M. Houston, *The Western Mediterranean World*, pp. 667–705.

CRESSEY, G. B. (1960) *Crossroads: Land and Life in South-west Asia*, Chicago.

DESPOIS, J. (1964) *L'Afrique du Nord*, Paris, 2nd ed.

EL-BADRY, M. A. (1965) 'Trends in the components of population growth in the Arab countries of the Middle East: a survey of present information', *Demography*, 2, pp. 140–86.

FISHER, W. B. (1971) *The Middle East*, London, 7th ed.

HOLLER, J. E. (1964) *Population Growth and Social Change in the Middle East*, Population Research Project, George Washington University.

ISNARD, H. (1966) *Le Maghreb*, Paris.

JONES, L. W. (1968) 'Accroissement rapide de la population de Bagdad et d'Amman', *Population*, 23, pp. 150–4.

KIRK, D. (1966) 'Factors affecting Moslem natality' in B. Berelson *et al.* (Eds.), *Family Planning and Population Programs*, pp. 561–79.

LAPIDUS, I. M. (Ed.) (1969) *Middle Eastern Cities*, Berkeley.

NARAGHI, E. (1958) *Recherches Démographiques dans les Pays Sous-Développés*, The Hague.

PEPPELENBOSCH, P. G. N. (1968) 'Nomadism on the Arabian Peninsula: a general appraisal', *Tijdschrift voor Economische en Sociale Geografie*, 59, pp. 335–46.

PLANHOL, X. DE (1957) *Le Monde Islamique*, Paris.

PLANHOL, X. DE (1962) 'Caractères généraux de la vie montagnard dans le Proche-Orient et dans l'Afrique du Nord', *Annales de Géographie*, 71, pp. 113–30.

STEPHENS, R. W. (1960) *Population Factors in the Development of North Africa*, George Washington University.

TIANO, A. (1967) *Le Maghreb entre les Mythes*, Paris.

UN ECONOMIC COMMISSION FOR AFRICA (1966) *Demographic Projection for North African Countries*.

WIRTH, E. (1969) 'Das problem der nomaden in heutigen orient', *Geographischen Rundschau*, 21, pp. 41–51.

Chapter 2
Turkey: recent population trends
J C Dewdney

Data sources

Enumerations of the population of Turkey were carried out many times during the period of the Ottoman Empire from the sixteenth century onwards, including at least five occasions during the nineteenth century (Alpat, 1968) as well as in 1900 and 1914 (Lefebvre, 1928). The modern period of census-taking, however, can only be said to date from the establishment of the Turkish Republic in 1923. The first modern census was carried out in 1927, to be followed by a second in 1935, since when censuses have been taken at regular intervals of five years, increasing in scope and quality with the passage of time. The most recent of this quinquennial series was carried out on 20th October 1970 (Pasiner, 1968). Other types of official demographic data are fragmentary and generally unsuitable for detailed historical study. The State Institute of Statistics (SIS) has collected and published marriage data since 1927 and divorce data since 1930, while mortality statistics have been published since 1931. In each of these cases, however, the record is incomplete, details being given only for towns with a particular administrative status. Although records have been kept of such births as are registered, the figures have not been published in view of the fact that registered births are believed to constitute less than a quarter of the total (Şengölge, 1968b). Fertility has, however, been the topic of a number of special studies in recent years, notably those by Demeny and Shorter (1968) and by Shorter (1968), but no acceptable long-term series of birth rate data exists. A table of estimated birth and death rates based on census data was published in the Second Five Year Development Plan (State Planning Organization, 1969) but this diverges considerably from other estimates.

The inadequacy of the available demographic data and the paramount importance of accurate information in this field for use in the formulation of development plans have now been recognized by Turkish statisticians and others (Şengölge, 1968a) and considerable advances have been made in recent years. In 1963, a system of continuous demographic survey (the Turkish Demographic Survey—TDS) was established, involving monthly interviews of a sample population in selected areas, and in 1967 this was extended to a nation-wide sample (Avralioğlu, 1968). Proposals have recently been made for compulsory vital registration and for the establishment of a population record to cover change of residence, occupation and educational attainment as well as vital events. It is now recognized that 'the attainment of an efficiently functioning vital registration system should be a long-term objective in Turkey. Since complete vital registration is not likely to be achieved for some time, the Turkish Demographic Survey will continue to be the principal source for measures of birth and death rates' over much of the coming decade (Şengölge, 1968b). For years prior to the establishment of the TDS, we must continue to rely heavily on the published volumes of the quinquennial censuses.

Population growth

Table 2.1 shows the available data on population growth in Turkey during the twentieth century. In view of the deficiencies in some of the earlier enumerations, average annual growth rates are given only for the period since 1927. The figures show that, since 1900, the population of Turkey has multiplied by a factor of 2.25, though this has involved a good deal of fluctuation in the rate of increase. Thus there appears to have been a large decline in numbers between 1914 and 1927, followed by growth at a diminishing rate between 1927 and 1945. Since 1945, population growth has greatly accelerated, with a slight decline in the rate of increase after 1960.

TABLE 2.1 POPULATION GROWTH IN TURKEY, 1900–65

Year	Population (thousands)	Population growth		
		Numbers (thousands)	Per cent	Annual average (per thousand)
1900	13,958	—	—	—
1914	15,703	+1,745	+12.5	—
1927	13,648	−2,055	−13.1	—
1935	16,158	+2,510	+18.4	+21.3
1940	17,821	+1,633	+10.3	+17.3*
1945	18,790	+969	+5.4	+10.6
1950	20,947	+2,157	+11.5	+22.9
1955	24,065	+3,118	+14.9	+28.9
1960	27,755	+3,690	+15.3	+29.3
1965	31,391	+3,636	+13.1	+24.9

* Excluding the addition of 208,116 persons by the annexation of Hatay in 1939.
Sources: 1900, 1914: Lefebvre, 1928; 1927–65: Census reports.

One of the most striking changes indicated by the figures in Table 2.1 is the large-scale population decrease between 1914 and 1927, when the number of people living within the 1927 boundaries of the Turkish Republic declined by some two million. A large part of this decline may be attributed to the massive migration movements which took place during that period. Between 1922 and 1924, at least 1.5 million Greek- and Armenian-speaking inhabitants left the territory of the Turkish Republic while the inward flow of Turkish speakers from Greece amounted to only 400,000, a net loss of population from Turkey exceeding one million. In addition, there was a large but unmeasured exodus of minority peoples from Turkey during the First World War and the War of Independence. Other factors included war losses and the effect on the eastern provinces of the Kurdish revolt of 1925.

As a result of these upheavals, many provinces in the east lost a quarter and some more than half of their population, while those in the west, where the emigrants were to some extent replaced by immigrant Turks, lost between 10 and 20 per cent. Only in the central Anatolian region, where minority groups were very small, was there a significant population increase between 1914 and 1927. While the population losses of this period had serious effects, leading to the wholesale abandonment of agricultural land over large areas and the removal, from many of the towns, of a large part of the commercial element, they were, in one sense at least, of advantage to the newly-established Turkish Republic which acquired a much greater degree of ethnic homogeneity and thus of internal cohesion than its Ottoman predecessor. Whereas, on the eve of the First World War, the territory which later constituted the Republic was the home of an estimated 2.5 million Greeks and 1.5 million Armenians (nearly 40 per cent of the total), in 1927 there were only about 75,000 belonging to each of these minority groups (Pallis, 1938). The only sizeable minority were the 1.2 million Kurds who at least were of the same religion as the Turks. Since 1927, immigration has been almost entirely by Turkish speakers and most minority groups have continued to decline so that the ethnic homogeneity of the Republic has been maintained. Thus the establishment of the Republic marked a new phase in the development of the population as it did in the country's economic and political development.

The upheavals, political and demographic, which occupied the first quarter of the twentieth century, were virtually at an end by the time of the first census in 1927 and Turkey embarked on a period of sustained though fluctuating population growth. It is impossible to be precise regarding the extent to which natural increase and migration gain respectively have contributed to the growth of the Turkish population over the last forty years, since the necessary data do not exist. We can, however, be sure that, over the period as a whole and in marked contrast to the situation before 1927, the dominant factor has been natural increase, and migration has played a minor role except in a small number of individual years. According to Darkot (1955), the net migration grain between 1927 and

1950 amounted to only 426,000, less than 6 per cent of the total population growth during that period.

Doubts as to the validity of some of the earlier census data are raised by the very high rate of population growth recorded between 1927 and 1935. The average increase of 2.1 per cent indicated by the figures in Table 2.1 was very much higher than those recorded in neighbouring territories and much of the apparent increase between 1927 and 1935 would appear to be attributable to deficiencies in the 1927 census, which almost certainly under-estimated the total population at that date (Pallis, 1938; Darkot, 1955). If this is so, then the decline between 1914 and 1927 may well have been smaller than indicated in Table 2.1. Whatever the precise facts, modern studies of the Turkish population, together with statistical summaries in recent census volumes, generally omit the 1927 data and deal only with figures from 1935 onwards.

In view of the more accurate nature of the 1935 and subsequent censuses, it can be stated with confidence that the rate of growth between 1940 and 1945 was very much lower than that between 1935 and 1940. According to the State Planning Organization (1969), whose precise figures are open to doubt but probably give a fair indication of trends, the rate of natural increase fell from 18.9 per thousand between 1935 and 1940 to 9.9 per thousand between 1940 and 1945, largely owing to a rise in the death rate from 19.4 to 27.2. Although not directly engaged in hostilities, Turkey experienced considerable economic difficulties during the war years as a result of her isolation from the outside world and the mobilization of a large part of her male labour force (Shorter, 1968). In addition to the considerable increase in mortality, there was also a slight decline in fertility, the birth rate falling from 38.3 to 37.1 per thousand. As a result of these changes in vital rates, the annual numerical increase of the population, which topped 300,000 in 1940, fell below 200,000 in each of the years 1941-4 (Darkot, 1955).

Whatever the uncertainties regarding the situation before 1945, there can be no doubt that the post-war years have witnessed a demographic upsurge sufficient to place the Turkish population among the more rapidly growing in the world. On no occasion over the past twenty-five years has the annual growth rate been less than 2 per cent, and between 1950 and 1960 it was close to 3 per cent. The average numerical growth rose to 620,000 between 1950 and 1955 and nearly 740,000 between 1955 and 1960, well over double the pre-war rate. This acceleration in the rate of growth was due in part to an increase in the birth rate which climbed from its war-time trough of 37.1 in 1940-45 to 44.0 between 1955 and 1960, but is attributable mainly to a decline in the death rate from 27.2 to 12.6 (State Planning Organization, 1969).

Since 1960 there has been a slight but significant decline in the annual rate of population growth which fell from 2.9 per cent between 1955 and

1960 to 2.5 per cent between 1960 and 1965. Preliminary results from the Turkish Demographic Survey quoted by Shorter (1968) indicate a birth rate of 44.2 and a death rate of 16.0 in 1966, giving a natural increase rate of 28.2 for that year. These figures, which incidentally call into question the accuracy of the State Planning Organization's estimates, particularly their death rate figure of only 12.6 for 1955–60, suggest that the decline in the rate of growth after 1960 was due mainly to a change in migration trends. Prior to 1960, Turkey experienced a small net migration gain resulting from the movement into the country of Turkish speakers from the Balkans. This reached a peak at the time of the Korean War (Tanoğlu, 1955) when more than 150,000 Turkish speakers were expelled from Bulgaria in 1950–51. Since 1960, immigration has been more than offset by the emigration of Turkish workers to western Europe, mainly to the Federal Republic of Germany. This movement, as a result of which some 200,000 Turkish citizens are temporarily resident abroad, has been large enough to bring about a net migration loss in recent years.

At the same time it would appear that, despite the contradictory nature of the available evidence, there has been some decline in the birth rate during the 1960's. According to the State Planning Organization (1969), 'A large proportion of the fertile female population during the period 1960–65 was born in the period 1940–45. This female population, which affects the births in the 1960–65 period, is small because their parents belonged to a small population group born during the First World War and the War of Independence.' In short, part of the birth rate decline is due to a temporary reduction in the number of women of child-bearing age. It seems likely, however, that some real decline in fertility has also occurred. Shorter (1968) suggests that there are marked fertility differentials between the major cities, smaller towns and rural areas, which, according to his estimates based on census data, had birth rates of 23.7, 35.1 and 48.9 respectively in 1960. A process by which reduced fertility, along with other urban cultural traits, is diffused among ever greater sections of the population is now in progress and future fertility trends depend to a large degree on the speed with which this diffusion takes place.

Fertility decline may well be accelerated over the next few years as a result of changing attitudes towards family-planning. Over most of the period since the establishment of the Republic, the attitude of the authorities has been firmly in favour of rapid population growth. Assuming, quite reasonably, that a population of twelve or thirteen millions in 1923 was dangerously small for a territory of 780,000 sq. km., they applied the usual populationist measures. A law passed in 1930 charged the Ministry of Health with instituting 'necessary measures in order to increase and facilitate births' (Yaşer, 1968), the import, manufacture, advertisement and sale of contraceptives were made illegal and tax reliefs were granted for each child born. Only during the 1960's, as pressure of rapidly growing numbers on available resources has become increasingly apparent, have traditional attitudes been challenged sufficiently widely to bring about a change in official policies. Since 1965, the latter have swung over to the restrictionist approach, exemplified by the passage in that year of a Family-Planning Law, which among other things, removes the ban on the distribution of contraceptive information and appliances. A nationwide system of birth-control clinics, many of them mobile, is now being established with the aim of reducing the very high fertility of the rural masses. Clearly it is too early to estimate the effect of these new developments on the birth rate and it will be most interesting to see what the 1970 census reveals.

Against a possible decline in fertility as a factor affecting the rate of natural increase must be set the possibility of a further reduction in mortality. As already indicated, current mortality rates cannot be stated with complete precision. If, as seems likely, the Turkish Demographic Survey estimates for 1966 are reasonably accurate in showing an overall death rate of 16 per thousand, with a range from 10–13 in urban areas to as much as 21 in poorer rural areas, there is still room for improvement. This is particularly true of infant mortality, which is estimated at 155 per thousand live births for the population as a whole with a range from 81 in Izmir (but 123 in Istanbul) to 204 in some rural districts.

Expectation of life at birth has shown a marked improvement in recent decades, rising from an estimated average of 44.9 years in 1935–40 to 57.6 by 1960–65. The latter figure suggests, however, that mortality levels are still appreciably above those of Western Europe and that a further decline in the death rate is possible.

A number of population projections were prepared in connection with the Second Five Year Plan (State Planning Organization, 1969). The highest of these, which assumes no significant decline in fertility before 1985, indicates a total population of 41 million in 1975 and 55.3 million in 1985. The low fertility estimate, assuming a 10 per cent fertility decline every five years, gives 39.4 million in 1975 and 48.8 million in 1985, while the medium fertility projection suggests 40.4 million in 1975 and 52 million in 1985. The last of these, postulating an increase of 9 million between 1965 and 1975 and a further 11.6 million between the latter date and 1985 is the one on which the Plan's proposals for economic development are based. In short, the Turkish population is expected to grow over the twenty-year period by at least 55 per cent, probably by 65 per cent and possibly by as much as 76 per cent.

Regional variations in population growth, 1935–65

The expansion of the total population since 1935 has involved considerable regional variations in rates of growth. These are summarized in Table 2.2

which gives details for the eight statistical regions used in Turkish censuses and are mapped on a provincial basis in Figure 2.2. These regional contrasts are the product of complex interactions among a variety of factors which include regional differences in rates of natural increase, movements from rural to urban areas and inter-regional migration, none of which can be accurately measured. Thus any attempt to explain the patterns of change shown in Figure 2.2 is inevitably somewhat subjective.

TABLE 2.2   POPULATION CHANGE IN TURKEY, 1935–65, BY REGIONS

Region	Population (thousands)			Change 1935–65		Change 1960–65	
	1935	*1960*	*1965*	Numbers (thousands)	Per cent	Numbers (thousands)	Per cent
I Thrace	1,268	2,285	2,656	1,388	109.5	371	16.2
II Black Sea	2,637	4,451	4,961	2,324	88.1	510	11.5
III Marmara and Aegean	3,131	4,877	5,480	2,349	75.0	603	12.4
IV Mediterranean	870	2,063	2,407	1,537	176.7	344	16.7
V Western Anatolia	1,504	2,373	2,570	1,066	70.9	197	8.3
VI Central Anatolia	4,001	6,943	7,883	3,882	97.0	941	13.6
VII South-eastern Anatolia	743	1,190	1,360	617	83.0	170	14.3
VIII Eastern Anatolia	2,003	3,573	4,074	2,071	103.4	501	14.0
Total	16,157	27,755	31,391	15,234	94.3	3,636	13.1

Between 1935 and 1965, the population of Turkey as a whole increased by 15.2 million or 94.3 per cent. Of the eight statistical regions, three— the Mediterranean coastlands (IV) Thrace (I) and Eastern Anatolia (VIII)—experienced rates of growth well above the national average. In the first of these, where the increase over the thirty-year period was 176.7 per cent, allowance must be made for the addition, in 1939, of the province of Hatay (31) with a population at that date of 208,116. If this province is excluded from the calculation, the remainder of the region experienced a growth of 116 per cent, still well above the national average. The Mediterranean region in 1935 was very thinly settled, particularly in view of its agricultural potential, and population density was below that of Turkey as a whole. Agricultural and, in recent years, industrial development, the latter particularly important around the Gulf of Iskenderun, have supported a high rate of growth. The province of Adana (1), for example, where development has been most effective, increased its population by 518,000 (135 per cent). Hatay, since its annexation, has also been the scene of rapid growth with an increase of 260,000 (105 per cent) since 1940. Expansion has been a good deal slower in the central and western parts of the region, where İçel (33) and Antalya (7) provinces barely doubled their populations in thirty years, but the latter particularly is now a growth area. Continued development of irrigated agriculture and a variety of industries in recent years has meant continued rapid population growth and the rate of increase between 1960 and 1965 was higher than in any other region.

The second most rapidly expanding region between 1935 and 1965 as

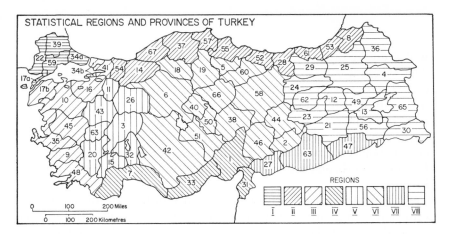

FIGURE 2.1

Statistical Regions: I. Thrace; II. Black Sea; III. Marmara and Aegean; IV. Mediterranean; V. Western Anatolia; VI. Central Anatolia; VII. South-eastern Anatolia; VIII. Eastern Anatolia.

Provinces: 1. Adana; 2. Adiyaman; 3. Afyon; 4. Ağrı; 5. Amasya; 6. Ankara; 7. Antalya; 8. Artvin; 9. Aydın; 10. Balıkesir; 11. Bilecik; 12. Bingöl; 13. Bitlis; 14. Bolu; 15. Burdur; 16. Bursa; 17. Çanakkale; 18. Çankırı; 19. Çorum; 20. Denizli; 21. Diyarbakır; 22. Edirne; 23. Elâzığ; 24. Erzincan; 25. Erzurum; 26. Eskişehir; 27. Gaziantep; 28. Giresun; 29. Gümüşhane; 30. Hakkârı; 31. Hatay; 32. Isparta; 33. İçel; 34. Istanbul; 35. Izmir; 36. Kars; 37. Kastamonu; 38. Kayseri; 39. Kırklareli; 40. Kırşehir; 41. Kocaeli; 42. Konya; 43. Kütahya; 44. Malatya; 45. Manisa; 46. Maraş; 47. Mardin; 48. Muğla; 49. Muş; 50. Nevşehir; 51. Niğde; 52. Ordu; 53. Rize; 54. Sakarya; 55. Samsun; 56. Siirt; 57. Sinop; 58. Sivas; 59. Tekirdağ; 60. Tokat; 61. Trabzon; 62. Tunceli; 63. Urfa; 64. Uşak; 65. Van; 66. Yozgat; 67. Zonguldak.

Throughout the text, a number in brackets after a place name, e.g. Ankara (6), refers to this map.

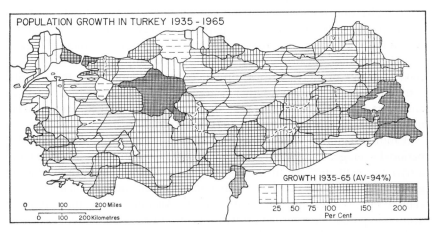

FIGURE 2.2

Boundary changes and the creation of new provinces between 1935 and 1965 have necessitated the amalgamation of certain groups of provinces in the compilation of this map. Where this has been done, the 1965 boundaries of the provinces involved are shown by broken lines.

47

well as during the last intercensal period was Thrace or European Turkey. This situation is, however, almost entirely due to the growth of Istanbul (34). The European part of this province increased its population, mainly within the urban area itself, by over a million (158 per cent), while the increase in the rest of Thrace amounted to only 313,000 (53 per cent) in thirty years. A significant proportion of the natural increase in the fairly densely populated rural areas of Thrace has been lost by migration to the Istanbul conurbation and only partially replaced by immigration from the Balkans.

A striking percentage increase was recorded in Eastern Anatolia (VIII), with an overall growth of 103.4 per cent and there were marked variations within this region. The seven provinces of Ağrı (4), Bingöl (12), Bitlis (13), Hakkâri (30), Muş (49), Siirt (56) and Van (65) experienced a growth of more than 160 per cent from 522,000 in 1935 to 1,364,000 in 1965. These are provinces which, according to Lefebvre (1928), suffered declines ranging from 30 to 80 per cent between 1914 and 1927 and where the rapid growth since 1927 has been described (Brice, 1954) as 'the successful filling of a vacuum left after widespread devastation during and immediately after the First World War'. The mechanism by which this rapid growth came about is uncertain. It seems probable that fertility among the predominantly rural, largely non-Turkish and, in the inter-war period at least, semi-nomadic population of these provinces was well above the national average, as indeed it still is today (Shorter, 1968) and that, despite rather high mortality, the natural increase rate has been above that of Turkey as a whole. The total growth in these provinces is, however, too large to be accounted for by natural increase alone and, in the earlier part of the period at least, there must have been an appreciable net migration gain as abandoned agricultural land was recolonized. It is significant that, in the period 1960–65, the rate of population growth in Eastern Anatolia was only slightly above the national average and well below that in Thrace and the Mediterranean region. It must also be emphasized that, despite their high rate of increase, these provinces are still among the most thinly settled parts of the country. Other eastern provinces, such as Erzurum (25) and Kars (36), where the 1914–27 decline was less marked, experienced much less rapid growth between 1935 and 1965.

A fourth region in which growth between 1935 and 1965 was above the national average, though only marginally, was Central Anatolia (VI), with a 97.1 per cent increase in thirty years. This was almost entirely due to growth in Ankara (6) province, with a 207 per cent increase mainly in the capital city. Other provinces of Central Anatolia, with their limited economic potential, recorded growth rates well below the national average and remain very thinly populated.

The Black Sea region (II) experienced only moderate growth and this was unevenly distributed. In a few provinces, rapid growth can be attributed to specific economic developments which attracted migrants from other areas. Thus the population of Zonguldak (67) province, which contains the bulk of Turkey's coalmining and steel industries, doubled between 1935 and 1965, while in Samsun (55) province port development and the expansion of commercial agriculture in the Kızılırmak delta supported an increase of 124 per cent. Elsewhere, the growth of predominantly rural populations pressed heavily on limited land resources and was checked by a persistent migration loss, mainly to Samsun, Zonguldak and Istanbul. Thus the population of Trabzon (61) province grew by only 65 per cent and that of Kastamonu (37), where land resources are particularly restricted, by only 22 per cent. Growth between 1960 and 1965 in this region was significantly below the national average.

The Marmara and Aegean (III) and Western Anatolia (V) regions formed another zone of relatively slow population growth. Here again there was marked contrast between the region as a whole and a restricted growth zone within it. The latter embraced the two provinces of Izmir (35) and Aydın (9). Containing some of Turkey's most valuable areas of commercial agriculture as well as her second port and industrial centre, these two provinces doubled their population, experiencing a numerical increase of 900,000. Rapid increase was also recorded in the Asiatic section of Istanbul province (34b) and in the adjacent province of Kocaeli (41) between 1935 and 1965. In the most recent intercensal period, 1960–65, the Marmara and Aegean region recorded a rate of growth somewhat below the national average, while Western Anatolia had the slowest growth rate of all the regions.

Finally, growth between 1935 and 1965 was relatively slow in the three provinces of Gaziantep (27), Urfa (63) and Mardin (47) which constitute the South-Eastern region (VII). Here there was relatively little industrial development and, over large areas, the agricultural potential is limited. On the other hand, between 1960 and 1965 the south-east experienced a growth rate above the national average.

Population distribution

According to the census of 1965, the total population of Turkey in that year was 31,391,421, an increase of 3,636,601 or 13.1 per cent over that recorded five years earlier. Despite this rapid increase, however, the average density remains quite low, standing in 1965 at 40.2 per sq. km. In this respect, as in so many others, Turkey occupies an intermediate position between the more densely settled lands of the Balkans (e.g. Greece: 65; Bulgaria: 74 per sq. km.) and the more thinly populated countries of the Middle East (e.g. Iran: 14; Iraq: 16; Syria: 24 per sq. km.). The distribution of population within Turkey shows strong regional contrasts with large areas recording densities well below the national average and a number of zones of concentration where densities are well above that level. As a prelude to more detailed consideration of density and distribution patterns, Table 2.3 indicates the situation for each of the eight statistical regions.

TABLE 2.3   POPULATION DISTRIBUTION AND DENSITY IN TURKEY, BY REGIONS, 1965

Region	Area		Population		Urban	Density per sq. km.	
	Thousand sq. km.	*Per cent*	*Numbers (thousands)*	*Per cent*	*Per cent*	*Total pop.*	*Rural pop.*
I Thrace	25.7	3.1	2,656	8.5	67.5	103.3	33.6
II Black Sea	81.7	10.5	4,961	15.7	14.5	60.5	51.7
III Marmara and Aegean	88.4	11.4	5,480	17.5	40.3	61.6	36.8
IV Mediterranean	59.3	7.6	2,407	7.7	36.1	40.8	26.1
V Western Anatolia	77.2	9.9	2,570	8.2	21.3	33.4	26.3
VI Central Anatolia	236.6	30.4	7,883	25.1	27.7	33.3	24.1
VII South-eastern Anatolia	39.9	5.1	1,360	4.3	30.6	34.0	23.6
VIII Eastern Anatolia	171.1	22.0	4,074	13.0	16.0	23.7	19.9
Total	779.9	100.0	31,391	100.0	29.8	40.2	28.2

Source: Census, 1965.

In this table, the Thrace, Black Sea and Marmara and Aegean regions stand out clearly as areas of population concentration, with densities well above the national average, even when the urban element, particularly swollen in Thrace by the presence of Istanbul, is discounted. These three regions together cover 25 per cent of the national territory but contain 41.7 per cent of the population and have an average density of 68 per sq. km. This is in striking contrast to the low density areas of the interior. The four Anatolian regions (Western, Central, Eastern and South-Eastern) together make up rather more than two-thirds of the area of Turkey but are the home of only 50.6 per cent of the total population. A more even balance is struck in the Mediterranean region with 7.6 per cent of the area and 7.7 per cent of the population.

The distribution of the population among the 67 provinces, together with the urban proportion in each province is indicated in Figure 2.3 while a more detailed picture of regional variations is provided by the density map (Fig. 2.4). The latter has been drawn on the basis of the 637 districts, the smallest sub-divisions of provinces for which the necessary data on area and population numbers are available. The most significant feature revealed by the density map, and already foreshadowed by the brief discussion of regional distribution above, is the tendency for high density areas to be found mainly around the coastal fringes of the country, the only exception being the western part of the Mediterranean region.

The Black Sea coast, despite the fact that it is the least highly urbanized of the eight regions, with 85 per cent of its population living in rural areas, is among the most densely populated sections of the country. This is particularly the case in the more easterly part where, along practically the whole coastal strip from Rize to Samsun, densities exceed 80 per sq. km. Trabzon (61) province, with an overall density of 127 per sq. km. and only 18 per cent of its population classed as urban, is the most densely settled in the country with the exception of the predominantly urban province of Istanbul. This is a region in which, despite the restricted nature of the coastal plain, rural densities exceed 100 per sq. km. over considerable areas. The mild climate, with rain all the year, supports intensive forms of agriculture with maize, livestock and such export crops as tea, tobacco and hazelnuts. Population growth, as already mentioned, is relatively slow and there is a steady flow of migrants to other parts of the country, suggesting

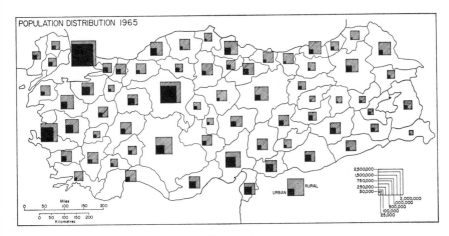

FIGURE 2.3

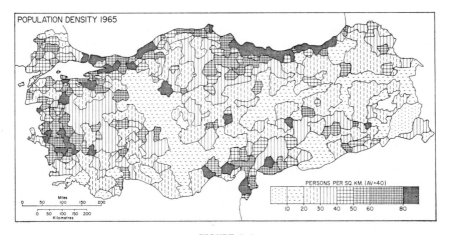

FIGURE 2.4

51

that the supportable limits of population density have been reached. For the most part, the Black Sea coastal zone of concentration is narrow, with densities falling off rapidly inland as altitude increases. High densities extend farther south, however, in the provinces of Amasya (5), Çorum (19) and Tokat (60), where the valleys of the Kızılırmak and Yeşilırmak break through the mountain barrier. The high density zone narrows again in Kastamonu (37) province where the coastal plain is very restricted, but widens in Zonguldak (67) to embrace the inland industrial areas.

A second high density zone occurs around the Sea of Marmara, particularly on its eastern and southern sides. A belt of territory from the Bosphorus eastwards to Izmit and Adapazarı and south through Bursa to the lower Simav is particularly highly urbanized and contains a large share of Turkey's manufacturing industry. In addition, there are fairly extensive lowlands, which support productive forms of agriculture serving the urban markets of the area as well as the export trade: rural densities reach 50 per sq. km. in several places. In Thrace, too, rural densities are generally well above the national average, particularly in the Ergene basin.

High rural densities and numerous towns are also characteristic of the Aegean provinces of Izmir (35), Aydın (9) and Manisa (45). Concentration is most marked around the port and industrial centre of Izmir itself, but high densities also extend inland up the fertile Gediz, Küçük Menderes and Büyük Menderes valleys. These are the scene of intensive, highly commercialized farming, accounting for a large share of Turkey's cotton, tobacco, vines and fruit production. Rural densities between 50 and 100 per sq. km. are common, with very much lower figures on the intervening uplands.

The south coast of the provinces of Muğla (48), Antalya (7) and western İçel (33) stands in contrast with the other coastal zones in being for the most part characterized by low densities. To some extent, this reflects the presence of the difficult mountain terrain of the Taurus, but there are also sizeable lowlands which, until recently at least, were also thinly settled. These Mediterranean coastlands, important in classical times, have long suffered from a degree of underdevelopment and their full potential is only now beginning to be realized. Neglect, possibly due in part to physical isolation, has been replaced by rapid development, particularly in Antalya (7) province, and the growth of population has accelerated. Rural densities, however, are still well below the national average and more akin to those of the Anatolian interior than the other coastal zones

The eastern part of the Mediterranean coastlands, on the other hand, comprising Adana (1), Hatay (31) and part of İçel (33), is a third zone of concentration. The extensive lowlands of the area, particularly those of the Seyhan and Ceyhan in Adana province, are now the scene of intensive agriculture and rural densities of 50 to 60 per sq. km. occur in many districts. In addition, there has been a considerable degree of industrial development in recent years and this is among the more highly urbanized parts of the country.

Practically the whole of the interior of Turkey is characterized by low densities, which also show a pronounced decline from west to east. The lowest densities of all are recorded in two distinct areas of environmental difficulty. The first of these low density zones is to be found in Central Anatolia, mainly in the provinces of Konya (42) and Ankara (6) where rainfall is scanty and extensive cereal growing and stock-rearing are the dominant activities. There are several large districts in these provinces where rural densities fall below 10 per sq. km. The second very thinly populated area is in the extreme east, where the climate is harsh and the terrain very mountainous. The provinces of Van (65) and Hakkâri (30) with densities of only 10 and 7 per sq. km. respectively, are the most thinly settled in the whole country.

Throughout the interior, small pockets of higher density occur, generally marking the position of the larger towns, particularly the provincial capitals. These are frequently situated in small basins which also form local pockets of high rural density in the midst of the thinly settled mountains and plateaux.

From this brief account it will be seen that, although in some areas the overall population density is considerably increased by the presence of cities or towns, the general distribution of the population is still very much influenced by the quality and availability of agricultural land and the intensity of agricultural development. This is only to be expected in view of the fact that nearly 70 per cent live in rural areas and a somewhat higher proportion is dependent on agriculture for its livelihood. Nevertheless, towns and urban activities are playing an increasingly important role.

Urban population and towns

Turkish censuses make two different divisions of the population, either of which may be used to distinguish urban and rural elements. The first of these is a division into *Şehir Nüfusu* and *Köy Nüfusu* (lit. city or town population and village population). The former includes the inhabitants of all settlements, regardless of size, which have the administrative status of province or district headquarters. In 1965 there were 621 such centres* with a combined population of 10.8 million, 34.4 per cent of the total. Well over 400 of these centres had populations below 10,000 and no fewer than 280 had less than 5,000 inhabitants. Many of these smaller 'towns' had predominantly agricultural populations and very poorly developed urban functions, though it is true that they contained the bulk of what little non-

---

* The actual total was 637, but each of the three largest cities included a number of districts—13 in Istanbul, 4 in Ankara and 2 in Izmir—which were administered together as a single municipality.

agricultural employment was to be found outside the larger towns. Furthermore, since new districts are constantly being created, a particular settlement may well become 'urban' by administrative decision, thus giving a false impression of the speed of the urbanization process. In addition, only total numbers, sex and literacy are tabulated on the basis of this *Şehir/Köy* classification.

The great majority of demographic characteristics are displayed on the basis of a division of the population living in settlements with more or fewer than 10,000 inhabitants. Consequently, throughout the discussion which follows, the term 'urban' is applied only to localities with a population above 10,000. In 1965, there were 200 such localities, with a combined population of 9.3 million, 29.8 per cent of the total. Thus, whatever the basis of definition, the urban population of Turkey remains relatively small and has only begun to grow rapidly in the post-war period. Between 1935 and 1950, the urban population as a proportion of the total rose only from 17.6 to 18.7 per cent, involving a numerical increase of 1.3 million or 47.1 per cent, compared with a total population growth of just below 30 per cent. Between 1950 and 1965, on the other hand, while the population of Turkey rose by nearly 50 per cent, the urban element increased by 138 per cent, a numerical growth of 5.4 million. This acceleration in the rate of urbanization is further illustrated by changes during the intercensal period 1960–65, when the total population rose by 13.1 per cent but growth in urban areas amounted to 23.5 per cent and in rural areas was only 7.4 per cent. Of the numerical increase of 3.6 million, 2.2 million or 60.1 per cent took place in towns. From these figures it is clear that migration from rural areas plays an important role in urban growth. The State Planning Organization estimate that, by 1985, at least half the total population will be urban, suggesting a numerical growth of more than 16 million over the next twenty years.

Despite the recent rapid growth of the urban population, there are still very marked regional differences in the degree of urbanization, some of which are indicated by the data for statistical regions given in Table 2.3. Even at this level of generalization, there is a clear distinction between the Thrace, Marmara–Aegean and Mediterranean regions, where the degree of urbanization is well above the national average, and the remainder of the country, where it is relatively low. Central Anatolia is close to the average only because of the presence of Ankara and, if this single centre is discounted, the urban element is reduced to 17 per cent, a figure more akin to those for most other parts of Anatolia. Thus the interior of Turkey is characterized by a low degree of urbanization as well as low overall densities while the coastal regions as a whole have both high density and a high level of urbanization. The outstanding exception is the Black Sea region with a unique combination of high density and low urbanization.

The map on a provincial basis (Fig. 2.5) shows the situation in more

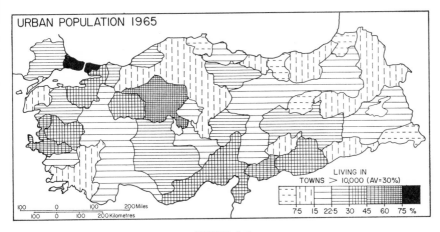

FIGURE 2.5

detail. Particularly striking is the small number of provinces—only 12 out
of a total of 67—which have more than 30 per cent of their population living
in localities with more than 10,000 inhabitants. These 12 provinces occur
in four quite clearly defined zones: Istanbul (34)—Kocaeli (41)—Bursa
(16), Eskişehir (26)—Ankara (6), Izmir (35)—Manisa (45) and İçel (33)—
Adana (1)—Hatay (31)—Gaziantep (27)—Urfa (63). Together, these provinces contain rather less than one-third of the towns over 10,000 but nearly
two-thirds (5.6 out of 9.3 million) of the people living in such centres.

There are nearly 2.5 million town-dwellers in the provinces of Istanbul
(34), Kocaeli (41) and Bursa (16), where there are a dozen towns of over
10,000. Throughout the modern period, Istanbul has been Turkey's
largest city by a wide margin, a position which it continues to occupy,
containing nearly a fifth of the country's urban population. Despite the
removal of the capital to Ankara with the establishment of the Republic,
Istanbul remains the primate city, main port and leading commercial centre.
Between 1935 and 1965, its population grew by just over a million, from
741,000 to 1,743,000, although there are increasing difficulties presented by
its overcrowded site. The second major centre in this region is Bursa, with
a population of 212,000, Turkey's fifth largest city, which had an early
origin as an Ottoman capital and owes its recent growth to its functions as
the leading textile centre, commercial focus for the region south of the
Sea of Marmara and tourist resort. With a population increase of 58,000
(38 per cent) between 1960 and 1965, Bursa is among the country's most
rapidly expanding cities. Industrialization and some decentralization of
foreign trade have led to rapid expansion of a number of other towns in this
region, notably Izmit (36,000 in 1950; 90,000 in 1965).

The second region with a high proportion of town dwellers is that
centred on Izmir (228,000 in 1950; 412,000 in 1965). Rapid growth con-

tinues on the basis of shipbuilding, textile, chemical and engineering industries and overseas trade. Other towns of this region are numerous but much smaller, the next largest being Manisa (72,000). The provinces of Izmir and Manisa together contain no fewer than 16 other towns over 10,000, which are agricultural markets, small industrial centres and transport foci in a part of Turkey with a high level of commercial activity.

The provinces of Eskişehir (26) and Ankara (6) are very different from the two areas discussed above. Although they register a degree of urbanization well above the national average, this can be attributed almost entirely to the growth of the administrative centres of two otherwise thinly populated provinces, which contain only three further towns of more than 10,000. From a town of some 50,000 in 1923, Ankara has grown to a city of 906,000 in 1965. Only since 1945 has the capital become Turkey's second largest town. Prior to that date it took third place to Izmir and Istanbul and still has little more than half the latter's population. However, Ankara is now one of the most rapidly growing Turkish cities and experienced an increase of 40 per cent between 1960 and 1965. Eskişehir (174,000) is Turkey's sixth city and owes its importance to locational advantages and the establishment of alimentary industries, particularly flour-milling and sugar-refining.

A fourth region in which the degree of urbanization is well above the national average is the group of provinces around the Gulf of Iskenderun. Included in this zone are the country's fourth and seventh cities, Adana (290,000) and Gaziantep (160,000), but the high and increasing level of urbanization is due to the growth of an unusually large number of medium-sized towns. These include the ports of Mersin (87,000) and Iskenderun (69,000), the commercial centres of Antakya (58,000) and Tarsus (57.000) and a further eighteen towns in the 10–50,000 range. In addition to the importance of this region in the sphere of intensive commercial agriculture, a good deal of industry has been attracted here in recent years.

As an illustration of the situation in interior regions of low urbanization, it is instructive to examine the case of Eastern Anatolia, where only 16 per cent of the population live in towns over 10,000. Even this region supports two of Turkey's large cities, Erzurum (105,000) and Diyarbakır (103,000) and there are five other centres with populations over 25,000. These seven centres together contain two-thirds of the region's urban population, the remainder being distributed among a further thirteen centres of 10–25,000. Altogether there are only twenty towns over 10,000 in a total area of 171,100 sq. km.

Language and religion

As already indicated, the Turkish Republic has, since its inception, displayed a high degree of ethnic homogeneity and this is tending to increase.

Turkish censuses divide the population according to 'mother tongue', and it is on this tabulation that the following discussion is based. According to the 1965 census, 90 per cent of the population claim Turkish as their mother tongue and the only sizeable minorities are those speaking Kurdish (2,219,000) and Arabic (365,000), 7.1 and 1.2 per cent of the total respectively. While comparisons from one census to another are unreliable owing to the contradictory nature of some of the evidence, it would appear that Kurdish-speakers are increasing slightly more rapidly than the population as a whole, presumably because of their higher natural increase rate, while the Arabic-speaking group, though still increasing numerically, is a diminishing proportion of the total.

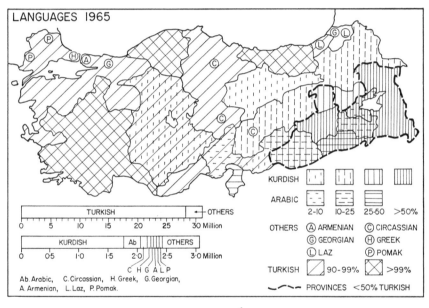

FIGURE 2.6

Kurdish-speakers are present in substantial numbers throughout the eastern part of the country (Fig. 2.6), forming a majority in the seven provinces of Ağrı (4), Bitlis (13), Diyarbakır (21), Hakkâri (30), Mardin (47), Siirt (56) and Van (65), and more than one-third of the total in Adıyaman (2), Bingöl (12), Muş (49) and Urfa (63). The eleven provinces named contain three-quarters of the Kurdish-speakers. The bulk of the remainder are to be found in Elâzığ (23), Erzurum (25), Kars (36) and Malatya (44), but there are small contingents as far west as Ankara (6) and Konya (42).

Arabic-speakers are more concentrated in the south-east. They constitute 30 per cent of the total in Hatay (31) and between 10 and 20 per cent in

Mardin (47), Siirt (56) and Urfa (63). These four provinces together contain more than 80 per cent of the Arabic-speakers and most of the remainder are in Adana (1), İçel (33), Bitlis (13) and Muş (49).

The distribution of these two groups is such that Turkish-speakers are in a minority in nine provinces: Ağrı (4), Bingöl (12), Bitlis (13), Diyarbakır (21), Hakkârı (30), Mardin (47), Siirt (56), Urfa (63) and Van (65). Kurdish- and Arabic-speakers are, however, much less common in towns than in rural areas and the urban population is predominantly Turkish-speaking in every province except Hakkârı, where it is mainly Kurdish and Mardin where there is an Arabic majority. While approximately one-third of the Arabic-speakers live in towns, only about 100,000 Kurds, some 5 per cent, are found in urban areas.

Other minority linguistic groups are no longer of any significance nationally and rarely constitute more than 1 or 2 per cent of the population at the provincial level. The Greek- and Armenian-speaking groups who, before the First World War, constituted more than a quarter of the total, numbered only 48,000 and 33,000 respectively in 1965 and are now almost entirely confined to Istanbul. Both are in fact outnumbered by the 58,000 Circassians, who form small communities in several provinces of Central Anatolia. The 34,000 Georgians are also widely distributed, the largest contingents living in the frontier province of Artvin (8) and in Kocaeli (41), Sakarya (54) and Bursa (16). The 26,000 Laz are found mainly in the eastern part of the Black Sea region and the majority of the 23,000 Pomaks in Thrace.

Religious minorities are very much smaller than linguistic ones, since both Kurds and Arabs as well as several of the smaller groups are Moslems. In 1965, nearly 99 per cent of the population professed allegiance to Islam and there were only 270,000 people of other faiths. These include 207,000 Christians, of whom 70,000 were of the Orthodox persuasion, 70,000 Gregorian, 26,000 Catholic and 23,000 Protestant, and there were 38,000 Jews. The bulk of the Christians and Jews lived in Istanbul, and non-Moslem groups were of negligible size in most other provinces.

Age and sex

The unreliability of Turkish age data is discussed by Taeuber (1958), who mentions in particular the inaccuracy of age reporting among the illiterate section of the population. It may be noted that, in 1965, 51 per cent of the population was classed as illiterate, the percentage being higher among women (67 per cent) than among men (36 per cent) and higher in rural areas (61 per cent) than in towns (33 per cent). The same author also suggested a tendency towards under-reporting of girl children, females of marriageable age and young men liable to conscription. All these deficiencies are likely to be more serious in rural than in urban areas and particularly in the more remote parts of the country. Although there has no doubt been progressive improvement in age-recording with successive censuses, the 1965 data, particularly those on a provincial basis, cannot safely be used for detailed analysis. Consequently discussion of age structure will here be limited to a number of reasonably valid general points.

As might be expected, the age structure of the Turkish population is markedly youthful, with 41.9 per cent below 15 years and only 4.0 per cent aged 65 or over. Urban areas show a distinctly less youthful structure, with 35.2 per cent below 15 and a proportion of adult males well above the national average, reflecting the significance of migration to towns by this group as part of the urbanization process. Regionally, there would appear to be a fairly close relationship between age structure and degree of economic development. The most youthful populations (Fig. 2.7) are found in predominantly rural areas, particularly those of the east, where agriculture has been least modernized and human fertility is above average. The youthful structure in these areas is probably also affected by the presence of the Kurdish element which would appear to have particularly high fertility and below average life expectation.

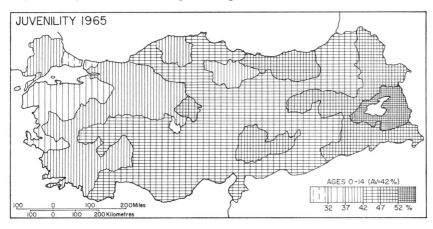

FIGURE 2.7

Sex ratio data from successive censuses, suggest a progressive diminution in the proportion of females which, according to Tümertekin (1958), stood at 1,035 per thousand males in 1935 and 1,002 in 1940. In the post-war period there has been a marked male surplus, the sex ratio reaching the low figure of 959 females per thousand males in 1960. Since 1960 there has been a slight increase to a sex ratio of 962 in 1965. This somewhat unusual sequence of changes may be related to historical events touched on elsewhere in this chapter. The predominance of females until 1940 may be attributed to high male mortality during the First World War and War of Independence and possibly also the masculinity of the net migration loss

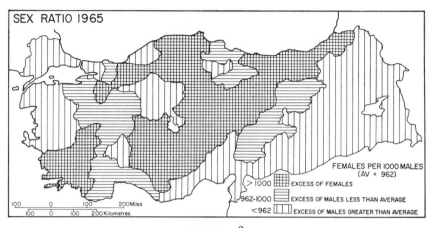

FIGURE 2.8

over the same period. In the years since 1945, with a more rapid population growth and a much higher male survival rate, there was a swing over to a male surplus produced by the normal masculinity of births and a youthful age structure. The slight increase in sex ratio since 1960 suggests that, as fertility begins to decline and life expectation increases, the female proportion is rising and will eventually become dominant, as it is in most developed countries. There is still considerable potential for an increase in the average expectation of life, a trend which will inevitably affect both age and sex structures. According to the figures given by the State Planning Organization (1969) life expectancy at birth rose from 42.3 years for men and 47.3 for women in 1935–40 to 56.1 and 59.2 in 1960–65.

There are marked differences in sex ratio between urban and rural areas. In 1965, the population living in towns over 10,000 had only 856 females per thousand males, while rural areas showed a marked female surplus, with a ratio of 1,103, a situation which was clearly the result of male-dominated migration to the towns. Provincial data show some interesting regional contrasts (Fig. 2.8). Male preponderance was particularly marked in Istanbul, the Aegean coastlands, the eastern part of the Mediterranean region and the provinces of Ankara and Zonguldak, areas already identified as zones of relatively rapid population growth, supported by the modernization of agriculture, a degree of industrialization and a high level of commercial activity. There is, however, also a large area of male preponderance in the under-developed eastern and south-eastern parts of the country. This could reflect a variety of factors including the high fertility and mortality already suggested, the failure of the Kurdish element to migrate towards areas of economic expansion and, possibly, some under-recording of females. Areas with a marked female surplus include much of the Black Sea region and the majority of provinces in Central Anatolia, from which migration on a considerable scale appears to have taken place.

Economic activities

In 1965, some 75 per cent of the population aged 15 years and over were classed as 'economically active', including 92 per cent of the men but only 56 per cent of the women in that age range. The economically active numbered 8.4 million males and 5.1 million females, a total of 13.5 million workers, whose distribution among the major groups of economic activities is shown in Table 2.4. The leading role of the agricultural sector as a source of employment is immediately apparent. Of all those engaged in Group I activities, only about 50,000 are in hunting, forestry and fisheries, leaving some 70 per cent of the total working population in agriculture alone. Agricultural employment is almost equally divided between the sexes, but is the predominant activity among women to a much greater extent than it is for men.

TABLE 2.4   ECONOMICALLY ACTIVE POPULATION IN TURKEY AGED 15 YEARS AND OVER, 1965

	Males		*Females*		*Total*	
	Numbers (thousands)	*Per cent*	*Numbers (thousands)*	*Per cent*	*Numbers (thousands)*	*Per cent*
I Agriculture, forestry, hunting and fishing	4,914	58.4	4,836	94.1	9,750	71.9
II Mining and quarrying	86	1.0	1	n.	87	0.6
III Manufacturing	884	10.5	77	1.5	961	7.1
IV Construction	349	4.2	2	n.	351	2.6
V Electricity, gas, water and sanitary services	26	0.3	n.	n.	26	0.2
VI Commerce, banking, insurance and real estate	372	4.4	20	0.4	392	2.9
VII Transport, storage and communications	281	3.3	6	0.2	287	2.1
VIII Services	732	8.7	104	2.0	836	6.2
Not adequately described	777	9.2	91	1.8	868	6.4
Total	8,421	100.0	5,137	100.0	13,558	100.0

n. = negligible.
Source: Census, 1965.

Thus, of a non-agricultural labour force of 3.8 million, only about 300,000 are women. Regional variations in the importance of agricultural employment (Fig. 2.9) are relatively slight, only three provinces—Istanbul (34), Ankara (6) and Izmir (35)—showing proportions substantially below the national average. Even so, Ankara and Izmir provinces each have more than 40 per cent in farming, leaving Istanbul, where the population is in any case predominantly urban, as the only province where farm workers, at 14 per cent of the total, are in a minority. If these three, containing

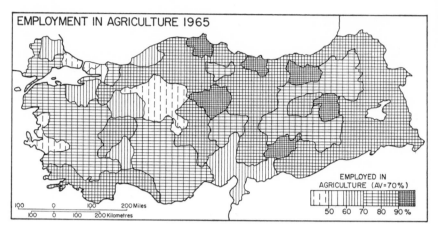

EMPLOYMENT IN AGRICULTURE 1965

EMPLOYED IN
AGRICULTURE (AV=70%)

50 60 70 80 90%

100   0   100   200 Miles
100   0   100   200 Kilometres

FIGURE 2.9

Turkey's largest urban agglomerations, are discounted, the figure for agricultural employment over the remainder of the country rises to 79.2 per cent. Proportions for individual provinces range from 58.6 per cent in Kocaeli (41) to 91.7 per cent in Yozgat (66), but no fewer than 46 (out of 67) provinces have more than 75 per cent of their labour force in the agricultural sector.

Of the 28.1 per cent of the working population outside the agricultural sector, 6.4 per cent are unclassified (at least half of these are in the armed forces) leaving 21.7 per cent in other activities. Non-agricultural employment has increased considerably in recent years; between 1960 and 1965, the number of farm-workers remained almost stationary, while the total employed in other activities increased by 552,000.

Mining and quarrying employ only some 87,000 workers, or 0.6 per cent of the working population, of whom 37,000 are found in the coal-mining province of Zonguldak (67), though even here they make up only 13 per cent of the labour force. The remaining 50,000 are dispersed in small numbers over a dozen provinces, the largest contingents being found in Elâzığ (23), Manisa (45) and Siirt (56). This distribution reflects the varied but scattered nature of Turkey's mineral resources.

Manufacturing industry is expanding rapidly and now employs 961,000 people, an increase of 335,000 (45 per cent) over the past 10 years. The most important branches are textiles and clothing (270,000), metallurgy and engineering (218,000) and food, drink and tobacco (158,000). Appreciable numbers are employed in some kind of manufacturing in almost every province, but the bulk of the labour force is concentrated in a small number of provinces. Istanbul province contains 255,000 manufacturing workers followed, at a considerable distance, by Izmir (84,000), Ankara (59,000), Bursa (40,000) and Adana (35,000). Thus nearly half the manufacturing labour force is found in these five provinces and the bulk of the remainder are in the Marmara, Aegean and Western Anatolia regions. Elsewhere only a few provinces, such as Zonguldak (metallurgy), Gaziantep (textiles) and Samsun (tobacco) have above average proportions in this sector. In contrast, manufacturing is very poorly represented in eastern areas; the Eastern Anatolia region, with a total population of 2 million, has only 36,000 manufacturing workers.

The tertiary sector (Groups IV–VIII in Table 2.4) employs 1.9 million people, 14 per cent of the labour force, and has grown rapidly in recent years. A special feature is the low level of female employment in this sector. Service activities, for example, employ seven times as many men as women, and in commerce the ratio is 18:1. The distribution of employment in the tertiary sector shows close similarities to that in manufacturing. The provinces of Ankara, Istanbul and Izmir together contain some 40 per cent of the total, a further 20 per cent are to be found in the Marmara–Aegean and Western Anatolia regions and some 10 per cent in the provinces on the Gulf of Iskenderun.

Migration

In the preceding paragraphs, reference has frequently been made to the process of internal migration as a factor leading to regional variations in population growth and structure. This topic now requires further investigation, though the possibilities are limited in that the only data available from censuses are those recording place of birth on a provincial basis. Taeuber (1958) commented on 'the high degree of residential stability in the Turkish population' in the period before 1955, a feature which has only been slightly modified in recent years. In 1945, of the total population living in Turkey, only 14 per cent were living outside their province of birth (including the foreign-born) and this proportion rose only to 14.2 per cent in 1955 and 15.7 per cent in 1965. However, the foreign-born element showed a progressive decline (4.4 per cent in 1945, 3.5 in 1955, 2.9 in 1965) so that the proportion of the Turkish-born population living outside the province of birth rose from 9.6 per cent in 1945 to 10.7 in 1955 and 12.8 in 1965. In numerical terms, this group comprised 1.7, 2.5 and 4.0 million at the three census dates.

A more detailed examination of the 1965 data reveals the extent to which particular areas were affected by these movements. At that date, there were 4 million Turkish-born living outside the province of birth and a further 900,000 born abroad, a total of 4.9 million. Notwithstanding the large but uncounted numbers who changed their place of residence within the boundaries of a single province, it is only these 4.9 million who can be studied as 'migrants'. Among the foreign-born migrants, the sexes were fairly evenly balanced, but the internal migrants showed a heavy

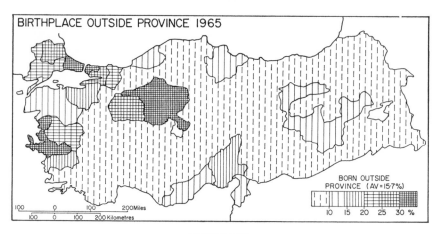

FIGURE 2.10

male preponderance, comprising 2.5 million men and 1.6 million women, a sex ratio of 640. Migrants also showed a heavy concentration in urban areas, particularly when compared with the population as a whole, 65 per cent of the foreign-born and 76 per cent of the internal migrants being found in towns. As a result, there was a predictable tendency for provinces with a high level of urbanization and recent rapid urban growth to have a high proportion of migrants, though the correlation was by no means complete (Fig. 2.10). Furthermore, a small number of provinces attracted a large share of the total movement. Of the 67 provinces, only three had more than 30 per cent of their population born elsewhere. These were Istanbul (59.0 per cent), Ankara (38.0 per cent) and Izmir (35.2 per cent). The province of Istanbul contained just over a quarter of the foreign-born and a similar proportion of the internal migrants, a total of 1.4 million who had arrived from elsewhere. Among the foreign-born, the largest numbers were from Yugoslavia (91,000), Bulgaria (49,000) and Greece (47,000). Among the 1.1 million internal migrants who had taken up residence in Istanbul, there were individuals from every province, the most important source areas being the Black Sea coast, Thrace and the Marmara region. Ankara had relatively few foreign-born, the majority of whom were, in any case, foreign nationals, and about 15 per cent of the internal migrants. The latter were again drawn from all provinces, but in this case Central and Eastern Anatolia were particularly well represented. Of the migrants to Izmir province, nearly half were born abroad and the bulk of the internal movement was from Western Anatolia and the Marmara–Aegean region.

Only ten other provinces showed a migrant element above the national average of 15.7 per cent. Six of these—Kocaeli (41), Kirklareli (39) Sakarya (54), Tekirdağ (59), Edirne (22) and Bursa (16)—were in the north-west. Two others—Manisa (45) and Aydin (9)—were provinces adjacent to Izmir and the remaining two were Adana (1) and Eskişehir (26).

Conclusion

This study has revealed a number of points. The Turkish population, in the post-war years, has been increasing at an unprecedented rate and only since 1960 has there been a slight slackening in this growth. Demographic expansion has resulted almost entirely from natural increase, with immigration playing only a very minor role, and future developments depend on fertility and mortality trends. Growth in recent years has been much more rapid in urban than in rural areas and, although rural population continues to increase, employment in agriculture has remained almost stationary. Thus the great bulk of the population increase has taken place in towns and the increase in the labour force has been almost entirely in the non-agricultural sector. Certain areas—the Marmara and Aegean coasts, the zone around the Gulf of Iskenderun and a few isolated centres such as Ankara—have taken the lion's share of urban growth and industrial employment, thus tending to strengthen the contrasts between modernizing regions and those which remain heavily dependent upon the traditional and only slowly-changing agricultural sector of the economy. These contrasts are, in the first instance, between the coastal fringes and the interior. Secondly, within the interior, there are contrasts between west and east. Both sets of contrasts are further strengthened by the fact that modernization of agriculture has proceeded much further in the coastal zones than in the interior and has been more effective in the west than in the east. In short, there are marked regional differences in the level of economic development and these are reflected in the population characteristics of the various regions.

The significance of this situation is indicated by national income data (State Institute of Statistics, 1969). Although the proportion employed in agriculture remains stable, farming contributes a declining share of the national income. Between 1948 and 1967, the value of agricultural production (at constant prices) rose by 70 per cent, but that of industrial output rose by 236 per cent, and agriculture's contribution to the national income dropped from 53.2 to 35.6 per cent, while that made by industry rose from 10.5 to 18.7 per cent. This draws attention to the low productivity of the agricultural worker, whose *per capita* output is little more than one-fifth that of a worker in industry, and emphasizes the contrasts between regions.

A further point requiring discussion is the extent to which expansion in agriculture has kept pace with population growth. During the 1950's, the food supply for the rapidly increasing population was maintained primarily by expansion of the cultivated area which increased by 55 per cent compared with a population growth of 32 per cent. As a result, *per capita* availability of foodstuffs increased during that decade. This form of expansion, however, was only a temporary palliative which, incidentally, involved the conversion of much pasture into cropland and overutilization of the remaining grazing land, particularly as there was no significant increase in the per hectare yield of the basic crops. By 1960 it was becoming apparent that further large-scale increase of the cultivated area was impossible and attention is now focused on intensification of production from existing farmland by the greater use of fertilizers, by irrigation and by improved farming methods. Continuous development along these lines will be necessary, even if the rate of rural population growth declines still further, in order to improve the living standards of the people in rural areas and to lessen the contrast with urban conditions, quite apart from the overall need to produce more food for a growing total population and for vital exports. At the same time, continued industrial growth will be necessary to provide employment for those moving out of the agricultural sector and to support the modernization of agriculture itself. Unless a positive policy is pursued towards the development of the less favoured parts of the country, the regional contrasts which are so clearly visible in the population geography of Turkey will become yet more marked.

REFERENCES

ALPAT, S. (1968) 'Current practices and problems in demographic statistics', *CENTO Symposium on Demographic Statistics, Karachi, Nov. 1968*, Ankara, State Institute of Statistics.

AVRALIOĞLU, Z. (1968) 'A review of Turkish Demographic Survey', *CENTO Symposium on Demographic Statistics, Karachi, Nov. 1968*, Ankara, State Institute of Statistics.

BRICE, W. C. (1954) 'The population of Turkey in 1950', *Geographical Journal*, 120, pp. 347–52.

DARKOT, B. (1955) 'Sur les mouvements démographiques en Turquie', *Review of the Geographical Institute, University of Istanbul (International Edn.)*, 2, pp. 38–44.

DEMENY, P. and SHORTER, F. C. (1968) *Estimating Turkish mortality, fertility and age structure: application of some new techniques*, Institute of Statistics, Faculty of Economics, University of Istanbul.

LEFEBVRE, T. (1928) 'La densité de la population en Turquie en 1914 et en 1927', *Annales de Géographie*, 37, pp. 520–6.

PALLIS, A. A. (1938) 'The population of Turkey in 1935', *Geographical Journal*, 91, pp. 439–45.

PASINER, S. (1968) '1970 population census programs of Turkey', *CENTO Symposium on Demographic Statistics, Karachi, Nov. 1968*, Ankara, State Institute of Statistics.

ŞENGÖLGE, O. (1968a) 'Needed studies and research subjects in demography in Turkey', *CENTO Symposium on Demographic Statistics, Karachi, Nov. 1968*, Ankara, State Institute of Statistics.

ŞENGÖLGE, O. (1968b) 'Vital registration in Turkey', *CENTO Symposium on Demographic Statistics, Karachi, Nov. 1968*, Ankara, State Institute of Statistics.

SHORTER, F. C. (1968) 'Information on fertility, mortality and population growth in Turkey', *Population Index*, 34, pp. 3–21.

STATE INSTITUTE OF STATISTICS (1969) *Türkiye Istatistik Yıllığı 1968 (Statistical Yearbook of Turkey, 1968)*, Ankara.

STATE PLANNING ORGANIZATION (1969) *Second Five-Year Development Plan, 1968–1972*, Ankara.

TAEUBER, I. B. (1958) 'Population and modernization in Turkey', *Population Index*, 24, pp. 101–122.

TANOĞLU, A. (1955) 'The recent emigration of the Bulgarian Turks', *Review of the Geographical Institute, University of Istanbul (International Edition)*, 5, pp. 94–106.

TÜMERTEKIN, E. (1958) 'The distribution of sex ratios, with special reference to internal migration in Turkey', *Review of the Geographical Institute, University of Istanbul (International Edition)*, 4, pp. 9–32.

YAŞER, Y. (1968) 'Family planning practices', *CENTO Symposium on Demographic Statistics, Karachi, Nov. 1968*, Ankara, State Institute of Statistics.

Chapter 3
Iran: changing population patterns
B D Clark

Iran, with an estimated population of 30 million in 1970 and an area of
1.65 million sq. km. (Plan Organization, 1966), has a complex range of
demographic characteristics. Great contrasts reflect not only the past
history of the country and the different physical environments of a land
that is three times larger than France, but also the increasing influence of
central government and private entrepreneurs, by their investment decisions, upon the distribution and characteristics of the population. With
over half of the total government revenue in recent years provided by the
oil industry (Plan Organization, 1968) in a country where economic growth
has averaged 6 per cent during the last 15 years, and where the industrial
sector has achieved a 12 per cent annual average growth rate for the last
5 years, it is inevitable that the concomitant economic and social changes
are having a marked effect on population.

Perhaps the greatest impact on the population geography of the country
has been as a result of the increased government investment in health and
welfare services, educational facilities, infrastructure planning and industrial and agricultural development policies. In some rural areas there has
been an increase in the population density, yet at the same time a growing
number of people are leaving the land and migrating to the towns and cities
where there are prospects of higher wages and more varied employment
opportunities. Increasing mobility among the population is now apparent
in response to either known or believed advantages of urban areas, and
this is again leading to greater contrasts in the demographic patterns of the
country. Iran therefore shows many of the classic features associated with
the population of a developing country: a rapid growth of the population
due to high fertility and declining mortality, a redistribution of the population from rural to urban areas, spatial population readjustment within
cities, the growth of a primate city, Tehran, and overall a marked contrast
between rural and urban populations in terms of income, job opportunities,
degree of literacy and standards of living, all of these being higher in urban
areas. It is worth noting, however, that Iran has avoided some of the worst
physical manifestations of rapid population growth, such as massive areas
of slums or shanty-towns, and the processes of change which are occurring,
and the experience gained may well be of relevance to other countries
within the developing world.

The changes which are now occurring are in a country which has experienced fluctuating fortunes over the centuries, but which has nevertheless maintained a degree of continuity perhaps best seen in an urban culture extending over 5,000 years, a period which has witnessed great alterations in the size of the state and the nationality of its rulers, and competition of outside powers to attempt to control and influence. Control can be seen in the Russian and British role in the nineteenth century whereas at the present time many countries are attempting to influence a state which is increasingly becoming more politically and economically independent as a result of oil revenue and internal reform. Although present developments are dominated by a real desire to advance social and economic reforms, the past has still a very important influence on Iran's population geography. This can be seen in the way that the historic trade routes have influenced the urban settlement pattern and in the way that investment in water supply over hundreds of years still affects the density of rural settlement. Another example of the very real significance of past events in the country can be seen in the attitudes of residual ethnic and racial groups, some now settled, others still nomadic, who often have more loyalty to their tribal leaders than to the anonymous and unidentifiable state. They present to a strongly centralized government great problems of integration. To appreciate fully the population geography of Iran one must be constantly aware of these past influences upon the composition, growth and distribution of population.

Statistical sources

Until 1956, there are no comprehensive sectoral or areal data available for a study of the demographic characteristics of the population. Prior to this date a variety of sources have to be used (Clark, 1967 and de Planhol, 1968). Most important are the estimates of travellers and diplomats of many nationalities, and some Arab geographers, who give figures of numbers, type and distribution of the country's population. Much of the information was based on hearsay or by the counting of tents or houses and by the use of a multiplier, in the case of towns, usually 5–8 persons per unit. Many of the figures arrived at in the eighteenth and nineteenth centuries were based on estimates by the local ruler. At times these figures appear inflated when he wishes to give a glowing impression of the numbers that he ruled; at other times low figures are given in an attempt to reduce the calls on his manpower by the national ruler. Nevertheless, towards the end of the nineteenth century and from then on total estimates do appear reasonably accurate, particularly when compared to backward projections from later censuses (Bharier, 1968). By careful manipulation it is possible to grasp the broad population figures prior to 1956, particularly for the early part of the twentieth century.

As well as these unofficial figures, certain government surveys were undertaken. Limited in scope and areal coverage, the most important was an urban head count conducted between 1939 and 1941, when 25 major cities incorporating an area up to six miles from the city centre were enumerated, the aim being to extend coverage to include other towns and then the rural areas of the country. Because of the Second World War, this was not done. Figures from the survey are included in the 1956 census volumes but most authorities are suspicious of their reliability.

Of other pre-1956 government sources, the only one of any real significance is the vital registration data which were collected from 1928 onwards after the establishment of civil registration offices throughout the country. Unfortunately data from this source are sporadic and unreliable, and regrettably the situation was still the same in 1970 despite a major drive to improve the collection and recording of demographic data (Plan Organization, 1968). This precludes many techniques of demographic analysis and emphasis has to be placed on the national censuses of 1956 and 1966, which obtained a wide range of data on age, sex, marital status and migration together with social and economic characteristics of the population, such as employment, occupation, housing, literacy and religious affiliation.

There are two drawbacks to the census data. First, most of the 1956 data cannot be compared with the 1966 data as statistical units have been altered and different questions asked. Secondly, there is considerable doubt as to the accuracy of the figures (Bharier, 1968). The census totals for 1956 are believed by various authorities to be low and have been variously corrected upwards by 2.6 per cent (Swan, 1967), 5 per cent (Jamei, personal communication) and 7.5 per cent (Bharier, 1968). Bharier believes the 1966 results to be more accurate, but authorities talk of a 3.5 per cent under-enumeration (Bartsch, 1970) and a 10 per cent over-estimation shown in a post-enumeration survey in urban areas.

In the post-war period many government departments have produced statistical data which includes information on certain characteristics of the population. The most important data have come from the Iranian Statistical Centre (Ministry of the Interior, 1960 and 1963), the Ministry of Labour (1958 and 1962) and the Ministry of Labour and Social Affairs (1968). Virtually all other ministries and departments have statistical offices which produce information of relevance to a study of the population geography of Iran. Unfortunately, there appears to be little co-ordination between the different statistical departments and in many cases data collected on the same topic are contradictory (Clarke and Clark, 1969).

Of equal importance are individual studies that have been made of smaller statistical units, such as on Abadan (Vieille, 1965), Tehran (Tamrazian, 1968) and selected rural areas (Mashayekhi *et al.*, 1953 and

Amani, 1968). Although limited in areas and topics covered and therefore general applicability, they do give an insight into detailed aspects of population geography. So also do the data which are increasingly in evidence from the various consultants now operating in Iran, for example survey data from integrated development work on Khuzestan, Jiroft and Gorgan, and town-planning studies where enumeration district data are used (Gruen).

In sum, with the exception of the 1966 census, the accuracy of much of the now prolific Iranian data is doubtful. As this is the case at the level of the total population figures there are clearly great dangers when using the areal and sectoral data from which total figures are derived. Figures and percentages used are therefore more a declaration of approximate amounts than categoric statements. With careful handling a great deal may be gleaned from Iranian statistical sources but many researchers may find rather disconcerting the comment found in the 1966 national census that 'users of the report may make any adjustments which they find appropriate'.

Race, religion and language

The inhabitants of Iran have neither racial nor linguistic unity, but over 95 per cent profess to be Moslems. The most important ethnic groups are the Persians, accounting for nearly three-quarters of the total population, and the Turkish, Baluchi and Arab elements. There is a considerable number of Armenians, and a small number of Jews, Assyrians, Brahuis and Hazaras. In general, racial mixture is greatest in those parts of Iran which have formed the historical zones of passage for invading armies such as Azerbaijan, Khurasan, Sistan, Khuzestan and Kermanshahan. The transfer of tribes and the incursion of wandering Arab groups from Iraq have also had an effect on the racial mixing within the country. With the exception of Arab, Turkish and Kurdish tribes appearing as relatively homogeneous groups in parts of Khuzestan, Fars and Mazandaran, there is a large block of people speaking Persian or allied languages throughout the central and southern Zagros chain, in the Elburz mountains and on the Caspian lowlands. The Kurds are found in the northern Zagros chain and north Khurasan, while the Turkish ethnic groups live in Azerbaijan and eastwards towards Tehran, with other groups in eastern Fars and north Khurasan. While the majority of the Armenians are predominantly an urban population element, a number still live in Azerbaijan and are engaged in agricultural pursuits Historically, almost all of the ethnic groups in Iran trace their origin to a pastoral tribe or tribal confederation that invaded Iran at some time in the past (Field, 1939)

Out of the total population of 25.07 million in 1966, 24.8 million were Moslems of whom 90 per cent were Shi'a, which is the official religion of the state. The Shi'a Moslems became the majority group under the Safavid kings; prior to this the Sunni Moslems were the dominant group. Sunnis are found mostly among the Kurds, Baluchis, north Khurasan Turkomans and Arabs. It is of interest to note that the Sunni religious leaders did not join with many of the landowners to oppose the Land Reform and social reforms of the 'White Revolution' as did a great number of the Shi'a leaders. There is a small number of Ismaili Moslems and a slightly greater number of adherents of Sufism. The Zoroastrians of Iran number approximately 25,000 and are concentrated in Yazd, Kerman and Tehran where they have five temples. Bahais, although not recognized by the state, are estimated to have 60,000 followers who practise illegally throughout the country (Echo of Iran, 1969).

Christians form the largest non-Moslem religious minority group in Iran. Armenians number approximately 190,000. For many centuries Armenia was part of the Persian Empire and Armenians spread through the northern provinces of the kingdom. As well as being forcibly moved, for example by Shah Abbas to Esfahan, many willingly migrated to the southern oilfields after 1920. However, most settled in Tehran, Julfa (Esfahan), Tabriz, Rezaiyeh and Rasht where they have been important in commerce and the development of industry. Assyrian Christians were estimated to be 19,000 in 1966 with over 50 per cent in Tehran and 40 per cent in or near Rezaiyeh. The Jews are found in most of the major cities (Fischel, 1950) and in 1966 numbered 67,000, but their numbers have been greatly reduced by the migration to Israel of approximately 45,000 members since 1948. Despite political pressure being brought against the Jews by Iran's Arab neighbours, they are recognized by the Constitution and have a seat in the Majlis. It has been estimated that there are virtually no illiterate Jews at school age and above in Iran, which is in marked contrast with every other ethnic, racial or religious group.

The languages native to Iran are Persian, spoken by a majority of the population and the official language of the country, and various languages closely akin to Persian which are spoken north of the Elburz in Gilan and Mazandaran and by Lur and Bakhtiari tribesmen. Kurdish and Baluchi are related languages of the Indo-European group and are spoken in the rural areas and towns where these tribal groups are still an important entity. Arabic dialects are spoken by some 2 million people particularly in Khuzestan, along the Persian Gulf and by some of the nomadic tribes in Fars province. Turkish dialects, unrelated to Persian or Arabic, are spoken by approximately 4 million people: the Azeri in Azerbaijan, the Qashqai, some of the Khamseh tribes in Fars and the Turkomen in Khurasan. Of the other languages, the Assyrians near Lake Rezaiyeh speak Aramaic dialects and the Armenians retain their native language, although most of them, particularly the urban-dwellers, can also speak Persian.

Age and sex

Of the total population of 25.07 million in 1966 there were 12.98 million males and 12.09 million females giving a ratio of 107.3 males per 100 females (Table 3.1). This very high ratio may partly be due to the fact that it is known that many girls were not declared to the enumerators. In both 1956 and 1966 sex ratios in the urban areas were higher than in the rural areas, but there has been a narrowing of the urban/rural gap in the intercensal period. The other major point is that in almost all age groups there is a marked excess of males to females which is in great contrast to most urban and rural areas of the western world.

TABLE 3.1   IRANIAN SEX RATIOS, 1956–66

Sex	Total population			Urban population		Rural population	
	1956	*1956 adjusted**	*1966*	*1956*	*1966*	*1956*	*1966*
Males	9,644,944	9,847,294	12,981,665	3,070,149	5,096,654	6,574,795	7,885,011
Females	9,309,760	9,593,895	12,097,258	2,883,414	4,697,592	6,426,346	7,399,666
Sex ratio	103.6	102.6	107.3	106.4	108.4	102.3	106.5

Source of data: Ministry of Interior, 1956, vol. 2, and *Plan organization*, 1966, vol. 168.
* Adjusted 1956 population (Maroufi-Bozorgi, 1965).

Age–sex pyramids for the total population in 1956 and 1966 (Fig. 3.1) indicate a broadening at the base of the pyramid; in 1966, 34.1 per cent of the population were under 10 years of age and 54.6 per cent were under 20 years while the 1956 figures are 32.6 per cent and 49.7 per cent respectively. In 1966 the mean age of the population was 22.2 years and median age was 16.9. The pyramids for urban and rural areas in 1966 reveal in particular a shortage of males aged 20–29 in rural areas, a reflection of the numbers undergoing military service or pursuing education courses or working away from home, usually in urban areas.

One common tendency is for age groups ending in 0 or 5 to be disproportionately high, particularly in the over 20 age groups. Under-enumeration of children below one year is also believed to be considerable (Amani, 1965).

Despite these statistical errors, there is clear evidence of a growing proportion of young persons owing to a decline in infant mortality and a continuing high birth rate, particularly in rural areas. This age distribution is putting great pressure on the country's educational system and increasingly imposing a greater dependency burden on those of the population in working age groups.

Manpower characteristics

As Table 3.2 shows, there have been marked changes in the composition of employment in different industries in the intercensal period. Worth

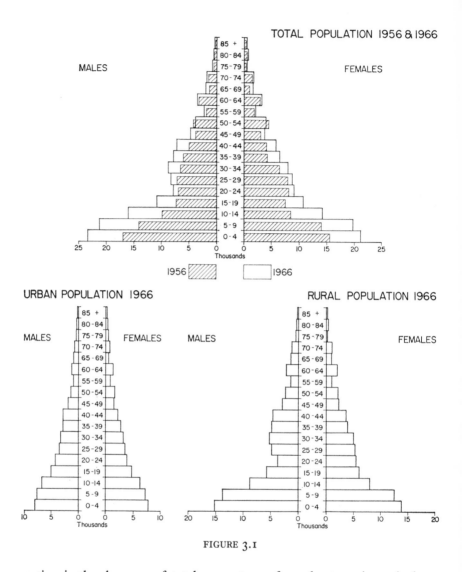

FIGURE 3.1

noting is the decrease of total percentage of employment in agriculture and this has important implications, as will be shown later, for rural–urban migration. Although manufacturing in the whole of the country has increased by 4.7 per cent, there has only been a small increase in the manufacturing percentage of total urban employment.

In tertiary activities there has been little change in the percentages of employment in the different service industries during the intercensal period. The figures shown give the relationships between employment in different industries, but overall there has been an increase from 5.90 million employed in 1956 to 6.85 million in 1966.

TABLE 3.2 PERCENTAGE EMPLOYED POPULATION OF IRAN 10 YEARS OF AGE
AND OVER BY MAJOR INDUSTRY GROUPS, 1956 AND 1966

Area	Agriculture		Mining and quarrying		Manufac- turing		Construction		Electricity gas, water		Commerce, transport, services, etc.	
	1956	1966	1956	1966	1956	1966	1956	1966	1956	1966	1956	1966
Urban	12.1	7.6	0.5	0.3	26.2	27.7	9.9	10.2	0.5	1.8	50.8	52.4
Rural	75.8	70.0	0.4	0.4	8.3	12.8	3.8	5.7	0.1	0.1	11.6	11.0
Total	56.3	46.2	0.4	0.4	13.8	18.5	5.7	7.4	0.2	0.8	23.6	26.7

Source of data: Plan organization, 1966.

Of the male population aged 10 years and above in 1966, 77.0 per cent
were economically active. In the economically inactive class, school children
and students were the major group and accounted for 15.5 per cent of the
population. Table 3.3 showing urban and rural age-specific activity rates
for Iran develops this important theme. For males there is a higher activity
rate in the rural areas, but this belies the fact that a great deal of agricultural
employment is seasonal in nature and for much of the year there is high
under-employment. In the 15–19 age group the great difference in the
rates in urban and rural areas indicates not only greater education opportunities in towns and cities but also the belief held among many
rural dwellers that when children are old enough to work they should do
so.

TABLE 3.3 PERCENTAGE MALE AND FEMALE AGE-SPECIFIC ACTIVITY RATES
IN IRAN, 1966

Age-group	Male		Female	
	Urban	Rural	Urban	Rural
15–19	48.6	84.7	9.8	19.8
20–24	85.9	96.0	12.1	15.6
25–44	96.3	98.2	10.4	13.7
45–54	91.6	95.3	11.0	11.7
55–64	74.3	81.7	8.9	7.5
65 and over	45.5	47.5	5.7	3.9

Source of data: Plan organization, 1966.

Figures for female activity rates can be best summarized by the statement that 'Iran was a patriarchal society for a long time and it still remains
part of the male psychology to wish for the upper hand. It has been said
that the movement for the emancipation of women has shattered the bonds
of second class citizenship, but the road to complete equality is long and
arduous' (Kooros, 1970). Despite attempts to increase female participation,
particularly in government employment, rates are low and although some

have argued that Iran will not reach economic maturity until this source of potential labour is more fully utilized, there is perhaps an even greater need to create male employment opportunities to reduce the high level of unemployment in both rural and urban areas.

Vital rates

According to the United Nations, there was a crude birth rate of 48 per thousand between 1945 and 1954. This is calculated by a reverse survival method from the 1956 census (United Nations, 1963), and compares with recorded Iranian figures of 28.8 for 1945–9 and 33.7 for 1950–4. Between 1955 and 1959 United Nations' estimates are 45 per thousand with recorded rates ranging from 34.8 to 44.3. Between 1960 and 1964 the United Nations' figure rises to 48 per thousand and is again based on the 1956 census and 'current rates in neighbouring countries with similar demographic fertility patterns' (United Nations, 1967). While many other figures are quoted for the crude birth rate in the 1960's, including 44 per thousand in the current development plan (Plan Organization, 1968), it is probable that the rate is nearer 49 per thousand.

Bearing in mind the recent demographic history of Iran the, child–woman ratio would be expected to be high and in 1956 was 886.7 per thousand women aged 15–44 (1956 adjusted figures 882.5), and in 1966 915.1; the rise may largely be accounted for by declining infant and child mortality. Rural Iran had even higher ratios in 1956 and 1966 of 921.3 and 989.3; for urban Iran the figures are 750.3 and 802.9, although there is some variation from town to town and in different rural areas.

Iranian data are particularly unsatisfactory in establishing crude death rates and infant mortality. Recorded crude death rates are 9.9. per thousand between 1945 and 1949 and 8.2 between 1950 and 1954, which are un-realistically low (Clarke and Clark, 1969). Between 1955 and 1964 the United Nations arrived at a figure of 25 per thousand which was based on calculations from the 1956 census against an average recorded rate for this period of 7.6. The United Nations publish a rate of 22 per thousand for the latter half of the 1960's, but the rate used by the Iranian planners is 18, which would appear to be too low.

Infant mortality rates have been calculated in special surveys as 217 per thousand at Shahrier in 1950, 188 in villages in Sabzevar in 1955, 170 for the whole of Iran and 120 per thousand in Shiraz in 1958 (Institute for Economic Research, 1968). Bearing in mind that infant mortality is one of the most difficult rates to establish, any final rate must be something of an approximation. Plan Organization use a rate of 160 per thousand in the current development plan and most Iranian demographers would accept this figure. Apart from infant mortality, other important causes of death are diseases of the digestive system (142 per thousand deaths), diseases of the respiratory system (121 per thousand deaths) and infectious and parasitic diseases (94 per thousand deaths).

It would seem likely that the crude death rate declines as more babies survive the first year of life and as a higher percentage of the population lives longer. This reduction in mortality is due to a great increase in medical facilities and better sanitation, particularly in the urban areas where mortality rates are now believed to be far lower than in rural Iran. Life expectancy in Iran has been variously calculated at between 40 and 45 years (Institute for Economic Research, 1968) and 46 years (Plan Organization, 1968).

In 1966, 56.5 per cent of the male, and 61.0 per cent of the female population were married. A higher proportion of young women are married compared to men, and as in most Moslem countries females marry younger. For example 45 per cent of girls aged 15 to 19 were married but only 4.2 per cent of the men in the same age group. The large number of women aged 40 and over who are widowed also shows this age discrepancy of marriage partners in Iran.

Population growth

Inevitably, there are wide discrepancies in the population estimates of Iran which have been made from the seventeenth century onwards. Great fluctuations would appear to be the normal pattern up to the start of the twentieth century. From then on there has been a steady increase through Reza Shah's rule (1925–41) with a rapid rise in population after the Second World War, the rate of population growth in the mid 1960's being estimated at 26 per thousand (Plan Organization, 1968).

One of the first estimates of the total population is a figure of 50 million at the time of Darius in the fourth century B.C. (Gupta, 1947)! At the height of the Safavid dynasty it was said to be 40 million! Chardin, quoting this figure, nevertheless believed the country to be 'but sparsely inhabited' because of 'unnatural vice, immoderate luxury, early marriages and constant migration to the Indies' (Chardin, 1686). Only in the nineteenth century do the figures appear more reasonable and, an oft quoted figure for the start of the century is 6 million. By 1850, total population was estimated to have grown to 10 million but by 1873, after cholera epidemics and famine it had again been reduced to 6 million (Rawlinson, 1880). Other writers in the 1870's and 1880's give figures of between 5 and 10 million (Field, 1939). By 1892 Curzon assumed the population to be between 8 and 9 million. This was based on a calculation of General Houtum-Schindler in 1884, the 'most available approximation to the truth', and then by applying a three-quarter per cent annual increase for the succeeding years (Curzon, 1892). Curzon believed that the population must have been greater in former times because of the visible evidence of 'ruined cities, abandoned villages and deserted bazaars, long lines of choked kanats, public works that once assisted to fertilize large districts now mouldering to decay and wide areas of cultivation since relapsed into sand and stones'. While this may have been the case, there are two recurrent themes in Iranian history that Curzon appears to ignore. First, the desire to move and create a totally new urban centre, as for example when a new dynasty became established, and second, the forced movement when land became exhausted or a qanat was blocked or dried up and it was more economical to move to a new locality. What Curzon describes as visible evidence of decline was often linked to greater growth elsewhere. There can be no doubt, however, that the most important demographic checks during the nineteenth century were famines and epidemics.

From the start of the twentieth century estimates of the population of Iran can be checked by a variety of techniques. By relating published estimates, postulated growth rates, life expectancy and a retrogression from a corrected 1956 census total, Bharier (1968) arrives at annual figures for the 1900–66 period. The most critical factor is the assumed growth rate, and this must be considered before looking at population figures. Amani has postulated growth rates of 0.2 per cent during 1900–25, 1.5 per cent during 1926–45 and 2.5 per cent during 1946–56. The low rate of growth, 0.2 per cent, in the early period is supported by several estimates of the country's population during these years and by the circumstantial evidence of political and economic instability. Some authorities imply that the population was decreasing in this period (League of Nations, 1926). Bharier believes that Amani's figure is too low and instead suggests a growth rate of 0.75 per cent, based on a forward projection of Houtum–Schindler at the end of the nineteenth century and a backward projection from the 1956 census. According to Bharier the most difficult period to postulate growth rates for is between 1920 and 1946, when certain events had an important bearing on the population situation. First, greater mobility was possible after the introduction of lorries from 1920 onwards. This enabled more efficient transfer of food to famine areas and therefore helped to reduce mortality. Secondly, during this period growth began to occur at certain urban centres which in the past had only acted as local service centres for an agricultural hinterland. Thirdly, a major drive was made by Reza Shah to improve living conditions in major towns and cities with some likelihood of a reduction in mortality (Banani, 1961). For this period Bharier feels that Amani's rate of 1.5 per cent fits most of the observed facts and can be related to both forward projections from 1900 and backward projections from 1956. Between 1946 and 1956 an annual growth rate of 2.5 per cent is accepted and reflects something of the post-war boom after a period of deprivation. The intercensal growth rate calculated from the published figures of the 1956 and 1966 censuses is 2.9 per cent (see Table 3.4).

TABLE 3.4   POPULATION GROWTH OF IRAN, 1900–66

Year	Total population		Urban population		Rural population	
	Numbers (millions)	Growth (per cent)	Numbers (millions)	Growth (per cent)	Numbers (millions)	Growth (per cent)
	Published data (a)					
1956	18.95	—	5.95	—	13.00	—
1966	25.32	2.9	9.79	5.1	15.29	1.6
	Calculated and corrected data (b)					
1900	9.86	—	2.07	—	7.79	—
1926	11.86	0.08	2.49	0.08	9.37	0.08
1934	13.32	1.50	2.80	1.50	10.52	1.50
1940	14.55	1.50	3.20	2.30	11.35	1.30
1956	20.38	2.20	6.32	4.40	14.06	1.40
1966	27.07	2.90	10.56	5.30	16.51	1.70

Source of data: (a) Ministry of the Interior, 1956; *Plan organization*, 1966.
(b) Bharier, 1968.

The table also emphasizes the relative and absolute increase of the urban population since the 1950's. A straightforward projection of these population totals and growth rates, ignoring for the time being changes in fertility and mortality patterns, and using published figures, gives a total estimated population in 1969 of 27.5 million (urban population 11.4 million, rural population 16.1) and in 1980 37.9 million (urban population 19.7 million and rural population 19.2 million). The projection of Bharier's adjusted figures suggest a population in 1969 of 29.4 million (urban population 12.2 million, rural population 17.2 million). A more detailed discussion of these figures will follow later.

Rural population distribution

In general, the areas with a high density of rural population at the present time are those parts of the country that have always been the most attractive for agricultural development. The densities shown on Figure 3.2, which includes both the rural and urban populations, are clearly a reflection of the availability of water. Although in some areas the government is now able to stimulate agricultural development by the provision of water and hence increase rural densities, the traditional supply of water from rivers, springs and *qanats** in particular, is still of paramount importance in explaining distributions. Moreover, the traditional division of the population of Iran into nomadic, rural and urban groups is to a lesser or greater extent a response to water availability. Indeed, there is a strong correlation

* Man-made underground water supply channels.

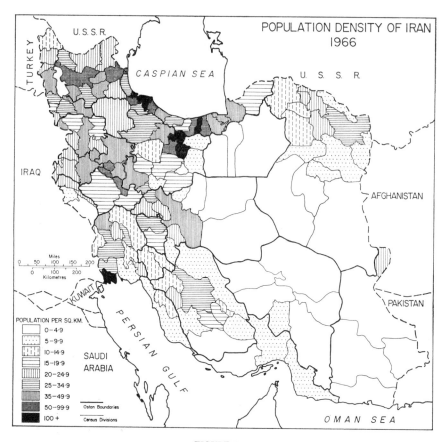

FIGURE 3.2

between urban settlements and high rural densities, whether one considers the Caspian littoral where intensive agriculture, high rural densities and an intensive network of towns are prevalent, or oasis areas such as Kerman, Yazd or Esfahan where again rural and urban densities are high in limited areas, but with the overall significance of this intensive settlement being lost on a density map of large administrative units.

Water availability is linked to broad physical and climatic regions and the associated population distributions are closely related to the major mountain ranges of the country (Fisher, 1968; Plan Organization, 1968). The Elburz mountains, stretching from Azerbaijan to the south of the Caspian and with outliers in Khurasan, and the Zagros mountains, incorporating agriculturally important intermontane basins, both greatly influence through their climatic régimes the major rural settlement patterns of the country. In the north-western provinces of Azerbaijan, where there is a reliable rainfall, are some of the highest rural densities, but even higher, if more restricted, densities are found in areas along the Caspian littoral. Climatically and hydrologically suitable for the growth of a wide range of crops, many of which need high labour inputs, this area makes a major contribution to the agricultural output of Iran.

Density patterns in the Zagros chain are far more complex. Settlement varies from intensive oasis-type agriculture carried out by a settled population, as for example in parts of Kermanshahan, Hamadan and Kordestan, to more extensive agriculture on the higher slopes with seasonal migration and transhumance, particularly in the southern Zagros, and a far lower rural density.

Khurasan is a region where there is a wide range of agricultural production. The climate is very varied, and in the north and north-east of the province a combination of temperate crops, dry farming and irrigated agriculture occurs. Only in a few restricted areas is there a higher density of population, but lower than the Caspian littoral and Azerbaijan. In southern Khurasan, oasis-type agriculture is most common with date-farming being very important, but overall densities are low.

In the rest of the country rural population density is low. Lowest densities occur on the central plateau particularly in the Dasht-e-Kavir and Dasht-e-Lut which are virtually uninhabited. To the south-west of these deserts and located on the main route between Tehran and Baluchestan is a number of major settlements such as Qom, Kashan, Yazd, Rafsanjan and Kerman. Important in themselves as urban nodes, they also act as major agricultural centres for scattered smaller oasis settlements (English, 1966).

At the present time, therefore, something like 60 per cent of the population of Iran are living in rural areas. This includes nearly one quarter of a million people who were described in the 1966 census as 'unsettled' or migratory. The percentage of the population classed as rural has been given as 79 per cent in 1900, 78 per cent in 1940 (Bharier, 1970), and 69 per cent or 13 million in 1956. At present there are 46,000 villages in Iran with a population of over 50, in comparison to about 15,200 villages in 1900 and 39,000 in 1956. Moreover, many places statistically defined as towns (a locality of over 5,000 inhabitants or a *shahrestan* (district) centre smaller in size) can in both a functional and morphological sense be considered rural, so that the rural percentage of the total population ought to be higher. Nevertheless, it is as much the contribution of agriculture to the national economy as the availability of oil revenues which explains why the government is making strenuous efforts to improve the efficiency and output of the agricultural sector by land reform and investment and why an understanding of rural population is of vital importance.

Tribal and nomadic population

The great historical nomadic movements into the area of Iran help to explain much of the ethnic and racial diversity that still exists. During the last fourteen centuries three major movements have occurred. The Arabs came in the seventh century to be followed in the eleventh century by the Seljuks. The last and perhaps most important group were the Mongols under Ghengiz Khan who occupied much of the territory. To these major movements must be added what Field calls 'minor incursions and slow infiltrations'.

The nomadic tribes of Iran are the most difficult population group to enumerate not only because of their life-style but also because many of them live in the remoter parts of the country. Increasingly many of the tribal groups have permanent or semi-permanent quarters, but for an ever-decreasing number the pattern of their seasonal migration makes this impossible. The tribal system, as it evolved, and in those areas where it is still operating today, particularly in the central and southern Zagros, is clearly a response to lack of adequate and regular water supplies for crops and livestock. Movement is seasonal and is geared to migration between winter and summer quarters. Nomadic tribes of the southern Zagros, for example, move to the warm plains of the Persian Gulf in autumn to sow grain. In the spring they return to the highest mountain pastures where grass is available for their livestock but leave some members of the tribe to gather the harvest. The actual pattern of migration varies in different parts of the country, but the above example is the most common type, often involving moves of several hundreds of miles between winter and summer quarters (Field, 1939; Monteil, 1966; Sunderland, 1968).

The most important tribal groups in Iran are the Kurds, Lur, Bakhtiari, Qashqai, Khamseh, Shahsavan, Baluchi and Turkoman. The first five of these are found in the Zagros region.

Population figures of the tribal population can be no more than rough estimates. Curzon in 1892 stated that there were then '2 million in the nomadic state', and an estimate of 1910 quotes a figure of 2.65 million (United Kingdom, Foreign Office, 1919). In the latter case it is not clear whether this includes a settled tribal component. By 1932 it was estimated that the number of tribal nomads had declined to around one million and numbers continued to decline until 1940. Although the figures may not be correct, there can be no doubt that a reduction did occur as a result of Reza Shah's policy to settle the tribes. As Lambton has stated, 'the settled population regarded the tribes as a potential threat to their security', and Reza Shah no doubt felt a nomadic group to be an anachronism in his policy of modernization. During his reign he attempted to destroy tribal organization, prevent seasonal migration and convert the tribal nomads into agriculturalists. Many were settled and many were killed, but, as Lambton has said, 'the tribal policy of Reza Shah, ill conceived and badly executed, resulted in heavy losses of livestock, the impoverishment of the tribes and a diminution of their numbers' (Lambton, 1953).

During the 1940's, as central government control was weakened, many tribesmen who had been forced to settle reverted to a nomadic or semi-nomadic existence. By the early 1950's the government was again in a position to attempt greater control over tribal activity, and a Higher Tribal Council under the direction of the Ministry of Court was established in 1953. Its aim once more was to force sedentarization and increase the economic contribution of the tribes to the national economy. Although the census of 1956 gives a figure of 240,000 migrant tribesmen, it adds the proviso that groups 'may have been incorrectly identified as temporary residents or even as members of the village near or in which they were enumerated'. Many people believe this figure to be too low. Likewise the 1966 census figure of 240,000 unsettled population is believed by several authorities to be too low and in one case a figure of 3 million tribesmen is quoted (Echo of Iran, 1969). Here the problem arises that many people described as tribesmen are in fact now permenently settled but still continue to live along tribal lines in their new villages and towns.

There can be no doubt that the number of tribesmen practising seasonal migration is declining, either voluntarily or enforced by the government. Increasingly the government's policy of only providing schools, health and communal facilities to those tribesmen living in permanent settlements appears to be working. Indeed many former tribesmen are spontaneously settling in villages and towns and buying land. It is probable that the death rates in the tribal rural areas will decline as more medical facilities are made available, and population will increase. For those who wish to continue a nomadic existence there is now the serious problem that their claims to large areas of land that were given to them in the past as a form of fief for military service have not been legally registered and are therefore no longer recognized. This together with greater control of their routes between winter and summer quarters is further evidence of the desire to eliminate seasonal migration, although some believe that this land system allows land to be used that would be otherwise unproductive.

Urbanization

During the last 25 years one of the most important population trends has been the rapid growth of the urban population. Just as villages have played a vital role in the community of social and economic organizations so towns and cities can be seen as part of a complex urban continuum extending over several thousand years. What has been significant in the past few years is the accelerating pace of urbanization as shown in the number, size and functional growth of towns and cities and the growing percentage of the total Iranian population living in towns or markedly influenced by this urbanization process.

While it is possible to talk about the continuity of an urban culture, it has not been an uninterrupted evolution of certain towns and cities. The changing political power over the centuries has led to a wide variety of patterns of growth and decay. Cities which have experienced changing political and economic vicissitudes have occasionally maintained their status, albeit with fluctuating population totals as at Esfahan, while other cities have flourished, declined and then in some cases disappeared. Political and economic locational advantages have altered with time, and in Iran this can be best seen in changing capital cities and the decline of cities located on major land trade routes after sea routes to the East were developed. In some cases these cities continued to perform local service functions for their surrounding agricultural areas, and some writers (English, 1966) would go so far as to say that these functions have always been more important than the external trade relationships so often quoted as the major causal factor of the growth of towns and cities in the Middle East. Fluctuating fortunes appear to be the most important theme in the urban past of Iran and in many ways this concept is still valid today.

It has been calculated that by 1900 21 per cent of the population were living in urban areas (Bharier, 1970). This percentage persisted until the 1940's although the number of urban dwellers increased from 2.07 million to 3.20 million. The latter part of this period coincides with the period of reform under Reza Shah and the development of motor transport. This increased mobility probably accounts for some of the migration to the towns during the period, but the fact that the urban–rural ratio remained the same during these 40 years may partly be explained by the need for the agricultural sector to produce more food for the growing rural and urban population by an increase not only of cultivable land but also of the labour force.

The urban population increased to 31 per cent in 1956 and 39 per cent by 1966. In 1956 there were 186 urban settlements with a population over 5,000. This compares with 100 settlements in 1900, although in the 56 years 13 of these settlements lost urban status so that the 1956 urban settlements comprised 87 that existed in 1900 plus 99 new ones (Bharier, 1970). These latter were either villages which had increased in population or entirely new creations such as oil towns, ports, mining communities or tourist resorts.

In the 1956–66 intercensal period the number of settlements with more than 5,000 inhabitants increased by 37, although Figure 3.3 includes all *shahrestan* centres, which are defined by the Iranians as urban although their population may be under 5,000. Certain broad patterns are discernible. The most striking is the correlation between urban settlements and areas of high rural population densities. With the main role of many urban

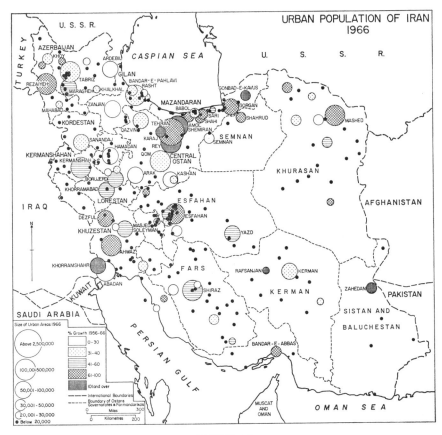

FIGURE 3.3

centres being the performance of higher order functions for rural areas, it is not surprising that the greatest networks of towns and cities are found in Azerbaijan, north and south of the Elburz and in intermontane basins along the Zagros mountains. Many of these settlements are on the historic trade routes, such as the Silk Road (Boulnois, 1966), and this route network is again being re-emphasized by current road-building programmes.

In 1966, approximately one-third of the total urban population was living in the Central *ostan*. Other ostans (administrative regions) making a major contribution to the total urban population are Khuzestan (11.1 per cent) and Esfahan (10.2 per cent). The significance of the Central ostan is again emphasized by the urban growth in the years from 1956 to 1966 when the total urban population increase was 3.8 million with 1.1 million occurring in this ostan.

Table 3.5 shows that the percentage of the urban population in cities of 100,000 and more has increased from 51.3 in 1956 to 60.6 in 1966. The

TABLE 3.5   THE NUMBER, SIZE AND GROWTH OF IRANIAN TOWNS, 1956–66

Size of locality	1956 Cities		Percentage distribution of urban population	1966 Cities		Percentage distribution of urban population	Annual rate of increase 1956–66
	No.	Per cent		No.	Per cent		
5,000–9,999	90	48.4	10.6	97	43.5	6.6	4.20
10,000–24,999	56	30.1	14.7	64	28.7	11.7	4.50
25,000–49,999	22	11.8	12.8	35	15.7	11.7	3.40
50,000–99,999	9	4.8	10.6	13	5.8	9.4	3.10
100,000–249,999	6	3.2	16.7	8	3.7	12.4	3.95
250,000–499,999	2	1.1	9.1	5	2.2	19.0	4.20
500,000+	1	0.5	25.5	1	0.4	29.2	7.15
Total	186	100.0	100.0	223	100.0	100.0	6.01

Source of data: Ministry of Interior, 1956 and *Plan organization*, 1966.

lowest annual rate of growth has been in towns with a population of 50,000 to 99,999.

The annual rates of increase by size categories conceal a very great range in rates of growth among individual towns and cities. Figure 3.3 shows the total percentage increase in towns over 20,000 in the intercensal period. If all urban areas below 20,000 were included, only nine towns in the whole of Iran had a decline in population during this period and most of these had fewer than 5,000 inhabitants in 1966. An analysis of intercensal growth in all urban areas showed that there was virtually no correlation between town size and percentage growth. In the case of towns in the size categories 5,000–9,999 and 10,000–19,999, a few increased by less than 20 per cent but most grew by more than 25 per cent, the highest absolute and relative growth being in towns over 10,000. When growth of small towns is considered in different parts of the country there is again a random pattern although two trends are discernible: high rates of growth occurred in towns remote from a major city (because of a great increase in government services), and in towns close to major provincial cities and part of their embryonic city regions.

It is, however, at the other end of the urban hierarchy where the important developments are taking place. The rapid growth of the country's largest cities is creating a vast number of social, economic and planning problems with which the Iranians will be forced to come to terms. This growth can be best seen in the case of Tehran, which is markedly primate, although its position in the urban hierarchy has not led to quite the same degree of urban primacy as exists in some Latin American and African countries. Cities such as Esfahan, with a population now approaching half a million, form a second tier of major centres. This in no way suggests that the size and status of Tehran is not of vital importance. Growing from approximately 200,000 in 1900 to 500,000 in 1940, its annual rate of increase between 1956 and 1966 was 6 per cent, with an increase from 1.5 million in 1956 to 2.7 million in 1966 (Tamrazian, 1968). By 1966 Tehran contained 10.5 per cent of the country's total population and 30 per cent of the total urban population, and was six times larger than the next city.

All other cities with a population over 200,000 have had considerable intercensal growth. These cities, important as regional capitals with major administrative and commercial functions and in some cases now seen by the economic planners as major growth poles of development, have grown, with the exception of Abadan, by more than 30 per cent in the intercensal period. Abadan's growth in this period was only 20.7 per cent, which is accountable to a reduction of labour demand in the oil industry. For the other cities of over 200,000, growth between 1956 and 1966 was high: Esfahan 66.4 per cent, Mashed 69.2, Tabriz 39.1, Shiraz 63 and Ahwaz 71.9. These cities, with Tehran and Abadan, contained 4.7 million people in 1966 or 48 per cent of the total urban population.

A few comments will be made on the distribution and growth of towns and cities in selected parts of the country. In Azerbaijan there is a high population density yet there are very few small towns, major settlement being in villages or large cities such as Tabriz, Rezaiyeh, Maragheh and Ardebil, but while there is a high rate of urban population increase in West Azerbaijan, in East Azerbaijan rates of growth are lower. Reasons for this may be the isolation—Ardebil, for example, having tortuous links to main communication networks—little growth of new industry and a long history of out-migration, particularly to Tehran.

Farther south in the central Zagros it is the major regional cities that have continued to grow at the expense of the smaller towns. Cities such as Kermanshah, Khorramabad and Borujerd have all grown more than 40 per cent between 1956 and 1966 while Hamadan and Arak are the only large cities throughout the whole of the Zagros mountains that have had a growth of less than 30 per cent At the present time Hamadan is experiencing net out-migration It is likely that Arak, with the recent building of a major machine tool plant, will show greater growth during the 1970's It is in this region, particularly surrounding Hamadan and near the Iraq border, that, in comparison with the rest of Iran, some of the slowest urban growth rates of small towns have occurred, and several towns, including Qasr-e-Shirin, have even declined in population In contrast, the province of Esfahan, as well as having a rapidly growing city, has also experienced over 30 per cent growth in the small and medium-sized towns.

In Khuzestan there are few small towns, but what is noticeable is the impressive growth of large- and medium-sized cities. Khuzestan is the third most highly urbanized province after the Central ostan and Esfahan and, with the exception of Abadan, the large cities have grown very quickly during the 1956–66 period: Khorramshahr 101.9 per cent, Ahwaz 71.9, Dezful 62.1 and Masjed Soleyman 44.4. Reasons for this are recent heavy investment in port installations by the government, and inland, further developments in the oil industry. Ahwaz is likely to grow still further as an increase of employment in the tertiary sector of the oil industry occurs and the government is establishing one of the country's first industrial estates there. On the other hand, Masjed Soleyman is likely to decline as readjustments take place in oil production which will reduce the number employed.

In both coastal and inland parts of the south-east Caspian area, the major towns, Amol, Shahi, Sari, Gorgan and Gonbad, all grew by more than 60 per cent between 1956 and 1966. This area has always been important for agricultural production and some of the growth of these towns has been linked to their continued expansion as market centres, as investment, mechanization and development schemes have increased production in the region. A more recent phenomenon is the growth of resort and tourist functions, which initially catered for wealthy Iranians who had summer residences there, but are now being developed for the growing middle class by the construction of hotels, villas and holiday camps. Access to the area, particularly from Tehran, has been greatly facilitated by heavy investment in improving roads across the Elburz Mountains. There are now very few areas on the south and south-east Caspian coast which are not staked out for development, and with a continuing rise in wages and more leisure time it is inevitable that there will be rapid population growth.

Urban populations

As yet little work has been done on population distributions within urban areas. Data at enumeration district level are only available for the 1966 census so that it is difficult to analyse trends of population movements and changing social areas as a reflection of internal population readjustment. Partial evidence does suggest, however, that the recent growth of urban population, by both natural increase and migration, is leading to great population contrasts within the urban area.

Traditionally, the urban area was very compact with a high density of residential population. Reasons for this were on the one hand the need to enclose towns with defensive walls (and from a cost point of view compactness was at a premium), and on the other hand the nature of extended family life which would often absorb many members into a small area. Within the city were found the traditional features of Iranian urban life such as the bazaar, caravanserai, arg (citadel) and mosque, and occasionally quarters for ethnic and religious groups (Clarke, 1963 and English, 1966). Peripheral development occurred after the need for defence declined and a demand for better standards of housing arose, and this was facilitated in the major cities of Iran by the opening up of the towns with new roads at the time of Reza Shah. The residential density of these new areas is generally far lower than in the central part of the cities, although there are exceptions such as the new high rise flats in Tehran (de Planhol, 1968) or the peripheral Kurdish quarter of Kermanshah (Clarke and Clark, 1969). Change and readjustment of the population are also occurring in the older residential quarters of the cities. As pressure for more higher-order central area functions increases, so much older residential property is being destroyed. Now in some of the largest cities of Iran there is a blighted zone near the central area where poor quality housing has a high residential density. These areas, together with poor quality peripheral housing, act as the reception centre for in-migrants to the city. Multi-occupancy is common, facilities are poor and these areas are major planning problems of the present time.

There are now great contrasts between different sections of the urban population and they can be measured in a variety of ways. Expression of this can be seen in contrasting residential land values (Clarke and Clark, 1969; Darwent, 1966), and in contrasting shopping areas which reflect the purchasing power of different socio-economic groups (de Planhol, 1968). Figure 3.4 shows some of these contrasting demographic areas that exist in one particular Iranian town, Kashan (Costello, 1970). By using enumeration district data for principal component factor analysis, a social area study has been made. Using 33 social, economic and demographic

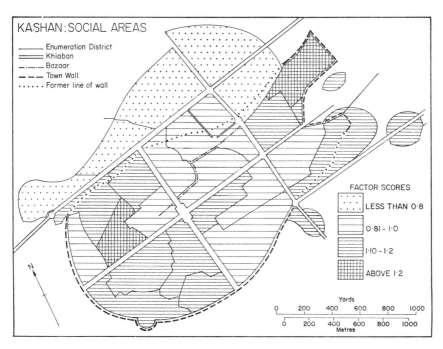

FIGURE 3.4

variables, including persons per acre, sex ratios, literacy, persons per household, activity rates and household industry, 70 per cent of the total variance is explained by one factor. The factor scores of the enumeration districts on the varimax factor one are thus mapped using 4 classes. Immediately, broad contrasts are seen. Areas with a score of less than 0.8 stand out as areas of recent development outside the walls, with low population density and with a high percentage of long-distance migrants (often technicians in the factories), higher literacy rates and a small percentage of households with household industries. Other work in Iran (Power, 1970) suggests that the same kind of demographic contrast exists.

Mobility and migration

A recurring theme in this chapter has been migration and mobility. This has already been considered in relation to the tribal population and included the seasonal migrations and the transfer of tribal groups. There remains the largely voluntary migration within the country, which is having a great impact on the contemporary demographic structure. Little work has been done on the detailed measurements of migration, or indeed on motivations, but there is enough evidence to indicate major patterns.

In the past there has been a tendency to think of migration as a simple rural-to-urban move. Bharier has shown that in Iran the movements are far more complex, and that the concept of a rural–urban continuum is only part of the pattern. By taking the total urban population increase, which was 105 per cent between 1900 and 1956, he argues that any individual town or city which had an increase above that figure had net in-migration. Only 25 of the 100 existing towns of 1900 had net in-migration well above this figure, totalling approximately 728,000 persons, and in fact Tehran's total net in-migration was greater than into all other receiving areas. Bharier has calculated from an analysis of the relative significance of natural increase and migration that the total rural–urban migration during the period 1900–56 amounted to 685,000 and that 61 per cent of the internal population movements were between urban areas and 39 per cent between rural and urban centres.

This work by Bharier can be placed in a wider context by looking at the life-time migration figures in the 1956 census. Of the total population 89 per cent had either never moved from their shahrestan of birth, or had now returned. Of the remainder, 4 per cent had moved to an adjacent shahrestan and only 7 per cent were living in a shahrestan not contiguous to the one of their birth. The greatest volume of migration from shahrestans was from Tabriz to Tehran 94,306, Arak to Tehran 78,318, Tehran to Karaj 62,303, Ardebil to Tehran 53,033 and Esfahan to Tehran 50,882. Tehran, as expected, experienced the largest gain with a total net in-migration of 690,778. Largest net out-migrations were from the shahrestans of Esfahan 134,161, Tabriz 118,146, Arak 88,578, Hamadan 75,654 and Ardebil 66,531. At the province level only the Central ostan, Khuzestan, West Azerbaijan and Kordestan had net gains and the rest had a net loss with heaviest losses recorded in East Azerbaijan 287,000, Esfahan/Yazd 190,000, Gilan 167,000 and Kermanshahan 94,000. Towns with the highest recorded percentages of migrants in their population were Abadan 52 per cent, Tehran 48, Ahwaz 45 and Mashed 25.

For the period from 1956 to 1966, Bharier using similar techniques as in the earlier period, calculates that there has been a sharp rise in the amount of rural–urban migration as a percentage of total migration. It now accounts for 90 per cent compared to 39 per cent in the earlier period. Tehran has again been the leading recipient of in-migrants but the number has now been reduced to 38 per cent. Mashed has retained its drawing power, and Esfahan, after suffering a net loss of population in the pre-1956 period, has made a net gain in the intercensal period.

TABLE 3.6 BIRTHPLACE OF POPULATION OF IRAN, 1966

Ostan, governorate or farmandorikol	Percentage born in shahrestan of enumeration			Percentage born in other shahrestan of ostan of enumeration			Percentage born in other ostan		
	Total	Urban	Rural	Total	Urban	Rural	Total	Urban	Rural
Central	65.1	54.5	90.4	11.3	13.9	5.0	22.8	30.5	4.5
Gilan	95.0	86.7	97.4	2.7	7.5	1.4	2.2	5.5	1.2
Mazandaran	83.5	74.5	86.4	4.0	5.9	3.4	12.3	19.3	10.1
East Azerbaijan	96.2	90.5	98.5	2.5	6.3	0.9	1.2	3.0	0.5
West Azerbaijan	92.4	82.0	96.0	3.4	6.3	2.3	4.2	11.5	1.6
Kermanshahan	90.8	83.4	94.9	4.0	5.3	3.3	4.8	11.1	1.3
Khuzestan	79.5	69.6	92.1	8.5	11.0	5.3	11.7	19.0	2.5
Fars	93.5	89.3	96.4	3.2	4.8	2.2	3.2	5.8	1.5
Kerman	95.1	88.3	97.5	2.6	6.1	1.4	2.2	5.5	1.1
Khurasan	92.5	81.6	96.9	5.4	11.3	2.4	2.6	6.8	0.6
Esfahan	95.9	94.2	97.6	2.0	2.6	1.4	2.0	3.1	0.9
Sistan and Baluchestan	93.7	69.1	98.3	2.7	12.2	0.9	3.4	18.1	0.7
Kordestan	94.8	85.3	96.7	1.6	4.3	1.1	3.3	10.3	1.9
Hamadan	97.3	93.9	98.4	0.9	1.4	0.7	1.8	4.6	0.9
Chahrmahal	97.9	96.7	98.4	0.2	0.2	0.2	1.9	3.1	1.4
Lorestan	94.7	84.6	97.9	1.5	4.6	0.5	3.7	10.7	1.5
Ilam	95.8	89.0	96.9	0.4	0.8	0.3	3.6	9.9	2.5
Kohkiluyeh	94.2	58.9	97.9	0.4	1.2	0.3	5.3	39.6	1.7
Ports and Islands, Persian Gulf	94.3	81.0	98.0	1.2	3.6	0.6	4.3	15.0	1.3
Ports and Islands, Oman Sea	94.9	78.7	97.8	1.3	4.5	0.7	3.7	16.4	1.3
Semnan	93.2	87.0	97.5	1.5	2.9	0.6	5.1	9.9	1.9

Note: Percentages do not add up to 100 as persons born in foreign countries are excluded.
Source of data: Plan organization, 1966.

Unfortunately the 1966 census did not publish detailed information on life-time migration similar to that of 1956, so intercensal changes of residence cannot be measured. Information on place of birth is only given as summary findings and these are shown in Table 3.6. Of the total population

86.9 per cent were born in the shahrestan of enumeration, compared to 89 per cent in 1956, although shahrestan boundaries have been altered between the two censuses. The percentage of the urban population born in the shahrestan of enumeration was 73.6, and of the rural population 95.4. Contrasts between different ostans and urban and rural areas of ostans are shown clearly. The most significant figures are for the Central ostan, which includes Tehran, Rey and Shemiran with only 65.1 per cent of the total population born there. Of the urban population of this ostan, 30.5 per cent or 1.07 million people were born in other ostans, implying long-distance migration into Tehran and its suburbs. Only the Central ostan has a considerable number of persons (33,386) born abroad living there. Apart from the Central ostan, only Khuzestan and Mazandaran have lower than average figures of persons born in the shahrestan of enumeration. However, over 10 per cent of the urban population in most ostans were born in a different shahrestan or ostan.

Reasons for these migration figures are many, and although little research has been done on causes of movement, many of the classic features operating in developing countries can be seen. It is in the agricultural sector that the greatest push factors are found. Movement from the land has been caused by a relative decline in agricultural productivity, some increase in mechanization and land reform with redistribution of land, leaving a group who no longer can find employment in rural areas. It would appear that many of these people are drifting into small towns, only to find lack of employment there also; and some then move on to the largest cities. The attraction of the cities, whether it be real or notional, is the prospect of a job for those unemployed, better wages for those already employed, the availability of better health and educational facilities, and a belief that standards of living can be improved. The general effect has been to spread unemployment more evenly between urban and rural areas. In the short term many of these migrants are suffering abject poverty, whereas in the rural areas that they have left they were at least able to obtain work in periods of intense activity such as harvesting and could be more easily supported in kind, if not in cash, by more affluent relatives.

One major study, while statistically suspect (Ministry of Labour and Social Affairs, 1968) suggested that 18.7 per cent of the Iranian population were migrants, and of these 42.5 per cent were principal migrants, others being secondary migrants including wives, children and dependant relatives. Of the total migrants 40 per cent were in the 25–44 age group and in total 10.4 per cent had migrated in the year prior to enumeration, 46.9 per cent 1–5 years before and 42.7 per cent over 10 years before. Economic reasons for migration are most important among the principal migrants and include 'seeking a better job' (43.6 per cent), 'seeking work' (10.7 per cent), with 'marriage' (24.6 per cent) also very important. It would appear that many of those 'seeking a better job' are unemployed, as a further tabulation in the study states that 2.8 million persons, 66.2 per cent of all migrants, were so categorized. Numbers unemployed were reduced to 2.5 million after migration but the length of unemployment is not made clear.

Information on those temporarily absent from home was also collected. There were 420,000 people in this category, with 92 per cent in working age groups. Many were male villagers who had taken seasonal employment in the large cities, particularly in the building trade. Military and Corps service were also important, while among younger age groups the reason for absence was often educational. Over 100,000 Iranian immigrants have been enumerated in the States of the Persian Gulf, but this figure is undoubtedly lower than reality as illegal entrance is common (Bharier, 1971).

Contemporary population trends

The Iranian population experiences high fertility and relatively high mortality, although the latter is decreasing and will continue to do so as more of the population live in urban areas where medical facilities and living conditions are better. There is yet little evidence of declines in fertility except among upper socio-economic groups and these are few in number (Behnam, 1968).

Population projections have been made for Iran based on different assumptions of growth characteristics (Maroufi-Bozorgi, 1965). Assuming decreasing fertility and moderately decreasing mortality between 1966 and 1986, population figures of 34.48 million in 1976 and 47.8 million in 1986 are forecast; with constant fertility and a rapid decrease in mortality figures of 35.1 million and 51.25 million are given. The implications of even the lowest figures are very great indeed.

Many of the great improvements made in health and education will be nullified. Literacy increased from 14.9 per cent of the population in 1956 to 29.4 per cent in 1966, not least because of the effect of the Literacy Corps as one of the arms of 'The White Revolution', and further heavy investment in education will be needed in the 1970's. Only in the Third National Development Plan was 'attention paid to the fact that illiteracy and the lack of sufficient technical training in secondary and higher levels can impede the economic and social growth of the country and reduce the productivity of development investments'. To this end the Fourth Plan is attempting to increase the literacy rate of the 10–45 age group from 35 per cent in 1968 to 60 per cent by 1972, and to provide compulsory primary education facilities for 93 per cent of school age children in urban areas and for 53 per cent in rural Iran. Calculations suggest that this is not possible (Bharier, 1971).

It is forecast that by 1972 nearly one million additional jobs will be required in the country. This figure is based on the assumption that there will be an annual rate of increase of population of 2.6 per cent. As the country was not able to achieve the employment targets set in the Third Plan and as this rate of 2.6 per cent is probably too low, it is unlikely that this one million figure can be attained, and consequently higher unemployment and greater under-employment is likely to occur.

A further critical need is for a population policy which can be based on more reliable demographic data. Many of the country's policies in a large number of spheres are based on suspect population projections. It is to be hoped that the 'fundamental review of the country's civil registration organization' will lead to the better collection, analysis and use of data to achieve more reliable forecasting. Prior to this, however, there are certain policies of population control that the government is attempting to implement, including the spread of family-planning to a greater number of people (Population Council, 1967). To make this more available to those with low income, poor nutritional standards and large families, family welfare centres are now being established throughout the country and there is now a serious possibility of legalized abortion.

A further attempt to manipulate and control population is by restricting the growth of pressure points such as Tehran, and by encouraging population and economic growth in areas away from the capital. To this end certain restrictions have been placed on the development of new manufacturing industry in the Greater Tehran region. It is hoped that new development will occur in selected regional industrial areas, such as Esfahan, Ahwaz, Tabriz and Arak, ports and also in agricultural growth poles. It is unlikely, however, that restrictions in Tehran will be effective and that sufficient industrial entrepreneurs will locate in smaller provincial towns to help mitigate rising unemployment. Current economic and population trends indicate that the largest cities will grow still faster and absorb an even greater percentage of talent and income, and that smaller towns will become provincial backwaters to a greater extent than at present, being largely supported by tertiary activities. While the educated, cosmopolitan Tehrani may decry these trends and suffer from the chaos and congestion in the quickly growing unplanned capital, he is rarely prepared to move to the provinces.

REFERENCES

AMANI, M. (1965) *Évaluation de la sous-estimation des moins d'un an dans le Recensement Iranien de 1956.* Tehran.

AMANI, M. (1968) Fecondité actuelle des femmes mariées dans quatre zones rurales d'Iran in *Some Demographic Aspects of the Population of Iran*, Institute for Social Studies and Research, Tehran.

BANANI, A. (1961) *The Modernization of Iran, 1921–1941.*

BARTSCH, W. H. (1970) *Employment Creation in the Urban Areas of Iran, 1956–1966*, unpublished Ph.D. thesis, University of London.

BEHNAM, D. J. (1968) 'Population policy and family planning in Iran' in *Some Demographic Aspects of the Population of Iran*, Institute for Social Studies and Research, Tehran.

BHARIER, J. (1968) 'A Note on the Population of Iran, 1900–1966', *Population Studies*, 22, 273–9.

BHARIER, J. (1970) 'The growth of towns and villages in Iran, 1900–1966', *Middle Eastern Studies*, in press.

BHARIER, J. (1971) *Economic development in Iran*, London.

BOULNOIS, L. (1966) *The Silk Road*, London.

CHARDIN, SIR J. (1686) *Travels in Persia*, London.

CLARK, B. D. (1967) 'Problems of urban research in Iran', *I.B.G. Study Group in Urban Geography.*

CLARKE, J. I. (1963) *The Iranian city of Shiraz*, Durham.

CLARKE, J. I. and CLARK, B. D. (1969) *Kermanshah, an Iranian Provincial City*, Durham.

COSTELLO, V. (1970) *Settlement Relations in the City and Region of Kashan*, Ph.D. thesis, University of Durham.

CURZON, G. N. (1892) *Persia and the Persian Question*, London.

DARWENT, D. (1966) *Urban Growth in Relation to Socio-Economic Development and Westernization. A Case Study of the City of Mashed*, Ph.D. thesis, University of Durham.

DE PLANHOL, X. (1968) 'Geography of Settlement', *The Cambridge History of Iran, Vol. 1. The Land of Iran*, ed. by W. B. Fisher.

ECHO OF IRAN (1969) *Iran Almanac*, Tehran.

ENGLISH, P. W. (1966) *City and Village in Iran*, Madisen and London.

FIELD, H. (1939) *Contributions to the Anthropology of Iran*, Anthropological Series, Field Museum of Natural History, 29.

FISCHEL, W. J. (1950) 'The Jews of Persia 1795–1940', *Jewish Social Studies*, 12, 119–60.

FISHER, W. B. (ed.) (1968) *The Cambridge History of Iran, Vol. 1. The Land of Iran.*

GRUEN, V. *Tehran Master Plan*, in progress.

GUPTA, R. N. (1947) *Iran: An Economic Study*, New Delhi.

INSTITUTE FOR ECONOMIC RESEARCH (1968) 'A prediction of Iran's future population according to age and sex', *Tahqiqat é Eqtesádi*, 5, Nos. 13 and 14, pp. 62–124.

KOOROS, A. (1970) 'Economic growth and labour participation in Iran', *Tahqiqat é Eqtesádi*, 7, No. 17, pp. 29–39.

LAMBTON, A. K. S. (1953) *Landlord and Peasant in Persia*, London.

LEAGUE OF NATIONS (1926) *Commission of Enquiry into the Production of Opium in Persia.*

MAROUFI-BOZORGI, N. (1965) *Population Projection for Iran, 1956–1976,* Tehran.

MASHAYEKHI, M. B., MEAD, P. A., and HAYES, G. S. (1953) 'Some demographic aspects of a rural area in Iran', *The Milbank Memorial Fund Quarterly,* 31, 149–65.

MINISTRY OF INTERIOR (1956) Public Statistics, Iran. *National and Province Statistics of the First National Census of Iran,* 2 vols.

MINISTRY OF INTERIOR (1960) Department of Public Statistics, *First National Census of Agriculture.*

MINISTRY OF INTERIOR (1963) General Department of Public Statistics, *Report on the Industrial Census of Iran.*

MINISTRY OF LABOUR (1958) *Survey of Manpower Resources and Requirements.*

MINISTRY OF LABOUR (1962) *Establishment Survey.*

MINISTRY OF LABOUR AND SOCIAL AFFAIRS (1968) *A Study on Manpower in Iran.*

MONTEIL, V. (1966) *Les Tribus du Fârs et la Sédentarisation des Nomades,* Paris.

NAVAL INTELLIGENCE DIVISION (1945) *Persia.*

PLAN ORGANIZATION (1966) Iranian Statistical Centre, *National Census of Population and Housing,* 168 vols.

PLAN ORGANIZATION (1968) *Fourth National Development Plan, 1968–1972,* Tehran.

POPULATION COUNCIL (1967) 'Iran: report on population growth and family planning', *Studies in Family Planning,* No. 20.

POWER, M. (1970) *The Region of Esfahan,* Ph.D. thesis in progress, University of Durham.

RAWLINSON, G. (1880) *The Five Great Monarchies of the Ancient Eastern World,* London.

SUNDERLAND, E. (1968) 'Pastoralism, Nomadism and the Social Anthropology of Iran', *The Cambridge History of Iran, Vol. 1, Land of Iran,* ed. by W. B. Fisher, Chap. 20.

SWAN, E. P. (1967) *Highlights of the 1966 Census of Iran,* mimeographed, Tehran.

TAMRAZIAN, S. (1968) Some demographic and sociological characteristics of a fast expanding city: Tehran, in *Some Demographic Aspects of the Population of Iran,* Institute for Social Studies and Research, Tehran.

UNITED KINGDOM, Foreign Office (1919) *Persia.*

UNITED NATIONS (1963–7) *Demographic Yearbooks.*

VIEILLE, P. (1965) *Abadan: Tissu urbain, attitudes et valeurs,* Institute for Social Studies and Research, Tehran.

Chapter 4
Iraq: changing population patterns
R I Lawless

Iraq, which was created as a political entity after the First World War from the three Ottoman vilayets (provinces) of Mosul, Baghdad and Basrah, became independent in 1932. Since that time three population censuses have been carried out, in 1947, 1957 and 1965, so that the information available for demographic study is probably more abundant than for most other Middle Eastern countries. Nevertheless, while the accuracy of the statistics has improved they are still far from satisfactory. For the period before 1947 some population figures are available. The British Consular Reports for the mid-nineteenth century and the partial census of population made by the Ottoman administration in 1890 provide some information. Other population estimates are available for the years between 1900 and 1908, and for 1919 when Iraq came under British rule. Finally there is the general enumeration of population made by the Iraqi Government in 1934, soon after independence. These are, of course, only estimates and the margins of error involved are considerable, but they are sufficient to indicate the general trend of population growth in Iraq.

Evolution of population

It has been suggested that during the period of Abbasid rule (A.D. 754–1258), when Baghdad was the centre of the civilized world, the present state of Iraq may have supported a population of some 20 million people (McCrary and Sa'eed, 1968). However, following the Mongol invasion of the thirteenth century and the accompanying insecurity and destruction, from which the country has only recently begun to recover, population declined rapidly. In the middle of the nineteenth century it has been estimated (Hasan, 1958) that the population numbered only 1.28 million, though by the beginning of the twentieth century it appears to have increased to around 2.25 million (Table 4.1). An estimate in 1935 on the basis of population registers gave a total count of 3.6 million. At the first census taken in 1947 the population numbered 4.8 million, though the results are generally regarded as too low (Adams, 1958). The results of the second census in 1957, however, were more satisfactory and gave a total count of 6.53 million including 42,000 Iraqis abroad and 221,000 estimated

TABLE 4.1   TOTAL AND REGIONAL GROWTH OF IRAQ'S POPULATION, 1867–1965

Year	Total population (thousands)	Northern Region		Central Region		Southern Region	
		Number (thousands)	Per cent	Number (thousands)	Per cent	Number (thousands)	Per cent
1867	1,280	265	20.7	491	38.4	524	40.9
1890	1,726	401	23.2	575	33.3	750	43.5
1905	2,250	540	24.0	855	38.0	855	38.0
1919	2,848	703	24.7	966	33.9	1,179	41.4
1935	3,605	1,041	28.9	1,319	36.6	1,245	34.5
1947	4,816	1,347	28.0	2,043	42.4	1,426	29.6
1957	6,298	1,722	27.3	2,764	43.9	1,812	28.8
1965	8,220	2,184	26.6	3,966	48.2	2,070	25.2

Source: Hasan, 1958.

under-enumerated persons. By 1965 the total population had increased to 8.2 million including 40,818 Iraqis abroad. The latest estimates suggest that the population reached a total of almost 9 million in 1970.

The rate of population growth, which appears to have risen from the mid-nineteenth century to 1905, fell slightly until 1935 but since that time has increased substantially (Hasan, 1958). Between 1867 and 1890 the population grew at an average rate of 1.3 per cent per annum, rising to 1.8 per cent between 1890 and 1905 (Table 4.2). This acceleration in the annual rate of population growth was checked between 1905 and 1935 when the rate fell first to 1.7 per cent and after 1919 to 1.5 per cent. Since 1935, however, the population has increased at a much higher rate because of falling mortality and steadily high fertility. Between 1935 and 1947 the average annual rate of population growth was 2.4 per cent, rising to 3.1 per cent between 1947 and 1957 and to 3.5 per cent during the last intercensal period. Population growth will probably remain high for some years to come, and may even increase, for the decline in mortality, especially infant mortality, is likely to continue, while birth rates may well be increasing

TABLE 4.2   ABSOLUTE INCREASE AND ANNUAL PERCENTAGE RATES OF INCREASE OF IRAQ'S POPULATION, 1867–1965

Period	Total population		Northern Region		Central Region		Southern Region	
	Absolute increase (thousands)	Annual per cent increase	Absolute increase (thousands)	Annual per cent increase	Absolute increase (thousands)	Annual per cent increase	Absolute increase (thousands)	Annual per cent increase
1867–90	446	1.3	136	1.8	84	0.7	226	1.6
1890–1905	524	1.8	139	2.0	280	2.7	105	0.9
1905–19	598	1.7	163	1.9	110	0.9	325	2.3
1919–35	758	1.5	339	2.4	354	2.0	65	0.3
1935–47	1,211	2.4	306	2.2	724	3.7	181	1.1
1947–57	1,482	3.1	375	2.8	721	3.5	386	2.7
1957–65	1,922	3.5	462	3.4	1,202	5.4	258	1.8

Source: Hasan, 1958.

with rising standards of living. Fertility is already higher in urban centres than in Iraq as a whole, and in time this increase may affect the rural areas (Jones, 1969).

Like most other countries in the Middle East, Iraq is a very young nation—44.9 per cent of the total population was, in 1957, below the age of 15 years; and only 7.4 per cent over the age of 59 years. The economically active section of the population in the age group 15–59 years was therefore only 47.7 per cent of the total population, and within this group the proportion of females was slightly higher than that of males. Although no more recent figures are available on population structure it seems probable that the proportion of the total active population gainfully employed is low; according to one estimate in 1951–2 the working population in Iraq was only 40 per cent of the total (El Badry, 1965).

Changes in the communal structure of the country

Iraq is not a nation in the Western sense of the word, but rather a conglomeration of ethnic, linguistic and religious groups, which gradually and not without difficulty are being welded into a whole (Qubain, 1958).

Settled since earliest times, Mesopotamia, the land between the rivers Tigris and Euphrates, was perhaps the cradle of world civilization. Village life was already well developed in the fifth millennium, and it was here that the arts of agriculture and livestock rearing were first practised. Unfortunately for much of its later history the region became a frontier province between powerful empires, and experienced a succession of conquests—Persian, Greek, Roman, Arab, Mongol and Turkish among others—and migrations. Consequently, there has been a constant movement of peoples into and within the region so that the ethnic composition of the population is deeply mixed and from many different sources. Moreover, the invaders also introduced new languages, new religions and new social habits which were accepted by some of the indigenous peoples and rejected by others. In this context the Arab conquest of the seventh century A.D. had the most profound and lasting results.

The newcomers, numbering fewer than a quarter of a million, rapidly converted a majority of the inhabitants to Islam, though some Christian and Jewish communities did survive. Arabic, the language of the invaders, became dominant in the plains where it was adopted by Moslems and also by many Christians and Jews, but it made little progress among the peoples of the mountains and foothills of the north. Few Arab colonies were settled there, and although a majority of the inhabitants became fervent adherents of Islam, they retained their own language, Kurdish. An already complex ethnic, religious and linguistic pattern became still more complex as a result of heresies, conversions and schisms, of which the most important was the split in Islam during the seventh century which created the large Shi'a community concentrated mainly in the central and southern parts of the country.

Islam, having produced this complex pattern, by its very organization served to maintain and even reinforce it. Moslems recognized and tolerated the presence of the main monotheistic religions, and as Islam does not differentiate between religion and state the Christian and Jewish communities had to be allowed to administer their own affairs according to their own laws. Under the Ottoman empire this principle found expression in the millet system whereby these communities were allowed a substantial degree of political and social autonomy (Baer, 1964). Heretical Moslem sects were not allowed the status of millet, and instead it was constant persecution—especially by the Turks—which strengthened the bonds uniting their members. Geographical segregation, poor communications, isolation in mountain regions difficult of access, and distance from an often weak central authority are other factors which helped the numerous religious and linguistic communities to remain coherent units and to retain their identity. Over the centuries it was these groups rather than ephemeral empires or kingdoms which continued to be the main focus of political and social loyalties, of a sense of belonging. When in 1926 these divers communities found themselves a part of the state of Iraq they did not immediately transfer their loyalties to the new political unit.

Thus, Coon's (1951) analogy of the Middle East as a mosaic is particularly apt in the case of Iraq. However, since the creation of the state, new pieces have been added to the pattern of the mosaic and others removed, changing the size and importance of the remaining pieces; and boundaries have become less distinct. New groups, the Assyrians and Armenians, have come to settle within the borders of the state, while almost the entire Jewish community has departed. Changes have taken place in the distribution of the various communities within the country and as between rural and urban areas leading to less segregation and greater contact between members of different groups. The central government has become much stronger and some aspects of its administration touches all the population, though with varying intensity. Finally the educational system has been greatly expanded with the declared aim of fostering national consciousness. Strong forces have been and are still at work, therefore, to bring about a transference of primary loyalties from the traditional groupings to the nation state. Some progress has been made, and the political functions of many of the communities, especially the religious groups, have certainly been much weakened. This is not so in the case of the Kurds, however, who have been successful recently in obtaining the promise of a measure of political autonomy from the government in Baghdad. In time, one of the results of the rapid urbanization which has taken place during recent decades must be the formation of new allegiances founded not on religion or language but according to occupation, wealth and social class. However, this will be a slow process, and at present the traditional groupings retain much of their former importance as a social framework. Because the linguistic and religious communities have played such a pre-eminent role in the lives of the people of Iraq in the past, and because they are still important, the evolution of each major group is examined in more detail below.

The Moslem communities

About 95 per cent of Iraq's population are Moslems, the remainder being mainly Christians or Jews. Unfortunately, the census returns give no details of the membership of the two main branches of Islam, Sunni and Shi'a, but reliable sources indicate that the latter, the majority of whom speak Arabic, represent about 55 per cent of the total population. As membership of the Sunni branch is further divided between Arabic and Kurdish speakers, and as the first loyalty of a Kurd is to the Kurdish community, the Shi'a form the largest religious community in the country. The Shi'a sect, though dominant in Iran, is more numerous in Iraq than in any other Arab country.

The split in Islam which resulted in the formation of the Shi'a sect took place in the seventh century because of political rivalry between Ali, the fourth Caliph, a cousin and son-in-law of Mohammed, and the Umayyades of Syria. After the political fall of Ali, whose capital was at Kufa in present-day Iraq, his supporters founded the Shi'a sect which later developed a doctrine distinct from that of the orthodox Sunni branch of Islam. The Shi'a are concentrated in the centre and the south, in the provinces of Karbala, Hilla, Kut, Diwaniya, Nasiriya and Amara where it is estimated they make up 98 per cent of the population (Baer, 1964). The Shi'a are in a majority in the province of Basrah, though the city of Basrah itself contains an important Sunni community. There is also a considerable Shi'a group, estimated at more than 25 per cent of the population, in the province of Baghdad which has recently been strengthened by the migration of many Shi'a from the south to the capital.

Traditionally the majority of the Shi'a were either farmers, who were rarely attached to the land they cultivated, or herdsmen, and conditions of life in their villages were often extremely wretched. Disease, especially malaria and bilharzia, was rife, and their lands and villages concentrated along the lower reaches of the Tigris and Euphrates and their tributaries were subject to periodic and disastrous flooding. They were mostly organized in a tribal system, but in some parts of the south, though the tenants were Shi'a, their shaikhs belonged to the Sunni branch of Islam. Only a small proportion of the Shi'a were urban dwellers, and their share in government offices, the army and urban occupations was low compared with their share in the total population. Their mainly rural distribution illustrates admirably Lewis' thesis that heretical sects in Islam install themselves at a distance from the centres of urban power and orthodoxy (Lewis, 1953).

After centuries of underprivilege as a result of Sunni rule the condition of the Shi'a community is hardly surprising. Under the Abbasid Caliphate the Christians and Jews often received better treatment than the Shi'a; four centuries of Ottoman rule under the Sultan-Caliph with its immense patronage and endowments greatly strengthened the Sunni community at the expense of the Shi'a; and until the revolution of 1958 the independent state of Iraq was ruled by a Sunni king. The Sunni Arabs of Iraq, on the other hand, who engage in a wide range of occupations, came to be heavily represented in the urban centres. They were generally better educated than the Shi'a; they made up a high proportion of the middle classes; and most of the members of the political, economic and intellectual élite were drawn from this group (Qubain, 1958). The Sunni Arabs, who count among their number the bedouin tribes, make up perhaps 20 per cent of the total population.

Today the social gap between Sunni Arabs and Shi'a is narrowing. One of the main causes is the rapid urbanization which has taken place in Iraq in recent years. Many Shi'a have migrated from the southern provinces to Baghdad while others have moved to Basrah. The conditions under which they live in the shanty-towns in and around these two cities is often very poor, but detailed surveys carried out among Shi'a migrants in Baghdad have shown that their income and standard of living is much higher than in their former homes (Phillips, 1959; Azeez, 1968). In the towns, moreover, there are opportunities for them to further improve their economic and social position. A second cause is the extension of the state educational system in the Shi'a provinces. Good progress has been made in primary education and by 1968 the number of primary schools in relation to population in these provinces compared not unfavourably with the national average. Nasiriya remains the most backward province in this respect.

However, centuries of underprivilege do not disappear overnight. In secondary education the contrast between the southern provinces and Baghdad province is still pronounced and the various institutions of higher education remain heavily concentrated in the capital. Finally, a great improvement is necessary in the social services, especially in the southern provinces. These areas, for centuries ravaged by disease, still possess fewer dispensaries, hospital beds and doctors in proportion to their population than the rest of the country.

Of the non-Arab Shi'a in Iraq, the Iranians have an importance which surpasses their total number, for they belong to a powerful neighbouring state, the only one in Islam which is almost exclusively Shi'a and where the ruling group belongs to this sect. Each year thousands of Iranians make a pilgrimage to the holy cities in Iraq, and no doubt over the centuries some have chosen to settle there. In 1968 Iraqi sources estimated that the number of Iranians with Iranian passports resident in the country was 22,860—well over half the total number of resident foreigners in that year. Other sources, however, put their number as high as a million (Kinsman, 1970). The Iranians in Iraq are essentially an urban community, and of those officially recorded in 1968 59 per cent were living in and around Baghdad and 25 per cent in the holy cities in the province of Karbala where, according to one source, their number has declined in the last fifty years (Longrigg, 1970). The insecurity of their position was well illustrated during the recent disagreement between Iraq and Iran over the Shatt-el-Arab in May 1969 during which it is reported that 1,500 Iranians had been expelled from Iraq.

No official figures are available for the present Kurdish population in Iraq. In 1932, 14.5 per cent of the population were Kurdish speakers according to official figures (Baer, 1964); Edmonds estimated that in 1947 the Kurds numbered 900,000 or 18.6 per cent of the total population (Edmonds, 1957); and the 1957 census recorded one million Kurdish speakers—16.4 per cent of the total population. On the other hand, the Kurdish nationalists (Blau, 1963) and others (Vernier, 1963) maintain that this group represents at least 28 per cent of Iraq's population. The most realistic estimate for the Kurdish community, however, appears to be between 15 and 20 per cent of the total population. The Kurds form a majority of the population in the northern provinces of Sulaimaniya, Arbil and probably Kirkuk, and they also inhabit parts of the provinces of Mosul and Diyala. Edmonds, on the basis of personal knowledge of the area, estimated that in 1947 the entire population of the province of Sulaimaniya was Kurdish, and that Kurds composed 91 per cent and 53 per cent respectively of the population of the provinces of Arbil and Kirkuk, but only 35 per cent and 27 per cent respectively of the population of the provinces of Mosul and Diyala (Edmonds, 1957).

The Iraqi Kurds represent only a part of a much larger group of Kurdish-speaking peoples—claimed by various sources to number anything between 4 and 13 millions—who occupy the highlands of Eastern Anatolia and the north-western Zagros. Their territory, sometimes known as Kurdistan, stretches in a wide arc from Kermanshah in western Iran across north-east Iraq to the southern parts of Soviet Armenia and Azerbaijan to north-east Syria and south-east Turkey, but at no time have the Kurds coalesced into a single united community. Their origin is still a problem, and much remains to be learnt. Various theories have been put forward and to summarize it appears that either by assimilating or displacing the previous inhabitants the central parts of what is now Kurdistan were settled by Iranicized tribes probably as early as the seventh century B.C. (Kinnane,

1964). These tribes are the cultural progenitors of the modern Kurds. They developed a common language which has a basic unity in spite of the existence of numerous dialectical forms in the high and isolated mountain valleys, and apart from the feeling that they are Kurds, their language has become the chief common bond between them. Although it has close affinities with Persian, linguists have shown that Kurdish is quite distinct, not merely a Persian dialect. Since the Arab conquest in the seventh century A.D., Islam, and essentially the Sunni branch, has been a profound civilizing force, and, though the Arab language made little progress, the religion of the newcomers has to a large extent determined the social and political evolution of the Kurds.

Kurdish society in Iraq is essentially tribal, with each tribe divided into clans and sects. In recent years, however, the old social order has been considerably weakened, and one of the effects of the conflict between the Kurdish nationalists and the Baghdad Government has been to accelerate the shift of power away from the tribal and feudal upper class to the urban intelligentsia. The Kurds are mountain peoples and traditionally they migrated each year between northern Iraq and Iran. In spring they travelled to the Iranian plateaux to avoid the heat and drought of the Iraq plains, returning in the autumn to escape the severe cold of the Iranian uplands (Fernea, 1969b). Today the majority of the Kurdish tribes are settled in villages, and movement of tribe and livestock is restricted to the nearby mountain slopes in summer and the lowlands in winter. Agriculture is also important, especially arboriculture, and there is often deep attachment to the land. Nevertheless as early as the Ottoman period there was some small-scale migration to urban centres, especially to Baghdad and even to Istanbul. Some Kurds left to seek employment as labourers, others to obtain a higher education. However, until recent years the majority of the Kurdish people lived in the countryside. Sulaimaniya and Arbil were the only Kurdish towns of any importance, and they were quite small. The Kurdish element in other northern towns such as Mosul and Kirkuk was relatively insignificant. During the last decade, however, a number of urban centres in Kurdish areas have grown rapidly (see Fig. 4.3), and a substantial part of this increase in population is the result of an influx of migrants from rural areas. Insecurity during the conflicts between the Kurdish nationalists and Iraqi government forces, the destruction of villages by the Iraqi air force, and a severe drought between 1958 and 1961 are the major factors which have precipitated or reinforced this trend towards greater urbanization.

The migration of Kurds to the major urban centres of the Ottoman empire during the years before the First World War resulted in a 'Kurdish renaissance'. The Kurdish educated class which grew up there brought about a revival of Kurdish national consciousness. It was due to their efforts that the peace treaty signed at Sèvres between the Sultan's government and the Allies in 1920 provided for a commission to draw up a scheme for local autonomy for much of Kurdistan. Unfortunately, with the subsequent rise of Ataturk and the Turkish Nationalist party this treaty was never implemented, and when a new peace treaty was signed at Lausanne in 1922 between Turkey and the Allies, no mention was made of the Kurds who found themselves divided between four states—Syria, Turkey, Iraq and Iran—together with a small enclave in the USSR. Statistics are unreliable but it is clear that the Kurds formed a higher proportion of the total population of Iraq than of the other three states, and initially the British, then ruling in Iraq, attempted to set up an autonomous administration for the Kurdish areas. However, this plan met with difficulties and was finally abandoned in favour of a new policy of integration in the Iraqi state. When the British relinquished their mandate in 1932, pressure was exerted on the new government to issue a declaration acknowledging the special position of the Kurdish people in the state. It is the opinion of the Kurds, both the tribal leaders and the intelligentsia, that this guarantee of Kurdish rights has never been honoured satisfactorily. Already before the complete transfer of power, hostilities had broken out in the Kurdish areas and they have continued with varying intensity, but with some relatively peaceful interludes, until the present. Since 1961, however, the conflict has escalated, and the increasing costs involved have compelled the Baghdad Government to divert capital resources, badly needed for economic development, to finance the war. Villages, crops and livestock have been destroyed in Kurdish areas, many Kurds have been displaced, and social and economic development has been much retarded. Detailed information about present conditions in the north is lacking, but figures published in 1968 reveal a marked shortage of secondary schools, doctors and hospitals in Kurdish areas and especially in the province of Sulaimaniya.

In March 1970 it was announced from Baghdad that a settlement had been reached which recognizes Kurdish autonomy, the adoption of Kurdish as the official language in areas where Kurds constitute a majority, and proportional representation of Kurds at all levels of the administration of Iraq. A settlement of the Kurdish question has been attempted many times before, and success in implementing this programme will depend on agreement concerning the delineation of the autonomous area, and the establishment of an acceptable figure for the proportion of Kurds in the population. On this depends not only Kurdish representation in the central government but also use of oil revenues, about 64 per cent of which come from the Kirkuk region. The Iraqi Government, it is reported, maintains that Arabs and Turkomans constitute two-thirds of the population of the Kirkuk region and Kurds only one-third; the Kurds, however, insist that historically and demographically it is predominantly Kurdish. They assert that during the hostilities Kurds were forced to migrate and were replaced with Arab settlers by previous régimes. There has now been a demand for a new population census carried out with the assistance of a United Nations team.

The Yezidi, who are of Kurdish stock and speak a Kurdish dialect, form a distinct community because of their curious religion. Few details are known but it appears to have originated in the thirteenth century, uniting elements of paganism, Zoroastrianism, Christianity and Islam. The sect gained numerous adherents throughout Mesopotamia, Kurdistan and in parts of Syria, but since the fifteenth century it has declined. At present, apart from a few scattered communities in Syria, Turkey and Iran, the majority (estimated in 1957 at 55,885) are found in northern Iraq in the Jebel Sinjar and at Shaikh Adi, north of Mosul. There they obtain a poor livelihood as cultivators and herdsmen, though recently several families have migrated to the towns. The Yezidi have little contact with their neighbours and are extremely suspicious of strangers. Over the centuries the community has often been persecuted. The most recent occasion was in 1935 when government troops were sent to attack their enclave after they had failed to submit to conscription.

Finally, communities of Turkomans, the majority of whom belong to the Sunni branch of Islam, are found in a series of villages and towns at the foot of the northern mountains, especially along the old Baghdad–Mosul road from Qara Tepe to Arbil. These groups, who appear to have originated in Seljuk or post-Seljuk times, are Turkish-speaking with a dialect intermediate between Turki and Ottoman. The Ottoman rulers may have settled groups of Turkomans at the entrance to valleys leading into Kurdistan in order to guard against incursions of the turbulent mountain peoples (Vernier, 1963). Once nomadic some are now farmers in the region around Tel Afar and Neni Younis between the Jebel Sinjar and the Tigris, and around Kifri, while many are found in urban centres in the north, Mosul, Arbil, Altun Kopru, Kirkuk and Khanaquin. Over the years others have migrated to cities elsewhere in Iraq to engage in commerce and to enter government service. During the Ottoman period and even to the present day their community has provided far more than its proportion of government officials. Their tribal organization has long since disappeared, yet they have preserved their identity against their Kurdish and Arab neighbours.

Other Turks came to the towns and cities of Iraq during the four centuries of Ottoman rule as administrators, both civil and military. They settled down and founded families, some of which still survive. According to the 1957 census, the number of Turkish speakers in Iraq was 136,806 or 2.1 per cent of the population.

The non-Moslem communities

In 1957 the Christian communities in Iraq numbered 206,206 or 3.2 per cent of the population, 53 per cent being concentrated in the province of Mosul, while 18 per cent were to be found in Baghdad province. Their survival in an area so deeply Islamized is not without interest. Many found shelter in the mountainous areas of the north, where they were able to maintain their identity in spite of successive invasions; others found security in the urban centres where, as 'people of the book' recognized by Islam, they came under the protection of the ruler. Later, during the Ottoman period each Christian sect was recognized as an autonomous millet, under its own elected head and with considerable freedom in the conduct of its internal affairs. However, since Iraqi independence, and especially in recent years with the rise to power of régimes extremely hostile to the (Christian) West, their position has become more vulnerable.

Most Christians speak Arabic as their main language, though another is often used for Church services. Reliable statistics suggest that their rate of increase is lower than that of Moslems, and certainly the status of women is higher among Christians (Baer, 1964). Apart from the Assyrians, a high proportion are urban dwellers, especially the Uniate communities, and they still constitute a significant element in the major Iraqi cities. Generally better educated than the Moslems, many have become clerical workers or entered the professions. With the expansion of the state educational system, however, they may now meet with more competition for employment in these fields from well-qualified Moslems.

Although Christians are relatively few in number, they belong to many different sects—a result of past heresies and schisms and because a part of each sect later decided to recognize the Pope's authority. They include the Greek Orthodox community, Assyrians, Armenians and Syrians (Jacobites) established well before the Arab conquest, together with the corresponding uniate communities, the Melkites, Chaldean, Armenian and Syrian Catholics, which came into existence between the sixteenth and eighteenth centuries (Vernier, 1963). There are no reliable estimates of the numbers in individual sects but after the First World War the Assyrian and Armenian communities were strengthened by refugees from Turkey.

The Jewish community in Iraq is one of the oldest of the diaspora, dating back to the sixth century B.C. Until the Arab conquest many Jews were farmers living in rural areas, though even at that time there was a significant urban group made up of merchants and craftsmen. After the conquest, which left the political structure and social hierarchy of the community intact, there is some evidence of a substantial migration of Jews to urban centres, especially to Baghdad, where they have remained heavily concentrated (Vajda, 1962). In 1947, 82 per cent of the Jewish population lived in the four major towns, 65 per cent in Baghdad. This urbanization may have resulted in part from their desire as 'people of the book' to seek the protection of the authorities, and it is clear that the Abbasid caliphs recognized their talents and used them in the administration as financial advisors and bankers. By the ninth century A.D. a well-organized Jewish bank in Baghdad had made that city the financial capital of the Middle East and Mediterranean. Other groups were able to maintain their identity in the northern mountains and, unlike the urban communities farther south who adopted Arabic, Kurdish became their main language. During Ottoman rule they had, on the whole, a recognized and protected place in society, though they were rarely popular. Some Jews from Baghdad and Basrah emigrated to India, China and Hong Kong during the 1830's, where they founded strong and prosperous communities (Vajda, 1962). In Baghdad, where they constituted almost a half of the city's population before the Second World War, Jews were bankers, tradesmen and clerks, and some became extremely wealthy. In Kurdistan, however, their position appears to have been less prosperous. In the towns they practised the unpleasant occupations of dyeing, tanning and the distillation of spirits, while others, with only a humble position, continued to live on the edges of Kurdish villages (Edmonds, 1957).

Following Iraqi independence the position of the Jewish community remained relatively secure. Some became civil servants, and one of the first ministers of finance was a Jew. However, with increasing Zionist activity in the Middle East, German propaganda during the Second World War, and finally the defeat of the Arab armies in the Palestine war, the condition of the Jews in Iraq—many of whom were anti-Zionist—rapidly deteriorated (Vernier, 1963). Since 1949, when the community numbered 120,000 or 2.5 per cent of the population—the largest Jewish community in the Middle East outside the Maghreb—the majority have departed. Many have gone to Israel, taking with them skills which were difficult to replace. In 1957 only 4,907 Jews remained in Iraq, of whom over two-thirds were living in Baghdad. In the future this community may well disappear completely.

Changes in the ecological structure of the country

It has been estimated that in the mid-nineteenth century out of a total population of 1.25 million in Iraq nearly half a million were nomadic, just over half a million settled cultivators and under a third of a million urban dwellers (Hasan, 1958). By the middle of the twentieth century the population had risen to 4.8 million and was composed of only a quarter of a million nomads, 2.9 million 'rural' dwellers and 1.6 million urban dwellers. Since 1947 these trends have continued. In 1957 out of a total population of 6.3 million only 65,000 were classified as nomadic, 3.7 million as 'rural' and 2.4 million as urban. At the last census (1965) the population had risen to 8.2 million of whom 4.6 million lived in rural areas and 3.6 million in urban areas. No estimate is available for the present nomadic population.

The nomads

These figures show that there has been an absolute as well as a relative decline in the nomadic population since the middle of the nineteenth century, their number falling absolutely from half a million in 1867 to 65,000 in 1957, and relatively from 35 per cent to 1.1 per cent of the total population. Several writers have pointed out that these estimates—and they are no more—are too low, but they are all agreed that a sharp decline in nomadism has taken place. For example, in 1955 Abdel-Gehl El Tahir estimated that 8 per cent of Iraq's population were nomads, 48 per cent bedouin living in villages, 22 per cent settled rural population and 28 per cent in communities with 20,000 or more persons (El Badry, 1965; Adams, 1958). The decline appears to have been more dramatic in the central and southern parts of the country than in the north. Between 1947 and 1957 the nomadic population of the centre and the south declined from 180,000 to 26,660, that of the north from 70,000 to 39,241. In 1957 almost two-thirds of the nomads, who belong to two main groups, the 'Aniza and the Shammar, were in the province of Mosul, where they made up 5.2 per cent of the population; the majority were concentrated in the region between the upper Tigris and Euphrates known as the Jazirah. The remainder were in the western and south-western deserts, and constituted 6.7 per cent and 1.9 per cent respectively of the populations of the provinces of Ramadi and Diwaniya.

The transition from a nomadic to a settled life is not new, and periods when the nomadic tribes were dominant have been succeeded by periods during which the sedentary population expanded. With a strong central government capable of maintaining the irrigation systems the settled population prospered, and many nomads became cultivators. Severe droughts or the expansion of more powerful tribes are other forces which in the past have encouraged sedentarization. Periods of weak central government, on the other hand, have invariably resulted in a return to nomadism. From the early twentieth century the forces in favour of sedentarization have been greatly strengthened.

Traditionally the economy of the bedouin was based on livestock rearing, especially the camel, and as grazing land is scanty and springs and wells are infrequent in the desert and steppelands, the tribes had to move from place to place in search of pasture. Their home was the tent. Animal products were exchanged with the villagers for grain and for certain manufactured goods, and their camels were often hired out for use in desert caravans which might also be raided by the nomads or compelled to pay for protection. However, the establishment of a strong central government in the early twentieth century, commanding armed forces and police equipped with modern weapons, discouraged the nomads from raiding. New and improved communications resulted in a decline in the caravan trade, and the demarcation of new political boundaries limited the tribes' freedom of movement. Equally important, the government in Iraq, as in many other Middle Eastern countries, has pursued a definite policy of settling the nomads. Their way of life conflicts with the efficient administration of a modern state, making tax collection, conscription and the improvement of health and education among the tribes extremely difficult, while their continued presence is a potential source of internal insecurity and may lead to disagreements with neighbouring states. Nevertheless, if all the nomadic tribes are settled in areas of permanent agriculture the scant resources of the desert (almost half of the total area of the state) will remain unproductive, for nomadism represents perhaps the only way of utilizing the limited agricultural possibilities of such areas.

The villagers

The decline in the number of nomads contributed to an increase in the settled rural population, which rose absolutely from just over half a million in 1867 to nearly 2.25 million in 1930, and relatively from 41 per cent to 68 per cent of the total population. Since 1930, however, though the total rural population in Iraq has continued to rise, there has been a relative decline from 61 per cent in 1947 to 56 per cent in 1965. Moreover, between 1957 and 1965 an absolute decline in the rural population was recorded in the four southern provinces of Amara, Basrah, Diwaniya and Nasiriya. This trend, together with the decline in the relative importance of the rural population in most parts of the country, is a result of a sharp rise in the level of urbanization. In 1965 the provinces which had the lowest proportions of their populations living in rural areas included Karbala (27 per cent), Basrah (37 per cent) and Baghdad (48 per cent); those which had the highest proportions included Nasiriya (73 per cent), Amara (70 per cent) and Kut (69 per cent), closely followed by Sulaimaniya (68 per cent) and Diwaniya (67 per cent).

The rural population and indeed almost the entire sedentary population of Iraq is concentrated in two regions, the plains and uplands of the north-east, and the alluvial plain of the Tigris and Euphrates, to which cultivation is confined and which support most of the country's livestock. It has been estimated (Azeez, 1968) that the amount of cultivable land in Iraq is about 90,000 sq. km. or 21 per cent of the total area, but according to the 1958–9 agricultural census the area actually cultivated is only 75,000 sq. km. or 17 per cent of the land area. The density of rural population to cultivated area—less than one-half of which is cropped in any one year—is therefore approximately 61 inhabitants per sq. km., a much lower figure than for many Middle Eastern countries. Although some writers (Warriner, 1969) have suggested that this estimate of the cultivated area is too high and that the true figure is nearer 50,000 sq. km., the census provides details of the cropland by province, and is therefore extremely useful (Treakle, 1966).

It reveals that just under half the total cropland is found in the north-eastern part of the country, which receives a moderate and highly variable rainfall. Extensive grain production with widely fluctuating harvests is the chief form of land use. Within this zone the main agricultural areas are in the southern foothills, the broad valleys and the lower slopes, and rural settlement is more evenly distributed than in the southern irrigated zone (Lebon, 1953). This region, however, contains less than a third of the rural population of Iraq, and the average density of rural population to cultivated area is below the national average of 44.3 inhabitants per sq. km. In contrast, the alluvial plain of the Tigris below Samarra and the Euphrates below Hit, with just over half the country's cropland, is an arid region where agriculture is almost entirely dependent upon irrigation. Since the 1950's the completion of a number of dams and reservoirs to regulate and store more water has greatly enlarged the cultivated area. However, because there is little or no natural drainage in this zone, large areas of irrigated land have been going out of cultivation through soil salinization, and this problem has not yet been solved. The main cultivated areas, which produce barley, dates and rice, lie along the two rivers, their distributaries and artificial channels. Unlike the Nile, where cultivable areas are limited to the floor of the valley itself, potentially cultivable land extends for many kilometres on both sides of the Tigris and Euphrates (Fisher, 1961). Rural settlement is highly concentrated in riverine areas, though the close concentration of population on actual river banks, so marked in Egypt, is much less a feature. More than two-thirds of the country's rural population are found in this zone, and densities of rural population to cultivated area are considerably higher than in the north-east; there are wide variations but the average density is 121 inhabitants per sq. km.

The village is the typical form of rural settlement in Iraq, as elsewhere in the Middle East. In the past, when there was no strong central authority to maintain public order, rural dwellers were compelled to live in a compact settlement for protection. This form of settlement also enabled the land-owner and his agents to carry out the tasks of agricultural management and supervision more easily and more effectively. Now, social customs developed over the centuries in such an environment present obstacles to any change to a more dispersed pattern. The majority of Iraqi villages are small. In 1957 there were 14,288 villages and the occupants totalled 3,853,517, an average of 265 occupants per village, or 40–45 households. Villages in the

111

north-eastern part of the country with an average of only 160 occupants, are much smaller than the villages of the southern irrigated zone. All rural settlements, however, have the same monotonous appearance, and there are few prominent buildings. The houses are constructed of mud or reeds in the south, but in the north, because of the severe winters and the availability of building stone, they are more substantial. Few villages are able to support commercial enterprises other than a teahouse or small shop (Adams, 1958).

Until recent years the way of life of their inhabitants had not changed significantly for centuries. Their level of living was deplorably low, they had few possessions, and medical and educational facilities, a pure water supply, electricity and similar amenities were almost totally lacking. Their diet was monotonous and generally deficient, many were undernourished, and disease was rife. In 1958, 95 per cent of the inhabitants of one southern village had at least one endemic disease, 80 per cent at least two, and 60 per cent three (Quint, 1958). There was illiteracy and there was ignorance. In fact the villages had been scarcely touched by the twentieth century; they were in the twentieth century but not of it.

These depressed conditions prevailed among the vast majority of the rural population, because until the revolution in 1958 agriculture provided no more than a bare subsistence for the average Iraqi farmer. Farming techniques were certainly primitive, and had hardly changed for centuries. Cultivation was extensive and yields were low. Agricultural implements remained traditional, and the hoe and the digging stick were still widely used. Only a very small proportion of the arable land was worked by machine, and human labour was employed in most agricultural work. Yet as the density of population to cultivated area was relatively low one might have expected the Iraqi peasant to be in a more advantageous position than, for example, his Egyptian counterpart. In fact, most experts agree that, until the 1958 revolution, inequality in the ownership of land and land tenure relationships contributed in large part to the low level of living of the peasants. Warriner in 1957 stated the case clearly when she wrote, 'The fellah's income is low, because the land produces little, and because the landowner takes most of what it produces'.

This oppressive land tenure system had only been established as a legal institution in 1932. Before that date the rural population had been organized for protection in a tribal system which probably originated during the unstable conditions following the fall of the Abbasid Empire. Each tribe occupied a piece of land and used it for either cultivation or pasture, the size of the tribal domain depending upon the size and strength of the tribe. Slight changes in population densities were accommodated through the expansion or contraction of tribal holdings. A man obtained the right to farm and graze his animals by his contribution to the defence of the tribe. A tribal chief or sheikh was an ordinary member of the tribe who held the position because of special qualities of leadership (Fernea, 1969a).

The Land Settlement Laws of 1932–8, which stipulated that all people must register the titles of the land they possessed, radically altered this traditional pattern of land tenure. As the tribesmen were not fully informed about the new law, the sheikhs were able to register in their own names the tribal lands, which became in effect enormous private estates. The tribesmen, formerly holding customary rights of occupation and cultivation, were therefore reduced to the status of sharecroppers and farm labourers. The relationship between sheikh and tribesman now became one of landlord and tenant (Baali, 1969).

In this way large agricultural holdings came to be concentrated in a few hands. In 1958–9 only 2 per cent of the landowners owned 68 per cent of the total agricultural holdings, whereas 89.4 per cent of the total peasants owned no land (Baali, 1969). Although a law of 1933 set out the rights and duties of cultivators, in fact it gave the landlord great authority over the peasants, for they and their agents directed and supervized much of the agricultural work, and took a large share of the annual crop: in the southern irrigated zone three-fifths on land under flow irrigation, two-thirds if seed was provided by the landowner, and five-sevenths on pump-irrigated land. The more powerful the landlord, the larger was his share. The peasant's income was therefore inadequate and he was unable to live without credit, which could only be obtained at extortionate rates of interest. Until he paid his debts a peasant was not permitted to leave the land, and many lived and died in debt. Conditions were particularly oppressive in the provinces of Amara and Nasiriya where extremely complex land tenure systems existed.

Before 1958 the government was controlled by the landowners so that any change in the existing land tenure system was impossible, though a number of foreign experts stressed that an improvement in the agricultural sector of the economy could only be achieved by raising the status and standard of living of the rural population. Instead, model land development and resettlement schemes were created, but the number of people involved was too few for the schemes to have any real effect on the rest of the rural population. Secondly, government revenues from oil royalties were invested in a number of flood control and water storage projects to extend the irrigated area. It was hoped that more intensive cultivation would lead to an increase in production, and thus raise the income and living standards of the peasants. From the mid-1930's to the mid-1950's agricultural production did rise, though there was little improvement in crop yields, and Iraq became an important exporter of grain. However, conditions of life for the majority of the rural population remained much the same, and may even have deteriorated. This period saw an acceleration in the movement of cultivators from the countryside to the towns.

The revolution in 1958 broke the landowners' control over the government, and one of the first measures carried out by the new administration of Abdul Karim Qassem was an Agrarian Reform Law. The declared aims of the law were to destroy the political influence of the landowners; to distribute land to the peasants; to raise their standard of living in order to stop the rural exodus; and to improve agricultural production. In detail, one person was to possess no more than 1,000 dunums (the Iraqi unit of area, the dunum, is equal to 0.25 ha. or 0.62 acres) of irrigated land or 2,000 dunums of non-irrigated land, and the land confiscated was to be allocated to the peasants in holdings of 30–60 dunums on irrigated land and 60–120 dunums on non-irrigated land. The law dealt with the making of agricultural contracts, especially the distribution of crop shares. It laid down the rights of the agricultural worker, and made provision for the formation of co-operative societies (Baali, 1969). Unfortunately, agrarian reform became a focal point in the conflict between the three rival groups within the government—Nationalists, Baathists and Communists—and each political faction had its own ideas about how the new law should be implemented. Consequently, though expropriation was rigorously enforced, constant changes of policy and personnel resulted in delays in the redistribution of land. Because of the problem of organizing co-operatives, there was failure to replace functions formerly carried out by the landowner and his agents, especially in the maintenance of irrigation works and in marketing produce. There were also delays in supplying agricultural machinery (Warriner, 1969).

As a result of this uncertainty and confusion, together with a period of serious drought in the north from 1958 to 1961, rural migration has continued, and a number of writers have pointed out that it may have reached its peak after 1955 (Dauphin, 1960; Thesiger, 1964). Nearly all rural areas have lost some of their inhabitants, but the largest movement has been from the southern provinces and especially from Amara. Moreover, because migration is age selective and involves the reproductive and economically active section of the population it has affected the rate of fertility in rural areas, and created an acute shortage of labour in the agricultural sector. Some land has certainly gone out of cultivation. Crop production has fallen, and has not kept pace with the increase in population, so that oil revenues are now being diverted from development projects to pay for food imports. Finally, according to one report, the number of agricultural agents in the field has fallen since 1958, as many returned to Baghdad to take up posts in the new administration (Fernea, 1969a).

But what of the condition of those who remain in rural areas? On paper a large number of peasants have obtained land either as owners or temporary tenants—though no information is available about the number actually cultivating their land. Also, very little is known about the present condition of the remaining sharecroppers. Moreover, it has been suggested recently that the redistribution of confiscated land in the irrigated zone in plots of 30–60 dunums may result in rapid deterioration of the soil, which appears to be more suited to extensive rather than intensive cultivation in small units. The physical problems of this zone have not changed with the reform, and some engineers have pointed out that on land with poor natural drainage which must be irrigated the only way to prevent salinization and permit more intensive land use is to lay tile drains under the fields (Fernea, 1969a). At present, the cost of such an operation is prohibitive.

The post-revolutionary governments have spent considerable sums in order to improve conditions of life in rural areas, no doubt to try and persuade the people to remain there. Reports indicate that some villages now have electricity, and that their inhabitants are better fed and better dressed (Warriner, 1969). They are, however, probably in a minority. There is certainly less isolation, owing to the diffusion of radios, and some progress has been made in expanding rural education. New hopes have been aroused, especially after the speeches of Qassem, the first political leader to address himself to a rural audience. Yet much remains to be done to improve communications, means of transport, housing, basic amenities, and above all the health of the people in rural areas. At least one survey has shown that, unless changes in the land tenure system are accompanied by projects of social transformation, migration from rural areas is likely to continue (Azeez, 1968).

The urban dwellers

Between 1867 and 1930 although there was an increase in the absolute level of the urban population, which rose from 310,000 to 808,000, its relative position appears to have remained constant at 24–25 per cent of the total population (Hasan, 1958). Since 1930 there has been both an absolute and a relative increase in the number of urban dwellers, of whom there were 3.6 million at the last census (1965), 43.9 per cent of the total population. The annual rate of urban growth was 5.1 per cent between 1947 and 1957, and 5.7 per cent between 1957 and 1965.

An urban place is defined in the Iraq census as a place having a municipal government, but some settlements included in this category cannot be regarded as genuinely 'urban'. In some centres a substantial proportion of the population is dependent upon agriculture; others fulfil few urban functions. On the other hand, there are some settlements, especially close to the major cities, where a majority of the inhabitants are engaged in urban occupations, but which are not municipalities. On balance, therefore, the level of urbanization which the census data reveal is probably reasonably accurate, so that today roughly one person out of four in Iraq lives in an urban place.

The relatively high proportion of town dwellers in Iraq before the First

World War, when little economic development took place, may be attributed to a number of factors: the importance of pilgrim and transit traffic; the absence of a strong rural-based aristocracy, the landowners prefering amenities which only the cities could provide; and the fact that the Ottoman ruling class, few in number, chose to govern the new provinces from the security of the urban centres (Issawi, 1969). Today, the four largest cities in Iraq, Baghdad, Basrah, Mosul and Kirkuk were all administrative centres during the period of Turkish rule.

After the First World War the change from subsistence to commercial farming and the export of agricultural products meant new employment opportunities in the countryside, and until 1930 migration from rural areas was on a relatively small scale. During this period the commercial element in the towns was certainly strengthened, but competition from cheap machine-made imports resulted in a sharp decline in the local handicraft industries, especially those in Baghdad (Hasan, 1958). Consequently, though the total population of Iraq increased during this period there was little change in the level of urbanization.

After the 1930's and particularly since the Second World War, massive rural-to-urban migration together with a high rate of natural increase in towns and cities resulted in rapid urban growth. Rural migration, which began in Iraq as elsewhere in the Middle East during the First World War, accelerated during this period to reach serious proportions. Today, it is perhaps the major socio-economic problem facing the government. During the 1940's and 50's more capital from oil royalties and agricultural output became available for investment, and new industrial and commercial enterprises were established in the major cities, creating greater employment opportunities there than at any time before. This period also saw a dramatic improvement in the range of social services available in urban centres. At the same time, conditions of life for the majority of the rural population had deteriorated as the sheikhs gained control of tribal land and reduced the tribesmen to the status of poor tenants. Both the push and the pull factors had therefore become stronger simultaneously, and rural dwellers flocked to the towns. The insecurity and confusion created by the Agrarian Reform Law of 1958 merely strengthened the force of this movement.

Unfortunately rural migration in Iraq is a problem which is difficult to define in statistical terms, because the data available are scarce and unreliable. Many rural dwellers left the countryside secretly and illegally during periods when the government had placed restrictions on such movement. Another difficulty is simply how to define a migrant. Thus, estimates of the number of migrants for any particular period differ widely. Nevertheless, official estimates indicate that out of a total of 19,497 rural dwellers who migrated to cities in 1958–9 almost 50 per cent came from the four southern provinces, 44.5 per cent from the single province of Amara (Baali, 1969). Other statistics also reveal the importance of the southern provinces as the major source of migrants. Between 1957 and 1967 the total population of the provinces of Amara, Diwaniya and Nasiriya grew at a much lower rate than the rest of the country— 6.7 per cent, 7 per cent and 9.9 per cent respectively. In contrast, during the same period the population of the provinces of Baghdad and Basrah (the two major destinations of the migrants) grew at the high rates of 73 per cent and 41 per cent (Figs. 4.1 and 4.2).

As we have seen in the previous section, conditions of life in the countryside are everywhere low, but there is some evidence to suggest that until 1958 they were slightly better in the north than in the south. In the northern provinces there were some independent peasant proprietors, rental shares were lower and the relative sparsity of the rural population improved the

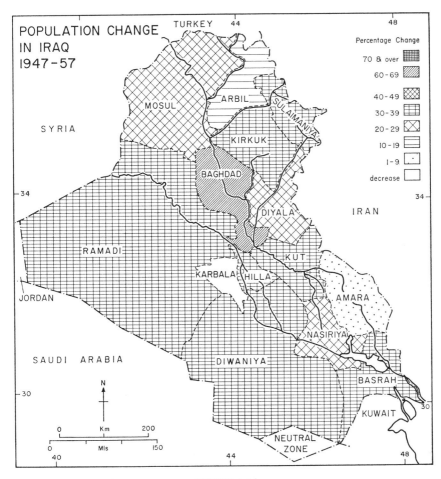

FIGURE 4.1

117

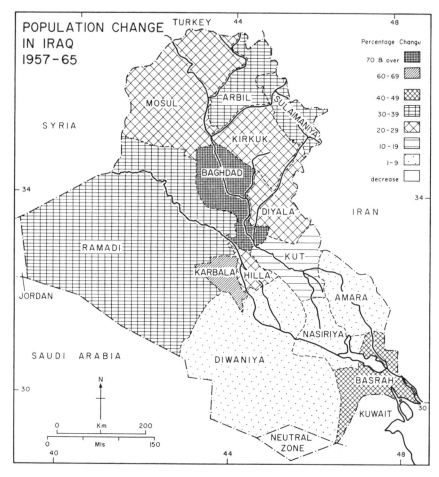

FIGURE 4.2

bargaining power of the tenants (Phillips, 1959). However, in the southern provinces the conditions of life of the cultivators were wretched, especially in Amara with its unique and oppressive land tenure system. Two surveys carried out in Baghdad among migrants from the south report that over half the interviewees stated that they had left the countryside because of their low economic status there; they had come to the capital for better employment opportunities and to improve their standard of living. A smaller, but still significant proportion of interviewees indicated that for them the lack of social amenities in the countryside was the most important cause (Phillips, 1959; Azeez, 1968). This is in complete contrast to several Middle Eastern countries where it is an increase in the supply of agricultural labour exceeding the increase in demand which has forced people from rural areas.

118

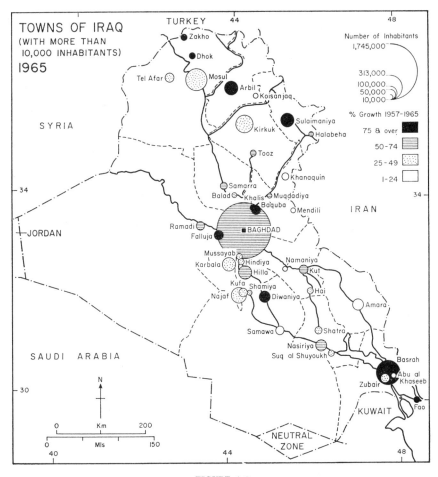

TOWNS OF IRAQ
(WITH MORE THAN
10,000 INHABITANTS)
1965

FIGURE 4.3

These surveys also show that in Iraq permanent migration of complete families is the most important type of movement. It includes not only cultivators—although they are in a majority—but also shopkeepers and traders. Most of the migrants, moreover, have no intention of ever returning to their former homes. This is very different from the situation in most African and Asian countries where migration involves a high proportion of single, male workers and is often only temporary, the men returning to their villages after a certain period of time or after they have accumulated sufficient money.

Urban growth since 1930 has been distributed throughout the country, but unevenly (Fig. 4.3). In the centre and south Baghdad and Basrah, Ba'quba, Khalis and Falluja (towns near the capital), Diwaniya (a provincial capital), and Fao (the new oil terminal) have grown rapidly, particu-

119

larly during the last decade, whereas Amara, Samawa and Namaniya have experienced a much lower rate of increase. The vast majority of migrants from the southern irrigated zone, however, go to Baghdad or Basrah, a trend already well established as early as 1947 (Adams, 1958). Many towns have grown more rapidly than Baghdad and Basrah during the last inter-censal period, but the absolute numbers involved were much smaller. In Basrah, the port, the oil installations and the date industry provide employment opportunities, but the capital offers a greater attraction. Baghdad and surrounding towns contained in 1967 over half of all the country's large industrial establishments employing ten or more persons each; most government organizations, which have expanded rapidly since the 1950's, are found there; and much of the investment in social services has been concentrated in this city. The capital may well have grown by about 8 per cent per annum during the last ten years and though natural growth has probably been slightly above average for the country as a whole, there has obviously been large-scale migration into the city at about 5 per cent a year (Jones, 1969). In 1960, at least a quarter of the city's population were rural migrants. Because of the scale of this movement, the problems created by the influx of rural dwellers are more acute in Baghdad than elsewhere in Iraq. It is, moreover, the only city for which detailed information about the condition of rural migrants is available.

Twenty years ago the population of Baghdad was just over half a million and by 1965 it had grown to 1,745,000. This dramatic increase has been accompanied by an expansion of the built-up area, made possible by greater security and by a series of water-control measures which reduced the danger of flooding. With little overall planning areal expansion has been somewhat haphazard, leaving many open spaces within the city limits. In the 1940's the hutments of rural migrants were mainly confined to the eastern outskirts of the city, though there were some scattered groups on the west bank of the Tigris to the south of the old city district of Karkh. By the late 1950's, however, such dwellings could be seen everywhere. A belt of shanty-towns had grown up behind the East Bund—a dyke built in the early part of this century two kilometres to the east of the Tigris—even though this area was subject to periodic flooding until 1956, and was crossed by polluted and foul-smelling streams. It also lacked all essential amenities. Other migrants settled in available open spaces in the area to the west of the Tigris, which was less affected by flooding and where numerous industrial and commercial establishments were concentrated. Even in the central district of the city squatters erected their hutments in open spaces around houses belonging to wealthy urban families, who often helped the newcomers by supplying them with free electricity and water (Azeez, 1968). This pattern, which remained until the early 1960's, is interesting because it differs from that found in many developing countries where areas of squatter settlement are often confined to the city fringes.

In the shanty-towns the migrants built mud or reed huts known as
serifas—the typical form of rural dwelling in the southern provinces—
and in the late 1950's such dwellings numbered 44,000, 44.6 per cent of the
total number of houses in Greater Baghdad. The newcomers retained
many social characteristics generally associated with rural societies, such as
loyalty to tribe, the importance of religion and marriage customs, but
perhaps more significant the high rate of fertility characteristic of rural
areas was also transferred to Baghdad where it was much higher in the
shanty-towns than in the older urban districts of the city. Thus, migrant
families tended to be large and densities within their settlements high,
leading to much overcrowding and congestion. Housing conditions and
sanitation were often much worse than in their former villages.

Nevertheless, it has been shown that the economic condition of the
migrants had greatly improved (Phillips, 1959; Azeez, 1968). They had
no difficulty finding unskilled employment, especially in building construction—heavily concentrated in Baghdad—and in municipal services, though
such jobs were extremely insecure. Most members of migrant families,
moreover, were able to obtain some form of employment and this helped
the family budget. In 1957, rural migrants constituted 57 per cent of all
industrial workers in Baghdad. Their annual income was now many
times greater than in the countryside, and they were able to afford more
food, better clothes and more household goods.

The presence in the capital of a vast number of rural migrants living in
extremely squalid conditions became, however, a danger to the health of the
rest of the urban population. They placed a strain on public services and
they competed with other workers for lower paid jobs. Therefore, during
the last ten years the government has had to take some action to deal with
the problem. Between 1961 and 1963 the shanty-towns were destroyed
and their occupants transferred to two new settlements on the outskirts
of the city—Madinat al-Thawra (now believed to contain 350,000 people)
and Al-Nur—where houses built of brick, and schools, clinics and markets
have been constructed. The new towns are also linked to the central
districts of Baghdad by regular bus-services. The schemes have been
costly, and by widening the gap between the condition of migrants in the
city and their friends in the countryside they have probably encouraged
further migration. In 1965, according to one report, there were still many
serifas in the city (Gulick, 1967). Secondly, the government attempted to
divert migrants away from the capital by establishing industries in provincial towns. Unfortunately this policy is unlikely to do more than absorb a
small proportion of the local unemployed and underemployed labour
force, which is generally agreed to be considerable (Jones, 1969).

Such projects have dealt only with the consequences and not with the
real causes of rural-to-urban migration which are to be found in the poor
conditions of life in the countryside, and they have done little to deter the

movement of rural dwellers to the capital. Yet action must be taken and quickly. The number of children in rural areas receiving primary education continues to grow each year, and the volume of migration may increase as young people move to the towns to make use of their new qualifications. The government rehousing schemes of the early 1960's have ensured that a large part of future migration will be directed to Baghdad which, according to one estimate, could have a population of 4.5 million in 1980 (Jones, 1969).

In the north a number of towns—Arbil, Sulaimaniya, Dhok and Zakho— have experienced very rapid growth during the last intercensal period (Fig. 4.3), and rural migrants must represent an important part of this increase. Although very little information is available about rural-to-urban migration in the northern provinces, several reports indicate that a substantial rural exodus has taken place in recent years (Warriner, 1969). Insecurity, always a strong force for urbanization, as a result of the war between the Kurdish nationalists and the central government, and the long and severe drought between 1958 and 1961 which reduced incomes and employment in the countryside have been perhaps the major factors contributing to this movement. It is interesting, however, that in the north much of the migration appears to have been directed to urban centres within the region rather than to the capital, and to the small- and medium-sized towns rather than the major northern cities such as Mosul or Kirkuk (Fig. 4.3).

The rank-size hierachy (Table 4.3) reveals one dominant feature in the urban pattern of Iraq—strong urban primacy. The capital, Baghdad, towers above all other urban centres, and there is an enormous difference between the size of this city and the next largest town. This feature already existed in 1947 when the capital contained 10 per cent of the country's total population and 30 per cent of the urban population; more people lived in Baghdad than in the next seven largest cities combined (Adams, 1958). By 1965 the population of Baghdad and its surburbs was estimated at 1,745,000 or 21 per cent of the total population of Iraq (Jones, 1969) and 47.8 per cent of the urban population; the population of the capital was greater than that of the combined populations of all other urban centres with over 25,000 inhabitants. By 1980 the population of the capital may almost double in size to reach 4.5 million, 33 per cent of the total population of Iraq, a degree of concentration found in only a few countries of the world (Jones, 1969).

Some of the reasons for the dominance of Baghdad have already been discussed. They include political instability, a highly centralized government leading to the concentration of the vast number of government posts in the capital, and a similar concentration of a high proportion of industrial employment and of investment in public services. As the chances of finding employment are proportionaly better in the capital than in the provincial

TABLE 4.3   RANK-SIZE OF TOWNS OF IRAQ WITH MORE THAN 10,000
INHABITANTS, 1947–65

1947		1957		1965	
Baghdad	515,411*	Baghdad	1,056,604	Baghdad	1,745,000
Mosul	133,625	Mosul	179,646	Basrah	313,327
Basrah	101,535	Basrah	164,623	Mosul	243,311
Kirkuk	68,308	Kirkuk	120,593	Kirkuk	167,413
Najaf	56,261	Najaf	88,809	Najaf	128,096
Karbala	44,150	Karbala	60,804	Arbil	90,320
Amara	36,907	Hilla	54,095	Sulaimaniya	86,822
Hilla	36,577	Amara	53,311	Hilla	84,717
Sulaimaniya	33,510	Sulaimaniya	48,450	Karbala	83,301
Arbil	27,036	Nasiriya	39,060	Amara	64,847
Nasiriya	24,038	Arbil	34,751	Diwaniya	60,553
Tel Afar	19,951	Diwaniya	33,204	Nasiriya	60,405
Diwaniya	19,878	Zubair	28,699	Kut	42,116
Zubair	17,884	Samawa	26,838	Zubair	41,408
Kut	16,237	Kut	26,524	Falluja	38,072
Samawa	15,292	Tel Afar	25,543	Tel Afar	36,837
Kufa	13,700	Kufa	21,880	Ba'quba	34,575
Abul Khasib	11,598	Falluja	20,009	Samawa	33,473
Hindiya	11,077	Khanaquin	19,312	Kufa	30,862
Falluja	10,981	Ba'quba	18,527	Ramadi	28,723
Ba'quba	10,511	Ramadi	17,747	Samarra	24,746
Hai	10,199	Samarra	16,398	Khanaquin	23,522
Khanaquin	10,090	Hindiya	12,839	Shatra	18,822
		Shatra	12,835	Dhok	16,998
		Mussayab	12,179	Hai	16,988
		Hai	11,806	Suq al Shuyoukh	16,465
		Suq al Shuyoukh	11,642	Hindiya	16,436
		Abu al Khaseeb	11,245	Mussayab	15,955
		Ana	11,070	Fao	15,399
		Namaniya	10,004	Zakho	14,790
				Habbaniya	14,405
				Tooz	13,860
				Shamiya	13,334
				Abu al Khaseeb	12,194
				Muqdadiya	12,181
				Balad	12,034
				Namaniya	11,943
				Khalis	11,877
				Mendili	11,262
				Halabeha	11,206
				Koisanjaq	10,338

* The figures for Baghdad are not strictly comparable. The capital has grown
beyond the old city limits incorporating other settlements which had formerly
been independent. Consequently, it is difficult to calculate the present population
of the city and its suburbs, or to compare figures for different years.

towns, much of the migration from rural areas in the south has been directed to this city; a movement only reinforced by government resettlement schemes for the migrants. Natural growth has also been higher than in the country as a whole, for mortality is probably lower and fertility higher in urban than in rural areas (Jones, 1969).

A second feature of the urban pattern is the small number of urban centres with over 100,000 inhabitants, and the relatively large number of small towns. Baghdad is over five times as big as its nearest rival, Basrah, which in 1965 had a population of 313,327, and which has grown at a rapid rate during the last intercensal period as a result of migration. It has replaced Mosul (243,311), which has lost the important position it held during Ottoman rule, as the second largest city in Iraq. Kirkuk, at the centre of the country's major oil-producing region, and Najaf, an important holy city of the Shi'a sect, are next in size with populations of 167,413 and 128,096 respectively. In 1965 there were only seven medium-sized towns with 50–100,000 inhabitants including Arbil and Sulaimaiya, which have grown rapidly during the last intercensal period, Karbala, a holy city which has declined in relative importance since 1947, and the larger provincial capitals, Amara, Diwaniya, Hilla and Nasiriya. There were, however, 29 small towns with 10–50,000 inhabitants—of which 19 had fewer than 20,000 inhabitants—including the smaller provincial capitals such as Ramadi, Samarra, another holy city, and Fao, the new oil terminal.

The faces of many towns and cities in Iraq, especially the largest centres, have been transformed since the Second World War. Broad avenues have been cut through the maze of narrow, twisting alleyways of the old town centres, and the suburbs which have grown up during the last two decades are laid out on a more open plan. New bridges have been constructed to accommodate the increase in modern traffic, and public services, particularly sewerage, water supply and electricity, have been greatly improved and extended. Urban architecture has also changed with the advent of reinforced concrete construction, and now reflects western influences (Longrigg, 1958).

Changes in the composition of the urban population have not been as profound as in some parts of the Middle East and North Africa, for Iraq never had a large European community. Nevertheless, some changes have taken place. Rural migration has resulted in a substantial increase in the proportion of Shi'a Moslems and Kurds in the urban population, communities which were until recently little urbanized. The relative importance of other groups in the urban population, such as the Christians, has declined, and the strongly urban Jewish community has almost disappeared. In physical terms the spatial pattern of the various communities has undoubtedly been modified, but traditional groupings do not appear to have been completely replaced by socio-economic groupings. The evidence available from Baghdad indicates that most people idealize and try to maintain the old pattern of *haras* (quarters). In modern districts, however, the presence of and contact with other groups cannot be avoided, and adjustments have to be made (Gulick, 1967).

Seventy-five per cent of Iraq's urban population is concentrated in the southern irrigated zone. According to official figures (1965), the level of urbanization within this zone is lowest in the province of Nasiriya (27.2 per cent) and highest in the province of Karbala (72.6 per cent). However, the figure given in the census returns for the urban population of Baghdad province (1,108,497 or 51.2 per cent of the total population of the province) appears to be too low. It has been estimated that the population of Baghdad City and its suburbs alone was 1,745,000 in 1965 (Jones, 1969), so that the proportion of urban dwellers in the province must be at least 80 per cent. In the four northern provinces the level or urbanization is only slightly below the average for the country as a whole; it is highest in Kirkuk province (48.5 per cent), and lowest in Sulaimaniya province (32.1 per cent).

Conclusion

The central theme which emerges from a study of the changing pattern of population in Iraq during recent decades is that of rural-to-urban migration. This movement has brought about important changes in the spatial distribution of the ethnic, religious and linguistic communities, the most notable being the massive migration of Shi'a, formerly concentrated in the south, to the central provinces and especially to Baghdad; it has radically altered the composition of the urban population hitherto made up of a surprisingly high proportion of non-Moslems; and increasing urbanization in itself is beginning to weaken traditional groupings, and encourage new loyalties determined by wealth, occupation and social class.

Rural-to-rural migration, which involves essentially the economically active section of the population, has greatly modified the occupational structure of the country. No recent figures are available so that these changes cannot be defined in statistical terms, but it seems clear that there has been a decline in the proportion of the active population employed in the agricultural sector and an increase in the proportion employed in industries and services. An acute shortage of agricultural labour has characterized some parts of the country in recent years, as a result of which crop production has declined and oil royalties are being diverted from development projects to subsidize food imports.

Migration has also been one of the major factors contributing to the rapid growth of the capital and its dominant position in the urban hierarchy, and to the present concentration of almost half the total population of the country in the central provinces. Since the mid-nineteenth century over 70 per cent of all Iraqis have lived in the southern irrigated zone, for Iraq

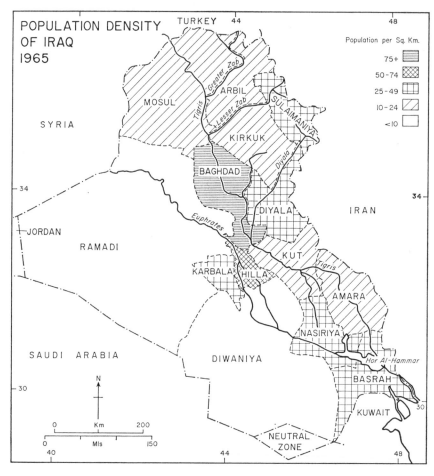

FIGURE 4.4

is truly the gift of its rivers, but until the early twentieth century over 40 per cent were concentrated in the four southern provinces. Today only 25 per cent of the population live in the south (Table 4.1). Average densities for the northern, central and southern regions are 25, 45 and 25 inhabitants per sq. km. respectively (Fig. 4.4), but as there are large uninhabitable areas average densities to cultivated area (72, 273 and 276 per sq. km. respectively for the three regions) are more meaningful. For the country as a whole the contrast between density of total area (19 per sq. km.) and density of cultivated area (110 per sq. km.) is marked. Compared with Egypt, however, the other major irrigated area in the Middle East, where the corresponding figures (1960) are 24 per sq. km. and 980 per sq. km. (Berger, 1963), there is no real population pressure. The total population of Iraq is still relatively small in relation to natural resources.

TABLE 4.4 COMPARISON OF PERCENTAGE AGE-STRUCTURES IN AMARA, BAGHDAD, BASRAH AND IRAQ, 1957

	Infants and adolescents 0–14			Adults 15–59			Aged 60+		
	Male	Female	Total	Male	Female	Total	Male	Female	Total
Amara	49.3	44.0	46.6	42.8	47.2	45.0	7.9	8.8	8.4
Baghdad	44.0	43.7	43.8	49.4	49.1	49.3	6.6	7.2	6.9
Basrah	44.6	42.4	43.5	49.1	50.2	49.6	6.3	7.4	6.9
Iraq	46.0	43.8	44.9	46.8	48.6	47.7	7.1	7.6	7.4

Source: Azeez, 1968.

Finally, as migration is age-selective the proportion of the reproductive section of the population is higher in areas of in-migration than in Iraq as a whole, and lower in areas losing population. Consequently, natural growth, which is likely to remain high for some years, is uneven, and the distribution of population is becoming more irregular. The increasing concentration of population in the central provinces, which have recently grown annually by 5.4 per cent compared with 3.4 per cent in the north and 1.8 per cent in the south, owing to in-migration and high rates of natural increase (Table 4.2 and Figs. 4.1 and 4.2), is politically attractive but is creating enormous economic and social problems. Yet unless effective action is taken by the government to deal with the main causes of the rural exodus and to encourage some migrants to return to their former homes, there appears to be no doubt that this trend will continue.

REFERENCES

ADAMS, D. G. (1958) *Iraq's People and Resources,* University of California Publications in Economics, Vol. 18, Berkeley.

AZEEZ, M. M. (1968) *Geographical Aspects of Rural Migration from Amara Province, Iraq, 1955–1964,* unpublished Ph.D. thesis, University of Durham.

BAALI, F. (1969) 'Agrarian Reform in Iraq: Some Socio-economic Aspects', *The American Journal of Economics and Sociology,* 28, pp. 61–76.

BAER, G. (1964) *Population and Society in the Arab East,* London.

BERGER, M. (Ed.) (1963) *The New Metropolis in the Arab World,* New Delhi.

BLAU, J. (1963) *Le Problème Kurde,* Publications du Centre pour l'étude des problèmes du monde musulman contemporain, Brussels.

COONS, C. S. (1951) *Caravan: the Story of the Middle East,* New York.

DAUPHIN, J. (1960) 'Les Ma'dan de Basse-Mesopotamie', *Annales de Géographie*, 49, pp. 34–49.

EDMONDS, C. J. (1957) *Kurds, Turks and Arabs: Politics, Travel and Research in North-Eastern Iraq, 1919–25*, London.

EL BADRY, M. A. (1965) 'Trends in the components of population growth in the Arab countries of the Middle East; a survey of present information', *Demography*, 2, pp. 140–86.

FERNEA, R. A. (1969a) 'Land Reform and Ecology in Post-Revolutionary Iraq', *Economic Development and Cultural Change*, 17, pp. 356–81.

FERNEA, R. A. and E. W. (1969b) 'Iraq', *Focus*, 20, 2.

FISHER, W. B. (1961) *The Middle East*, London.

GULICK, J. (1967) 'Baghdad, Portrait of a City in Physical and Cultural Change', *Journal of American Institute of Planners*, 34, pp. 246–55.

HASAN, M. S. (1958) 'Growth and Structure of Iraq's population 1867–1947', *Bulletin of Oxford University*, 20, pp. 339–50.

ISSAWI, C. (1969) 'Economic Change and Urbanization in the Middle East' in I. M. Lapidus (Ed.), *Middle Eastern Cities*, University of California Press, Berkeley, pp. 102–21.

JONES, L. (1969) 'Rapid population growth in Baghdad and Amman', *Middle East Journal*, 23, pp. 209–15.

KINNANE, D. (1964) *The Kurds and Kurdistan*, Institute of Race Relations, London.

KINSMAN, J. (1970) 'Kurds and Iran: Iraq's changing balance of power', *The New Middle East*, 22, pp. 25–7.

LANGLEY, K. M. (1967) *The Industrialization of Iraq*, Harvard Middle Eastern Monographs.

LEBON, J. H. G. (1953) 'Population distribution and the agricultural regions of Iraq', *Geographical Review*, 43, pp. 223–28.

LEWIS, B. (1953) 'Some observations on the significance of heresy in the history of Islam', *Studia Islamica*, 1, pp. 43–63.

LONGRIGG, S. H. and STOKES, F. (1958) *Iraq*, New York.

LONGRIGG, S. H. and JANKOWSKI, J. (1970) *The Middle East: A Social Geography*, London.

MCCRARY, J. and SA'EED, M. (1968) 'The Social Characteristics of the Population of Iraq', *Bulletin of the College of Arts, University of Baghdad*, 11, pp. 69–124.

PHILLIPS, D. G. (1959) 'Rural to urban migration in Iraq', *Economic Development and Cultural Change*, 7, pp. 405–21.

QUBAIN, F. I. (1958) *The Reconstruction of Iraq, 1950–57*, New York.

QUINT, M. N. (1958) 'The Idea of Progress in an Iraqi Village', *Middle East Journal*, 2, 368–84.

THESIGER, W. (1964) *The Marsh Arabs*, London.

TREAKLE, H. C. (1966) *The Agricultural Economy of Iraq*, Washington Foreign Regional Analysis Division, Economic Research Service, USDA.

VAJDA, G. (1962) 'Le milieu juif à Baghdad', *Arabica*, 9, pp. 389–93.

VERNIER, B. (1963) *L'Irak d'aujourd' hui*, Paris.

WARRINER, D. (1957) *Land Reform and Development in the Middle East*, London.

WARRINER, D. (1969) *Land Reform in Principle and Practice*, Oxford.

Chapter 5
Syria: patterns of population distribution
J C Dewdney

Enumerations of the population of Syria were carried out on a number of occasions during the period of the Ottoman Empire and again under the French mandate, but the results are of varying reliability and do not form a comparable series on which to base any detailed study of population change. The most recent census was carried out in 1960 (Directorate of Statistics, 1964–5). While this may be assumed to give a reasonably accurate picture of total numbers and their geographical distribution, the information which it contains on various aspects of population structure is often highly suspect. In addition to data available from the census, Syria also has a system of civil registration, the results of which are published regularly in the official *Statistical Abstract*. The civil registration data are 'computed on the basis of the 1922 population census after allowing for additions and subtractions at the end of each year' (Central Bureau, 1969) and it is therefore not surprising that there are serious discrepancies between the census and civil registration figures. Thus, according to the census in 1960 the total population of Syria was 4,565,121 while the figure

TABLE 5.1 POPULATION DISTRIBUTION OF SYRIA BY PROVINCES, 1960

Province	Population (thousands)			Area (thousand sq. km.)	Density per sq. km.	
	Total	Urban (per cent)	Rural		Overall	Rural
Damascus	985.4	603.6 (61.3)	381.8	19.5	50.5	19.6
Homs	380.5	150.3 (39.5)	230.2	42.2	9.0	5.5
Hama	313.1	118.4 (37.8)	194.7	8.3	37.7	23.5
Latakia	515.6	111.1 (21.5)	404.5	4.5	114.6	89.9
Idlib	309.2	50.6 (16.4)	258.6	7.1	43.5	36.4
Aleppo	933.3	474.1 (50.8)	459.2	15.9	58.7	28.9
Raqqa	137.9	14.6 (10.6)	123.3	22.0	6.3	5.6
Deir ez Zor	214.1	57.4 (26.8)	156.7	33.1	6.5	4.7
El Haseke	309.5	58.3 (18.8)	251.2	23.4	13.2	10.7
Es Suweidiya	92.0	24.3 (26.4)	67.7	5.6	16.4	12.1
Dera	162.9	22.4 (13.8)	140.5	4.2	38.8	33.5
Total	4,353.5	1,685.1 (38.7)	2,668.4	185.8	23.4	14.4

Notes: 1. The bedouin population, totalling 211,670 and classified as entirely rural, is excluded from this table.
  2. 'Urban' population as officially defined, i.e. the inhabitants of *mohafaza* (province) and *mantika* (district) centres.
  3. Areas and densities based on them are approximate.

from the civil register for the same year was 4,840,539, a difference of some 275,000 or 6 per cent of the census total. A discrepancy of this order is of relatively minor significance, since the census itself is unlikely to be accurate to within 6 per cent, but unfortunately there are much more serious discrepancies in the case of individual administrative areas. In Raqqa province, for example, the census gave a 1960 population of 178,417, compared with a civil registration figure of 120,056, which may be largely accounted for by the presence of 40,000 bedouin who are not registered. There is no such explanation in the case of Aleppo province, where the census recorded 957,339 people and the civil register 1,085,316 (Zimpel, 1966). If confusion is to be avoided, a choice must be made between the two sets of data, and the account which follows is for the most part based on the 1960 census.

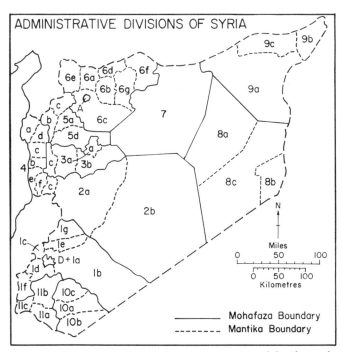

FIGURE 5.1 ADMINISTRATIVE DIVISIONS OF SYRIA, as used in the 1960 Census. Provinces (*mohafaza*) are indicated by numbers 1–11, and districts (*mantika*) by letters a–g. D = Damascus city; A = Aleppo city.

1. Damascus: a. Ghouta; b. Duma; c. Zebdani; d. Qatana; e. Quteifa; f. El Quneitra; g. En Nebk. 2. Homs: a. Homs; b. Palmyra; c. Telkalakh. 3. Hama: a. Hama; b. Selemiya; c. Masyaf. 4. Latakia: a. Latakia; b. Baniyas; c. Jeble; d. Haffe; e. Tartus; f. Safita. 5. Idlib: a. Idlib; b. Jisr esh Shughur; c. Harim; d. Maarret en Numan. 6. Aleppo: a. Azaz; b. El Bab; c. Jebel Saman; d. Jerablus; e. Afrin; f. Ein al Arab; g. Membij; 7. Raqqa. 8. Deir ez Zor: a. Deir ez Zor; b. Abu Kemal; c. Meyadin. 9. El Haseke: a. El Haseke; b. Dijlah; c. El Qamishliye. 10. Es Suweidiya: a. Es Suweidiya; b. Salkhad; c. Shahba. 11. Dera: a. Dera; b. Izra; c. Fiq.

131

Population growth

In view of the limited and contradictory nature of the available data, no firm statement can be made concerning the growth rate in recent years, save that it has been rapid and now probably stands in the region of 3 per cent per annum. According to estimates published in the United Nations *Demographic Yearbook*, the total has more than doubled over the past 25 years, rising from about 2.5 million in 1940 to 5.3 million in 1965. The same source gives an average annual increase rate of 2.9 per cent for the period 1963–7, and this seems a not unreasonable approximation. The same cannot be said of the birth and death rates which also appear in the *Demographic Yearbook* and are based on data drawn from the civil register. These indicate a steady rise in the crude birth rate from 22.5 per thousand in 1950 to 33.1 in 1965 and a decline in the death rate over the same period from the incredibly low level of 7.3 to the even less likely figure of 4.6. Clearly there is gross under-registration of deaths and a significant under-registration of births as well. A clue to the situation is given in a note which accompanies these figures to the effect that they 'exclude live-born infants dying before registration', an exclusion which will affect both birth and death rates and does much to account for the implausibly low infant mortality rate of 28.1. If the UN estimate of a natural increase rate of 27.6 per thousand in 1967 is accepted as something near the truth, then a birth rate in the region of 45–50 and a death rate around 17–22 per thousand would appear, by analogy with other Middle Eastern populations, to be reasonable approximations. It follows that rapid population growth is likely to continue during the 1970's.

Population distribution: broad patterns

Table 5.1 shows the distribution of the population among the eleven provinces (*mohafaza*) into which the country is divided. Unfortunately, as Figure 5.1 illustrates, these are particularly unsatisfactory units on which to base any detailed study, not only because of their large average size (16,860 sq. km.), but also because several of them, notably Damascus and Homs, include large expanses of empty territory as well as densely settled areas, so that provincial population density and other figures are very misleading. The position is somewhat improved if the smaller district or *mantika* is adopted for density or distribution mapping, as in Figures 5.2 and 5.3, but the problem is by no means eliminated, particularly in the case of the very large districts in the centre and east of the country. The existence of this problem, together with the actual patterns of district and provincial boundaries, which give a few large units in the east and numerous small ones in the west, draws our attention to a basic feature of the distribution of the Syrian population. This is the contrast between

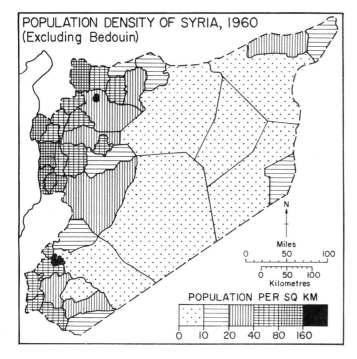

FIGURE 5.2

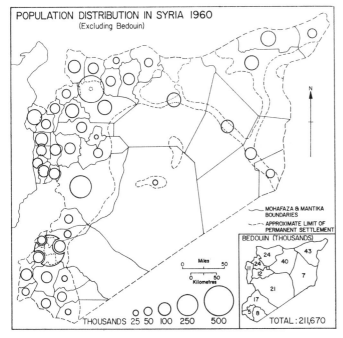

FIGURE 5.3

(a) the large areas of arid territory in the central and eastern parts of the country, devoid of settled population and inhabited only by small numbers of nomadic bedouin, and (b) the settled zone which contains all the crop-land and 95 per cent of the country's population. The approximate limit of the settled zone is shown in Figure 5.4 where it can be seen to lie mainly in the west of the country, covering virtually the whole of Aleppo, Latakia, Idlib, Hama and Dera provinces, together with the western sections of Homs, Damascus and Es Suweidiya. Settlement is also widespread in the far north-eastern province of El Haseke, but in Raqqa, Deir ez Zor and eastern Homs it is wholly confined to river valleys and oases.

This distribution pattern, in its general outline at least, can be described fairly simply in terms of the physical environment as it affects agriculture, since over 60 per cent of the population is still classed as rural and at least 50 per cent of the male labour force is employed in agriculture. Thus the distribution of the numerically predominant rural section of the population to a very large degree reflects the agricultural productivity of the land which, in turn, as throughout the Middle East, is largely bound up with the availability of water. The interior of Syria is cut off from the Mediterranean coast by the mountain systems of the Jebel el Ansariye and the Jebel ez Zawiye in the north, and the Lebanon and Anti-Lebanon ranges in the south. As a result, average annual precipitation, which is about 750 mm. along the coast and reaches 1,000 mm. or more in the coastal ranges, falls off rapidly to the east of the mountains. It is about 450 mm. at Homs, Hama and Aleppo, 250 mm. at Damascus and only 125 mm. at Palmyra and Deir ez Zor. Over most of the country, the isohyets run from north to south, but towards the Turkish border they turn to run from west to east along the southern flank of the Taurus ranges, thus giving a zone of rela-tively plentiful precipitation along the border, with annual totals of some 350 mm. at Jerablus and El Qamishliye. Speaking in very general terms, the density of population tends to vary with annual rainfall, diminishing across the country from west to east and from north to south.

This is, of course, a gross simplification of the actual state of affairs. and local features of relief, soil and drainage have a marked effect on local patterns of population distribution. Thus, within the settled zone itself, there are at least three contrasting elements. The highest rural densities are recorded in intensively farmed valleys and basins, where irrigation sometimes adds greatly to the carrying capacity of the land; intermediate densities are found over large, open, often steppe-like areas of rain-fed cultivation; and there are thinly-settled districts where steepness of slope, poverty of soil or absence of water militate against a productive agriculture. Again, in the centre and east, the picture of overall low density given by data on a provincial or district basis must be modified to take account of the high densities recorded in places along the valleys of the Euphrates and its tributaries.

In addition to the physical factors, account must also be taken of the extent to which the agricultural potential of the various areas has been realized, for not all cultivable land is in use, nor is all potentially irrigable land irrigated. Estimates as to the amount of land under cultivation vary widely, and here again there are major discrepancies between the data given in the *Statistical Abstract* and figures suggested by outside bodies. According to United Nations estimates published about the time of the 1960 census (FAO, 1960), some 5.5 million hectares, 30 per cent of the total area, was classed as arable (including tree crops) of which about a third would be fallow in any one year, giving about 3.6 million hectares actually under crops. This represented an increase of between 1.5 and 2 million hectares during the 1940's and 1950's when Syria, along with several of her neighbours, was able to support rapid population growth by progressive extensions to the cultivated area. This expansion, assisted by a rising level of mechanization, was most effective in areas of rain-fed cereal cultivation, notably in Aleppo province and in the Jazirah district of El Haseke. This gave the relatively favourable balance, in 1960, of roughly one hectare of arable land per head of the population and 1.5 hectares per head of the rural element. A further 3 million hectares were classed by FAO as 'potentially productive' at the same date, sufficient to support an additional 2 million rural population at the same density. Since about 1960,

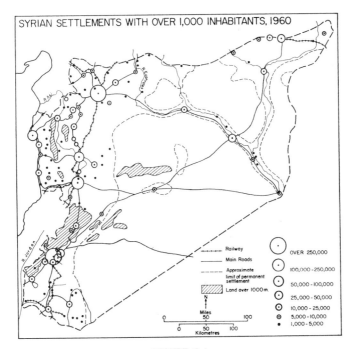

FIGURE 5.4

expansion of the sown area has proceeded more slowly and attention has been focused on increasing productivity from land already in the area under irrigation, which in 1960 was about 500,000 hectares, less than 10 per cent of the cultivated area, and a doubling of this figure is not beyond the bounds of possibility. New projects have so far been mainly in the west, but there remain large areas of potentially irrigable land in the valley of the Euphrates. Thus regional variations in population density have been affected by the process of agricultural expansion as well as by variations in agricultural potential.

A further factor affecting rural population density is the location of commercial centres and transport arteries, proximity to which may intensify agricultural production and raise population densities well above those of physically similar but more remote areas. Thus the patterns of population distribution and density shown in Figures 5.2 and 5.3 are the product of complex interactions among a variety of physical, economic and human factors, and both maps mask wide regional variations which are discussed below.

Urban population and towns

According to the census of 1960, 1,684,956 people, 37 per cent of the total population, lived in urban settlements, which for this purpose included only *mohafaza* and *mantika* centres. Many of the latter were too small to be classed as urban settlements by any realistic criterion, while the inhabitants of a number of larger towns which did not have the appropriate administrative status were excluded from the urban total. Using the data assembled by Zimpel, it is possible to identify the numbers living in settlements of various sizes. These are set out alongside the officially defined urban population in Table 5.2 and the 126 places with over 1,000 inhabitants are mapped in Figure 5.4.

TABLE 5.2   URBAN POPULATION OF SYRIA, 1960

Size of centre	Mohafaza and Mantika centres only			All settlements over 1,000		
	Number of centres	Population		Number of centres	Population	
		Number	Per cent		Number	Per cent
> 250,000	2	955,430	20.1	2	955,430	20.1
100–250,000	1	137,217	3.8	1	137,217	3.8
50–100,000	2	164,994	3.6	2	164,994	3.6
25–50,000	2	76,234	1.7	3	103,523	2.3
10–25,000	15	233,881	5.1	17	257,583	5.6
5–10,000	11	82,653	1.8	27	196,894	4.3
1–5,000	10	34,547	0.8	74	174,606	3.8
Total	43	1,684,956	36.9	126	1,990,247	43.5

It will be seen from these figures that the great bulk of the urban population lives in a small number of major centres. About half the town-dwellers and roughly one-fifth of the total population of Syria are to be found in the cities of Damascus and Aleppo which, in 1968, had well over half a million inhabitants each, an increase of some 16 per cent over the 1960 figure. There is a marked break in the urban hierarchy between these two leading cities and the three second-grade centres of Homs, Hama and Latakia. These three towns appear to be growing more rapidly than Damascus or Aleppo: by 1968 their populations had reached 190,000, 148,000 and 87,000 respectively, an average growth of some 40 per cent from the 1960 level. The remaining 121 centres with over 1,000 inhabitants had, in 1960, a combined population of only 732,000, less than 20 per cent of the total population of Syria, but many of these minor centres are also experiencing rapid growth.

Population distribution: regional variations

Of all the eleven provinces, the most densely populated is Latakia, which extends from the Mediterranean coast to the crest of the Jebel el Ansariye and thus conveniently illustrates the features of the coastal zone. Despite a relatively low level of urbanization (21.5 per cent), the overall density reaches 114 per sq. km. and the rural density of just below 90 per sq. km. is six times the national average. The only large town is Latakia itself (67,604 in 1960) which has grown rapidly in recent years as Syria's main port, since the traditional outlets via Aleppo–Iskenderun and Damascus–Beirut pass through Turkish and Lebanese territory. Tartus (15,353) and Jeble (10,668), both small ports, are the only other centres with more than 10,000 inhabitants, but there are no fewer than eighteen other settlements of 1,000–10,000, the majority of them in the lower half of that range (Fig. 5.4). The presence of so many minor centres reflects the intensity of land use in this well watered zone and the highly commercialized nature of its agriculture with cereals, vegetables, citrus fruits, olives, vines and tobacco.

To the east of the coastal ranges, the settled zone forms a band of territory which varies in width from 50 to 100 km. and lies between the mountains to the west and the deserts to the east. This falls readily into two sections which are separated by a thinly settled area where the Anti-Lebanon ranges cross the western frontier. To the north of this divide lie the four provinces of Aleppo, Idlib, Hama and Homs, which together contain some 43 per cent of the population of Syria. The level of urbanization, overall density and rural density are all close to the national average.

Aleppo province, though it accounts for little more than 8 per cent of the national territory has 20 per cent of Syria's population and an overall density of 59 per sq. km., second only to that of Latakia. This is in part accounted for by the high degree of urbanization which, at 50.8 per cent, is exceeded only in Damascus province, but Aleppo ranks fourth in rural density, which is twice the national average. This reflects the presence of large areas of rain-fed cultivation on the open plains of the province. In the post-war years there has been a large-scale expansion of the sown area and more than 80 per cent of the cultivable land is now in use. Cereals are dominant over most of the province, but it is also a major producer of sugar-beet and cotton. Population distribution is dominated by Aleppo itself, Syria's chief commercial centre, which in 1960 had 425,000 inhabitants, compared with about 300,000 in 1945. There is only one other town (El Bab: 16,783) with a population over 10,000 but there are nearly a score in the 1,000–10,000 range. Rural densities are highest in the northwest of the province, in the basins of the Afrin and Quweiq Rivers, falling off rapidly towards the south-east.

The province of Idlib, which was separated from Aleppo about ten years ago, has no major urban centre. The provincial capital has a population of only 25,000 and the degree of urbanization is very low. The average rural density, however, is high, about two and a half times the national average, and Idlib is second only to Latakia in this respect. The highest rural densities are found in the western part of the province where some 35,000 hectares have recently been reclaimed and irrigated in the Ghab, a large marshy basin in the Orontes valley. On the northern and eastern slopes of the Jebel ez Zawiye, particularly around Idlib itself, a varied agriculture, producing olives, figs, almonds and vegetables as well as cereals, also supports high densities. Densities fall to very low levels east of the Aleppo–Damascus railway.

To obtain an accurate impression of the situation in the provinces of Hama and Homs, it is necessary to detach from the latter the large Palmyra district which, except in the Palmyra oasis, is devoid of permanent settlement. If this is done, the settled area of the two provinces contains a population of 680,000, with an overall density of 34 and a rural density averaging about 18 per sq. km. The level of urbanization is slightly above the national average. Open plains devoted to rain-fed cereal and cotton cultivation occur widely in the west of these provinces and support rural densities in the vicinity of 25 per sq. km. over large areas, particularly in the zone between the two cities. Higher densities are recorded on irrigated land along the valleys of the Orontes and its tributary, the Sarut. There is again a decline towards the east with diminishing rainfall, and densities also fall off southwards into the foothills of the Anti-Lebanon ranges. Homs (137,217) and Hama (97,390) are Syria's third and fourth largest cities and are rapidly-growing commercial and industrial centres. Both benefit from their position at points where the main north–south road and railway are joined by routes from the coast to the interior which use the gap between Jebel el Ansariye and the Lebanon and Anti-Lebanon ranges.

The intrusion of the Anti-Lebanon ranges into Syrian territory is marked by a thinly settled zone in the En Nebk and Quteifa districts of Damascus province, where rural densities average less than 15 per sq. km. To the south of this zone, the three provinces of Damascus, Es Suweidiya and Dera have an aggregate population of 1,240,000. This gives an overall density of nearly 45 sq. km. and a rural density of 20, but these figures should be raised to 70 and 30 respectively to allow for the large areas of empty territory in the east of Damascus and Es Suweidiya. About 50 per cent of the population of the three provinces is urban. Most of the urban element is to be found in the capital itself, which had a 1960 population of 530,000, but there are seven other towns over 10,000. Three of these, Jaoubar (27,000), Duma (23,000) and Daraya (15,000) are in the Ghouta oasis (see below), Qatana (10,000) and El Quneitra (17,000) are district centres in the west of Damascus province, and two are the provincial capitals Es Suweidiya (18,000) and Dera (17,000). The smaller centres of 1–5,000 are mainly in the Hauran plain between Damascus and Dera and in the Jebel ed Druze.

The three provinces of Damascus, Es Suweidiya and Dera contain great variations in population density. The highest values are recorded in the Ghouta oasis to the south-east of Damascus, where intensive irrigated agriculture is supported by the Barada River, which emerges from the Anti-Lebanon ranges to flow south-eastwards for some 40 km. before disappearing into the desert. Ghouta Nahia, which does not cover the whole of the oasis, has a population of 120,000 in an area of 400 sq. km. The majority live in large nucleated settlements which, though they are larger than many 'towns' elsewhere in the country, are essentially agricultural in function. A smaller zone of irrigated agriculture and high population densities occurs in the extreme south of Dera province in the upper part of the Yarmuk valley, and extension of this irrigated zone downstream is under way. Elsewhere, densities are much lower and show the usual relationship to precipitation. Above average densities (40–50 per sq. km.) are recorded on the better-watered uplands towards the Lebanese and Israeli frontiers and on the western flank of the Jebel ed Druz, moderate (20–30) values in the intervening Hauran plain, and very low densities to the east of the Jebel ed Druze.

The remaining three provinces of Raqqa, Deir ez Zor and El Haseke are in strong contrast to the areas so far discussed. Covering more than 40 per cent of Syria's land area, they contain only 15 per cent of the country's population, with an overall density of 8.4 and a rural density of 7.8 per sq. km. Only 20 per cent of the population is classed as urban. The most densely populated of the three provinces is El Haseke where, in the area known as the Jazirah, there has been a large-scale expansion of the land under rain-fed cultivation during the post-war period. The sown area of the Jazirah has risen from an estimated 20,000 hectares in the 1940's to a present total of about 1.6 million hectares. Most of this expansion has been in a zone within 80 km. of the Turkish frontier where Melikiye and El Qamishliye districts now have rural densities of 14 and 20 per sq. km. respectively. This agricultural expansion has resulted in the rapid growth of El Qamishliye town, the main commercial centre of the region, which by 1960 had a population of 35,000 and ranked as Syria's seventh largest urban centre. In Raqqa and Deir ez Zor provinces, population is almost entirely confined to the narrow strip of fertile, well-watered alluvium along the Euphrates and Khabur Rivers, where densities in places exceed 100 per sq. km. Current plans envisage a major expansion of the area under irrigation in these valleys. Although the general level of urbanization in this region is low, it contains Syria's sixth city, Deir ez Zor, with 42,000 inhabitants. Sited at the junction of the main north-west to south-east and south-west to north-east routes across the country, Deir ez Zor has long been the main commercial centre of the Euphrates valley lands.

Population structure

Discussion of population structure will be confined to a brief review of the 1960 census data. The age structure of the Syrian population is very youthful, with nearly 85 per cent below the age of 45 and about 30 per cent less than ten years old. The main variations are between urban and rural areas, the former showing an above average proportion of adults (52.6 per cent as against 47.5 per cent in rural areas) and a rather lower proportion of children (43.3 per cent as against 47.5 per cent). The census data show a predominance of males with a general sex ratio of 947 females per thousand males, but here too there are differences between urban and rural populations, the former having a significantly lower sex ratio (940 compared with 952 in rural areas). These urban/rural differences in the age and sex structures of the population suggest migration to towns involving a preponderance of young adult males, but the data do not permit detailed investigation.

The data on economic activity are summarized in Table 5.3. The census tables on this topic cover the whole population aged six and over, a total of 3,348,000 people. The activities of 67,000 of these are 'not stated' or 'inadequately described' and a further 2,296,500 are categorized as being 'without activity'. This leaves a recorded labour force of 984,400, including 892,300 men, but only 92,100 women, whose allocation to eight groups of economic activities is indicated in Table 5.3. The surprisingly low figure of 52.7 per cent of the entire labour force employed in agriculture is clearly due to the fact that the great majority of females working on the land are not recorded. Suppose the number of female agricultural workers is at least equal to that of males, then the proportion of the labour force actually engaged in agriculture rises to about 66 per cent, a much more realistic figure.

TABLE 5.3 ECONOMICALLY ACTIVE POPULATION OF SYRIA, AGED 6 YEARS AND OVER

Nature of employment	*Males*		*Females*		*Total*	
	Numbers (thousands)	*Per cent*	*Numbers (thousands)*	*Per cent*	*Numbers (thousands)*	*Per cent*
1. Agriculture, forestry, hunting and fishing	468.0	52.4	50.9	55.2	518.9	52.7
2. Mining and quarrying	3.9	0.4	0.2	0.2	4.1	0.4
3. Manufacturing	116.5	13.1	8.3	9.1	124.8	12.7
4. Construction	56.9	6.4	0.7	0.8	57.6	5.9
5. Electricity, gas, water and sanitary services	7.2	0.8	0.1	0.1	7.3	0.7
6. Commerce	88.3	9.9	1.1	1.2	89.4	9.1
7. Transport, communications and storage	38.1	4.3	0.4	0.4	38.5	3.9
8. Services	113.3	12.7	30.4	33.0	143.7	14.6
Total	892.2	100.0	92.1	100.0	984.3	100.0

Data on the ethnic composition of the population are also incomplete. According to the census, 'Syrian Arabs' number 4,192,000 and constitute 92 per cent of the population. There are 211,670 bedouin (4.6 per cent), 122,600 Palestinian Arabs (2.5 per cent), 42,700 non-Syrian Arabs (0.9 per cent) and 6,000 persons of other nationalities. No mention is made of ethnic minorities known to exist in Syria who are presumably submerged in the 'Syrian Arab' total. According to one recent source (US Army, 1965), these number about 540,000, some 11 per cent of the total population. There are believed to be about 250,000 Kurds, many of whom arrived from Turkey in the inter-war period. They are found mainly in the north and north-east of the country, with perhaps 30,000 in the vicinity of Damascus. Armenians, again for the most part the descendants of refugees from Turkey, number about 165,000, the majority living in Aleppo province, but there are also sizeable contingents in Damascus and the other large towns. Some 60,000 Turkomans live mainly in Aleppo province, in the Jazirah and along the Euphrates. There are 50,000 Circassians, found in many western areas, particularly in the El Quneitra district and 15,000 Assyrians, mainly in the Khabur valley. The number of Jews has greatly declined in the post-war period and there are now believed to be only about 5,000, compared with some 30,000 in 1945. The Kurds, Turkomans, and to a lesser extent the Circassians, all of whom are Moslems, are being assimilated, but the Armenians, who are predominantly Christians, still retain a very separate identity.

The census distinguishes three religious groups: Moslem (3,987,000: 87 per cent), Christian (361,000: 8 per cent) and Jewish (5,000: 0.1 per cent), the bedouin being excluded from this classification. No mention is made of the division of the Moslem element into Sunni, who are overwhelmingly predominant, forming at least 75 per cent of the population, and the much smaller Shi'a, Alawi, Ismaili and Druze groups. Most of these are highly localized—the Shi'a (25,000) now live mainly in the Homs and Aleppo areas, Alawi (600,000) are dominant in Latakia province, most of the Ismaili (56,000) now live in the Selemiya district of Hama province and the Druzes (70,000) occupy the Jebel ed Druze in the extreme south. The majority of Christians are Greek Orthodox and live mainly in Damascus, Homs, Hama and Latakia provinces, while the Armenian population follows its own Gregorian rite. There are small communities of the Syrian Orthodox, Nestorian and Catholic persuasions.

Despite the great variety of ethnic and religious minority groups indicated above, the Syrian population is increasingly homogeneous in language and religion, deriving its unity from the Syrian Arabic tongue and the Sunni Moslem religion as well as from its political development over the past twenty years.

NOTE   Since this chapter was written, a few preliminary results of the 1970 census have been released by the Syrian authorities. These show a total 1970 population of 6,924,000, an increase of 1,729,000 over the 1960 figure. This represents an average annual growth rate of 3.3 per cent, slightly higher than the estimate made on page 132. Urban growth has been particularly rapid: the aggregate population of the provincial capitals has risen by 57 per cent, compared with 29 per cent growth in the remainder of the country. The population of Damascus city has increased from 530 to 835 thousand and that of Aleppo from 426 to 639 thousand.

REFERENCES

CENTRAL BUREAU OF STATISTICS (1969) *Statistical Abstract, 1967,* Central Bureau of Statistics, Syrian Arab Republic, Damascus.

DIRECTORATE OF STATISTICS (1964–5) *Census of Population, 1960,* Directorate of Statistics, Syrian Arab Republic, Damascus, 15 vols.

FAO (1960) *Production Yearbook,* United Nations Food and Agriculture Organization, Rome.

US ARMY (1965) *US Army Area Handbook for Syria,* Department of the Army Pamphlet No. 550–47, US Government Printing Office, Washington D.C.

ZIMPEL, H. G. (1966) 'Die Verteilung der syrischen Bevölkerung nach dem Zivilregister und der Volkszählung von 1960', *Petermanns Geographische Mitteilungen,* 110, pp. 57–67.

Chapter 6
Lebanon: an ecumenical refuge
W B Fisher

Physical fragmentation

The Lebanese state could be described as the roof of the Eastern Mediterranean, with not only a surprising number of attics and garrets located just
below, but also a splendid façade. Situated more or less centrally along the
Eastern Mediterranean coastlands, the Lebanon is characterized by two
imposing hill ranges, anticlinal in structure, that run more or less parallel
to the coast, but converge towards the south. The western anticline, the
Lebanon range, attains heights greater than any occurring in coastal Syria
to the north, or in Israel to the south. Two peaks, Qornet es Sauda
(3,083 m.) in the extreme north, and Sannin (2,548 m.) in the centre behind
Beirut, are without rival in Syria, Israel or Jordan, except for the single
crest of Mt. Hermon (2,814 m.) which is the culminating point of the
eastern, or Anti-Lebanon range, and lies on the Libano–Syrian frontier.

Between the Lebanon and Anti-Lebanon ranges there occurs the Beqa
valley. This is broad and open towards the north, but increasingly con-
stricted southwards, until the two mountain ranges come almost together
at what are now the frontiers of Israel–Syria–Lebanon. Here there is no
more than a tortuous defile, parts of which are occupied by the head-
streams of the Jordan River.

On the extreme west, the Lebanon massif is flanked by an extremely
narrow coastal plain, no more than 10 km. wide at its broadest near Beirut.
Elsewhere it is usually much narrower, and in a few places highland reaches
the sea, to produce a number of bold cliffs, as at Nakoura (the 'Ladder of
Tyre') near the Israeli frontier, or Ras Shekka south of Tripoli. Besides the
major folding movements of the Tertiary period which produced the
Lebanon ranges in their present form, there was episodic uplift during
late Pliocene and Quaternary times which gave rise to coastal benches and
erosion surfaces that were later to offer significant sites for human settlement. These can be seen at levels of 10–30 m., especially southwards from
Beirut as far as Nakoura, at 40–60 m. round Beirut itself, and at 70–100 m.
in the extreme north beyond Tripoli.

An especially significant element in the Lebanon is the occurrence of a
series of relatively thin and generally impervious sandstone and marls, of

lower Cretaceous age. These occur only in the Lebanon range, thinning out north and south, and thus are absent also in the east. Below them is often massive Jurassic limestone, whilst overlying is a complex of permeable Tertiary series—Miocene limestone particularly, which is relatively coarse, fissured and highly porous.

With a mountain range of exceptional altitude fronting the coast for several hundred kilometres and lying across the track of prevalent on-shore winds, it is hardly remarkable that most of the Lebanon experiences relatively heavy precipitation. The highest slopes of the Lebanon and even the Anti-Lebanon carry a snow cover for nearly half the year—hence the name of the region: *Lubnan* (whiteness); and annual falls of over 1,000 mm. or even in a few places 1,500 mm. are normal on the higher levels, with 500 mm. at least over most of the rest of the country, apart from a very small rain-shadow area in the north-eastern Beqa, where less than 300 mm. of rainfall is experienced. Snowfall with gradual melt spread over three to six months produces a more consistent and sustained sub-surface percolation throughout the year; and one may contrast these conditions with the flash-flooding, due to rapid surface run-off, that is more characteristic in areas farther south—for example, southern Israel, Jordan or the Sinai.

As well, and a matter of considerable local importance, is the existence of the impermeable rock complex, which gives rise to a series of spring lines located along the flanks of the Lebanon range at heights of 700–1,500 m. above sea level. These springs occur on both sides of the range, but, because of a slight westward dip of the impervious series, are rather more developed on the west. From these develop copious streams that become short, swift-flowing rivers directly consequent to the strike of the Lebanon massif—most important of these being successively from south to north, the Beirut River, Dog River (Nahr el Kelb), Adonis River (Nahr Ibrahim), Nahr Abu Ali and Great River (Nahr el Kebir). On the eastern, Beqa, side there rise the Orontes, the Yammouneh, the Litani and Hasbani Rivers, all of which are perennial. One may contrast these with conditions farther south in Israel, where the brook Kishon and the partly saline Jordan are the only major perennial rivers.

For part if not all of their courses, the Lebanese rivers tend to be deeply incised in narrow gorge-like valleys. Some of this encasement is an effect of the greater run-off that prevailed during wetter climatic phases in the Quaternary; some is due to present-day erosion. Exceptions are the Orontes, which for most of its course flows in flat, open country, and the upper (but not the lower) Litani. The general effect is thus of massive gorges some of them over 1,000 m. deep, which split the country into separate, generally small blocks of 20–30 sq. km. in extent.

This topographical subdivision—segmentation of a major upfold—produces a remarkable result when the effects of climate are added. From sea level, where frost is practically unknown, there is rapid transition successively from sub-tropical conditions to humid highlands where winters are severe, then farther eastwards to increasing aridity and continentality. In the 70 or so kilometres between Beirut and the Syrian frontier near Damascus one passes from steamy lowlands where bananas can be cultivated, through typically Mediterranean and then cool temperate conditions that become Alpine in the highest parts. Farther east, there are steppe conditions that pass into the semi-arid and then arid karstic regions of the Anti-Lebanon, where rainfall is scanty, and the Nubian Cretaceous intercalation of impermeable rocks that produces a spring-line is entirely absent.

Overall, the effect is of a series of strongly differentiated small-scale *pays*. While a few of these 'pays' are lowland, most are enclaves of various types within the highland massifs, and some, as in the Beqa, which varies remarkably from north to south, are steppe-zones. In many of these flattish basins or benches there is enough soil and water for agriculture, and the bold topography, with its sweep of mountain, gorge and tiny platform, and of vegetation-type that includes natural woodland (much, though by no means all of this now degraded to semi-scrub) produces scenery of great beauty and attractiveness, particularly on the western side overlooking the Mediterranean. The territory appears not only as a cooler refuge from summer heat, but also as an easily accessible winter sports centre.

A final geographical factor of importance is the key geographical location of the Lebanon, as an entry to much of the central zone of the Middle East. Besides having most of the relatively good harbours in the difficult eastern coast of the Mediterranean, there are a number of inland passes or corridors that give fairly direct access to the interior. Most striking of these is the Col du Baidar that provides a route from Beirut to Damascus; but there are others—via Tripoli and the Nahr el Kebir valley to central Syria, Iraq and Southern Turkey; and various routes over the southern Lebanon ranges by way of the upper Jordan valleys to the state of Jordan, to Kuwait, and the Persian or Arabian Gulf.

Lying at the most direct and, on the whole, easy way across the isthmus that links the Mediterranean to the Persian/Arab Gulf and thence to the Indian Ocean, there has been much contact in the Lebanon between on the one side, the Arab world, with beyond it, Iran and further Asia, and, on the other side, Europe and the West. This is, to use the historian's term, the 'mission' of the Lebanon, its social and geographical function, which it has performed over many centuries both in an economic aspect, through trading and exchange, and also culturally. No other Middle Eastern town even Cairo, has four separate universities as has Beirut; and it was a far from random choice that led to the setting up of UNESCO Headquarters in the same city. The modern importance of Beirut as a centre of air traffic is also well known.

Scenery, climate and location apart, there are few other major resources in the Lebanon. Tiny deposits of coal have been entirely worked out, there are no metallic minerals, and petroleum is absent. Its main export of Biblical times—cedar trees—is now reduced to a dozen or so stands of near-museum status, and its present day exports, mainly citrus fruit and apples, are not very extensive. Yet, the Lebanon continues to exist on a principal basis of international trading and commercial services, with a *per capita* income about double that of most other Arab countries. Eminent economic, political and geographical observers have summed the situation as 'we don't know how it works, but don't touch it—it seems to manage all right'.

We now propose to disregard such possibly sound advice by attempting an analysis of the population situation in this remarkable country.

Political evolution

The Lebanon achieved semi-autonomy in a very small territory—far less than its present size—during the latter part of the nineteenth century. Subjected to French Mandate after 1920, it at first formed one of six autonomous regions within the Mandate, but these six were soon reduced to Syria, and to a Lebanon enlarged to its present frontiers by the inclusion of the Beqa and certain Moslem districts north and south. Following a short period of dissidence and struggle, independence was gained in 1945 with the ending of the French Mandate, but for several years there was a customs union with Syria. This was dissolved in 1950, after which the Lebanon was able to pursue an entirely independent foreign policy, aligned, as its leaders regularly insisted, to the general aims of the Arab League. A special feature, the basic *raison d'être* of the Lebanon as a separate political unit, is the predominant part taken by Christian sects in the life of the country. Though undoubtedly Arab, the Lebanon is a Christian multi-confessional state, with a Christian Head of State, who so far has always been a Maronite.

The Lebanon attained its present frontiers because of the desire of the then Mandatory power, France, to include as many Christian sects as possible within a Lebanese state who would otherwise have been minorities in Moslem Syria. The fact that by taking in detached and small Christian communities on the Beqa and elsewhere meant also inclusion of large numbers of Moslems was held to be of lesser importance than erecting a territorial unit of viable size and with a numerical preponderance of Christians. The balance initially was thus quite fine: and since 1920 a consistently lower birth rate among Lebanese Christians together with a greater propensity to emigrate has tended to reduce the Christians' numerical predominance, even, some observers believe, to the point of extinction.

Consequently, the census is a crucial matter, and none has been taken in any total or wholly meaningful way. There were census operations in 1921 and 1932 but the totals given, 559,000 and 795,000 people respectively,

146

are thought to be low, especially the first one. During the Second World War, rationing led to an attempt at enumeration, and census operations were carried out over most of the country during 1941–2. The full results were, however, never published officially, and no census has been undertaken since. The Lebanon thus remains one of the few Middle Eastern countries for which there are no census data.

Various later estimates have appeared, however. In 1953 E. de Vaumas published an extensive analysis of the population situation, with detailed figures for various sects, and a few administrative units (*cazas*) and towns. There is, however, no statement in the article as to how these figures (which tend to suggest conditions round about 1950) are actually derived, or any discussion as to their reliability: they are *choses données*. The Lebanese Government gave estimations for 1958 in their *Recueil de Statistiques Libanaises, 1965*. The Population Reference Bureau of Washington gave an estimate for 1969 of a total population numbering 2.6 million, with a growth rate of 2.5 per cent annually; and various reference books quote figures more or less in line with these. The Lebanese Embassy in London stated during 1970 that the population of the Lebanon was 2,367,000, and the population of Beirut 700,000. The first figure would seem low; and the legal situation of being able to include non-resident migrant Lebanese as citizens (even though these may be permanently domiciled outside the Lebanon) is another source of difficulty.

Human settlement in the Lebanon

A consensus of view based on literary and archaeological evidence suggests that down to Roman times the greater part of the Lebanon ranges were largely forested, and therefore carried only a very small population. Whereas the lower and drier areas of upland Judaea and Samaria farther south were occupied by human groups organized as states of various sizes and influence, the region we know as the Lebanon contained only a few tiny coastal kingdoms or urban clusters that lived by commerce and craft industries—weaving, metal-working, glass and pottery-making. The interior highlands were a source of timber: a lumbering region exploited from such centres as Tyre (modern Sur) and Byblos and literally a backwoods area inhabited permanently only by a few lawless bandits and predators. Lebanese cedar wood was an important article used as far away as Persia, Mesopotamia and Pharaonic Egypt; but the absence of any large-scale archaeological remains of this period in the hills, strongly contrasting with conditions on the coast, clearly suggests a scanty landward population.

This situation appears to have continued largely through Roman times. Strabo mentions outlaws and robbers who at times came down from the Lebanese hills to pillage the coastlands, and only an exceptionally strong

147

emperor succeeded in any serious control of the relatively empty and lawless uplands.

After about the seventh century A.D., the demographic situation was greatly altered by the entry first of the Maronites, and somewhat later by the Druzes. The Maronites, a Christian sect of Syrian origin, and named after a monk John Maroun, originated round the lower Orontes, in the region of Antioch–Hama. Persecution in the fifth and succeeding centuries impelled them to colonize the upper part of the Nahr Abu Ali (Qadisha area) where they established a number of monasteries with associated agricultural settlements. In these latter elaborate terrace cultivation developed on the steep hillsides, with rain-fed growing of cereals. The springs were used for irrigated cultivation of fruit and cereals, with goats and sheep kept on the neighbouring scrub or stubble pastures, and more regular seasonal visits to higher natural pasture during summer. In this way, at the price of isolation and a frugal existence based on laborious terrace cropping, a sufficient degree of freedom and religious liberty could be obtained; and 'The Mountain' is still quoted by many Lebanese as the epitome and ideal of a plain, simple, but satisfying and meritorious way of life. The main cultural centre of the Maronites was the Qadisha, in the northern Lebanon below the culminating peak of Qornet es Sauda, but other settlements of a similar kind grew up based for preference on the valley edges at levels that were not too high for cultivation yet remote and sufficiently inaccessible to offer some defence against outsiders. These, mainly located in the hills just east and north of Beirut (i.e. the north-central Lebanon), became the areas where most Maronites lived.

The Druzes, a heterodox community deriving from Shi'a Ismaili, originated farther to the south-east, in the separate hill district east of Mt. Hermon, which still is known as the Jebel ed Druze. Groups of Druzes began to establish themselves during the eleventh century onward in the central part of the Lebanon, immediately south-east of Beirut. Here they developed a way of life very similar to that of the Maronites, and gradually as numbers of both communities grew, Maronites and Druzes found themselves in increasingly close contact. Up to the mid-nineteenth century, relations between the two communities were, according to Mikesell (1969), generally amicable, but from 1850 or so onward Druze attacks on the somewhat numerically greater Maronites led to considerable deterioration in relations, and the ultimate intervention by European powers, the French particularly.

As well as Maronite–Druze occupation of the hills, other communities settled in various other parts. Metwalis (a Shi'a sect) found asylum from attack originally in the hills of the Lebanon range, but were gradually forced out by the Maronites and Druzes, and are now mainly established in three other localities: on the plain of Akkar in the extreme north, in the northern Beqa round Hermel, and in the extreme south towards upper

Galilee. Other groups, mainly Christian, but much smaller in number, also established themselves in the hill districts: the Armenians (Gregorians and Catholics) in the Jbeil–Ghosta–Bzoumar district, Greek Catholics and Syrian Catholics (Jacobites), with others as small groups in the towns.

Two other communities, Sunni Moslems and Greek Orthodox, enjoyed a far greater degree of acceptance by the Ottoman authorities, and for them defence and remoteness were thus much less necessary. These groups established themselves on the lowlands: Sunni Moslems in the majority, and Greek Orthodox often as an urban minority of traders and artisans. Tripoli is almost entirely a Sunni Moslem town, whilst Beirut, though very cosmopolitan, has a strong Sunni nucleus of population (26 per cent of the total in 1948). Rivalry between all these communities was, and still is, a significant feature. Where a particular group was wholly dominant, defence could take second place: where intermixture occurred, settlements took on a more defensive aspect: for example, de Vaumas (1953) explains the relatively wide scattering of settlement in the Batroun area by the fact that the inhabitants were almost totally Maronites, but where juxtaposition with other groups occurred, then villages were much more nucleated, with tightly drawn boundaries and a defensive morphology.

An important adjunct to the economy of the hill zones was production of silk, for which extensive groves of mulberry trees were maintained. At the same time, growing population numbers would appear to have led to an extension of cereal-growing—the mainstay of the economy—into areas of thinner and rocky soils wherever rainfall was adequate or the rocks were not too permeable.

From about 1890 down to the 1920's a number of influences combined to alter the demographic character of the Lebanon. Civil unrest due in large part to weakening Ottoman control, the disturbances of the First World War, and a marked decline in the silk trade when this became exposed to French competition were factors that led to emigration and falling population, particularly in the hill zones of the Lebanon. At the same time, greatly improved communications and the opening up of the Americas, both North and South, provided incentives to overseas migration. Thus from at least the beginning of the present century there developed a stream of outward migration that affected most of all the communities of the higher hillsides. Terraces that had been maintained for centuries began to fall into disuse; the mulberry trees have by now all but disappeared; and the cereal cultivation on the poorer marginal soils retreated, leaving former cultivated zones in some instances to be occupied by scrub vegetation— dwarf beech, scrub oak, and bushes.

In more recent times there have been other changes. A number of areas, especially those of the middle slopes east and north-east of Beirut, have developed apple cultivation; while perhaps of greater importance has been the invasion of the higher hills by *estiveurs*—summer residents or tourists

149

who have built new or improved older houses as temporary resorts. The great influx of tourists, both in summer and to a less degree in winter, has helped to arrest the decline in population that might otherwise have greatly depopulated the hills.

The greater general security of the last few decades together with vastly enhanced commercial opportunities in the towns have contributed to considerable growth in the urban population. There is the familiar feature of the emergence of a single metropolitan centre, far out-distancing the rest. Less than a century ago, Beirut probably had under 60,000 inhabitants, and in 1921 it had 91,000. Now an 'official' city within defined municipal boundaries it appears to have 700,000 inhabitants, and if a surrounding agglomeration of suburbs and tributary villages is included, the population of 'Greater Beirut' appears to exceed one million—40 per cent of the country's total population, which is far greater in proportion than for any other neighbouring state, though less than Kuwait.

It is impossible in the absence of a census to speak with accuracy of the numbers and distribution of the sects now forming the Lebanese nation (Figs. 6.1 and 6.2). Since, however, the national Chamber of Deputies has been organized on a confessional basis, with the allocation of seats by sect, it is possible to have a broad view of the relative balance between the various groups. In 1952 there were 44 members of the Chamber of Deputies, and by 1959 this had been increased to 98, though still maintaining as a fundamental principle the balance of six Christians to five Moslems (inclusive of Druzes).

TABLE 6.1   PARLIAMENTARY SEATS BY RELIGION IN THE LEBANON

Religious group	pre 1952	post-1960
Maronites	13	30
Sunni Moslems	9	20
Shi'a Moslems	8	19
Greek Orthodox	5	11
Greek Catholic	3	6
Druzes	3	6
Armenian Orthodox (Gregorian)	2	4
Protestant	0	1
All others	1	1

These figures may be viewed alongside the statement made by de Vaumas that in 1950 the population of the Lebanon consisted of 678,104 Christians; 577,004 Moslems; and 12,471 'others' (including Jews). This gives a total of only 1,267,579, which again appears to be low statistically, but perhaps better founded politically.

Two other points must be mentioned. Unlike many Middle Eastern countries, the Lebanon does not have any really nomadic population.

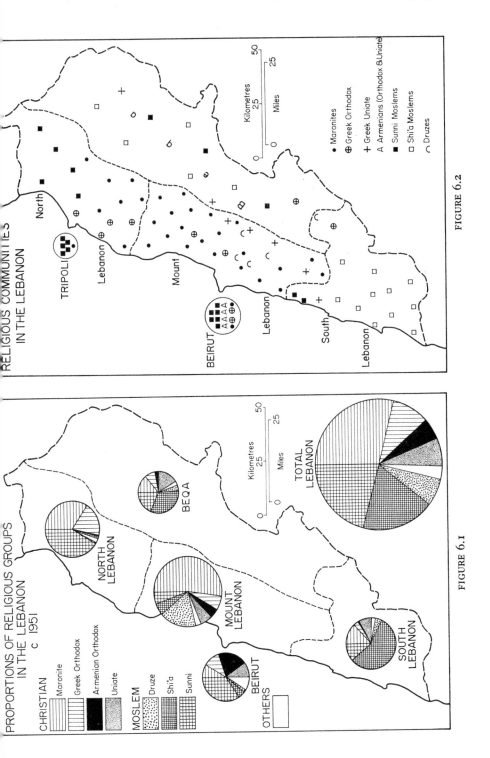

FIGURE 6.2

FIGURE 6.1

Animal husbandry is not anyway on a large scale, and the most that could be said to approach nomadism is a seasonal movement of pastoralists over a short distance to higher pastures on the same mountain side. There was until recently some seasonal migration into the northern Beqa by Syrian pastoralists but, with the erection of national frontiers since 1945–50, this movement has declined.

The Lebanon, like Jordan, has a number of Palestinian refugees, who are housed in camps or temporary villages close to Beirut and farther south. Numbers are, however, much less than, for example, in Jordan, and the possibility of finding jobs and training outside the camps has been greater in the Lebanon, hence the younger members particularly have tended to move away and find employment, sometimes even out of the Lebanon. Though this is not always accepted by Arab authorities, for practical and economic reasons, the Lebanese Government has been alive to the other political implications of a large, unoccupied, and possibly dissident group, hence it has not been unwilling to have some members of the camps develop a way of life outside the refugee areas.

Population movement

In the absence of a census, only a few general comments can be made. Population increase over the period 1955–70 is now estimated to be between 2.5 and 3.0 per cent annually, with the tendency for lower figures in most recent years. One important but highly sensitive element is the differential birth rate as between Christian and Moslem, but no general figures exist. A fragmentary view may, however, be obtained from a detailed study by D. Yaukey in 1958–9 (1961). This tended to show (a) that in general terms, fertility of both Moslem and Christian women was high. Figures suggested higher Moslem fertility, but only marginally, with a probable error as great as the difference between the two groups, (b) no significant change as between urban and non-urban groups of Moslem women, but a significant difference as among Christian women, the urban group having slightly lower fertility, and (c) education had some effect in leading to lower fertility. In this connexion it is apposite to recall that Christians are somewhat better educated than Moslems in the Lebanon.

Thirty years ago the country was once highly malarial in certain areas: this has almost totally altered. Increased national wealth has allowed the development of social services to the point that the towns, once regarded as less healthy than the Lebanese countryside, now have at least as good, if not better public health standards. There are no large, slow rivers or extensive irrigation schemes to spread parasitic diseases like bilharziasis, and most towns have a good water supply, as have many villages, at least in the west. Thus death rates have declined in recent years, which, given a high birth rate, produces the larger annual number of survivors, especially in towns. The larger proportion of Moslems in Lebanese towns—we have seen that the chief Maronite areas are the hill country—means that as public health improves in the towns, the number of Moslem survivors increases; but this is a minor factor, the main one being the higher specific birth rate of Moslems.

Migration

An important element in the demography of the Lebanon is the existence, since about 1880, of an important outward migration to Africa and the New World. It may well be that this movement only partially appears as statistics, since data are collected only by receiving countries, but a number of somewhat fragmentary figures support the probability of emigration on a significant scale. Whereas in 1869 there were only two arrivals in the United States of America of 'Syrians' (the term was applied equally to migrants from both Syria and the Lebanon), by 1899 the annual total had risen to 3,708; and it is estimated that a total of 120,000 'Syrians' emigrated over the period approximately 1865–1904—an average of 3,000 yearly. If we apply to this period proportions known to exist at a later time when statistics were fuller, it is reasonable to suppose that the substantial majority of 'Syrians' were really from the Lebanon. As with some other nationalities emigrating to the United States of America, there was a peak period up to 1913. In this year 9,210 'Syrians' entered the United States, and between 1904 and 1913, there were 46,003 arrivals of 'Syrians' in Brazil (Table 6.2).

TABLE 6.2   AVERAGE ANNUAL FLOW OF LEBANESE EMIGRANTS
TO THE NEW WORLD

USA		Brazil	
1871–80	67	1884–93	96
1880–90	2,220	1894–1903	7,214

During the same period West Africa began to draw 'Syrian' migrants, mostly temporary. Numbers were relatively small, but there were an estimated 4,000 arrivals during 1914–18. In all, it is estimated that 225,000 'Syrians' emigrated: an average of 15,000 per annum. Of these last, perhaps 10,000 were from the Lebanon.

After 1919 the number of migrants tended to fall, with an annual average during 1921–39 of 4,400 (Table 6.3). However, following the war of 1939–45 emigration began on a somewhat larger scale, then it again dropped to figures of little more than 1,000 per annum. After 1921 the political division under French Mandate meant that figures of Lebanese movements only became available.

Many Lebanese became workers in the car industry of Detroit and Dearborn, whilst store-keeping and trading were the predominant occupations in tropical Africa. Here, peak immigration probably occurred before the Second World War, and in 1939 approximately 11,000 Lebanese were living in tropical Africa mainly in the following countries:

British Colonies		*French Colonies*		*Portuguese Guinea*
Sierra Leone	1,000	Senegal	4,400	400
Gold Coast	1,000	Guinea	1,600	
Nigeria	700	Ivory Coast	700	
Gambia	350	Dahomey	40	

A number of Lebanese (Maronites and Greek Orthodox especially) migrated to Egypt. Some of these, however, have now returned to the Lebanon, following the hardening of opinion against Christians in Egypt over the last few decades.

Of these, as would be expected, by far the largest numbers were in the 15–29 age group, with a high predominance of men.

TABLE 6.3   DESTINATION OF LEBANESE EMIGRANTS IN SELECTED YEARS

Year	USA	Brazil	Argentina	Uruguay	British Africa	Senegal	Others	Total
1923	778	2,327	1,844	100	27	664	2,874	8,614
1928	341	1,797	838	1,158	283	268	1,413	4,998
1933	135	443	127	19	212	201	379	1,516
1938	61	139	145	11	229	436	418	1,419
1951	—	—	—	—	—	—	—	4,077
1953	—	—	—	—	—	—	—	3,315
1959	—	—	—	—	—	—	—	1,434

Source: League of Nations, Reports of Mandatory Authorities.

TABLE 6.4   REGION OF ORIGIN OF LEBANESE EMIGRANTS

	1951	*1959*
Beirut	469	301
Beqa	1,043	336
North Lebanon	1,334	216
South Lebanon	488	205
Mount Lebanon	743	376
Total	4,077	1,434

Distribution and densities

In view of the limited and provisional nature of demographic statistics relating to the Lebanon, charged as these are with political implications, one

can only offer generalities and hypotheses. The study of Lebanese population by de Vaumas (1953) nowhere gives an absolute overall total of
numbers for the whole country (though this can be inferred), but has considerable detailed breakdown, even to the 59,001 persons described as
the population of Tripoli during 1949–50.

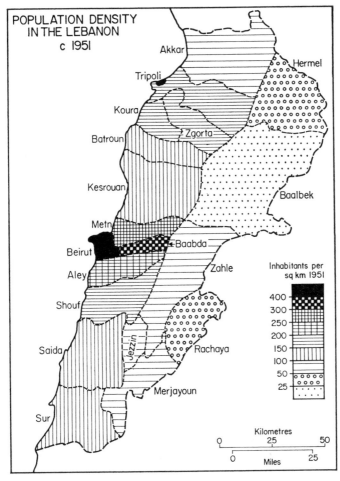

POPULATION DENSITY
IN THE LEBANON
c 1951

Inhabitants per
sq km 1951

400
300
250
200
150
100
50
25

Kilometres
0   25   50

0   25
Miles

FIGURE 6.3

De Vaumas gives an average population density (precise year not stated)
of 177 persons per sq. km., with 211 per sq. km. for a Lebanon area which
would exclude the low density Beqa and Anti-Lebanon regions (Fig. 6.3).
Taking the 1969 (Pop. Ref. Bureau) estimate of 2.6 million would give a
density of 250 per sq. km., a 42 per cent increase over approximately 20
years, which is perhaps rather low if we set this alongside a recently

155

estimated increase of 2.5 per cent per annum. If, however, this estimate of natural increase is regarded as reduced by a significant volume of emigration, then perhaps fairly close accordance is achieved, given the overall lack of a precise census.

It may therefore be instructive to follow out the densities stated by de Vaumas for the administrative sub-regions of the Lebanon (Table 6.5).

TABLE 6.5 POPULATION DENSITIES IN THE LEBANON, c 1950

		Densities per sq. km. (including towns)			
Akkar	90	Baabda	357	Rachaya	25
Tripoli	193	Aley	247	Zahle	92
Zgorta	184	Shouf	175	Baalbek	24
Koura	152	Saida	142	Hermel	20
Batroun	103	Jezzin	97	Anti-Lebanon	
Kesrouan	104	Sur	109		under 5
Metn	273	Merjayoun	86		

A number of points may be made.

(1) Densities are greatest in the central part of the Lebanon range, closest to Beirut city, which is not counted in any of the administrative districts (*cazas*) given above, since it is a separate unit. The population of Tripoli City is, however, included as part of the *caza* figures. We then see (the anomaly of the Tripoli area having thus been removed) how densities decline north and south. This is related to less favourable natural conditions: these are, in the north (especially in the Akkar area), poor drainage and relatively infertile soil; and in the south, a lower rainfall due to lower altitude, highly pervious limestone and marl outcrops, and a deeply dissected surface which prevents easy irrigation of what is anyway a difficult terrain.

Social and human factors also enter in: Akkar is remote and often held, unusually for the Lebanon, by absentee landlords; whilst the south has much share-cropping which could be held to be a factor inducing stagnation. Moreover, in the last few years, incursions of Palestine guerrillas into southern Lebanon have not assisted economic advancement, and migration outwards is now a marked feature.

(2) Densities for much of the western side of the Lebanon range are in absolute terms, very high—much above those for, say, similar mountain areas of Turkey, Iraq and Iran. They are also higher than for many European regions of similar altitudes. Thus, though overall figures are not large (as for instance by comparison with the populations of southern Asia) the situation emerges that even excluding the considerable effect of Beirut there is a remarkably high concentration of non-urban population in what is, after all, a 'difficult' terrain. Some of this population is still engaged in agriculture, but other groups are either of the 'commuter' type working

in the towns, or tenants on a small scale—hence it seems preferable to use the term 'non-urban' rather than 'rural' to describe them.

Above the levels of the impermeable strata, porosity, ruggedness and high altitudes combine to produce a region that is still remarkably empty, as it was down to Roman days. The high plateau of Cenomanian and later rock-measures is well developed in the north of the Lebanon, and can be traced, to a diminishing extent, as far as Merjayoun. Here, the topographical divide, visible as a line of bold cliffs or as a scarp, is also a clear demographic boundary between the well-populated middle hill zone and the almost uninhabited highland.

(3) The changeover to apple-growing and market gardening at middle levels, and to citrus and banana cultivation at lower altitudes have had certain significant though small-scale effects on population distribution, since larger scale cultivation units have been created in replacement of the former narrow terraces. A market-oriented system with some mechanization has replaced the older cereal-based farming especially in the Beirut hinterland, with consequent reduction in demand for manpower.

(4) The very low densities of the Beqa, and the almost uninhabited nature of much of the Anti-Lebanon will be noticed. The only *caza* with more than 30 inhabitants per sq. km. is Zahleh, which includes Zahleh town of 35,000 people. Moreover, village size appears to increase eastwards, being in some areas almost double in the east as compared with the west. Villages in the Rachaya *caza* have about 1,000–1,100 inhabitants per village, as compared with 600–700 as a mean for the western Lebanon. This closely nucleated settlement in an otherwise empty terrain which is increasingly characteristic of the east contrasts remarkably with the frequency of more evenly spread but smaller scale rural settlements in the west. An important further element is the changed nature of many accessible western villages (Fig. 6.4): they have become extensions of the Beirut suburbia, sometimes seasonal, sometimes all the year round; and the tourist element has also resulted in the inflation of some former villages (e.g. Aley) to the size of small towns.

Economic basis

It remains to consider how such a relatively sizeable population, unequally distributed throughout an extremely varied but on the whole rugged terrain, is able to support itself at standards of living much above those of many other Middle Eastern countries. For 1969 the country had a *per capita* Gross National Product estimated at $US 480, as compared with $180 for Syria, $220 for Jordan, and $280 for Turkey.

As we have noted, the Lebanon has no indigenous petroleum or other important mineral deposits, and its manufactures are on a restricted scale. There is an important export of fruit—chiefly oranges, bananas and apples

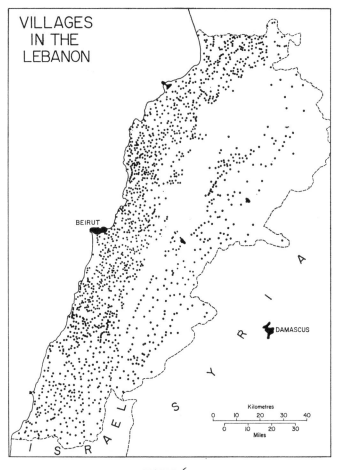

FIGURE 6.4

—but this is not on the scale of Israel's activities, and the outlets are highly competitive. At home, despite a large rural population, the country is not self-sufficient in essential foodstuffs, and must import wheat.

Like Israel, however, the Lebanon receives remittances from emigrants and well-wishers, to the amount of over $200 m. annually. By 'well-wishers' we include a small number of Lebanese emigrants, and now with the unrest and disturbance of the last few years a greatly declining number, who return in old age after a period spent abroad.

Tourism is also a very valuable resource, especially as many visitors stay for a period of several weeks, even months—this is especially true of visitors from oil-states. The Ruler of Kuwait, for instance, maintains a summer residence in the Lebanon. Receipts from tourism generally have exceeded $60 m. annually in some years.

Though probably less valuable than formerly, the attraction of the various Lebanese universities and colleges (especially the American University of Beirut) results in a sizeable import of funds; and the international relief organizations particularly those concerned with Palestinian refugees, also bring in small amounts of outside capital. Revenue from oil companies for pipeline wayleaves and use of terminals at Tripoli and Sidon (Iraq Petroleum Co. and Aramco respectively) amounts to $16 m. directly, and this figure rises as the oil companies are persuaded to increase the sums paid over.

Transit trade is an extremely important item, and in some years during the 1960's it produced several times the total revenues from exports. Main direction of this trading is with Jordan, Syria, Iraq and Kuwait, but there are connections with other Asian countries.

Highly important also is the general commercial reputation of Beirut, with its eighty or so banking firms. Open markets, total *laissez-faire*, a free port, and few questions, all in an extremely beautiful environment have for two decades attracted international trading, and the Lebanon has acted as banker, consultant and broker for many oil-rich developing states. It is this combination of commercial acumen, tolerance and opportunism in a pleasant physical setting that has produced the growth of Beirut and with this much of the prosperity of the country. We may note the significant level of Lebanese tolerance even after 1948, when most Jews were forced to leave many Arab countries. They remained in the Lebanon, to the number of several thousand.

In 1969, however, ominous strains appeared with the increasing activities of guerrillas, Palestinian, Arab and Israeli. The Lebanon with its sensitive network of commercial contacts and tourist traffic, is highly vulnerable to disorder, and some observers have recently detected a considerable decline in general confidence, with a flight of capital abroad. The demographic effects of this, if real and sustained over a period, could be considerable.

REFERENCES

ANNUAIRE GENERALE DU LIBAN, Beirut, since 1927.

DIRECTION CENTRALE DE LA STATISTISTIQUE (1968) *Recueil de Statistiques Libanaises, Année 1965*, Beirut.

LA DOCUMENTATION FRANÇAISE (1964) *L'Evolution de la Population dans les Pays du Proche-Orient*, No. 3093.

EL-BADRY, M. A. (1965) 'Trends in the components of population growth in the Arab countries of the Middle East: a survey of present information', *Demography*, 2, pp. 140–86.

MIKESELL, M. W. (1969) 'The deforestation of Mount Lebanon', *Geographical Review*, 70, pp. 1–28.

POPULATION REFERENCE BUREAU, Annual data sheets, Washington.

VAUMAS, E. DE (1953) 'La répartition de la population au Liban. Introduction à la géographie humaine de la République Libanaise', *Bulletin de la Société de Géographie d'Egypte*, 26, pp. 5–76.

YAUKEY, D. (1961) *Fertility Differences in a Modernizing Country*, Princeton.

Chapter 7
Cyprus: ethnic dualism
M P Drury

' "Cyprus is a small island. I think I have relations in every one of the six
hundred villages. At *least* six hundred free drinks".'

L. Durrell, *Bitter Lemons*, 1957.

The nature of the population

Cyprus, the first of the Mediterranean's islands to emerge as an independent state in the modern world, has been and remains a source of fascina-
tion to the representatives of a wide range of interests from beyond its
shores. Although this degree of external interest suggests the magnetism
of the island in a variety of distinct fields and confirms the importance of
its 'resources', nevertheless it is immediately apparent that the problems
which beset the people of Cyprus are largely a consequence of their island's
unfortunately overpowerful appeal.

As the island's name suggests, copper was the original attraction, and
these ores, in a country where agriculture forms the basis of the economy,
still retain their measure of economic significance. However, copper has no
longer the force that attracted early colonists some 3,500 years ago.
Instead, increasingly, the strategic significance of the island's location has
come to the fore, as successive peoples have regarded possession of the
island as a step towards the solution of their own diverse problems and the
achievement of their ambitions, and, in surmounting this step, have
created a further level of complexity for Cyprus and its own inhabitants.

Following in the wake of the Myceneans, the earliest known colonizers
in c. 1500 B.C., Cyprus has attracted in succession the Phoenicians,
Achaeans, Egyptians, Persians, Macedonians, Romans, Byzantines, Arabs,
crusading forces from the West, Franks, Genoese, Venetians, Ottoman
Turks, and the British. All were interested in Cyprus not so much for
what could be gleaned from the island itself, though this was far from
insignificant, but because of the implications and possibilities for expansion
and control which ownership of the island conveyed to the possessor. All
these peoples shared their common belief in the strategic usefulness of
Cyprus, and not least the latest of these, the British. Having on four
occasions in the fifty years preceding their takeover of the island refused to

accept it as payment for services rendered to their predecessors, the Otto-
man Turks, they finally saw fit to do so, at the fifth opportunity in 1878.
W. H. Dixon (1887) concisely summarizes the perpetual dilemma of
Cyprus and accounts for the British change of heart:

'A race advancing on the East must start with Cyprus. Alexander,
Augustus, Richard and Saint Louis took that line. A race advancing on the
West must start with Cyprus. Sargon, Ptolemy, Cyrus and Haroun-al-
Rashid took this line. . . . Genoa and Venice, struggling for the trade of
India, fought for Cyprus and enjoyed supremacy in that land by turns.
After a new route by sea was found to India, Egypt and Syria declined in
value to the Western nations. Cyprus was then forgotten; but the opening
of the Suez Canal has suddenly restored her to her ancient pride of place.'

Whether or not the Cypriots rejoiced to see their island's 'pride of place'
restored after several centuries of relatively quiet stagnation remains to be
seen. However, there can be no doubt that such a succession of occupying
forces is inevitably bound to have left its mark, not only in a physical sense
on the landscape of the island, but, more profoundly, on the present
inhabitants. In such circumstances the emergence of, at one extreme, a
highly nationalistic and xenophobic population intensely determined to
preserve its newly-gained independence, or, at the opposite extreme, a
polyglot cosmopolitan community devoid of a distinctive overall identity
save that derived from a complex admixture of alien types, would have
seemed equally probable. Neither of these, however, approaches an adequate description of the contemporary Cypriot population.

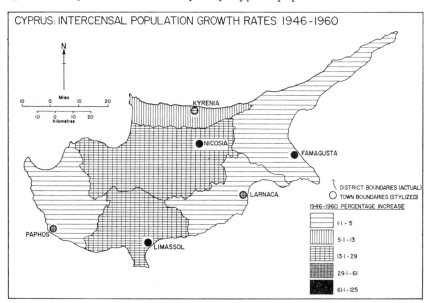

FIGURE 7.1

The island's 9,250 sq. km. of territory currently houses some 618,000 Cypriots (1968 est.). This steadily increasing total (Fig. 7.1) includes such minor ethnic communities as the Armenians, the Maronites, and the British, but essentially, these groups apart, the population is split into two unequal elements: the Greeks and the Turks. The distinctiveness of these two components was officially recognized in the Cypriot constitution when independence was achieved in 1960, and the determined efforts of both sides to secure and maintain their separateness and sovereignty have formed the basis of most of the recent problems of, and writings about Cyprus.

The population is largely divided between the 77 per cent who are Greeks, and who are virtually all members of the Orthodox Church, and the 18 per cent who are Turkish, and are mainly members of the Sunni branch of the Moslem faith, with only 5 per cent of the population belonging to one of the minor groupings. This division is recognized within the island at a variety of levels, not least the parliamentary one. Within the 50-seat House of Representatives there are 35 seats exclusively reserved for members returned by the Greek voters, under which heading are included the Armenian and Maronite minorities, and 15 seats for those returned by the Turks. The fact that the Turkish representatives, all members of the same party, currently led by Mr. Rauf Denktash, the aim of which is Turkish-Cypriot automony, have not chosen to sit with their Greek colleagues for several years is tangible evidence of the continuing state of animosity which exists between the two sides.

However, given the present distribution of the population, autonomy for the separate ethnic elements could only be achieved either by considerable movements of people, or by confounding all the known principles of successful administration. For, though there is a very strong tendency for settlements to be populated exclusively by members of only one ethnic group, there is no obvious regional clustering of these settlements into their two dominant component parts. Some 36 per cent of the population live in one of the six district capitals: Greater Nicosia, Famagusta, Kyrenia, Larnaca, Limassol and Paphos, and these are the only settlements recognized as being urban. In these six towns as a whole, Greek outnumbers Turk by a ratio of 3.6:1, the proportion ranging from just under 2:1 in Nicosia to over 5:1 in Limassol. Nicosia refers, in this context, to Nicosia proper, with 45,629 inhabitants in 1960. Greater Nicosia, which includes the suburbs (ratio 5:1), always omitted from the statistics for the rural population, had 95,515 inhabitants in that year. Whilst, therefore, no urban centre is either exclusively Greek or exclusively Turkish, the opposite is usually true in the rural settlements.

Rural settlement in Cyprus is, apart from a very few recent developments catering for the expatriate settler market, exclusively nucleated. This form of distribution, though possessing the usual range of economic disadvantages for the hindering of modern agricultural progress, presents the demographer with a rather simpler task of analysis than would otherwise have been the case. The 64 per cent of the Cypriot population which may be termed rural numbered 303,000 Greeks and 62,400 Turks in 1960, and inhabited a total of 620 villages, eight of which are either as populous as or more populous than Kyrenia, the smallest of the six towns. Of these 620 rural settlements, 458 are exclusively Greek, Maronite, or Turkish. Only 37 villages have no single group at least twice as numerous as the other, and in these Greeks form a majority in 23 and Turks in the other 14 of them. Consequently, in the rural environment, on the local scale, total separation of the two major ethnic components is the norm. The 43 per cent of the population recorded at the 1960 census as living in Mixed (i.e. Greek and Turkish) Settlements includes all the town-dwellers, and therefore leaves only 7 per cent of Cypriots in the category of 'rural inhabitants of an ethnically-mixed village'. This means that 89 per cent of the rural population, or all except 40,000 of the total, live in villages where only their own language will be heard and only their own religion practised. Table 7.1 summarizes this position, whilst Figures 7.2 and 7.3 show the regional proportion of Greek to Turk and the ethnic patterns among the 620 villages.

TABLE 7.1   CYPRUS: THE ETHNIC PATTERN IN THE RURAL SETTLEMENTS

Administrative district	Turkish villages		Greek villages		Mixed villages (no ethnic group twice as numerous as others)	Total
	Turk:Greek >2:1	No Greeks	Greek:Turk >2:1 (Maronite villages)	No Turks		
Nicosia	33	29	132 (1)	109	6	171
Famagusta	28	24	61	46	8	97
Kyrenia	8	6	37 (3)	28	2	47
Larnaca	13	10	37	24	9	59
Limassol	12	7	96	77	6	114
Paphos	39	31	87	67	6	132
Total	133	107	450 (4)	351	37*	620

Source of data: 1960 Census of Cyprus.
* Of the 37 'mixed villages', 23 have a majority of Greeks and 14 a majority of Turks.

The rural settlement pattern

Having stated the situation, it is now necessary to account for it. The length of time throughout which the Cypriot has had to suffer foreign interference in his island, and the variety of that interference, has already been referred to. Equally significant has been the attitude of the invaded to the invader. Until the present century there is little evidence to suggest that the Cypriots have ever seriously attempted to stem the tide as these successive

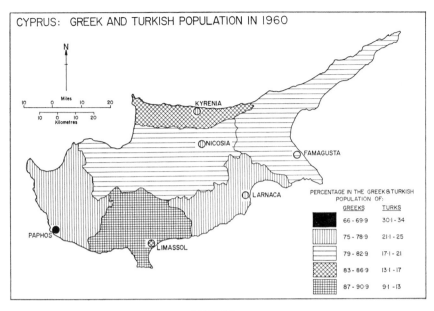

FIGURE 7.2

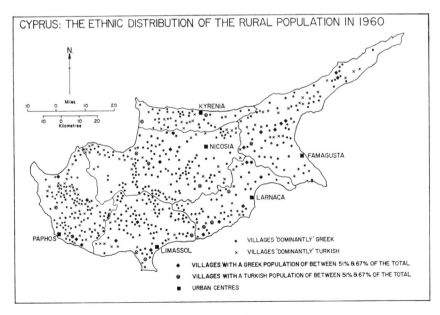

FIGURE 7.3

colonizing waves have swept over them. At their least active they have contented themselves with avoiding unnecessary contact with the outsider, and at their most active they have occasionally connived with or welcomed a new invader in the hopeful expectation, sometimes fulfilled, that their lot would improve following a change of master. A desire to be left to his own devices, with his back turned to the outer world and without the enforced superimposition of alien values and modes of life, coupled with an acceptance of his island's greater worth to outside forces, seems thus to have marked the Cypriot's attitude to the foreigner throughout the history of the island. Because this attitude clearly manifests itself in the form and distribution of settlement throughout the island, a consideration of this settlement pattern emerges as an issue vital to the understanding of the Cypriot population.

Apart from the five coastal towns, which must be excepted from these comments, the pattern of settlement in Cyprus displays a marked rejection of the possible benefits of insularity. All the rural settlements, and the capital itself, are not only inland, but entirely land-orientated. The sea has never featured prominently in the economic organization of the native Cypriot community. In many parts of the Mediterranean the vulnerable maritime site was eschewed for the purposes of settlement because of the obvious dangers from piracy. This strategic factor has obviously been of significance in Cyprus as elsewhere. However, whereas the tightly-knit hill-top community is the classic outcome of this desire for security, a desire which made men utilize sites far from ideal for the purposes of cultivation of the land, cropping of the sea, or collection of water, yet vital for survival against attack in many parts of the Mediterranean, this is not the corollary to the lack of coastal settlements which one finds in Cyprus. As far as is currently known, there is no evidence of walled, or otherwise strongly defended villages anywhere on the island, and everything in the general pattern of their form and distribution tends to suggest that, whilst the Cypriot will do all that is reasonably possible to make his settlements invisible from the sea, and whilst they will be so sited as to facilitate the early warning of the approach of strangers, little if anything will be done to preserve these villages from attack once they are discovered. This would seem to confirm the view that the Cypriot accepts what is deemed to be inevitable very readily, thus bringing about the inevitable more rapidly and less painfully than would otherwise have been the case. The siting of the rural settlements is not therefore dominated by the defensive needs of their inhabitants. To this factor must be added three others of greater importance: the availability of water, economic, and hence agricultural, convenience and gregariousness.

Of all these elements, water is the most significant. Not only has it largely determined the distribution pattern of the settlements, but it can also be seen to be a vital factor in influencing their degree of nucleation.

For although today piped water is supplied to most villages, 76,244 out of a total of 110,360 rural households having direct access to a piped water supply by 1960, this is largely an improvement dating from the Second World War. This greatly increased degree of rural availability of water, coupled with the fact that almost all settlements can trace their origins at least as far back as the Venetian occupation, only serves to emphasize the link between a source of water and the original choice of a settlement site. However, not only has Cypriot rural settlement shunned the sea: it has also avoided the river valleys. This is partly because such a location, in the local physical environment, has a tendency to become a frost hollow in winter and unhealthily hot in summer, but mainly because most of the island's surface watercourses are temporary. The river beds are usually dry, except when in spate following sudden downpours, and at such times the excess of water can be as great a hazard as the more normal lack of it. Village tales of the drowning of tethered animals abound. A spasmodic and unreliable supply is not the answer to an agricultural community's water problems, and consequently all such settlements have been sited close to the only permanent sources of water, adjoining springs or shallow aquifers where wells could conveniently be dug. The island's deserted villages are usually those which have been deprived of such a supply.

The annual rainfall totals reveal a high degree of variation over the island, ranging from in excess of 1,200 mm. in parts of the Troodos Mountain massif to under 300 mm. on the Morphou Bay lowlands some 30 km. to the north-north-east of this massif. It is not, however, the annual, but the seasonal rainfall totals which are of the most profound significance. 'The winter rainfall is probably the most important single element in the physical environment of Cyprus. The pattern of life is keyed to it. The life-cycle of vegetation is decided by it and man has had perforce to adapt farming practices accordingly. It is by far the greatest amount in the year and is certainly the most beneficial and most effective. It is generally more gentle and more concentrated; it occurs when vegetation cover is at its best, when temperature is lower, when cloudiness is at its maximum and consequently less is lost by evaporation and more percolates. . . . (In contrast) the summer rainfall is never an unmixed blessing and too often not a blessing at all. It is rarely effective owing to the high rate of evaporation; it usually comes in torrential outbursts and leads to floods, excessive soil erosion and damage to crops. Too often it is accompanied by destructive hail. In the past it encouraged mosquito breeding and high malaria rates' (Christodoulou, 1959).

Within this context of Cyprus's water supply two facts are particularly significant. Firstly, the frequency of droughts, which create the most serious problem in land management which the island has to face, and, following on from this, the fact that water is certainly the most precious of its natural resources. The Cypriot farmer has not only been fatalistic when considering his treatment at the hands of foreign invaders; he also adopts a singularly fatalistic attitude to these vagaries of the climate. With such a degree of climatic variation over the island, and with a dearth of statistical data to cover these variations, it is difficult to generalize, but in Nicosia, with a mean rainfall during the six winter months of 290 mm., there is an 8 per cent probability of receiving in excess of 150 per cent of this total, and an 18 per cent probability of receiving less than 75 per cent. Only one year in three receives a winter total within 10 per cent of the mean. Consequently, with rainfall totals so low in the main agricultural regions of the island, this degree of uncertainty is an added hazard which only an imaginative long-term water conservation policy will remove. In contrast, and confirming the significance of water availability to the settlement pattern, is the distribution of the underground water resources, which are easily exploited on the small scale, and can be tapped throughout much of lowland Cyprus. The island's most prolific spring, on the slopes of the Kyrenia Range, yields almost 2,000 million gallons of water per annum at a consistent rate throughout the year. The systematic exploitation of such supplies as this, the extension of the mechanically irrigated area, and the increased degree of co-operation between the farmers involved, have done much to reduce the total concentration of all rural settlement on the water sources, but such measures have yet to alter the basic pattern of settlement distribution, which confirms this dependence most markedly.

Whilst, therefore, the rural inhabitants of Cyprus were originally compelled to site their villages within easy reach of a water source, a second factor, that of the convenient exploitation of the land for their range of agricultural pursuits, also has always been of the greatest significance throughout the 5,000 years of agricultural practice in the island. In a land where soil erosion is, given the prevailing conditions of relief, climate and soil type, an inevitable problem, the actions of man on the land have done little, until the most recent times, to alleviate this situation.

'Cyprus is a living monument to man as a parasite on the soil. Beginning in the third millennium before Christ, the island's inhabitants worked with an uncalculated, yet skilful, rapacity to change the ecology and deplete the soil of the land. . . . Somewhere along the line man was joined by that picturesque and playful symbol of a depraved agriculture, the goat. Together man and goat, cutting, burning, and grazing, have done a tragically effective job on Cyprus' (Meyer and Vassiliou, 1962). Rates of soil erosion reach particularly high levels in association with such traditional elements of the agricultural system as autumn ploughing, fallow land and, worst of all, vineyards. The estimated rate of soil loss in the vine-growing districts of the Eastern Mesaoria is, according to Burdon (1950), 150 cu. metres per sq. km. per annum. However, although having done little to prevent this loss, the agricultural community is very conscious of the significance of the variety of soils to be found within the village lands.

Until recently, under conditions of a subsistence economy, the most desirable site for a village to occupy was obviously one which permitted the greatest range of agricultural possibilities, and it is a marked feature of the settlement distribution pattern, and the bounds of the lands involved, that the village limits incorporate the widest possible range of soil types.

If, then, 'agricultural convenience' is seen to be a significant factor influencing the general distribution of the population, so 'gregariousness' emerges in an equally important role as a concentrator of that population. Christodoulou (1959), who dedicates his book 'to my parents who tilled the land and lived its drama', observes: 'The climate has made the Cypriot people live much of their time in the street. Sociability is the order of the day and private, interior life is weak. A good deal of give and take goes on among neighbours and much co-operative work takes place. Aloofness is unknown and deplored. An insatiable curiosity will keep every Cypriot up to date in matters that concern him or may even be utterly irrelevent.' The farming family, not merely for the sake of the village water supply, nor in the hope of a greater degree of security from past external or present internal forces, but essentially because of the benefits which constant contact with the other members of the community offer, is only too eager to maintain its homestead within the nucleation. Thus, despite the financial advantages to be gained from closer contact with the farm lands, now increasingly made feasible by technological advances, economic efficiency is willingly sacrificed on the altar of social satisfaction.

The land policies of the occupiers

The rural distribution of the population is, however, not only a reflection of the interplay of these four forces of water availability, pedological variety, sociability, and defence: it is also closely connected with the sequence of occupance on the island, which in turn has had a profound effect upon the system of land tenure. Although today almost all the agricultural land, excluding the forests and rough grazing which are generally state-owned, is cultivated by its owners, this widespread peasant proprietorship is a relatively recent phenomenon dating back little more than a century.

The earliest records, from the fifth century B.C., indicate that large estates were owned by a series of priest-kings, with private land ownership being rare. The majority of the farmers, the priest-kings' tenants, held their lands only against a regular payment of taxes. Under Roman and Byzantine rule the rural population was divided into two separate classes; the free-men, or *Parici*, and the serfs, or *Enapographi*. The latter worked in village settlements under the direct supervision of the local landowner, their master, to whom all produce was given, and by whom all taxes were paid. The former, although more favourably off than this condition of slavery, were somewhat euphemistically named. They were not owners of their land but tenants within a village community the lands of which were owned by an absent landlord, often either the state or the church. In some respects their settlements resemble the modern co-operative concept, in that the farmed lands were divided into plots, responsibility for the cultivation of which would change from time to time from one *Parici* to another. The community was taxed as a whole, and each tenant was obliged to remain in the village in order to contribute his share of the general financial responsibility. This system thus gives a clear indication of the early establishment in Cyprus of the closely-knit rural community, bound at this stage by compulsion rather than desire, and justifies the villager's profound interest in the activities of his colleagues.

With the arrival of the Franks, Cypriot society underwent considerable superficial change. It was at this stage that the urban centres of the island began to emerge in cultural isolation from the rural environment. The contrast between the latter, now divided into a number of feudal estates for the purposes of controlling the peasant population, who were for the most part worse off than they had been under the previous régimes, and a city such as Famagusta is remarkable. Famagusta in the fourteenth century was 'the busiest mart of the eastern Mediterranean. If Rhodes continued the military tradition of the Crusades their commercial heritage fell to Famagusta where wealth and luxury astonished visitors to Cyprus and became for a while proverbial in Europe. . . . Truly Famagusta was then a cosmopolitan place. In addition to its native Greek-speaking population and the superimposed Frankish ruling class, it contained, so it seemed, colonies of every race of the Near East. Countless tongues were spoken in its streets, from Norse to Persian, Georgian to Amharic. Gregorian, Jacobite, and Nestorian shrines arose beside those of the Roman and Orthodox rites; "the blessed murmur of the mass" could be heard daily in Greek and Latin, Syriac and Armenian' (Luke, 1924).

Concurrently with this urban situation, the native population was continuing to support the feudal system. There were now three classes of rural inhabitant, apart from the Franks themselves. *Parici* became an increasingly euphemistic term, as this class replaced the *Enapographi* at the bottom of the scale. They had no rights, being subject to sale or exchange at the whim of their feudal lord to whom they had to offer considerable annual taxes, one-third of all their produce, and two days of free labour each week. They were somewhat bettered by the other two classes, the *Perpiarii* and the *Lefteri*, former members of the *Parici* who had respectively bought or been granted their 'freedom' from the more onerous of these obligations. With the substitution of Venetian for Frank, little in the above system changed, though the *Perpiarii* class vanished, leaving only the landless *Parici* and the *Lefteri*, a far less numerous group who owned the land they cultivated, but had to pay yearly rates equivalent to some three-quarters of their annual produce to the owner of the estate in which

170

their holding was situated. It is not surprising, therefore, that the prospect of Turkish control was seen as a welcome change by the rural population who, like Luke (1924), doubtless thought that 'nothing so well became Venice in Cyprus as the manner in which she left it'.

The Ottoman Turks, welcomed by the Greek population of rural Cyprus as liberators after centuries of Catholic oppression, undertook two significant acts which greatly altered the social status of the peasantry during their period of control. First, they restored the Orthodox Church to the position from which it had been toppled four centuries previously, and secondly, but not until the nineteenth century, they abolished serfdom. The Ottoman Empire chose the criterion of religion by which to classify its subjects. Under the *millet* system, the Ottoman method of colonial government, in which church and state were regarded as virtually synonymous, Greeks throughout the Empire fared rather better than did most other Christian communities. Cyprus was no exception to this, and the island's Greek community was granted total cultural autonomy within the framework of its church. The Archbishop thus emerged, not only as the spiritual leader of his people, but also as their political spokesman and guide: a position which was not challenged throughout the Ottoman presence, and one which has been restored, since his installation in 1950, by the present incumbent.

The restoration of the Orthodox Church was not, however, the only object of the Turks when they took over Cyprus in 1571. They also wished to profit from their latest possession, but, instead of continuing the system of crippling taxation of the peasantry employed by their predecessors, they hoped to increase the revenue collected by the more enlightened policy of stimulation of growth rates in the rural areas. Thus, they instigated policies aimed at increasing not only both the extent of the cultivated area and the yields from these lands, but also the size of the rural population itself. Contemporary population estimates suggest, however, that this last ambition was not achieved. The Ottoman authorities gave the population of the island as 290,000 in 1571 and 186,000 in 1868, this record figure being confirmed by the first British census in 1881. Until the middle of the nineteenth century, the peasants farmed their lands as tenants of either the state, on the *Sipahis* lands, or of religious institutions, the *Vakiflar* lands. The latter included the properties both of the Moslem foundations and the Orthodox Church, whilst the farmers were under the control and management of a resident native Turk. In addition, the Greek peasantry were permitted to hold some land of their own, known as the *Mulk*, whilst their usufructuary rights passed automatically to their heirs so long as the cultivated lands were not neglected and the taxes regularly paid. To organize this new rural order some 30,000 Turkish settlers arrived in Cyprus during the first years of Ottoman rule. These people, mostly soldiers and their families who were given estates in payment for their military services, became the *Sipahis* tenants' landlords and formed the original nucleus of the present Turkish element in the Cypriot population.

In addition to supervising the indigenous Greek population, these migrants were also expected to be farmers in their own right, and each estate was centred around the *Hassa Chiftlik*, the private farm which the Turkish owners worked themselves. It had been the original intention to employ Greek labour on these farms, but this became increasingly difficult, partly because of a continuous population decline throughout the seventeenth and eighteenth centuries, and partly because an increasing proportion of the Greek peasantry chose, and were allowed, to concentrate on the cultivation of their own lands. Consequently, the Turks could only continue to maintain a portion of the original large estates given to them, even though still in legal control of considerably greater areas, and their small settlements became more isolated and separate from one another. This tendency, which largely accounts for the contemporary dispersal of the Turkish villages throughout the island, was furthered by the arrival in the seventeenth century of more Turkish settlers, coming chiefly from the Anatolian mainland, to fill the gap on the Turkish lands which had been created by the voluntary withdrawal of so much of the Greek labour. Thus, the third chronological and second numerical ethnic element in the rural population of the island was established on a permanent basis. For, apart from the Greeks themselves, this Turkish element was preceded as rural settlers by the Maronites, Catholic mercenaries (from the Lebanon) who entered Cyprus during the Frankish rule to assist their fellow-Catholics in the policing of the state. By the time of the arrival of this second wave of Turkish settlers, the Maronite number and influence was already on the wane, but there were nineteen of their village settlements remaining. The Maronites, despite their numbers, have been just as determined as the two stronger branches of the Cypriot rural scene to preserve their distinctive institutions and religion intact and free from 'alien blemish'. No less than 97 per cent of the rural-dwelling Maronites are grouped together in four villages; a quartet which had in 1960 a combined non-Maronite population of 65 out of a total of 2,220 inhabitants.

It was during the later years of Turkish rule that the ethnocentricity of the Cypriot population as a whole was polarized. Such feeling invariably springs from a shared sense of oppression, and this feeling, to be expected among a small minority such as the Maronites, spread to the Greeks during this period. Despite the abolition of the feudal system of land tenure, and the consequent rapid expansion of land under peasant ownership, the nineteenth century was a particularly frustrating one for the Greek population of the island. Ottoman power was declining, as the emergence and steady expansion of an independent Greek state away to their north-west proved, and Constantinople clearly regarded the island, situated until 1869 in a backwater of the Mediterranean, and with its increasingly hostile Greek majority, as more trouble than it was worth. Several attempts had been made by the Sultans to dispose of it. By the time they finally managed to do so, their general mishandling of the island's internal affairs had so antagonized the Greek population as to create a lasting feeling of animosity towards their former Turkish masters. Thus, 'when the British took over Cyprus, the forces responsible for Greek Cypriot nationalism had already crystallized. The administrative policies of the British, which initially were not unlike those of the Turks, further aggravated the existing discontent' (Adams, 1964).

The Turkish system of land registration and re-allocation, which divorced land ownership from rights of usufruct, was based on the classification of all land into one of five categories: the *mulk* lands, state land, lands held by religious bodies, land for public use, and waste. Though theoretically sound, it was cumbersome and confused in its application. It caused relatively little hardship for the peasantry during the years of transition largely because it was implemented, if at all, in a grossly inefficient manner. The British, who inherited the system were, however, unused to inefficiency, and the vigour and determination with which they undertook to carry through the ideals of the reforms caused considerably more confusion and chaos for the peasantry involved than had all the years of Turkish indifference. Not until the end of the 1920's was the situation satisfactorily resolved, and only in 1946 was peasant proprietorship under the 'new' land code finally legalized.

A steady fragmentation of holdings has been the tendency throughout the history of agriculture on the island, and only the occasional spate of re-consolidation, usually following the arrival of a new régime, has helped to counter this trend. However, local inheritance custom has always prevailed over these spasmodic attempts, and so long as the present small size and fragmentation of holdings remains the norm, the development of modern agriculture on the island will be seriously impeded. The tendency in the fields is therefore the opposite of the tendency in the settlements which they support. The more compact the nucleated village, the greater the degree of dispersal of holdings. The one is a natural consequence of the other, for the farmer with numerous small plots scattered across the village lands will not only wish to remain settled close to his neighbours for social reasons, but would, given the position of the village in relation to his fragmented holding, have difficulty in increasing his economic efficiency by basing himself elsewhere. The consolidation of these plots would at least offer the possibility of an economic incentive to break away from the nucleation, and consequently any signs of a weakening of the degree of rural nucleation can be taken to be indicative of the strengthening of the rural economic base.

Whilst the four elements of water, soils, social needs, and, to a lesser extent, security were thus the influential factors in the evolution of the pattern of distribution of the rural population, it has been the peculiar history of the island which has been responsible for the ethnic dispersals within this framework. Deviation away from the mean proportions which, given a ratio within the rural population of 82 Greeks to 17 Turks to 1 Maronite and others, should approximate to one Turkish village for every five Greek settlements, can invariably be explained by reference to factors pertinent to this historical development of land ownership policies and patterns.

In the district of Paphos, for instance, where the incidence of Turks, at over 23 per cent of the total, is the highest for any rural division in the island, this figure owes its size to the string of Turkish villages in the low-lying areas which were, under the Venetians, centres of cotton and sugar-cane production. At that time these were the most important of Cyprus's products, and environmental conditions for their growth were at their most suitable in these areas. The cultivation of these cash crops was undertaken, not by the native population, but by Catholic communities who came into Cyprus from Western Europe with the Franks. Their removal following the Ottoman takeover allowed Turkish settlers to take their place in these favoured areas, and there they have remained. The 22 per cent Turkish element in Larnaca District's villages can be ascribed to exactly parallel causes. Conversely, there is a noticeable lack of a Turkish element among the settlements in the Troodos Mountains. Owing to conditions of climate and relief, this region did not attract early settlement or cultivation, and it was the only part of the island not to be included within the framework of the large estates during the Frankish and Venetian periods. It is unique within Cyprus in that the majority of its settlements are of post-Venetian origin. The modern colonization of this area did not take place until, wishing to escape from the proximity of their Moslem masters, the Greeks established communities in the Troodos during the second half of Ottoman control. In no other large area of the island are the Turks today so thinly scattered.

Such anomalies as these apart, there is a relatively small degree of regional variation in the pattern of the ethnic distribution, and that which does exist is tending to diminish. This reflects the changing economic conditions in the island which, at one extreme, are attracting Turks into the Troodos region for the first time, and at the other extreme are inducing an increasing number of Greeks to settle in the towns. The Troodos Mountains are no longer the retreat of escaping Greek settlers, but have emerged as the major resort area on the island, catering particularly for summer visitors from the Middle East states. The Turkish movement towards them is in recognition of the financial benefits to be earned from catering to the needs of their wealthier Moslem cousins. Similarly, the shift in emphasis away from agriculture in the Cypriot economy, and the consequent growth of urban-based occupations has had its greatest effect on the Greek population which, particularly in areas where land holdings are substantially below the lowland average of some 8 hectares, has migrated in considerable numbers to the towns. They have thus boosted their numerical representation in the six towns, whilst slightly redressing the rural imbalance.

Urban patterns

Despite this urban growth, and despite the very considerable emigration which, reflecting the lack of economic opportunity on the island, has taken place throughout this century, it must not be supposed that the rural population has numerically declined. On the contrary, the serious losses of the seventeenth and eighteenth centuries have been completely reversed, with the total rural population increasing between 1881 and 1960 from 155,000 to 368,000. This, although it does not match the urban growth rate of 31,500 to 206,000 over the same period, is still very substantial and indicates that, though the agricultural population has steadily lost a proportion of its manpower, traditionally the young single males, it has in no way been depleted.

Although the proportion of the population connected with the use of the land is still high, the percentage of the working population which derives its main source of income from agriculture has now, for the first time, fallen below 40 per cent. Despite this, every Cypriot is very little removed from the land, and total landlessness is a condition which has only recently appeared. The inhabitants of the six towns cannot therefore be expected to differ markedly from the rural Cypriots. Nevertheless, the capital and the five coastal towns, and the 36 per cent of the island's population which inhabit them, display certain distinctive characteristics which warrant their separate treatment.

The ethnic compositions of the six towns (Table 7.2) display a marked degree of statistical similarity, particularly among the Greek element, which in none of the towns is more than 2 per cent away from the urban mean of 71 per cent of the total. The Turkish element is less consistent than this, varying from 14 to 31 per cent, with a mean of 20 per cent. The balance is made up by a substantial number of 'others', including over 15,000 British, nearly 4,000 Armenians, and under 500 Maronites. The post-war levelling off of these figures is their most significant characteristic: complementing the state of affairs in the rural areas, this points to an increasing uniformity in the ethnic distribution pattern over the island as a whole, at least up to the attainment of independence.

As the former ruling class, the Turkish community is urbanized to a significantly higher degree than is the Greek. Some 40 per cent of the Turkish population, a total of 42,000, inhabit the towns, together with 142,000 Greeks, 26 per cent of their total number. Although, therefore, unlike the rural population, it is the rule rather than the exception for the

TABLE 7.2 CYPRUS: THE GROWTH AND ETHNIC COMPOSITION OF THE URBAN POPULATION

Towns (District capitals)	Population					Percentage ethnic composition					
						Greek		Turkish		Other	
	1881	1911	1946	1960	1967 (estimate)	1946*	1960	1946	1960	1946*	1960
Greater Nicosia	11,536	16,052	34,485	95,515	109,000	60	70	30	23	10	7
Limassol	6,131	10,302	22,799	43,593	50,000	80	73	15	14	5	13
Famagusta	2,564	5,327	16,194	34,774	40,000	81	71	17	18	2	11
Larnaca	7,833	9,262	14,772	19,824	21,000	72	69	20	21	8	10
Paphos	2,204	3,435	5,803	9,083	—	62	69	37	31	1	0
Kyrenia	1,192	1,726	2,916	3,498	—	76	69	19	20	5	11
All six towns	31,460	46,104	96,969	206,287	—	72	71	23	20	5	9

Source of data: Selected censuses, and for 1967 the estimates of the Department of Statistics and Research, Ministry of Finance, Nicosia.

* The 1946 figures include the Maronite community in the Greek column, rather than under 'Others'. This position was reversed in 1960.

town-dwellers to live in ethnically-mixed nucleations, this mixing, apparent when a town is considered as a whole, breaks down at the community level to resemble much more closely the rural pattern. Suburban Nicosia, for example, had in 1960 6,100 of its 7,400 Turkish inhabitants concentrated within the two suburbs of Kuchuk Kaimakli and Orta Keuy, these two centres having in addition a total Greek population of under 1,200 out of a total of 39,600 in all the nine suburbs. Thus, although the average ratio of Greek to Turk in suburban Nicosia is 84:16, this ranges from 100:0 in four suburbs, to 9:91 in Orta Keuy, and in only one of the nine does the minority population exceed 20 per cent of the total of the majority.

The differences in the proportion of the Turkish element in each of the towns would seem to be the outcome of two factors: their varying rates of growth, and the composition of the rural population in the Districts governed by these towns. For the five coastal towns, if not Nicosia, as is commonly the case in countries experiencing the early stage of urban growth, have drawn their immigrants largely from the areas for which they serve as the administrative, commercial, and social centres, and their ethnic compositions therefore reflect those of their rural Districts. Paphos displays most clearly the action of these two factors. It has grown at a rate considerably below the urban mean, and this, coupled with the highest proportion of Turkish villages in any of the six Districts, has maintained its position as the most Turkish of the towns.

Kyrenia and Larnaca have expanded at a rate similar to that of Paphos, and their lower Turkish proportions are a reflection of the relative lack of Turks in their catchment areas. The former's Turkish community of almost 700 has remained little changed in number since 1881, when it represented half of the town's small total population. Such increase as has taken place has been largely due to the excess of births over deaths, whereas the Greek community has expanded at a greater rate, not because of a higher level of fertility, but because of movement into Kyrenia from the predominantly Greek surrounding area. This is equally true of Larnaca, which has drawn the majority of its immigrants from the western interior areas of its District, a zone exclusively peopled by Greeks. Larnaca, the principal port of the island during Turkish rule, was then the most important commercial centre on Cyprus, but its administrative functions were few. Here, as elsewhere throughout their Empire, the Turks preferred not to soil their hands by engaging in trade with the infidel, choosing whenever possible to leave such tasks to the willing Greeks. Larnaca was thus never an important Turkish urban centre, even though the second largest town when the Turks left Cyprus, and its ethnic composition, which has for long included a significant foreign business element, reflects its early and continued commercial functions clearly.

Famagusta and Limassol, the island's only other ports of significance, have both grown at a more rapid rate than Larnaca, and both now surpass it in size and importance. With a ratio between the Greeks and Turks of over 7:1 in its District, the highest in the island, it is hardly surprising that, in increasing its population eight-fold since the 1881 census, Limassol has drawn almost exclusively on the Greek rural community. Its Turkish population of 6,000, representing 14 per cent of the total, is a significantly lower percentage than that of any other town. Famagusta, as a city, has experienced mixed fortunes. The heights, as described by Luke, have already been referred to: the depths were reached towards the end of Turkish rule, when the population of 2,500 was scarcely more than that of Paphos. At that time the Turks were well represented in the town, and the old centre, within the walls, remains predominantly Moslem. However, following the construction of a rail link to Nicosia, one of the first acts on the island of the British, who removed it in 1952, Famagusta regained its position of commercial pre-eminence. Greeks migrated to the town in positive response to the financial possibilities its growth presented, while, like Paphos, it also received an inflow of Turks, in negative response to the lack of opportunities in the northern Mesaoria plain where several of their villages were situated. The growth of Famagusta was thus more rapid than that of any other port, with most of the extra-mural development, notably in the suburb of Varosha, being occupied by Greek settlers, and the Turkish migrants strengthening their ethnic position in the old town.

Nicosia occupies a unique position within the urban framework of the island, not only by virtue of its location, but also because, as the capital, it has attracted immigrants from the whole of Cyprus, in addition to those from its district catchment area, the predominantly Greek south-western region on the edge of the Troodos massif. The administrative capital throughout Turkish rule, it has had, and retains, a large Turkish population which stood at just over 22,000 at the 1960 census. Without its suburbs, which, when included, now more than double the population, Nicosia has a ratio of Greek to Turk of just under 2:1. Although the relatively narrow margin of this differential is not maintained when the suburbs, with their preponderance of Greeks, are included, nevertheless the Turkish element recognizes that it is in the capital of the island that its greater strength lies. Admittedly, Paphos has a higher percentage of Turks in its population than has Greater Nicosia, but this involves under 3,000 people. In Nicosia are to be found over one-half of all the urban Turks on Cyprus. Hence Nicosia has, in recent years, epitomized the dominating problem of the Cypriot people: the mutual incompatability of the two main communities.

Mobility and intractability

These two communities are economically largely self-sufficient, with their agricultural, commercial and industrial activities rarely complementing each other. Inevitably, therefore, there is a constant overlapping in the occupational distributions of the two communities, a repetitiveness which does little to assist the progress of the island's economy. Apart from the presence of a mosque or an Orthodox church, it is difficult to distinguish the settlements of the two communities, whose agricultural practices and standards of living are almost identical. Yet socially the Greeks and Turks are totally separate, and so long as the two camps have basically opposing political aims, the one bent on domination and majority rule, coupled with infrequent overtures to the 'homeland' in recognition of former pleas for 'enosis', and the other seeking autonomy, separation, and the division of the island into two political entities, there can be little objective hope of co-operative progress. 'In successful federal régimes there develops in time something that has been called the "federal spirit" or the "federal behavior". It is a highly pragmatic kind of political conduct, which avoids insistence upon "agreement on fundamentals" and similar forms of doctrinaire rigidity. Such behaviour proceeds in the spirit of compromise and accommodation' (Friedrich, 1968). This time has not yet arrived on Cyprus, which continues to display all the dangers of a divided society striving for opposing goals.

The island's potential for economic growth is nevertheless high, and this in itself should act as some incentive towards a greater degree of co-operation. Despite the ethnic problem, which has turned Nicosia into a divided capital where, for long periods following independence, representatives of one community have seldom ventured into the territory of the other; and which, throughout the last decade, has induced a considerable movement of the rural population away from mixed or ethnically-isolated settlements towards the security of greater concentrations of their own kind—a move which has inevitably affected the Turkish villager more than the Greek—the population as a whole shares a rising *per capita* annual income. This stood at £58 in 1966, and it is expected to reach £355 by the end of 1971, being second only to that of Israel throughout the eastern Mediterranean. Certainly, this relative economic health has been assisted by the leasing of 260 sq. km. of territory to the British as the Sovereign Base Areas of Akrotiri and Dhekelia, and by remittances sent home by emigrants—neither a totally desirable prop on which to lean—but an annual growth rate of 6 per cent since the instigation of the first Five Year Plan in 1962, and the undoubted opportunities offered by agriculture, industry, and tourism, bode well for the future.

The mobility of the Cypriot population has not only revealed itself in these recent internal re-adjustments, which have tended to divide the island ever more rigidly; on the wider scale it has manifested itself in a willingness to emigrate. Emigration rates have fluctuated greatly throughout this century, partly in response to changing conditions on the island, and partly as a consequence of the varying regulations pertaining to immigrants in the recipient countries. As a Crown Colony of Great

Britain, Cyprus's population gained access without great difficulty into Britain, Australia and Africa, and left the island in considerable numbers in the years following the Second World War when, having experienced the comparative prosperity which that war brought to Cyprus, they were not prepared to return to pre-war standards of living. The majority of such emigrants were drawn from the rural areas undergoing the greatest degree of depopulation in favour of their district capitals. 'It was not the impoverished and apathetic section of the population with no drive to cut away from their dormant environment, but the disgruntled, frustrated and enterprising who could not see their ambitions being fulfilled within the socio-economic framework of their community that formed the ranks of the post-war immigration to the United Kingdom' (George and Millerson, 1967). This outflow reached its peak in 1960, when 14,000 Cypriots, the great majority of them Greek, left the island. Since independence, however, both the direction and the scale of migration have changed considerably. The Commonwealth is no longer so readily available, and the industrial regions of Western Europe have tended to replace it as the major attraction, whilst, in addition, the prospect of greater opportunities at home in the euphoric post-independence years has reduced the total number involved.

The direct financial return for the Cypriot economy of emigrants' remittances helps to offset the social and economic consequences which the persistent loss of many young, healthy and ambitious people can cause. Also offsetting such losses has been the buoyant natural growth rate of the population. Having, in common with most other Mediterranean areas, experienced a severe decline up to the middle of the eighteenth century, which carried the total, 50 per cent of which was then Turkish, down to a low of 80,000, the population has since risen steadily to its present level of over 600,000. The present rate of increase, of some 1.8 per cent per annum, is a result of a death rate of under 7 per thousand and a birth rate of 25 per thousand.

With ethnic enmities as the overriding political problem, and with the agricultural system (which absorbs 40 per cent of the labour force, yields 20 per cent of the GDP, and leaves the average income of a rural agricultural family some 50 per cent below the national average) as the major economic problem, there can be little doubt among the population of Cyprus about what needs to be done in order to establish the politico-economic viability of the island. It has yet to be shown, however, that the viability of the whole community as it now exists is the aim of either side. It would not be appropriate to conclude by discussing the merits of the claims of either Greek or Turk, but the Cypriot Turk, that 'most tolerant of men' (Luke, 1924) must surely be reflecting on the outcome of his ancestors' tolerance, so often indistinguishable from indifference, towards the activities of the Greek community. Had not the Turks, in their leniency, allowed the Greeks to farm more of their own lands at the expense of the care of the Turkish estates, the present extent of isolation of the Turkish communities need never have arisen. Their present vulnerability and dispersal is thus a direct consequence of their own earlier policies: policies of which the original inhabitants have never failed to take maximum advantage.

REFERENCES

ADAMS, T. W. (1964) *US Army Area Handbook for Cyprus*, Washington.

BURDON, D. J. (1950) 'Floods and Rainfall in the Eastern Mesaoria', Appendix 4 to the *Annual Report for 1949, Water Supply and Irrigation Department*, Nicosia.

CHRISTODOULOU, D. (1959) *The Evolution of the Rural Land Use Pattern in Cyprus*, Bude.

DIXON, W. H. (1887) *British Cyprus*, London.

DURRELL, L. (1957) *Bitter Lemons*, London.

FOLEY, C. (1962) *Island in Revolt*, London.

FRIEDRICH, C. J. (1968) *Trends of Federalism in Theory and Practice*, London.

GEORGE, V. and MILLERSON, G. (1967) 'The Cypriot Community in London', *Race*, 8, pp. 277–92.

HMSO (1960) *Cyprus*, London.

KIRIAZIS, G. N. (1952) *The villages of Cyprus* (in Greek), Nicosia.

LUKE, H. C. (1924) *Anatolica*, London.

MELAMID, A. 'The Geographical Distribution of Communities in Cyprus', *American Geographical Review*, 46, pp. 355–74.

MEYER, A. J. and VASSILIOU, S. (1962) *The Economy of Cyprus*, Cambridge, Mass.

NEWMAN, P. (1956) *A Short History of Cyprus*, London.

PERCIVAL, D. A. (1950) 'Some features of a peasant population in the Middle East', *Population Studies*, 3, pp. 192–204.

REPUBLIC OF CYPRUS (1962) *Census of Population and Agriculture, 1960*, Nicosia.

STAMPOLIS, A. (1963) *The Social Economic Development of Cyprus*, Nicosia.

SURRIDGE, B. J. (1930) *A Rural Survey of Cyprus*, Nicosia.

TAEUBER, I. B. (1954) 'Cyprus: the demography of a strategic island', *Population Index*, 21, pp. 4–20.

VAUMAS, E. (1959) 'La répartition de la population à Chypre et le nouvel état chypriote, *Revue Géographique Alpine*, 47, pp. 457–529.

Chapter 8
Israel: immigration and
dispersal of population
G H Blake

This chapter concerns the state of Israel as defined by the armistice lines before the war of June 1967. Territories in Syria, Egypt and Jordan occupied by Israel in June 1967 and still held in 1970 are discussed briefly at the end of the chapter. While it is unlikely that all the occupied territories will become an integral part of Israel, the old city of Jerusalem (population 65,800 in 1967) has been officially 'annexed' and is included in Israeli population statistics as part of the state of Israel (Central Bureau of Statistics, 1968a). In this chapter, however, 'Jerusalem' refers to Israeli Jerusalem only, unless otherwise stated.

It is a truism that among the countries of the Middle East and North Africa, Israel provides the exceptions to the rule. Thus in terms of population structure, ethnic composition, the degree of urbanization, and a rapid rate of growth largely through immigration, Israel differs radically from her neighbours. At first sight, Israel exhibits the same kind of uneven distribution of population between semi-arid and well watered zones as other countries discussed in this book, but there are important differences. While the Negev desert represents over two-thirds of the area of the country, Israel is still very small, and the south has many positive aspects, not least of which is its function as a corridor to the Red Sea. Unlike larger desert areas, a network of small towns can be envisaged in the Negev, while extensive agricultural settlement is planned in northern parts in addition to what has already been achieved. Israel is also unique in the degree to which population distributions and settlement patterns reflect deliberate planning policies, related to the needs of national security as well as recognized principles of social and economic theory.

Most of this chapter will be read in the context of Israel's political significance to the heart of the Arab–Islamic world, but it is worth remembering that the emergence of the only Jewish state of modern times has also had an important impact upon world Jewry. In 1948, less than 6 per cent of the world Jewish population lived in Israel, compared with some 17 per cent in 1968, while Israel's share of Middle Eastern and North African Jews rose from about 10 per cent to 95 per cent during the same period. Thus an almost total redistribution of Jews from these regions has occurred, resulting in their concentration in one state to a greater degree than at any time since A.D. 70. In 1967, 43 per cent of Israel's population were Israel born, 28 per cent were born in the Middle East or North Africa, and the rest were chiefly of European or American origin (Central Bureau of Statistics, 1968a).

Two population censuses have been taken in Israel. The first, in November 1948, was no more than a simple population count and cannot be regarded as wholly reliable, particularly regarding the Moslem minority which was under-estimated by some 10,000. In central upper Galilee no effective count was made as fighting had ceased only days before the census. A second census followed in 1961 which was complete and comprehensive; it also generally confirmed the accuracy of annual calculations made by the Central Bureau of Statistics (Orni and Efrat, 1964). The Bureau publishes a regular series of bulletins, technical papers, and an annual Statistical Abstract, all of which provide valuable sources of population data. In August and September 1967, following the occupation of territories in Syria, Jordan and Egypt, the Israelis conducted censuses of the Arabs remaining in these areas, the results of which are summarized at the end of this chapter. Several other sources of information are available relating to population and settlement in Israel, including the fine *Atlas of Israel*, available in English in 1970. The next full national census is due to be held in Israel in 1972.

Population growth since 1948

The population of Israel numbered 873,000 persons in November 1948 of whom 156,000 were Arabs (Moslems and Christians) and Druzes (Fig. 8.1). The estimated population, including East Jerusalem, at the end of 1969 was 2,918,000 including 422,000 non-Jews, more than a threefold total increase since 1948 (Central Bureau of Statistics, 1970). The Jewish population has increased at an average annual rate of about 2.7 per cent and the non-Jewish population at about 2.2 per cent. While natural increase accounted for 43 per cent of the increase in the population as a whole, it contributed 37 per cent of the increase in the Jewish population. Thus the nature and origins of Israel's immigrants provide the major theme for this chapter.

Jewish immigration into Israel has never been restricted but actually encouraged for political and idealistic reasons. The Proclamation of Independence in 1948 declared that the state would be 'open to the in-gathering of the exiles', while the Law of the Return of July 1950 provided that 'every Jew shall be entitled to come to Israel as an immigrant'. One result of this policy is the problem of predicting the nature and rate of future immigration. The Jewish Agency which assumes responsibility for bringing and settling immigrants has admittedly exercised some selectivity

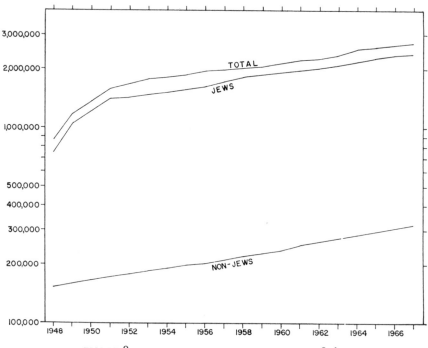

FIGURE 8.1 ISRAEL: POPULATION GROWTH, 1948-67

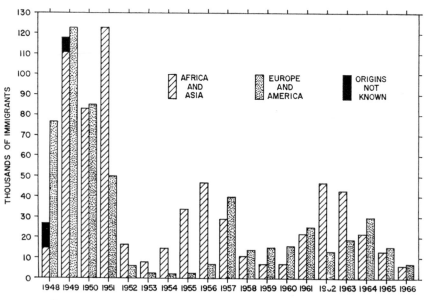

FIGURE 8.2 JEWISH IMMIGRANTS INTO ISRAEL BY CONTINENT OF BIRTH, 1948-66

in granting free passages to would-be immigrants, but this has never acted as a significant regulator of the flow. Table 8.1 shows how the number of immigrants has fluctuated from year to year, usually in response to political events in the host country, or in the Middle East. By the end of 1967, altogether 1,247,000 immigrants had reached Israel. During the same period rather more than 170,000 persons emigrated, approximately 13 per cent of the total number of immigrants. Apart from 1952 and 1953, the level of emigration has remained at around 8,000 per annum. The small number is not surprising since few immigrants have the means to go elsewhere even if they wish to do so.

TABLE 8.1   IMMIGRATION OF JEWS INTO ISRAEL, 1948–67

1948	101,824	1955	36,327	1962	59,600
1949	239,424	1956	54,996	1963	62,156
1950	169,720	1957	71,100	1964	52,456
1951	174,014	1958	26,093	1965	28,795
1952	23,408	1959	23,045	1966	13,610
1953	10,388	1960	23,644	1967	12,275
1954	17,485	1961	46,650		

Source: Central Bureau of Statistics, 1968a.

Immigration into Israel has occurred in two fairly distinct phases: from May 1948 until the end of 1951, and from 1955 to the present day, with a slack period from 1952 to 1954 (Fig. 8.2).

The rate of immigration during the first four years of the state was higher than at any period since. The average annual rate of population increase was 23.7 per cent. In this short period Israel received more immigrants than during the subsequent 17 years, and in 1949 when nearly a quarter of a million persons entered Israel, rates at times rose to as high as 5,000 a week and 20,000 a month.

Immigrants entering Israel during these early years were chiefly of three kinds. There were the survivors of concentration camps, perhaps 75,000 in number, and others released by the British from detention camps where they had been held during the war for attempting to enter Palestine illegally. Secondly, about 200,000 Jews came from Eastern Europe where the communist régimes had yet to reveal their attitude to minority groups, and many escaped while the going was good; the largest numbers were from Rumania, Czechoslovakia and Bulgaria. Thirdly, large numbers left the Arab countries of North Africa and the Middle East. In these regions the Arab–Jewish war of 1948 in Palestine had created tension between Jews and their neighbours, and many Jews concluded that there was no future for them in the Arab world. At the same time there was the strong emotional appeal of 'returning' to the 'promised land'. A remarkable feature of the exodus of Middle Eastern Jews at this time was the airlift of 145,000 Iraqi and Yemenite Jews in 1949 and 1950.

The colossal rate of immigration and the destitution of many of the immigrants in this period almost overwhelmed Israel, which had neither the manpower nor the material resources to cope adequately. Without the provision of large funds, chiefly from North America, the situation might have been disastrous. New arrivals were housed at first in abandoned British army camps, tents and empty Arab houses. Thousands drifted to the three large towns of Tel-Aviv, Haifa and Jerusalem which in 1948 already held 48 per cent of the Jewish population. In 1950 the government began to build huge transit camps (*ma'abarot*), sometimes adjacent to the sites of projected new towns, and these provided temporary housing of wood, concrete or corrugated iron, and all essential services. By the end of 1951 there were 125 *ma'abarot* in Israel, but in the course of 1952 they began to be replaced by permanent settlement in the form of new towns and villages up and down the country.

Fortunately for Israel, a much needed pause in immigration occurred from 1952 until 1954. For the first time natural increase contributed more than immigration to population growth, and in 1953 there was actually a net loss through emigration. Most refugees from the Second World War had reached Israel by the end of 1951 and the initial rush to leave the Arab countries had died down. These three years of consolidation were of vital importance to Israel, permitting the reappraisal of methods of absorbing and settling immigrants, administrative reorganization, and the construction of permanent housing beyond immediate requirements in anticipation of the next wave of immigration.

The second great phase began in 1955 and is still in progress. The first three years saw the arrival of large numbers of immigrants from the Maghreb largely as a result of nationalist movements culminating in independence for Tunisia and Morocco in 1956, and the war of independence in Algeria which began in earnest in 1954. In 1956 following the Suez and Sinai fighting more Jews fled from Arab countries, and all but a few left Egypt. The Hungarian rising of 1956 brought a fresh influx of European Jews to Israel, while in 1957 the Polish Government agreed to the departure of 40,000 Jews. Since 1957, immigration has been generally moderate, with the exception of 1962-4. The high figures for 1962-3 are associated with Algerian independence and the lifting of a ban on the emigration of Jews from Morocco at about the same time, resulting in the exodus of over 90,000 from these countries. With the exception of 1962 and 1963, immigrants from America and Europe have outnumbered those from Africa and Asia every year since 1956. It may be noted that 1966 and 1967 recorded the smallest number of immigrants for any two-year period in the history of the state; taking emigration into account there was a net gain of just over 6,000 persons in each year.

The gentler tempo of immigration and the experience acquired in earlier years have enabled the absorption of immigrants to go ahead relatively smoothly since 1955. Transit camps and other temporary accommodation are no longer used. Instead, immigrants are transported direct to 'development towns' or new rural settlements in what has been called the 'Ship to Settlement' technique. The Jewish Agency offers housing and some kind of employment to all who are prepared to go where these are to be found, and in this way the government has been able to expand and establish settlements in various parts of Israel in accordance with its physical master plan.

Natural increase

Figure 8.3 illustrates the natural increase of Jews since 1948 and non-Jews since 1951, reliable statistics for the latter being unavailable before 1951.

The high birth rate of the non-Jewish population is comparable with certain Arab states where the rate remains high; in 1967 the lowest ever rate of 44.9 was recorded, which may be compared with rates in excess of 50 in recent years. Birth rates are much lower among Arab Christians and Druzes. Death rates on the other hand have shown a steady decline since 1952, falling below those of the Jewish population since 1964, to 6.2 in 1967. This very low rate may be explained in part by incomplete registration of deaths, but in addition infant deaths have declined markedly, rates being between 42 and 44 per thousand among the non-Jewish population in recent years. The rate of natural increase for non-Jews rose from 37.8 in 1951 to 45.0 in 1964, but fell to 38.7 in 1967 (Central Bureau of Statistics, 1968a).

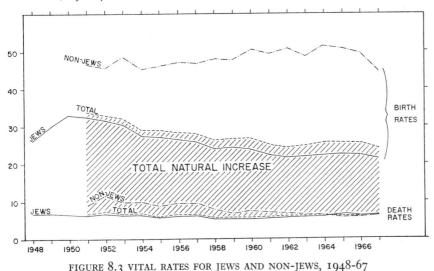

FIGURE 8.3 VITAL RATES FOR JEWS AND NON-JEWS, 1948-67

The Jewish birth rate has rarely exceeded 30 and has declined steadily to 21.5 in 1967. The Jewish death rate (6.6 in 1967) has shown only minor fluctuations since 1948, but infant deaths have decreased from the early years of the state to the very low rate of 20.8 in 1967. With a static death rate and declining birth rate the natural increase of the Jewish population has fallen from the peak rates of 1950–51 to 14.9 per thousand in 1967 (Fig. 8.3).

The contrast between the Jewish and non-Jewish rates of natural increase is sufficiently striking to raise questions of a political kind concerning the future of Israel. Comparison of gross reproduction rates confirms this contrast; among the Jews they have gradually declined to present figures of 1.65–1.68 while among non-Jews they have risen to more than 4.0, though with some signs of a decline since 1964. Furthermore, the age-structure of the Jewish population exhibits a mature profile akin to countries of Europe (Fig. 8.4), while the non-Jewish population exhibits

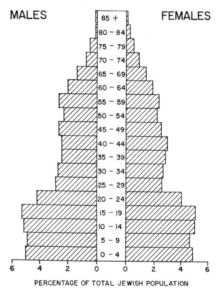

FIGURE 8.4 AGE-SEX PYRAMID OF ISRAEL'S JEWISH POPULATION, 1967

youthful characteristics similar to that of the populations of Morocco (Fig. 17.2) or Egypt (Fig. 13.1), just over 50 per cent being under 15 years of age. While detailed population projections are of little value because of uncertainties concerning immigration and the future frontiers of Israel, present demographic trends must clearly discourage the Israelis from seeking permanent control of the occupied territories and their large Arab populations. To do so in the absence of massive Jewish immigration could lead to a non-Jewish majority within twenty years (Smith, 1968), a very different situation from 1966 when 88.2 per cent of the total population were Jews (Table 8.2).

TABLE 8.2   PEOPLES OF ISRAEL, 1966

	Numbers	Per cent
Jews	2,344,900	88.2
Moslems	223,000	8.4
Christians	58,000	2.2
Druzes/others	31,000	1.2
Total	2,656,900	100.0

Source: Central Bureau of Statistics, 1968a.

The Jewish population

In 1967 approximately 43 per cent of the Jewish population were Israel-born (or born in Palestine before 1948); a further 30 per cent were immigrants from Europe and America, 14 per cent from Africa, and 13 per cent from Asia. Altogether, immigrants have reached Israel from more than 80 different countries, including all the Islamic states discussed in this volume. Of those born in Europe, the vast majority originated in the USSR, Poland and Rumania, which have supplied well over half a million immigrants. Other important sources were Germany, Austria and Bulgaria. North Africa has yielded more than 300,000 Jews notably from Morocco, Algeria and Tunisia. Rather fewer have emigrated from Asian countries, Iraq being easily the largest single source (125,000), followed by Yemen, Iran and Turkey. In fact, only about one-third of Israel's population was born outside the Middle East and North Africa, and the proportion is gradually declining.

It is a fallacy to regard the Jewish population as homogeneous; in reality it embraces groups of widely differing ethnic and cultural origin, and there can be little scientific justification for the idea of a Jewish race. The Jews of some Diaspora communities, it is true, differ slightly from their neighbours in certain physical traits possibly as the result of long periods of segregation and inter-marriage, but basic affinities of colour and build can only be explained by mixed marriages or proselytization centuries ago. Thus Israel's immigrant population is a rich tabloid of racial and cultural groups with some of the strengths and weaknesses of each; this is particularly true of the two major groups of European immigrants on the one hand and African and Asian immigrants on the other.

In 1948, nine-tenths of the Jewish population of Israel were of European origin, and the leaders of the young state together with its institutions and ideals were almost exclusively European. The subsequent influx of Jews from Africa and Asia has brought about radical changes in the composition of the population which can scarcely have been anticipated in 1948. Although European immigrants still constitute a majority of the foreign-born population, children born to African and Asian parents in Israel have been sufficiently numerous to bring about approximate numerical equality between the two groups. Eventually, no doubt, complete assimilation will occur as the number of mixed marriages increases, but the process will take time. Between 1955 and 1966, for example, only 14 per cent of Jewish marriages in Israel were between persons of different cultural groups. Meanwhile gross reproduction rates of African and Asian Jews (2.17 in 1966) remain higher than among European Jews (1.19 in 1966) and one can expect the dark-skinned element in the population to become increasingly dominant (Central Bureau of Statistics, 1968a). The problem posed by this situation is not at present essentially one of colour, but of the cultural and educational gulf between the 'European' and 'Oriental' groups. A high proportion of immigrants from Africa and Asia have little or no education. Many of them hailed from isolated villages and small towns, sometimes reaching Israel with the social structures of pre-immigration communities still intact. In their religious zeal, their previous levels of income, and the whole cultural environment from which they came, the Oriental Jews had little in common with their European counterparts. These differences are well illustrated by the pre-immigration occupations of the two groups. Generally the proportion of active immigrants is much higher among European immigrants, with a far higher proportion of female earners than among African and Asian immigrants. Between 1955 and 1959 some 37 per cent of previously active European immigrants were in professional, technical and managerial employment, compared with 17 per cent of the Oriental immigrants. On the other hand a higher proportion of the latter group were merchants, craftsmen, unskilled labourers and so on (Central Bureau of Statistics, 1968a). The danger of the emergence of a Western élite and an Oriental proletariat is therefore a real one, and strenuous efforts are being made at all levels to ensure that this does not occur. How far these efforts are meeting with success lies beyond the scope of this book, but the contrasting geographical distribution of the two groups is discussed later in the chapter.

The non-Jewish population

The bulk of Israel's minority population can be appropriately called Arabs, but for the sake of the few to whom this appellation does not strictly apply, the all-embracing term non-Jew is used in this chapter. Together, non-Jews constituted just under 12 per cent of the population of Israel in 1967, but like the Jews they are by no means a homogeneous group.

The largest minority group are the Moslems who, in common with nine-tenths of their co-religionists, belong to the Sunni sect. Most of Israel's Moslems can be assumed to be descendants of Palestine's various ancient inhabitants, converted largely during the early years of the Islamic conquest. Curiously, the Arabian racial elements which might have been introduced at that time do not appear to be important today. The Moslems are largely concentrated in Galilee and along the eastern margins of the plain of Sharon adjacent to the pre-1967 armistice line. A large Moslem community exists in Nazareth, with other important urban communities in Haifa, Akko, Ramla and Lod. In addition, some 34,000 bedouin live in Israel, most of them in the northern Negev around Beer Sheva, but some are also found in parts of lower Galilee.

Christians numbered 58,000 in 1966. The majority of Israel's Christians are Arabs, two-thirds of whom are urban dwellers. The largest sect is the Greek-Catholic, followed by Greek Orthodox and Roman Catholic communities, but besides these a bewildering variety of groups exist including Maronites and a number of Protestant denominations. The number of European clergy, nuns and monks associated with all these sects may be well over 1,000 (Orni and Efrat, 1964).

The only other minority of any size are the Druzes, followers of a faith whose origins can be traced to Egypt in the tenth and eleventh centuries when it broke with Islam. The main Druze settlements are in Lebanon and Syria, but Druzes have inhabited parts of Palestine for over four hundred years. Most are farmers in western and central upper Galilee and on Mount Carmel, while a few live in Haifa. The Druzes enjoy a rather privileged position compared with other minority groups, and are sufficiently trusted to serve in Israel's defence forces.

'Others' in Table 8.2 refers to fewer than 3,000 persons altogether. Most numerous are the Circassians, descendants of Moslem refugees from the Caucasus who reached Palestine towards the end of the last century. The rest are religious minorities: Ahmedis, Samaritans and Bahais.

Distribution of population

The distribution of population in Israel in 1948 strongly influenced subsequent plans for future disposition of population, particularly the contrast between a densely settled coastal zone and a sparsely settled hinterland, and a hierarchy in which small and medium-sized towns were unusually scarce (Fig. 8.5).

Table 8.3 shows the proportion of population in each of the six administrative districts (Fig. 8.5) of the country in 1948. Of greatest concern was the high concentration of Jews in Tel Aviv and its immediate hinterland. In spite of the ideological attachment of a minority to the idea of a return to the soil, the bulk of immigrants even before 1948 were refugee urban dwellers for whom Tel Aviv, Haifa and Jerusalem provided strong attrac-

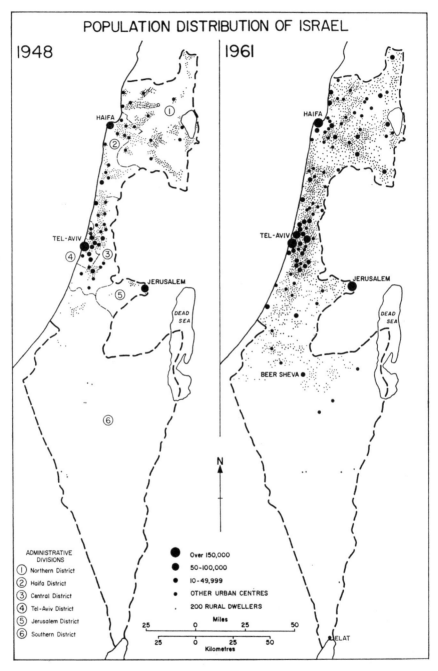

FIGURE 8.5

TABLE 8.3   PERCENTAGE OF POPULATION OF ISRAEL BY DISTRICT,
NOVEMBER 1948

Administrative district	Jews	Non-Jews	Total
Northern	7.6	58.1	16.8
Haifa	21.1	17.6	20.5
Central	15.2	10.3	14.3
Tel Aviv	43.2	2.3	35.7
Jerusalem	12.0	1.8	10.2
Southern	0.9	9.9	2.5
	100.0	100.0	100.0

Source: Central Bureau of Statistics, 1968a.

tions. Suitable land for agriculture was in any case difficult to acquire and rural colonization demanded arduous pioneering often in situations of great danger. Thus by 1948 the three largest cities themselves contained 58 per cent of the Jewish population, and a further 23 per cent lived in other towns, six of which were in the Tel Aviv region (Spiegel, 1967).

The uneven distribution of population posed a number of serious problems. The populous Tel Aviv region presented a vulnerable military target, while the south, comprising nearly 70 per cent of the county, lay almost empty. Much of the relatively well-watered north was also under-populated and possessed a substantial Arab majority, while the borders of the country were mostly unguarded by frontier settlement of any kind. The unbalanced settlement structure also clearly required change, nearly 27 per cent of the population living in settlements of fewer than 5,000 inhabitants and nearly 53 per cent in towns of over 80,000 inhabitants, while between these two extremes was a remarkable dearth of small and medium-sized towns (Table 8.4). Moreover, apart from Jerusalem and the Arab town of Nazareth, all centres of more than 5,000 inhabitants were in the Tel Aviv/

TABLE 8.4   STRUCTURE OF SETTLEMENT OF ISRAEL, NOVEMBER 1948

Size of settlement	Number of settlements	Per cent population
Over 80,000	3	52.7
20,000–25,000	1	2.7
10,000–19,999	5	9.8
5,000–9,999	8	8.4
1,000–4,999	63	13.8
0–999	362	12.6
	442	100.0

Source: Central Bureau of Statistics, 1961.

Haifa coastal zone. The polarity of city and village life evolved during the British mandate largely because small regional towns had no useful function to fulfil. Most Jewish villages had a wide range of internal social and economic facilities which rendered them almost independent for everyday services, while services at the highest levels could easily be obtained in one of the three big cities, which also provided the only important markets for agricultural produce. The majority of Jewish settlements were within 30 km. of Tel Aviv or Haifa, and only a few were as far away as 50 km. A factor which further discouraged the idea of local regional centres was doubtless the antipathy of most *kibbutz* and *moshav* members to town life in general (Kolodny, 1963).

Planned redistribution of population

Three master plans designed to bring about an eventual optimum spatial pattern and distribution of population have succeeded one another, in 1951, 1957 and 1963. These plans have differed in detail. The first assumed a 1982 population of 2.6 million, the second 3.2 million, while the 1963 assumption is 4 million. Since 1951 there has been a gradual erosion of the proportion assigned to villages and rural service centres. The 1963 plan puts the target for 1982 at only 13 per cent, which may be compared with an actual rural population of 18 per cent in 1967. Some Israelis have strongly opposed the reduction of the proportion of rural population on political and ideological grounds, but the reality of limited resources of water and soil has led to a gradual acceptance of the fact that Israel must increasingly become a nation of urban-dwellers. Thus the share of future population assigned to the urban sector in the various plans has increased since 1951 at the expense of the rural sector, the additional growth having been conceded to the major cities and other towns in approximately equal proportions. By 1981 it is planned that the three major cities and their satellite towns will possess about 38 per cent of the national population compared with approximately 35 per cent today. The share of the other towns, however, should increase from 47 per cent at present to 49 per cent in 1980 (Spiegel, 1967).

In spite of differences in detail, an objective of all three master plans has been the creation of a closely-knit hierarchy of settlement whose theoretical basis was derived from the work of Christaller and others in Europe (Brutzkus, 1966). The model was a fivefold hierarchy consisting of the following:

A — villages
B — rural service centres
C — rural/urban centres
D — medium-sized towns
E — cities

194

At the lowest level (A) the unit of settlement would generally be *kibbutzim* and *moshavim*. Rural service centres (B) were designed to provide services for clusters of from three to six *moshavim*, and accommodating non-agricultural specialists such as teachers, mechanics, doctors and administrators. In practice, such centres usually have fewer inhabitants than neighbouring *moshavim*, but there is talk of their ultimate expansion to 2,000 persons in conjunction with light industries (Halperin, 1963). Rural/urban centres (C) with populations of 6,000–12,000 were to provide services at a more advanced level than the rural centres. Such small towns were thought to be a way of bringing immigrants 'close to the soil' and were also to be a means of achieving dispersal of population where farming could only absorb limited numbers. They were to act as foci for small regions, processing agricultural produce and serving the local farming community. Experience has shown that these towns are rather too small to create a genuine urban atmosphere and they cannot easily maintain adequate services with the necessary personnel to operate them, so that future new towns will probably aim at over 30,000 inhabitants (Spiegel, 1967). Meanwhile several rural/urban centres have been founded, some of which remain very small. In addition to the towns shown in Figure 8.6, there were ten more urban centres in 1967 with fewer than 5,000 inhabitants, some of which appear in the 1961 map (Fig. 8.5). Medium-sized towns (D), on the other hand, have been far more successful. These are the urban centres of 21 of Israel's 24 planning regions. At the end of 1967 eight already had over 40,000 inhabitants, the largest being Nazareth, Netanya, Petah Tiqva and Beer Sheva. The three major cities of Jerusalem, Tel Aviv and Haifa are also centres of planning regions. With Ramat Gan (107,000 in 1967) they constitute the highest level of the hierarchy (E).

By no means every part of Israel now has every level of the hierarchy

TABLE 8.5   STRUCTURE OF SETTLEMENT IN ISRAEL, DECEMBER 1967

Size of settlement	Number of settlements	Per cent population
Over 100,000	4	35.0
50,000–99,999	6	14.6
20,000–49,999	15	16.4
10,000–19,999	22	10.3
5,000–9,999	20	5.3
1,000–4,999	88*	8.0
0–999	725	9.1
Bedouin tribes, etc.	—	1.3
Total	880	100.0

Source: Central Bureau of Statistics, 1968a.

* Including 10 'urban centres'.

represented; this was clearly never intended. On the other hand, no closely settled region is without an urban centre of some size, and the need for a network of medium-sized towns has been largely met, with 44 towns of between 10,000 and 100,000 inhabitants in existence today compared with seven in 1948 (Table 8.5). The dispersion of these towns in northern and central Israel and the beginnings of a loose network in the south are remarkable features of the present population distribution. In siting these new towns throughout the country, Israel's planners enjoyed great flexibility in the choice of site. Most important was the employment structure of the new towns, notably services, processing farm produce, and light manufacturing, none of which imposed severe limitations of choice in respect of raw materials, power, transport and markets. Until 1952 most new towns were in fact sited adjacent to old Arab centres, but since then completely new sites have been chosen (Fig. 8.6). The planners also enjoyed another unusual advantage in being able to direct a steady flow of immigrants to the developing towns, for few were able to decline the immediate offer of a house and a job wherever they were available.

Comparison of Tables 8.4 and 8.5 shows that the number of rural settlements in Israel has more than doubled since 1948, the bulk of the increase being in those with fewer than 1,000 inhabitants. The majority of new rural settlements are *kibbutzim* and *moshavim*, most of which were founded before 1961. Thus the 1961 distribution of rural population shown in Figure 8.5 indicates the same basic pattern as today. Four more *kibbutzim* were founded between 1961 and 1967, making a total of 233, while the number of *moshavim* and collective *moshavim* had increased by three to 368 in the same year (Central Bureau of Statistics, 1961, 1968a).

Altogether Israel's population is distributed more rationally than in 1948 from the standpoint of national security and development. Of the six administrative districts (Table 8.3) the Southern District has gained most with 10.5 per cent of the total population in 1967, while the Haifa District (16 per cent) and Tel Aviv District (29.6 per cent) between them have lost nearly 10 per cent of their populations since 1948. The Northern District (15.3 per cent), on the other hand, has a slightly smaller share of the national population than in 1948, and the Central District (17.9 per cent) nearly 4 per cent more, which is a disappointment to the planners. The master plan for 1981 envisages generally denser population everywhere, and further settlement of the sparsely populated parts of the north (Dash and Efrat, 1964). The most extensive rural developments are planned north and west of Beer Sheva, but it must be remembered that detailed plans for the future will depend a great deal upon the configuration of Israels' frontiers. In this connection, the extent of border settlement in 1961 is worth noting (Fig. 8.5). In the north, in the Hula and Jordan valleys, in the hill country of central Israel and the Jerusalem corridor, and

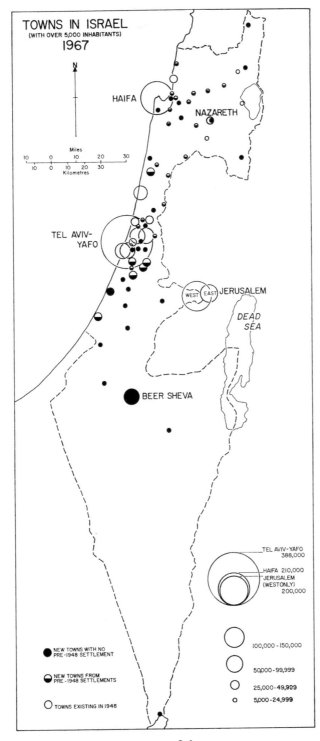

FIGURE 8.6

around the Gaza Strip in the south, *kibbutzim* in particular have been sited as much for strategic as economic advantage.

The deliberate policy of achieving redistribution of population by inducing immigrants to settle in peripheral areas, together with the fact that internal migration is not extensive (apart from some movement to the large towns), has resulted in local concentrations of particular immigrant groups. Veteran immigrants from Europe have tended to remain in the more central parts of the country where they were before 1948, but newer immigrants, many of them from Africa and Asia, are found more in peripheral developing areas and in the new towns of the north and south. Because of their comparatively high fertility and younger age distribution, birth rates tend to be higher in peripheral than central areas, levels of education are often lower, and Hebrew-speaking less dominant (Bachi, 1967). The challenge of integrating Israel's Jewish peoples thus has a geographical as well as a purely social dimension. The same remains true of relations between Jews and non-Jews, the latter being still very largely confined to the areas they inhabited in 1948. Some 57 per cent were rural-dwellers in 1967, chiefly in the highlands of Galilee and Judaea, the remaining 43 per cent inhabiting a handful of towns including Nazareth, Haifa, Akko, Ramla and Lod. Ninety-one per cent of non-Jews are in the north (Central Bureau of Statistics, 1968a). Israel's bedouin are shown in Figure 8.5 largely east of Beer Sheva.

Since the early days of Zionist settlement, the 'absorptive capacity' of Palestine has been the subject of much debate, with estimates tending to increase over the years. Israel's population today is probably only slightly greater than Palestine's in the time of Christ, and Israel's willingness to take in the 14 million Jews outside the country is undoubtedly based on real economic potential, although shortage of water is an increasingly serious problem. Thus there can be little doubt that the 1.3 million or so Palestine refugees could also in theory be settled in Israel.

Territories occupied by Israel in June 1967

A few weeks after occupying territory in Jordan, Egypt and Syria, Israel's Central Bureau of Statistics and the Israel defence forces conducted a full-scale population census in the Golan Heights on 10th August 1967, and elsewhere between 10th and 25th September 1967. Two volumes have so far been published giving basic population data (Central Bureau of Statistics, 1967) and information concerning housing conditions, household equipment, welfare and farming (Central Bureau of Statistics, 1968b). Further volumes are promised giving the results of a 20 per cent sample survey dealing with migration, levels of education, fertility, employment and many other details. How far this census material is reliable is uncertain. There can be little doubt that sound techniques were adopted, but the degree of co-operation received from the inhabitants is not known. In the shocked and somewhat fearful atmosphere of August and September 1967 it is quite probable that answers were generally honest and accurate. The material is in any case of sufficient importance to warrant a very brief summary of the findings in this book.

The West Bank

Of a total population of 498,637, 95 per cent were Moslems and 5 per cent were Christians. Only 56,440 persons were enumerated in actual refugee camps including those within towns; 345,270 lived in small villages or as nomads, and the rest in large villages with over 5,000 inhabitants or in towns. The largest towns were Nablus (44,223 including 2,424 in the refugee camp), Hebron (38,348), Bethlehem (16,313 including 1,874 in the refugee camp), and Tulkarm (15,275 including 5,200 in the refugee camp). The old city of Jerusalem (East Jerusalem) does not appear in the census, but elsewhere its population for 1967 is put at 65,800 (Central Bureau of Statistics, 1968a).

These figures do not, regrettably, specify the number of refugees registered with UNWRA remaining in the West Bank region. One report suggested that 200,000 persons left the West Bank in June 1967, half of whom were registered with UNWRA as refugees already (UNWRA, 1967a). The number remaining in refugee camps is clearly no indication, since two-thirds of all refugees lived outside camps. It was found, however, that 18.4 per cent of the total population could be regarded as having originated in Israeli territory, the origin of the household head being used to determine the origin of all its members. In this way more than 110,000 might reasonably be classified as Palestine refugees.

The Gaza Strip and North Sinai

The total population of the Gaza Strip in 1967 was 356,260, of whom 99 per cent were Moslems. This figure is almost exactly 100,000 fewer than the Egyptian estimate of 1966. Although 172,521 were counted in refugee camps, 61 per cent of the total were classified as originating in Israeli territory, which would mean approximately 217,300 Palestine refugees. Only 34,250 lived in villages, the rest being urban-dwellers in Gaza (87,793), Khan Yunis (29,522), and Rafah, Jabaliya and Deir el Balah, each with about 10,000 inhabitants apart from adjacent refugee camps. As in other regions, the population of the Gaza Strip is unusually young, 50.6 per cent being under the age of 15.

The total population of North Sinai was 33,440, of whom some 30,000 lived in El Arish, the rest in small villages. A similar number probably fled into the United Arab Republic during the 1967 hostilities (UNWRA, 1967b).

The Golan Heights

The total population of this small part of Syria was 6,396 in August 1967. Of these, 7 per cent were Arab Moslems, less than 1 per cent Christians, and the rest Druzes. The small town of El Quneitra was almost totally evacuated during the fighting.

Israeli *kibbutzim* have been established in the Golan Heights in the course of 1968 and 1969, a region not previously settled by the Jews. *Kibbutzim* have also been founded in the West Bank around Ezyon, a region of Zionist settlement which fell to the Arabs in 1948.

REFERENCES

ATLAS OF ISRAEL (1970), Amsterdam.
BACHI, R. (1967) 'Effects of migration on the geographic distribution of population in Israel', *International Union for Scientific Study of Population*, Conference Papers, Sydney, pp. 737–51.
BRUTZKUS, E. (1966) 'Planning of spatial distribution of population in Israel', *Ekistics*, 21, pp. 350–55.
CENTRAL BUREAU OF STATISTICS, Jerusalem:
   (1961) *Statistical Abstract of Israel, No. 12.*
   (1967) *Census of Population, 1967*, Vol. 1, Data from full enumeration.
   (1968a) *Statistical Abstract of Israel, No. 19.*
   (1968b) *Census of population, 1967*, Vol. 2, Housing conditions, household equipment, welfare assistance and farming in the administered areas.
   (1970) *Monthly Bulletin of Statistics* (January), Table 1.
DASH, J. and EFRAT, E. (1964) *The Israel Physical Master Plan*, Jerusalem.
HALPERIN, H. (1963) *Agrindus*, London.
KOLODNY, Y. (1963) 'Aspects et structures du peuplement urbain en Israel', *Méditerranée*, 4, pp. 21–47.
NOTESTEIN, F. W. AND JURKAT, E. (1945) 'Population problems of Palestine', *Milbank Memorial Fund Quarterly*, 23, pp. 307–52.
ORNI, E. and EFRAT, E. (1964) *Geography of Israel*, Jerusalem.
SMITH, C. G. (1968) 'Israel since the June War', *Geography*, 53, pp. 315–19.
SPIEGEL, E. (1967) *New towns in Israel*, Stuttgart and Bonn.
SUPER, A. S. (1961) 'Absorption of Immigrants', *Israel Today*, 18, Jerusalem.

TAMSMA, R. (1959) 'Changes in the Jewish population pattern of Israel, 1948–57', *Tijdschrift voor Economische en Sociale Geografie*, 50, pp. 170–82.

UNWRA, (1967a) *Emergency 1967*, Beirut.

UNWRA (1967b) *UNWRA and the Palestine Refugees*, Beirut.

Chapter 9
Jordan: a demographic shatter-belt
W B Fisher

The State

Since 1967 Jordan, alone of Middle Eastern countries and probably also uniquely in the world, has been a country where refugee and displaced persons form a near-majority of the population. Fluctuating political fortunes, with drastic alterations of territorial area as the result of conquest and occupation have had a greater effect in Jordan absolutely and proportionately, than in any other Middle Eastern state. Actual refugees, together with persons displaced from their original homes, amount to over 40 per cent, possibly 50 per cent, of the total population.

The country is of modern creation, dating from 1921 when the Emir Abdulla of the House of Hashem, son of the former Ruler of Mecca and brother of King Feisal of Iraq, was formally recognized as ruler of a newly defined territory lying entirely east and south of the River Jordan. This territory, named Transjordan, was expressly excluded and separated from the territory of Palestine to the west of the Jordan; both areas being allotted by the League of Nations under Mandate to Great Britain. Recognition of Transjordan as a separate political unit meant that it was excluded from the provisions of the Balfour Declaration regarding the establishment of a National Home for the Jews, which henceforward could apply only to Palestine. There were some Zionist protests at what was termed withdrawal and curtailment of the original Balfour Declaration, but the situation stood without alteration.

In 1924, the father of the Emir Abdulla, King Hussein of Mecca, became involved in fighting with the Wahhabi leader Ibn Saud, who eventually defeated and supplanted him as ruler of Arabia. Hussein was supported from Transjordan, and Wahhabi troops invaded this country, but soon withdrew southward. Abdulla then occupied the extreme southern areas around Ma'an and Aqaba, and proclaimed them part of Transjordan: a matter that was never formally resisted or disputed by Ibn Saud. The two incidents of the early 1920's—Zionist claims and Saudi dispute over the southern area—are mentioned here as adumbrating later attitudes which affected political trends in Transjordan. The fact of Zionist interest and possible claims east of the Jordan has never totally disappeared since;

and the Saudi rulers of Arabia, whilst making no overt moves to occupy Aqaba or Ma'an, nevertheless maintained a personal and national hostility to the Hashemite dynasty of Jordan down to a very few years ago. During the Jewish–Arab war of 1947–8 the presence of a Saudi Arabian military force in the south of Jordan that took little or no part in the fighting was an equivocal element that, in the opinion of some observers, introduced a disruptive factor into the Arab effort directed by the Hashemite rulers.

By 1946 the full independence of Transjordan was recognized by Britain, but admission to the United Nations was vetoed by Russia supported by the USA—both countries having reservations about Transjordan's independent status vis-à-vis Great Britain. Following the Arab–Israeli War of 1948, Transjordan annexed the area conquered by the Arabs (mainly by Transjordanian forces) which lay west of the Jordan, in the uplands of Judaea. This territory, taking in the Old City of Jerusalem, as well as the districts of Nablus and Hebron, though smaller in area than Transjordan, held considerably more population, and in 1949 the enlarged country was proclaimed the Kingdom of Jordan.

The last phase has been one of territorial loss. In 1967 Israeli forces occupied all Jordanian territory west of and up to the River Jordan; and the subsequent skirmishing, guerrilla activity and reprisals that have occurred have further led to a 'neutralizing' and partial demographic abandonment of the Jordan valley floor immediately east of the Jordan River, with groups of displaced persons moving eastwards into the hills of eastern Jordan.

These facts are mentioned in some detail in that they have exercised a close control of the population situation in Jordan. Several Middle Eastern states have, during the last fifty years, seen some movement or rectification of their national frontiers, but none on a scale comparable with that in Jordan, where the effects of alternate expansion and retraction have, as we noted, at times more than doubled the effective population of the state, and then turned a majority of these inhabitants into dispossessed refugees. Here is the reason for our choice of the expression 'shatter-belt'.

The country

Physiographically, Jordan consists of a considerable expanse of the plateau block of Arabia, with, on the west, portions of the Jordan rift, and a segment of the Judaean upland (Fig. 9.1). This last region, containing the towns of Jerusalem, Hebron and Nablus, is an anticline of Secondary and Tertiary rocks, chiefly calcareous, and generally permeable. Here, a westward situation gives rise to a moderate rainfall that in most years is sufficient for agriculture, especially in erosion basins where there are expanses of fertile soil. In places, however, especially eastwards, the series pass locally into marls that are extremely infertile, and rainfall declines

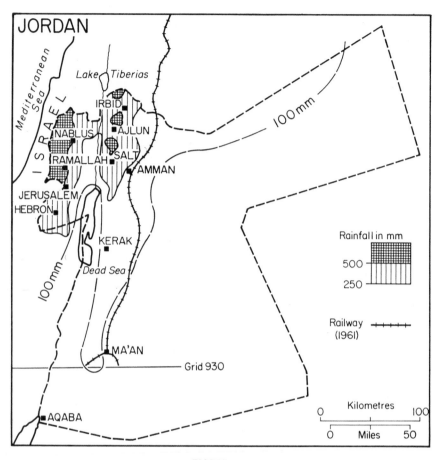

FIGURE 9.1

rapidly beyond the crest of the hills. The Jordan trough in its Jordanian portions lies between 200–400 m. below sea level, with the Dead Sea, part of which is Jordanian territory, lying at −400 m. The eastern edge of the Jordanian rift is formed by a series of imposing highlands that, within a few kilometres, attain 800 m. above sea level. This upraised and elevated edge of the main Arabian plateau is dissected by a number of streams, most of which flow directly westwards to the Jordan. A few, however, notably the Zerqa and Yarmuk, have cut back sufficiently extensively into the plateau surface to have developed subsequent or longitudinal sections. This deeply eroded highland zone is termed the north Jordan highland, and here, because of a rainfall that attains 500–600 mm. annually in the highest parts, settled agriculture is possible on the flatter, open slopes.

Eastwards, in the rain shadow of the Jordan highlands, rainfall rapidly declines to annual totals of 100 mm. or less, and except for a few localities such as Azraq and Mafraq where artesian water is available, the land can support only pastoral nomads.

In summary, rain-fed agriculture is possible within Jordan only in two districts—the greater part of the Judaean plateau except towards its eastern edge; and in the middle reaches of the northern Jordan highlands, especially those with a western aspect. Together these two areas amount to little more than 20 per cent of the total area of the country, and in north-west Jordan especially, soil erosion is a considerable danger. Irrigation is possible on the floor of the Jordan valley in areas away from the saline zone round the Dead Sea, and an important scheme based on the East Ghor canal, that used water from the tributary rivers, had been developed along the eastern floor of the Jordan valley north of the Dead Sea. The southern rift valley south of the Dead Sea as far as the Gulf of Aqaba remains arid and inhabited, at least in its Jordanian portion, only by a few nomads. The only other major resource is small but useful deposits of phosphate north and south of Amman; with a number of other minerals proved, but so far undeveloped. Petroleum is absent, though 'Tapline' from Saudi Arabia crosses Jordan territory. So long as Old Jerusalem and Bethlehem remained in Jordanian hands, there was a considerable tourist–pilgrim trade, both Christian and Moslem, that brought in around £10 million sterling annually; but with the alienation of Jerusalem since 1967 this source of revenue has greatly declined. As a result, *per capita* gross national product is low—$US 250 in 1967—and the country depends largely upon foreign subsidies from Britain, the USA, and from oil-rich states such as Kuwait; 1969 estimates of finance gave the total revenue as £J 15.3 million, expenditure £J 89.3 million, and foreign aid £J 49.3 million.

Population composition

During the period of maximum effective control of the national territory— i.e. between 1949 and 1967—two censuses were taken, one in 1952 that was really no more than an extended census of housing, with coefficients of occupation applied to give a national population; and a second, full national census in 1961. Besides these two sets of data, there are a number of estimations for different periods. In 1921 government sources estimated the East Bank population at 300–350,000 (at that time the so-called 'West Bank' formed a part of Palestine). In 1947, the East Bank territories were thought to have a population of 400,000 or 450,000.

It is not possible to follow in detail the changes in population that supervened as a result of the war of 1948. The frontier that emerged was no more than a solidification of a fortuitous military situation as it existed on a particular day. There was no negotiation or exchange of population, because the territorial basis could not easily be calculated, since the new frontier paid no attention to pre-existing administrative boundaries. Moreover, there was a massive movement of refugees within the Arab-held areas, originating from elsewhere in Palestine; and even when fighting stopped, a large number of Arabs formerly resident in the West Bank territories moved across the Jordan to the vicinity of Amman. This number is placed at over 150,000.

Thus we are forced to rely on the two sets of census data of the 1950's and 1960's. The 1952 enumeration gave a total population of 1,329,174; but this did not include Jordanian Army and Air Force personnel or their families living in military installations. Jordanian diplomats and families located abroad, and foreign residents were not included either. The 1961 census did, however, include all these categories, and given the small overall numbers—1,706,226 were counted—and the relatively high proportion of Jordanians in the armed forces (the country spends over 35 per cent of its budget on defence), the discrepancy is of some significance.

Another difficulty arises from the presence of nomadic pastoralists, who move regularly and seasonally, sometimes—though to a decreasing extent —across international frontiers. Most nomads tend to move either into or towards the hill areas (some of which also are cultivated, though not by the nomads) or to areas of wells where summer water is available. Besides these, however, are a considerable number of semi-nomads, who spend part or even most of the year as occupants of settled villages. In years of poor rainfall, the margin of occupation in the desert recoils, and numbers of Arabs who, in normal times, might move in search of pasture stay longer in the areas of cultivation, pasturing their animals on the stubble or fallow, and then in the scrub that almost always surrounds cultivation at only a short distance. There are few parts of Jordan where cultivation extends uninterruptedly over a wide area.

The 1952 census did not fully separate Bedouin 'tent dwellers' from the settled rural population. Closer enumeration in 1961 did, however, achieve a better separation, but figures for the two years are not as a result totally comparable. Moreover, because of their seasonal movement, tent dwellers were sometimes arbitrarily allotted to one or other census district, according to whether it appeared that they seemed to spend most of their cycle of movement in one or other district. This means that in the regions of the east and south, Ma'an and Kerak especially, total comparability between 1952 and 1961 is again not feasible. Nevertheless, with all the reservations as now given, it is possible to have a very meaningful view of population distribution (Table 9.1).

The 1961 census, being carried out under conditions of relative tranquillity, allowed a fair amount of detailed investigation, but there were the difficulties arising from nomadism and semi-nomadism, and the presence of refugees living in tents or in camps. The Jordanian Government designated a 'desert area', defined as lying south of parallel $29°57'30''$

TABLE 9.1   POPULATION OF JORDAN BY DISTRICT, 1952 AND 1961

District	1952		1961	
	Population	*Per cent of total*	*Population*	*Per cent of total*
East Bank	(586,885)	(44.1)	(900,776)	(52.8)
Amman	218,465	16.4	433,618	25.4
Belqa	64,926	4.9	79,057	4.6
Ajlun	213,877	16.1	273,976	16.1
Kerak	} 89,617	6.7	67,211	3.9
Ma'an			46,914	2.8
West Bank	(742,289)	(55.9)	(805,450)	(47.2)
Hebron	125,651	9.5	119,432	7.0
Jerusalem	301,402	22.7	344,270	20.2
Nablus	315,236	23.7	341,748	20.0
Jordan	1,329,174	100.0	1,706,226	100.0

North (Palestine Grid Line 930) and east of the Amman–Damascus rail-way line or any obvious settled villages, whichever lay farthest to the east (Fig. 9.1). This allowed division into three categories: fully urban, mainly rural, and scattered tents (Table 9.2). Fully urban populations were those resident in (a) all district capitals, (b) all localities of 10,000 inhabitants or more, (c) localities of 5,000–10,000 in which at least two-thirds of the active males were engaged in non-agricultural occupations and (d) suburbs of Amman and Jerusalem regardless of size in which the same conditions applied as in (c). Refugee camps, if located in urban areas as defined above, were classed as urban localities.

Mainly rural populations were defined as all persons other than those classified as fully urban, or as tent-dwellers. Thus besides the semi-nomads, mentioned above, the term *rural* also includes all the rural seden-tary population, together with all residents of army and refugee camps which were not located within the suburbs of large towns.

Scattered tent populations were regarded as comprising fully nomadic people and such semi-nomads as appeared to be on the move during the general period of the census. No distinction of this kind was made in the 1952 survey.

On a first examination, the most striking point is the importance of towns and urban populations, even in a country where there are no large manufacturing or international market centres, and where agriculture and pastoralism are the principal activities. The special position of Jerusalem, with its tourist/pilgrim function and conventual population is of impor-tance here, and there is the large refugee population in and around Amman. Nevertheless, the general situation reinforces the view of the Middle East, or at least this central part of it, as above all a region of towns and urbanism.

TABLE 9.2   MODE OF LIVING IN JORDAN, BY DISTRICT, 1961 CENSUS

Administra-tive district	Fully urban		Mainly rural		Scattered tents	
	Numbers	Per cent	Numbers	Per cent	Numbers	Per cent
Amman	359,979	83.0	53,353	12.3	20,286	4.7
Belqa	16,176	20.5	48,861	61.8	14,020	17.7
Ajlun	64,975	23.7	190,838	69.7	18,163	6.6
Kerak	7,422	11.1	51,634	76.8	8,155	12.1
Ma'an	15,551	33.2	11,500	24.5	19,863	42.3
Hebron	37,868	31.7	79,900	66.9	1,664	1.4
Jerusalem	154,059	44.7	185,485	53.9	4,726	1.4
Nablus	92,261	27.0	240,930	70.5	8,557	2.5
Jordan	748,291	43.9	862,501	50.5	95,434	5.6

Nomadism is probably slightly under-enumerated, mainly because of the difficulty of distinguishing degrees of partial nomadism, but also to a small extent due to the difficulty of being sure all scattered tents have been visited, and that some of the nomadic populations only partly located within Jordan (i.e. those that may move into arid Syria, Iraq or Saudi Arabia) were properly accounted for. Though the overall total is small, it will be remarked how, in the south (Ma'an District), nomads make up nearly one-half of the population; and the 15,000 or so pastoral nomads on the west bank were not confined wholly to the drier 'Wilderness' area, or the west Jordan valley floor. At least in 1961, whatever the situation ten years later under *de facto* Israeli rule, there were a few shepherds abiding in the fields around Jerusalem and Bethlehem.

Densities

In view of the large areas of desert, and the considerable concentration of population into the areas of higher rainfall, overall consideration by territory would largely be meaningless. Distinction is therefore made between the desert area and the rest of the country divided by district. This means (as the desert area lies entirely on the East Bank) that West Bank district densities include the 15,000 nomads living there, whereas the five East Bank districts are for population purposes regarded as excluding their desert areas and the populations living in them. The 'desert area', defined summarily by two lines, one east–west and the other north–south, does in fact include a number of small urban settlements, notably Azraq and Aqaba; and the populations of these have been included in the 'desert area'. In 1961 this was relatively unimportant, since all the towns were very small and therefore tended to balance the number of semi-nomads perhaps normally resident in desert areas but temporarily located in the cultivated areas and therefore enumerated with the 'mainly rural' population. However, with the growth of Aqaba in the 1960's such a procedure would now have much less validity.

TABLE 9.3   POPULATION DENSITIES OF JORDAN, BY DISTRICT, 1961

	Total population	*Persons per sq. km.*
Jordan	1,706,226	19
Settled area†	1,640,039	74
Desert area	66,187	1
East Bank*	834,589	51
West Bank‡	805,450	143
District		
Amman*	417,519	168
Belqa*	79,057	71
Ajlun*	256,017	66
Kerak*	63,064	13
Ma'an*	18,932	5
Hebron	119,432	110
Jerusalem	344,270	167
Nablus	341,748	136

Source: Official Census, 1961.
* Excluding the desert area and its population.
† Total area of Jordan *less* the desert area.
‡ Total area.

One point of interest is the northward concentration of the West Bank rural population. The province of Jerusalem, besides including the Old City, also takes in the substantial urban clusters of Ramallah (29,000) and Jericho (10,200), whereas the province of Nablus has fewer towns and Nablus itself had only 45,000 inhabitants in 1961. The closer rural settlement of the northern, less arid and more fertile West Bank area thus emerges. This pattern is, however, less apparent on the East Bank, since even allowing for the population of Amman City, there is a relatively dense rural occupation of the Belqa province (chief town Es Salt), which contains no large towns, and then a diminution in overall density northwards, even when the towns of Ajlun, Es Salt and Irbid are counted in.

Population composition

The 1961 census gives a detailed breakdown of age structure. Whilst Cyprus shows a preponderance of females, Jordan, like all its neighbouring Moslem countries (Iraq, Iran, Syria, Turkey, UAR), shows a greater proportion of males. It is possible that, in a strongly Moslem society, there is some under-enumeration of females, but this is hardly likely to be a total explanation, which must be sought in part at least in the higher survival rate of boys, and the tendency of many Moslem families to end a family with a boy. Males outnumber females in each age cohort with the exception of the groups 15–44 years, 50–54, and 70–74. Whilst the predominance of females among the working population (15–59) could well be expected, the almost exact balance between the sexes in the 60+ age groups (60,057 men to 57,113 women—respectively 6.9 and 6.8 per cent of the total number of each sex) may well reflect the harder way of life of many women and, possibly, their somewhat less favourable childhood circumstances as compared with the males. Figure 9.2 illustrates the details, and the curious slight aberration of a low 55–59 age group for both sexes will be noted. Whether this is a statistical anomaly or a real variation reflecting social influences is difficult to decide in the absence of comparable figures for other years.

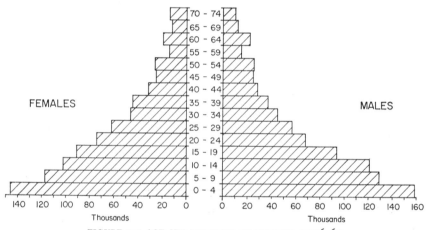

FIGURE 9.2 AGE-SEX PYRAMID OF JORDAN, 1956-65

If we consider the three broad categories of juveniles (0–14), working population (15–59) and elderly (60+) some interesting regional contrasts emerge. The West Bank (Jerusalem province especially) shows the highest proportion of old people, and Amman the least: the proportion of urban dwellers, the greater mobility of younger people, and differences in standards and ways of life enter in here. Nomadism might be held to have some but not a dominating effect upon longevity; but the situation cannot be analyzed because the totals given for age distribution do not always reconcile. In summary, however, the proportion of the population living in 'scattered tents' and over 60 given as 6.4 per cent of the total population group comes between the 5.7 per cent aged 60 and over of the 'fully urban' group, and the 7.9 per cent aged 60 and over of the 'mainly rural' group.

210

What is most apparent is the considerable uniformity of distribution throughout Jordan. With the one exception of the Aqaba area which, as a 'new' area of incomers has a high proportion in the adult working range (15–59), the rest of the country shows surprisingly little variation. Means for Jordan as a whole (1961) emerge as

Under 15 years   —   45.4 per cent of total population
15–59 years   —   47.7 per cent
60 and over   —   6.9 per cent

Provincial variation ranges as follows:

Under 15 years: Minimum (43.5 per cent) Belqa District; Maximum (48.0) Hebron District.
15–59: Minimum (46.2 per cent) Ajlun District; Maximum (50.8) Ma'an District.
60 and over: Minimum (4.8 per cent) Amman; Maximum (8.0) Jerusalem.

Homogeneity is thus a feature rather than variation, a situation that repeats in other aspects of the demography of Jordan.

Besides this, we have the familiar phenomenon of a 'young' population. As is obvious from the figures given, nearly one-half of the Jordanian population is aged 15 or less, and with rapidly rising population numbers, the tendency will be for the younger groups to increase their proportion of the total population. The effect of this on economic and social needs, beginning with the provision of educational facilities; and also the political implications, especially vis-à-vis Israel, where average age of population is now over 25 and tending to rise, are especially critical.

Minorities

Though the large majority of Jordanians are Sunni Moslems, there are a small number of others, located on both sides of the River Jordan. On the East Bank the Circassian element is the largest of the non-Arab, non-Moslem groups. These people, 20,000 to 25,000 in number, are descendants of colonists deliberately 'planted' by Ottoman Turkish rulers during the last third of the nineteenth century, and beginning of the twentieth. Transjordan itself was thought to have 81 per cent Sunni Moslems, 3 per cent Greek Orthodox, 3 per cent Roman Catholics, and the rest mainly Shi'a Moslems, Druzes, Jews and other Christians. The West Bank held 89 per cent Sunni Moslems and 7 per cent Christians; and refugees from Israeli Palestine were 93 per cent Moslem (Shi'as being very few) and 7 per cent Christians. This means that present day Jordan is about 82 per cent Sunni, 10 per cent Christian, and the rest about equally Shi'a and Druzes. Modern Amman itself owes its revival to Circassian colonization

(Hacker, 1960). Though a substantial city (Philadelphia) in Roman times, the site was later abandoned, and in the mid-nineteenth century was no more than a watering place for nomads. Its development began with the settling of Circassian immigrants in 1878, and though now overwhelmingly Arab and Moslem, there are still some Circassians both in the city itself and in the district. These people, partially though incompletely assimilated, still speak their own Caucasian languages usually but not entirely in the home, and employ Cyrillic orthography alongside Arabic, and are Orthodox Christians.

Other Christian groups were located in and around Jerusalem. A very small number of Arabs are Christian; these are, or were, to be found mainly in the towns—besides Jerusalem, also Bethlehem, Ramallah and Hebron. In addition there were the inhabitants of Christian shrines and monasteries, who for the most part represented a temporary element in the population. In addition, a number of Druzes live in northern Judaea and Samaria (district of Nablus). The disturbed conditions of the last thirty years have led to migration, especially by Arab Christians and Druzes, whilst the existence of a Circassian Guard for the Royal Household has tended to maintain a certain separate identity for the East Bank Circassians, who would otherwise gradually absorb into the Arab population. Besides working as farmers and merchants, some Circassians find employment in the motor repair trade and other activities of the capital. Numbers are difficult to obtain, hence one can do no more than accept the proportions given above, which refer to 1958–60 (Notes et Etudes Documentaires, 1964).

Towns

With only one set of census figures, any detailed analysis of town size and development cannot be profound—moreover the existence of large-scale refugee groups adds a further distortion and disequilibrium to the normal processes of town development. The position of Jerusalem is also anomalous. Jordanian territory included until 1967 the Old City, and nearby suburbs like Bethany. However, Jewish immigrants built a new settlement after 1948 in the Israeli corridor area which has come to add a considerable outer 'ring' to the Old City. Under British mandate, expansion of Jerusalem was not greatly encouraged, for political and to a less extent cultural, tourist, and archaeological reasons, but after 1948 considerable Israeli development took place, with an 'Iron Curtain' separating Arab and Jewish Jerusalem. In the present context, therefore, to regard Jerusalem as nominally only the third city of Jordan is in one sense factually and politically accurate, but in another it is hardly realistic. There is, however, the even larger example of East and West Berlin.

There is here a clear indication, though on a small scale, of a metropolitan primacy—at least, so long as one excludes the equivocal site of

TABLE 9.4   LOCALITIES IN JORDAN WITH OVER 15,000 INHABITANTS, 1961

Rank	Locality	Males	Females	Total	Males per 100 females
1	Amman	130,688	115,787	246,475	113
2	Zerqa	53,539	42,541	96,080	126
3	Jerusalem	31,563	28,925	60,488	109
4	Nablus	23,224	22,255	45,479	105
5	Irbid	23,064	21,621	44,685	107
6	Hebron	19,499	18,369	37,868	106
7	Bethlehem	17,253	18,482	35,735	93
8	Ramallah	14,402	14,867	29,269	97
9	Tulkarm	10,632	10,058	20,690	106
10	Es Salt	8,119	8,057	16,176	101

Jerusalem. Amman has developed as the dominant town of the country by a considerable margin, and although much of this could be held to be the result of refugee movement, there is the other matter that the town has wholly developed from nothing in less than a century. And it might be argued that it was the relatively stable, established functions of Amman— housing, infrastructure, means of defence and communication—that acted to draw in the large numbers of depressed and displaced Arabs.

It will further be noted that not all the district capitals are large: Es Salt is marginal, but Aqaba, Kerak and Ma'an, all with fewer than 10,000 inhabitants each, are smaller than towns like Zerqa, Tulkarm or Jenin. Some 43.7 per cent of Jordanians in 1961 lived in the 18 towns of 10,000 population or over, and of these, only one-third, or 14.4 per cent of the total, lived in Amman. This is far less in proportion than in the Lebanon; and with the two nearly equal cities of Damascus and Aleppo in Syria the situation is clearly very far from parallel—though one might regard Jerusalem as nearer in actual size and function than real numbers suggest. Some 26.5 per cent of the Jordanian population lived (1961) in localities of 1,000–5,000 size, and only 5.1 per cent in localities of the 5,000–10,000 range. This considerable hiatus in ranking size reflects the lack of economic resources.

Another index of some significance is that of males to females. In the largest towns there is a clear male predominance in numbers, but in the smaller towns this proportion is reversed. Part of this may be due to the relatively large accretion of population numbers in larger towns by inward migration, which tends to affect younger males, since they are the more mobile; but this is by no means a total explanation. Fragmentary results and inconsistency in age counts may also be another factor.

Population movement

Data on crude birth rates have been available since 1951 up to 1967 and these have fluctuated from figures of 35–39 per thousand in the early 1950's to figures of well over 40 in the 1960's; statistics for 1965–7 show a mean crude birth rate of 47 per thousand (Fig. 9.3). Commenting on these figures, the Demographic Yearbook for 1969 estimated that the 1950–60 figures were 20 per cent deficient, and that there had thus been no real increase in fertility. Birth rates of over 45 per thousand could hence be normal; and it is also relevant to note that in Arab refugee camps crude birth rates of over 50 per thousand have been recorded. Moreover, a survey by the International Bank in 1955 showed that in the irrigated area of the East Jordan valley a group of 100 women in childbearing age could be expected to have 80 children among them aged 0–4 years—this not counting older children. Evidence of a slightly different kind suggests that in some areas at least of Jordan, a family of between seven and eight children is the norm.

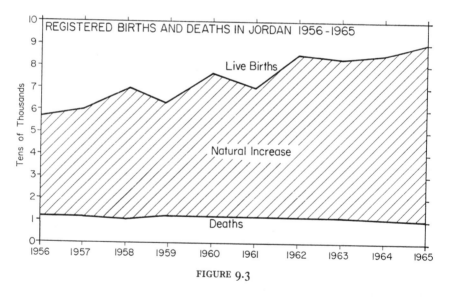

FIGURE 9.3

In some, but not all, Arab countries, birth rates in the towns are somewhat lower than among the rural population. Even, however, if this were in fact true of the state of Jordan, the highest birth rates among displaced persons and refugees (who are numerous in the large towns) could be held to offset this tendency. The rapid growth of Amman especially owes something to a high rate of births, as well as to inward migration.

Death rates again were probably seriously under-recorded in the 1950's when an average of 9.1 per thousand was officially given, yearly figures fluctuating between 12 and 7, with a marked decline to lower figures in the last years of the decade. Other, later figures suggest a figure of 16 per thousand in the period 1965–7, and these seem more credible. Outside surveys made among refugee camps have shown death rates in the neighbourhood of 20 per thousand, hence while one may well accept the tendency towards decline shown in official Jordanian figures, death rates of 15–17 per thousand would appear to be closely comparable with those of Syria, Turkey and Iraq, and, whilst there have been considerable programmes of aid and infrastructure development since 1950 that have greatly improved standards in the towns and adjacent countryside, the number of refugees, with their higher morbidity, has also increased.

Infant mortality has responded markedly to the improvements just mentioned. Hospitals are more widespread, sanitation has improved, communications are better, and greater tertiary education has increased the numbers of doctors and nurses. Jordan is more accessible to outside than some other countries of the Middle East, and in child care the effects are seen in a fall from 80–100 deaths per thousand live births to figures of 55–60. These again may be serious under-enumerations, but a downward trend is once more clear.

Migration has, as we have seen, played a predominant part in the population situation of Jordan. In 1948 some 350,000 refugees from western and northern Palestine moved into the West Bank area; and these refugees were formally accepted as Jordanian citizens in 1950. By a process of natural increase and accretion due to further inward movement, the refugee population grew to 631,000 in 1961, some 37 per cent of the then total population. As we have already seen, numbers of these transferred across the River Jordan to the East Bank after 1950, and then further large numbers moved during and after the events of 1967—precise numbers not being known, but official estimates give 200,000.

Governmental statistics also show a movement by Jordanians in and out of the country, of the order of about 65,000 annually. About 10 per cent more leave than arrive, and whilst many of these are 'displaced' individuals or groups formerly from Palestine, others are not. Many students of various kinds move abroad for training and a proportion of these do not return; Jordanians/Palestinians find employment in other Arab countries and some of this is temporary, leading to eventual return, but part is not. Other Arabs also migrate into Jordan in relatively small numbers, sufficient perhaps to make good the net loss of Jordanian nationals. There is also the presence of military and para-military units, which has been a feature of the period since 1967. Some of these are of Iraqi and Syrian origin, others are Palestinian Arab, and they are sufficiently numerous to have been able to challenge and even supplant the authority of Amman in certain districts. These groups also have followers, partly domestic, and in some cases clandestine, but they are highly temporary and a special phenomenon arising from the disturbed political situation, and their demographic importance is small, though not by any means negligible.

Population growth and resources

The confused population situation of the last few years, and gains and losses of territory, make detailed comparisons difficult. We have, however, the basic fact of a stable or even possibly increasing birth rate at high levels, together with a generally declining death rate. This means a net increment of 3.1 per cent in the years since 1965, as compared with an annual increase possibly of the order of 2.5 to 2.7 per cent at earlier periods. Latest estimates thus suggest that the population of Jordan could double itself in 21 years from 1969 to reach 5.6 millions by 1990. This is, of course, on the basis of the 1950 boundaries.

It might well be argued that, with the growing urbanization of the Jordanian population, there could be a fall-off in population increase because of a diminution of fertility. However, the investigations of Yaukey (1961) in the Lebanon, and conditions in Egypt where, according to El Badry (1965), there is only a slight variation in the long term between urban and rural rates of fertility, do not suggest that urbanization will dramatically or even substantially reduce net reproduction rates. Sedentarization of nomadic populations will also, by lowering death rates, lead to higher survival rates.

We thus reach the situation that unless there are major demographic calamities, and/or considerable population control, major economic development will be essential even to maintain existing standards. Should circumstances arise in the near future by which the Jordanian Government re-assumes effective control of the West Bank area, the problem would be slightly easier in that there is greater scope for agricultural development; and, moreover, with the movement of displaced persons eastward from this territory, it could be held that the possibility of ultimate return to the West Bank by those who left it after 1967 would in some limited degree help conditions on the East Bank, which now has an enormous demographic problem.

As we have seen, there are two small regions of the East Bank (the northwest highlands and the immediately adjacent Jordan valley floor) where further agricultural development could be undertaken. The key to development along the eastern rift valley floor is irrigation, and plans were well advanced to impound the waters of certain side valleys (the Wadis Ziglab, Shuaeb, Qufrain and Zerqa) to provide extra water supplies for the already existing East Ghor canal system. Soil salinity limits southward development towards the Dead Sea; but given political stability, the schemes already planned plus some further development involving total use of East

Bank wadi flow, and careful use of groundwater where this exists, much more could be done.

On the plateau, problems are different. Excessive near-monoculture of cereals and a limited range of other crops in an area of very broken relief and highly episodic rainfall result in locally severe problems of soil erosion. Slopes up to 40° are still cultivated, and the habit of summer grazing by animals, especially goats, brought in by nomads or semi-nomads prevents regeneration of vegetation that is subject to depletion by man and animals, and hence natural fixation of soil.

In some areas, the process has now gone too far, and whole hillsides are stripped to bedrock. Others, as yet cultivated, will go the same way in the very near future, unless rapid conservation measures can be taken. What are needed, in very bald outline, are:

(1) Selective afforestation of certain areas. There are still wide areas of dwarf oak forest that were once far more developed in type of tree, and extensive in area: these could be the basis of a forest policy that would be the basis of a conservation programme. Forest activities (including tourism) could develop.

(2) Cultivation of steeply sloping areas should either be stopped (in the zones of greatest slope) or physically stabilized by valley plugs. Gradoni terracing (contour-aligned low walls to retain soil wash) and a reconstruction of holdings should be undertaken where necessary. It might be necessary also to clear some land at present tree-covered, in order to compensate farmers for loss of steeply sloping land now cultivated. This latter, and grazing land, might be afforested as overall compensation and balance.

(3) A policy for animal husbandry that will allow closer use than at present of an area which, in the interests of cultivation, will have to be restricted. It would be unsatisfactory and for humanitarian, economic and political reasons, inept to attempt to exert pressure on pastoral nomads with the idea of extinguishing their way of life. Hence, in a wider scheme of environmental regeneration, the special needs and contributions of pastoralists should be provided for and encouraged. This could be achieved by selective improvement of grazing, marketing, and of social conditions among the pastoralists.

(4) Attempts to improve resource use by more careful crop programmes, bearing in mind land capabilities in relation to market orientation. Crops such as citrus fruit, tomatoes, export items like avocado, strawberries and celery are now successfully produced in Israel; and whilst conditions in East Jordan are not wholly comparable, there is sufficient geographical similarity to suggest that Arab cultivation could be at least partially successful.

(5) The aims detailed above imply an extensive programme of rural regeneration. To follow the economic pattern outlined, and develop

217

superior and more intensive use of a deteriorating natural environment involves both general education and technical improvement. Schemes of agricultural extension services, provision of simple, therefore cheap but improved equipment, and a revived pattern of general education are involved here.

Some of this has already been achieved, as the result of governmental action (e.g. the Development Plans of 1962–7 and later) and the co-operation of international agencies, based on aid schemes. Improvements can be seen in several sectors, ranging from contour terracing, stream control, and the provision of better plant strains and marketing organization. It is questionable, however, as to whether, in view of the intensely disturbed political and social conditions, such action will be vigorous, rapid and fundamental enough to answer the needs of the present Jordanian populations.

There remain the opportunities for commerce and industrial growth. These, given the interior situation of the country, and its enclosure by other sovereign states—even the approaches to the one Jordanian seaport of Aqaba are controlled by Egypt and Israel—offer no obvious considerable openings for development beyond a range of manufacturing for the domestic market that would not involve sophisticated or highly capital intensive plant. Tourism, even with the loss of Old Jerusalem, remains a possibility, though on a reduced scale; but a tranquil political climate is essential here. Exploitation of phosphates and potash are other natural advantages, but it is clear that Jordan will remain dependent on outside aid. As the example of Israel may demonstrate, aid in various forms is conducive to permanent economic development if rightly applied. Problems in Jordan are, unhappily, more severe—environmentally, politically and socially; and capital inflow is less. However, as the outside world bears a considerable responsibility for the unfortunate demographic situation that Jordan now experiences, it is only right to expect that foreign assistance should be forthcoming to attempt regeneration. The demographic shatter-belt that now characterizes Jordan is a direct effect of policies initiated and followed, in part at least, by outside powers—Jordan itself is in greatest measure an unfortunate victim of processes over which it has had no real control.

REFERENCES

DEPARTMENT OF STATISTICS, HASHEMITE KINGDOM OF JORDAN, Amman.
(1961) *The East Jordan Valley: a Social and Economic Survey.*
(1961) *First Census of Population and Housing.*

(1967) *Population and Labour Force in the Agricultural Sector. Statistical Yearbooks of Jordan.*

EL BADRY, M. A. (1965) 'Trends in the components of population growth in the Arab countries of the Middle East: a survey of present information', *Demography*, 2, pp. 140–86.

FISHER, W. B. *et al.* (1969) *Soil and Land Potential Survey of the Highlands of North-West Jordan*, Special Report No. 11 to the Ministry of Agriculture, Jordan.

HACKER, J. (1960) *Modern Amman A Social Study*, Durham.

INTERNATIONAL BANK FOR RECONSTRUCTION AND DEVELOPMENT (1957) *The Economic Development of Jordan*, Baltimore.

NOTES ET ETUDES DOCUMENTAIRES (1964) *L'Evolution de la Population dans les Pays du Proche-Orient*, La Documentation Française.

YAUKEY, D. (1961) *Fertility Differences in a Modernizing Country*, Princeton.

Chapter 10
Saudi Arabia: population and the making of a modern state
R McGregor

The late King Abdul Aziz Ibn Saud completed his conquest of the Hejaz in 1926 and by 1932 had consolidated his authority over eight-tenths of the Arabian Peninsula, thus bringing into being the Kingdom of Saudi Arabia. The establishment of a central authority in an area so vast and inhospitable, which had never known political unity, and over a people notable for their individualism and indiscipline must rank as one of the remarkable achievements of the first half of this century. His success was founded on military skill, religious fervour and adaptability to the physical environment, in which only the bedouin and his camel were mobile. The physical environment is, and is likely to remain, the dominant determinant of life in Saudi Arabia, although the possibilists can point to the increasing relevance of non-geographical variables, as the country's oil-based development brings modern technology to bear on the environmental situation.

Arabia is the largest peninsula in the world and Saudi Arabia occupies about 2.2 million sq. km. of the total 2.7 million sq. km. There are two distinct geological sections. The first consists of the Western Province, the Hejaz, and the western part of the central province, Najd. This area is composed of ancient crystalline rocks, which were part of the ancient Gondwanaland. The second of the major sections, in the eastern part of the peninsula, was once under the ancient sea called Tethys, a remnant of which is the Persian or Arabian Gulf. Today the Eastern Province is principally composed of sedimentary rocks.

The surface of the land takes the form of a north–south range of mountains down the Red Sea coast, rising steeply from a narrow coastal plain with an average elevation of over 1,200 m. The eastern slopes of the range are much gentler and give way to the central plateau, Najd, where the land gradually descends to the low-lying Eastern Province. In some places the decline in elevation is broken as a result of differential erosion by westward-facing north–south escarpments. There are three main areas of sandy desert—the Great Nafud (5,720 sq. km.), the Rub'al Khali or Empty Quarter (780,000 sq. km.) and the Dahna, a 25–30 km. wide river of sand extending for 1,300 km. and connecting the Great Nafud with the Empty Quarter. Other types of terrain are the *sabkhat* (salt flats) of the

Eastern Province, the *hadhabat* (gravel plains) also in the Eastern Province, and the more common *dikakah* areas, where the plains are covered with a thin mantle of sand which permits the growth of bushes and grass often forming hummocks. The extreme northern areas of Saudi Arabia are geographically closer to the Syrian than to the Arabian desert. In the western part of the country a common feature are the *harrat*, lava tracts of recent origin. One other feature worth mentioning is the Summan plateau lying between the eastern coastal strip and the Dahna, which is composed of hard rock with an average width of 150 km. and an altitude of 300 m.

The factor of climate is of major importance and is the cause of the aridity of the land, less than 0.2 per cent of which is cultivated and perhaps a maximum of 15 per cent cultivable (Mallakh, 1966). Rainfall is seasonal (winter months) and unpredictable and, except in the south-west, where the effect of the Indian Ocean monsoons are felt, varies on average between 10 mm. and 150 mm. and in certain areas is completely lacking in some years. The temperatures are high in the summer (as much as 47°C in the interior) and the summer heat is combined with high humidity in the coastal areas. In the winter months temperatures are between 10°C and 20°C in the coastal region, but fall below freezing on occasion at high altitudes. There are no perennial rivers and vegetation is of course sparse.

The early years

That was the harsh physical setting to the new Kingdom of Saudi Arabia. In the absence of reliable statistics the population of the country in 1932 might be estimated to be between 1½ and 2 million, of whom at least one-half would be rural settled, more than a quarter nomadic and the balance (perhaps one-fifth) could loosely be described as urban. (The populations of some thirty ports and inland towns mentioned in the *Admiralty Geographical Handbook* (1946) and based on estimates made at various times before the war add up to a total of 330,000 persons.) The largest town was Mecca, which is unlikely to have exceeded 50,000 souls. The country's economy was based upon oasis agriculture of a simple type, small-scale fishing along the coasts, pearling in the Persian Gulf, nomadic pastoralism, commerce (particularly in the Hejaz) and income from the Mecca pilgrimage (about £3 million annually). There were no metalled roads, no railways (the Hejaz railway had not been repaired) and only a limited telegraph and postal system started by the Turks. *Per capita* income was among the lowest in the world. The administrative structure was rudimentary and traditional. In 1926 Ibn Saud issued a statute which has been called the Constitution of the Kingdom of the Hejaz; although it has been modified frequently and some of its provisions have remained a dead letter, it is still fundamental to the current political structure. Article 5 reads: 'All administration is in the hands of His Majesty King Abdul

Aziz Ibn Saud. His Majesty is bound by the laws of the Sharia.' The Kingdom was divided into two viceroyalties, which were in turn divided into provinces. There were only two embryonic Ministries—Foreign Affairs and Finance. The system was in fact based on Islamic and Arabian traditions; the King had sole executive power, although he would seek the advice of tribal and privy counsellors and the Ulema (learned men). The legal system was the Islamic (Sharia) and the Hanbali School of Law was the officially recognized school. The King (as Imam) and the Qadhis (Judges) formed the judiciary. *'Urf*, customary tribal law, was prohibited (Shamma, 1965). It was in short a theocratic state.

Saudi Arabia did not essentially change until after the 1939–45 war. Although an oil concession was granted in 1933 to Standard Oil of California (subsequently joined by Texaco, Standard Oil of New Jersey and Mobil Oil to form the Arabian American Oil Company) and the first oil was exported in 1938, the war prevented the development of the oil resources and in 1944 production was the equivalent of only three days' production in 1969.

Nevertheless, despite its extreme poverty, backwardness and small population, Saudi Arabia in those years enjoyed considerable prestige in the Arab world. This was partly owing to its custodianship of the main holy places of Islam, but it also owed something to the outstanding personality of Ibn Saud and to the fact that most of the other Arab countries had still to achieve complete independence.

The post-war history of Saudi Arabia is closely related to the phenomenal expansion of its oil industry and the use to which the income from oil was put. How phenomenal that expansion has been can be seen from the fact that between 1946 and 1968 oil production rose from 60 million barrels to 1,114 million barrels and the government's revenue from oil from $10 million to $926 million.

Oil brought benefits and posed problems in the fields of domestic and foreign affairs. Domestically, it enabled the Saudis to free themselves from the limitations of a harsh environment in which, by our standards at least, life was 'nasty, brutish and short'. However, it created political and social problems associated with the adaptation of a traditional society to the requirements of modernization. Eventually it brought Saudi Arabia into greater contact with the world in general and other Arab states in particular. Increasing wealth made it feasible for the government to play a greater role in international affairs and on the Middle East stage, but at the same time economic dependence on oil imposed certain limitations on freedom of political action and coloured relations with the major powers and other Arab states. The place and influence of Saudi Arabia in the Arab world has been notably affected by the degree of success and failure in handling these problems.

The post-war years

The post-war years can be conveniently divided into the reigns of Ibn Saud, Saud and Faisal. During the last eight years of Ibn Saud's reign (1945–53) the personal system of government, which might be termed benevolent absolutism, showed itself increasingly ill-equipped to cope with the opportunities and problems created by rapidly growing wealth in a traditional society. Yet his great personal prestige enabled him to hold together the various strands in Saudi Arabian society or at least to prevent the tensions and dissensions breaking through the façade of order and harmony. He himself recognized in his last year the need for some devolution of executive authority and decreed the establishment of a Council of Ministers.

Ibn Saud also became increasingly preoccupied with foreign affairs. His long-standing friendship with, or respect for, Britain survived his dislike of British policy towards Palestine but was severely tested by British championing of the claims of Abu Dhabi and Muscat to the Buraimi oasis. His ancestral claims prevented any settlement of Saudi Arabian boundaries with most of his Arab neighbours. His traditional feud with the Hashemites affected his relations with Jordan and Iraq and contributed to his broad alignment with Egypt and Syria in inter-Arab policies and rivalries. Saudi Arabia has traditionally maintained and sought to maintain good relations with Egypt; this did not change with the advent of President Nasser but only after Nasser tried to export his brand of revolutionary socialism.

The personal system of government continued under Saud. Unfortunately, he did not have the capacity to make it work and, in fairness, the business of government became progressively more complicated, as growing oil wealth and the impact of the outside world made possible and stimulated the demand for economic and social development. There was no proper development planning and budgetary control, and some of the revenue from oil was dissipated in conspicuous and wasteful spending. The conservative elements disliked the effect which wealth and new ideas were having on the traditional society and the discontent in the Hejaz and the Eastern Province took the form of a stirring of separatist sentiments, which, if allowed to swell, would have threatened the unity of the state.

The crisis occurred in 1958. The primary cause was the levelling off of oil income (which had grown from $170 million in the year of Saud's accession to $341 million in 1955) and the inability of the government to adjust expenditure to available income. Prince Faisal was called upon to take over the government of the country and, with the help of the International Monetary Fund, a stabilization programme was drawn up, which by 1960 had put the country on a sound economic footing. Saud again took control of the government, but his health deteriorated and Faisal reassumed control in December 1961 and in 1964 replaced his elder brother as King.

The last decade of Saudi Arabian history is dominated by Faisal, both as *de facto* ruler from 1961 to 1964 and as *de jure* ruler since 1964. It is during this period that the country has made rapid economic progress, that the government has grappled seriously with the social problems inherent in transforming a traditional society into a modern state and that Saudi Arabia has assumed a major place in the Arab world, second perhaps only to the United Arab Republic. King Faisal has himself played the key role in all these processes. A by-product of the development of the decade has been the beginnings of serious documentation, statistical and other, which makes it possible for the first time to study the part played by human resources in the growth of the state or, in other words, the interrelation between demography and development.

The 1962–3 population census

The first and only census of population in Saudi Arabia was held in 1962–3 and the government repudiated the results. The United Nations' own estimates, based on conjecture, give figures of 6.53 and 6.99 million for the total population in 1963 and 1967 respectively, the annual rate of increase is said to be 1.7 and density per sq. km. to be 3 (United Nations, 1967). A sample survey of population was conducted in 1966 and a survey of establishments in 1967, the results of which may be published in the near future (Central Department of Statistics, 1967).

Although the Saudi Arabian Government has not published all the data obtained in the 1962–3 census, some statistics are available from the *Survey of Population and Establishments* published in April 1963 by the Department of Statistics of the Saudi Arabian Ministry of Finance and National Economy (Asfour, 1965; Abdo, 1969). These statistics contain information about sex, total population and (except for Riyadh) broad age groups of the population of the main cities; an unpublished age grouping of the population of the whole Kingdom is also available.

The total population according to the 1962–3 census was 3,302,330 and the age structure is shown in Table 10.1. An obvious source of weakness in these figures is the overlapping of the two middle age groups. The figures for the cities show, as one would expect, a higher proportion of young persons aged 10–30 than in the whole Kingdom, as well as an excess of males. The proportion of children under ten in Saudi Arabia is exceptionally high, even by South-West Asian standards. Additional information on the age distribution of the population is given in a World Health Organization report published in July 1963 (Asfour, 1965). Data furnished to the World Health Organization team by the Saudi Arabian authorities and obtained from sampling studies undertaken by the team itself revealed that in 62

TABLE 10.1   POPULATION OF FOUR MAJOR CITIES IN SAUDI ARABIA,
BY SEX AND AGE GROUPS, 1963

City	Age groups (numbers)					Sex (percentage)	
	Under 10	10–30	30–50	Over 50	Total	Male	Female
Mecca	55,873	57,285	33,936	11,547	158,641	53	47
Jedda	49,959	52,275	34,314	11,263	147,811	57	43
Madina	25,573	25,252	15,174	5,999	71,998	52	48
Taif	22,653	19,913	9,030	2,358	53,954	54	46
Total of cities	154,058	154,725	92,454	31,167	432,404	—	—
Percentage of total city population	35.6	35.7	21.4	7.3	100	—	—
Percentage of total population of kingdom	37.8	30.8	21.4	10.0	100	—	—

Sources: Department of Statistics, Saudi Arabia.
  Survey of Population and Establishments, April 1963.

villages in the Taif district 49.3 per cent of the population were under
15 years, while in Riyadh 41.2 per cent were under 15 years, 54.5 per cent
between 15 and 59 and 4.3 per cent were 60 and above.

The report also estimated on the basis of a few sample studies that the
crude death rate was about 24 per thousand and the infant mortality rate
in the region of 260 per thousand live births. The effect of malnutrition and
disease on the life expectancy of the people was referred to in the following
passage:

'Evidence of malnutrition and under-nourishment could be seen among
the patients in the out-patient clinics and among the children in the
streets, in cities and villages. Due to subsistence level of living and poor
diet of the majority of the population the growth and development of
their children could not be adequate. Incidence of tuberculosis among
the people seemed to be high. Many preventable diseases were still
consuming much of the strength and energy of the adult population.
Although it was not possible to collect data for constructing a life-table,
the life expectancy at birth among the people in Saudi Arabia could not
be more than thirty.'

The birth rates in two villages (Erga and Manfooha) were found to be
42.35 and 51.72 respectively. Owing to early marriage and high fertility
among females and the high percentage of children under 15 years of age
among both the rural and urban populations, the report considered that
rural population increase would be expected to be at least 1.5 per cent;
there can, however, be little doubt that much higher natural increase rates
occur.

The areal distribution of the population is clearly associated with environmental factors, particularly rainfall, underground water resources and land formation. Thus within an overall population density of 3 per sq. km., the south-western part of the country has the highest density of 29, while the three great sand deserts are unpopulated (Fig. 10.1). Many of the population live in desert oases that are separated by vast sparsely inhabited expanses, and settlements are generally small; the number of settlements with more than 20,000 inhabitants in 1962–3 was only 11, and the nomadic population represented 20.82 per cent of the total population (Abdo, 1969).

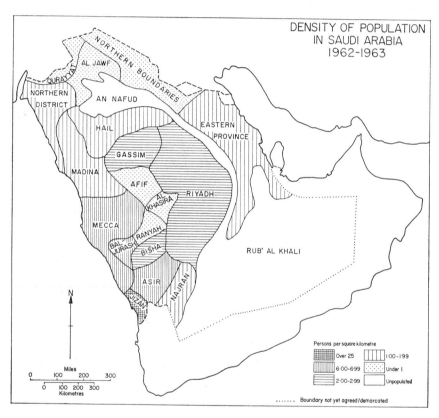

FIGURE 10.1

Published figures are not available to determine accurately the breakdown in 1962–3 between urban, rural settled and nomadic populations. On the basis, however, of the above-mentioned nomadic percentage and an estimated 50–60 per cent of the population employed in the agricultural sector (a small percentage of which was probably semi-nomadic) a rough breakdown would be:

	Number	*Per cent*
Urban	800,000	24
Nomadic	700,000	21
Rural settled	1,800,000	55
Total	3,300,000	100

Urbanization

The speed of urbanization can readily be seen from a comparison of the urban populations in 1932 and 1962–3. From the estimated 300,000 in 1932 the urban population increased by about 170 per cent to 800,000 in 1962–3; during the same period total population increased 120 per cent from a base of 1½ million. Riyadh (197,000) had replaced Mecca as the most populous city and six towns had populations of over 50,000 (Riyadh, Mecca, Jedda, Madina, Taif and Hofuf), whereas in 1932 only Mecca had perhaps just attained that figure. However, unlike many other developing countries, Saudi Arabia has low urban primacy, because Riyadh has not yet achieved marked numerical supremacy over Mecca and Jedda.

The location of towns in 1932 was essentially on an historical pattern, imposed primarily by physical environment. The 'break in transportation' theory—'population and wealth tend to collect wherever there is a break in transportation' (Cooley, 1894)—largely applied, and the Arabian peninsular trade routes were determined by the difficulties of the terrain and the availability of water. The primacy of Mecca, which was on the main trade route, owed much to its status as the first holy city in Islam and the place of pilgrimage. The port of Jedda also gained from the pilgrim traffic (although Yanbo was the main pilgrimage port at that time) and Madina was significant both as a transportation staging post and as the second city of Islam, where the prophet's tomb was located. Riyadh and Hofuf in the eastern province were also on the ancient trade routes and were market centres; in 1932 the growth of Riyadh as the capital and administrative city of the new Kingdom had only just begun.

The growth of oil income and transportation developments (made possible by the oil income) in the post-war years up to 1962–3 produced demographic responses. The most obvious response was the increasing urbanization concentrated on the existing east–west axis towns: Madina, Jedda, Mecca, Taif, Riyadh, Hofuf, Dhahran, Dammam and Al Khobar (Fig. 10.2). The growth of the last three towns was directly connected with the discovery and exploitation of oil; the surfacing and improvement of roads, the development of Jedda port and the establishment of an international airport at Jedda in 1967 benefited the Hejaz towns; the completion of the Dammam–Riyadh railway in 1952 opened the way to the rapid development of the capital.

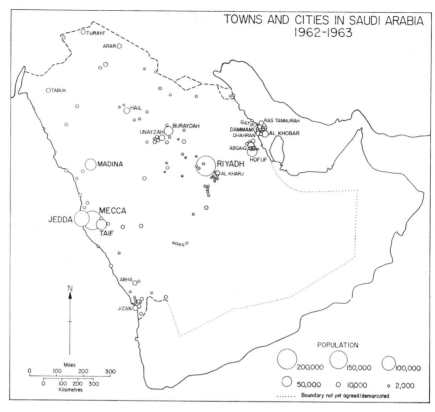

TOWNS AND CITIES IN SAUDI ARABIA
1962-1963

POPULATION

200,000   150,000   100,000

50,000   10,000   2,000

······· Boundary not yet agreed/demarcated

FIGURE 10.2

Health

Reference has already been made to the health of the population (World Health Organization, 1963). Some improvement certainly took place in the post-war years. Until 1950 medical care was confined to the major cities, but even in the capital, Riyadh, there was only one hospital in a mud-walled house with twenty mattresses on the floor for patients (Horniblow, 1966). Malnutrition, tuberculosis and malaria were endemic; trachoma and bilharzia were a serious problem; the rate of pre-natal and infant mortality was high (*Financial Times*, 1969). In 1951 Ibn Saud decreed that free medical care should be available to all Saudi citizens and a crash hospital-building programme was undertaken in the 1950's. A Ministry of Health was created in 1953 to supervize the programme and was also charged to take special measures to deal with the health of the pilgrims, whose annual arrival in hundreds of thousands created special problems and increased the danger of smallpox and cholera epidemics. By 1963 there were 41 hospitals, 119 health centres, 73 clinics, 4,236 beds, 395 doctors,

336 male nurses and 444 midwives (Central Department of Statistics, 1967). The building of hospitals outstripped the availability of doctors and trained staff and as a result of the reluctance of doctors to serve in the rural areas medical care was effectively restricted to the towns. The low standard of hygiene, caused by lack of education, sewerage and water supplies, and the poor housing conditions of the majority of the population, who lived in overcrowded and ill-ventilated mud brick houses (72 per cent of the population in Riyadh in 1962 according to the Survey of Population and Establishments, 1962) without sanitary fittings, were as important as the shortcomings of the medical services in causing high morbidity and mortality.

Education

Another key factor in determining the quality of the population is education. Before the 1939–45 war formal education in Saudi Arabia was almost entirely in the Islamic tradition of religious learning, and illiteracy was widespread. In the 1940's the government school system was formed and a Ministry of Education was established in 1954. Free public education for boys expanded rapidly and schools for girls were begun in 1959. University education dates from 1957, when the University of Riyadh was opened. Adult education schools were also started about the same time to reduce illiteracy. By 1963 the number of students at all levels was 216,000, of whom 191,087 were boys and 25,113 were girls (Central Department of Statistics, 1967). Nearly 75 per cent of the pupils were at the primary stage, and over 40 per cent of the boys and 6 per cent of the girls of primary school age were enrolled in schools. The government had to rely heavily on foreign teachers, mainly from Egypt, Syria, Jordan, Iraq and the Sudan, and in 1963 the non-Saudi teachers in primary schools still exceeded the Saudi teachers.

Economic and social development

That was the base from which for the greater part of the 1960's King Faisal's government began to develop and modernize the country. The human resources consisted of a population of some $3\frac{1}{2}$ million over 40 per cent of whom were under 15 years of age; the rate of natural increase was below 2 per cent; the expectancy of life at birth was crudely estimated to be 30; morbidity was high as a result of inadequate medical services and low living standards; and illiteracy was a major problem. The main economic resources were oil and agriculture, but the revenue from the former had touched only a relatively small section of the population and the majority were living in a subsistence economy based on oasis agriculture and nomadic pastoralism. The traditional way of life prevailed for all but a small minority.

The main achievement of the 1960's has been in the economic field. The underlying fact about the Saudi Arabian economy is that it is a one-product export economy. Apart from a limited and largely subsistence agriculture, contributing less than 10 per cent of the gross domestic product in 1963 (Central Department of Statistics, 1969), there was an extremely narrow productive base. Oil was the only significant export and contributed over 80 per cent of the government's revenue and 95 per cent of the foreign exchange earnings (Saudi Arabian Monetary Agency, 1964 and 1965) and value added to the oil industry accounted for more than 50 per cent of GDP (Central Department of Statistics, 1969). The expenditure of the government was largely reflected in a demand for foreign exchange for imports and other purposes. Declared policy has aimed at widening the productive base of the country to lessen the dependence of the economy on income from oil.

Because of the steadily rising income from oil the government has been able to finance economic development on those lines. Oil income rose from US $333.7 in 1960 to US $926.8 in 1968 and total government revenue from the equivalent of US $351 in 1379/80 (December 1959 to December 1960) to US $1,230 million in 1388/89 (September 1968 to September 1969); sharp upward trends were also recorded in foreign trade, monetary reserves and money supply (Fig. 10.3). About 40 per cent of each budget has been devoted to projects, and the principal development departments have absorbed about another 20 per cent; the other main item of expenditure has been defence and national security.

The main emphasis has been on building the infrastructure, which must precede the development of industry and agriculture, and on resource discovery (primarily water and minerals); but large sums have already been spent on major agricultural and water projects and industrialization has started, mainly in the oil and mineral resources sector under the aegis of Petromin (the General Petroleum and Mineral Organization), a public corporation established in 1962 to participate in the various phases of commerce and industrial activities connected with petroleum and minerals with the purpose of developing, promoting and improving both the petroleum and mineral industries and mineral products and by-products as well as related industries (Article 2 of Statutes of Petromin). Education, including technical and vocational training, has not been neglected, since human skills are scarce and this has been a major limiting factor to development—not least, of course, the development of education itself. Social services are gradually being expanded (health, community welfare, sport, pensions, etc.). Municipal improvements are being made, the machinery for town planning has been brought into being and a preliminary town plan produced for Riyadh. Economic departments and institutions multiplied

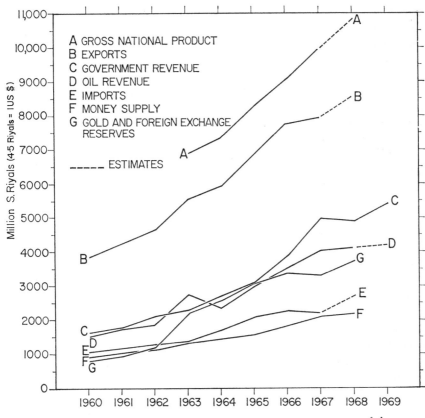

FIGURE 10.3 ECONOMIC RATES IN SAUDI ARABIA DURING THE 1960'S

during the 1960's and laws and regulations were promulgated to regulate commerce and encourage Saudi and foreign investment in industry. Monetary stability has been achieved as a consequence of the policy of balanced budgets and wise management of the money supply by the Saudi Arabian Monetary Agency through the steadily developing banking system, and there has been no need for exchange control or significant import restrictions.

Budgetary allocations, however impressive, do not necessarily mean real measurable progress. And budgetary surpluses have characterized most years owing to a persistent lag in development spending caused by administrative inexperience, shortage of skilled manpower and the time-consuming nature of feasibility studies. The most clearly visible progress has been in the communications sector, which was rightly given high priority in view of the vast and difficult nature of the terrain and the long distances separating the main urban centres. The length of asphalted roads more than trebled between 1963 and 1968 to 6,813 km., a further 3,033 km.

were under construction, and 3,643 km. were out to tender or under design (Saudi Arabian Monetary Agency, 1968). The design of nearly all these roads had, because of lack of native know-how, to be entrusted to foreign consultants and much of the construction was undertaken also by foreign contractors. A start has been made on a system of secondary roads, and a programme of low cost rural roads to act as feeders between the main roads and the villages is under study by foreign consultants. A major expansion of Jedda port was started in 1967 and the first phase of a similar scheme for Dammam was initiated in 1968. By 1969 there 26 airports in the country, two of which could handle international traffic, and the designs for new airports in Jedda and Riyadh were completed in 1969. Saudi Arabian Airlines expanded rapidly and has today the largest Arab air fleet; technical, operational and administrative assistance is provided by Trans World Airlines. Automatic telephone exchanges have been installed in Jedda and Taif and other main cities should be similarly served by the early 1970's. A television system reaches the main urban centres of the east–west axis and a satellite communications centre is planned.

Agriculture

In agriculture progress has inevitably been slower. It is still largely subsistence agriculture, based on oasis farming and nomadic pastoralism. Less than 0.2 per cent of the total land area is cultivated; the ratio of cropped to cultivated land is only 1.1 to 1; 80 per cent of the cultivated land is irrigated and 20 per cent rain-fed (Medawar, 1966). The land tenure system is characterized by small owner-operated farms; abour 50 per cent of the agricultural holdings are less than 0.6 of a hectare and 85 per cent are less than 1.6 hectares each. The results of agricultural censuses held by the Ministry of Agriculture between 1960 and 1964 revealed that 60.4 per cent of agricultural land was used for field crops, 23.3 per cent for palm trees and permanent crops and 16.3 per cent for vegetables (Central Department of Statistics, 1967). Dr Medawar estimated that domestic agricultural output comprised field crops and alfalfa (52 per cent), vegetables (28 per cent), dates (15 per cent) and fruits (5 per cent). A gradual move to cash crops such as fruits and vegetables at the expense of field crops and dates is an expected trend, as marketability improves with transport developments and dietary habits change with rising incomes. Crop yields are high relative to other Arab countries owing to the predominance of irrigation and, because of water scarcity, the exploitation of only the most fertile land (Asfour, 1965). Although such large schemes as the Faisal Bedouin Resettlement Project between Riyadh and Hofuf, the major drainage and reclamation scheme in Al-Hasa oasis and dam construction in the Wadi Jizan are in progress and the Ministry help farmers with advice, rent of equipment and financial assistance (directly and through the Agricultural Credit Bank), major developments in agriculture await the completion of the surveys of the underground water resources. In 1965 the country was divided into eight regions and hydrological studies entrusted to foreign consultants have been completed in four regions, are in progress in three regions, and only in one region (the Empty Quarter) no start has yet been made (Saudi Arabian Monetary Agency, 1969).

Industrialization

The main industry is, of course, oil and from 1966 to 1968 Saudi Arabia was the fourth largest producer in the world, after the United States, the USSR and Venezuela (in 1969 she dropped to fifth place after Iran). In addition to providing the government over 80 per cent of its revenue, the major oil company, ARAMCO, has benefited the economy by local purchase of goods and services at an annual average of over US $60 million. Oil, however, is a capital intensive industry and in 1968 employed only 11,525 persons, of whom 82 per cent were Saudi nationals (ARAMCO, 1968). For that reason, the government has sought to develop industries related to the oil (and mineral) resources. The chosen instrument has been Petromin, which currently has an approved programme involving capital expenditure of $500 million and plans which would raise that figure to $800 million. Oil refining, petrochemicals and a steel plant are projects already in operation. Nationalization of industry is not Petromin's goal; it is rather to provide and stimulate investment in industry, Petromin itself only taking that percentage of the share-holding which is necessary to get a project launched—although in some ventures such as the steel-mill Petromin had to provide all the capital (Taher, 1966). Foreign investment is welcomed primarily for the technology it brings with it, and obligations to train Saudi personnel are written into agreements with foreign partners. A programme of mineral discovery has been pursued by the Directorate General of Mineral Resources for some years, by means of geological and geodetic surveys, and iron, phosphate and copper have been discovered. Petromin has participated in the geodetic surveys and in 1969 signed an agreement with the Mitsubishi group to exploit the iron ore deposits in the Hejaz.

Industrialization outside the oil and mineral sectors exists on a limited scale—cement plants, electricity generating stations, pipe manufacture, shipbuilding and repair, paper factories, a tannery, bottling plants, furniture and detergent factories and numerous small workshops. Through its Industrial Research and Development Centre, the Ministry of Commerce and Industry studies the feasibility of industrial projects, carries out industrial surveys and is setting up industrial estates in Jedda, Riyadh and Dammam to assist and encourage the private sector to play a more active role in the industrial development of the country. By 1967, however, manufacturing contributed only 2 per cent to the gross domestic product (Central Department of Statistics, 1969).

Social services

Progress has also been made in the social services. By 1968 the number of hospitals had risen to 80 (with 6,299 beds), health centres to 303 and doctors to 686. The assistance of the Vickers Medical Group was obtained in 1969 to study the condition of the hospitals and make recommendations for their improvement, and the first students were enrolled in 1969 at the Medical College of Riyadh, which will be provided with a number of British teachers in agreement with the University of London (Saudi Arabian Monetary Agency, 1968). In the field of education, the primary schools continued to expand and in 1968–9 over 250,000 students attended them (Saudi Arabian Monetary Agency, 1969). Increasing emphasis has been placed on intermediate and secondary schools, on higher education, on vocational training centres, on female education and on the campaign against adult illiteracy. Yet by 1967 non-Saudi teachers were still slightly in excess of Saudis in the primary schools and greatly in excess in the intermediate and higher schools (Central Department of Statistics, 1967).

Politics and modernization

Economic and social development took place during the decade in an atmosphere of political stability and no essential change in the personal system of government, which has prevailed since the foundation of the Kingdom by Ibn Saud. At first sight this seems a surprising situation in view of the economic and social progress and the instability and political evolution of most of the other Arab states. The explanation lies primarily in the personality of the King and the strength of traditionalism, buttressed by a puritanical religious movement (Wahhabism), in Saudi Arabia. Ibn Saud consciously strove to associate, or at least weaken by consultation and conciliation, the opposition of the Ulema and the Wahhabi rank and file to the modest modernization which occurred during his reign. Saud was less successful, or tried less, to reconcile the traditionalists to progress, and the political unity and national cohesion were endangered. Faisal has reverted to his father's policy of consultation and conciliation in the more difficult circumstances of rapid economic progress. The aims and methods of Faisal were clearly interpreted in the following passage from an article written a few years ago by Professor Malone (1966) of the American University of Beirut:

'King Faisal is attempting to achieve a partnership with the Ulema in the development of his country. . . . As custodian of the Holy Places he is above all aware that Islam brought order and system to the Arabian Peninsula and that to ignore it is to invite the return to chaos. The strains upon the social fabric of the nation, which are being imposed by urbanization, industrialization and other facets of modernization must be countered by reinforcing the foundation of the community with the ideological cement of Islam. To the extent that King Faisal succeeds in obtaining the sanction of the Ulema for his programmes, and in transmitting the ethical standards of the faith to the bureaucracy, the military and the intelligentsia, he will also succeed in building a modern state on a largely theocratic basis.'

It has also to be remembered that despite the progress of the 1960's Saudi Arabia has today, as in 1960, a dual economy. A modern money economy has developed alongside a traditional, indigenous economy. The modern money economy is export-led, the impulse to development and the means of sustaining it coming from the production and export of oil. The traditional economy is based on subsistence agriculture and nomadic pastoralism and the majority of the people belong to the traditional sector, have very low money incomes and are not significant consumers of the products of the modern economy. The real test of the political system will come in the 1970's, particularly if the targets of the Five Year Plan (1970–75) are achieved. An outline of the Plan was given by the Director-General of the Central Planning Organization in September 1969 (Saudi Arabian Monetary Agency, 1969). The stated objectives of the Plan are:

a) to raise the rate of economic growth by increasing the GDP from SR 16,000 million to SR 26,000 million (4.5 Saudi riyals = 1 US $) during the five years;
b) to develop human resources so that different elements of the society can contribute to and participate more fully in the growth of the economy;
c) to diversify the economy and reduce its dependence on oil;
d) to lay the foundations for sustained economic growth.

The formulation of development plans is easier than their implementation, and in Saudi Arabia, which has no real problem of capital accumulation, it is the human factor which is the key. Economic growth depends ultimately on the character of the people, especially on their willingness and capacity to change and to learn and apply improved methods of production.

Population projections

Since no full census has been held since 1962–3 and the published information available from the 1962–3 census is limited, it is not possible to give a precise figure of total population in 1970. The consensus of informed opinion supports a figure of between 4 and 5 million in 1969 (*Financial Times*, 1969; BNEC, 1969). An interesting estimate of the rate of increase of population was made by Edmond Asfour in 1965. Using the data from the 1962–3 census he attempted two methods of estimation. One method was to make a comparison between the age structure of the Saudi Arabian population and the age structure of other developing countries with a similar level of socio-economic development. The second was to apply the age structure of the Saudi Arabian population and other available demographic rates to a standard demographic model. Both methods produced similar results. A range of 2.0 to 2.9 per cent was taken to represent the natural rate of increase and for the purpose of projection up to 1975 it was considered that the declining mortality rate would bring the rate of increase near the higher figure in the range by 1975. Assuming a steady rise in the rate of increase from 2.0 per cent per annum in 1965 to 2.9 per cent in 1975, an increase in relation to the base year (mid 1962) was arrived at (Table 10.2).

TABLE 10.2   PROJECTED POPULATION GROWTH IN SAUDI ARABIA, 1962–75

Mid-year	Index of size of population
1962	100.00
1965	106.12
1970	118.32
1975	135.17

On the basis of a population of 3.30 million in 1962, the figures for 1970 and 1975 would be 3.90 million and 4.46 million respectively. It might, however, be reasonable to assume that the 1962–3 census underestimated the population, since the Saudis had no previous experience of census operations. Moreover, suspicion of the motives behind the census could have induced uneducated Saudis to give false information and some bedouin are likely to have evaded enumeration at the water-holes. If, therefore, the undercount is assumed to be of the order of 10 per cent, the revised figures would be 3.63 million, 4.28 million and 4.90 million for 1962, 1970 and 1975 respectively.

Demographic responses to development

The effect of development on the distribution of the population can be most clearly seen in the growth of urbanization. While push factors, such as high natural increase creating population pressures on limited resources, must have accounted to some extent for the movement of bedouin and agricultural workers to the towns, the pull of job opportunities, higher wages and urban amenities would seem to have been the chief cause of migration from the rural to the urban sector. Although official figures are not available for the population of the main towns (over 50,000), estimates for 1970 (Table 10.3) gleaned from the local press and other sources, are likely to be accurate within a range of 10 per cent:

TABLE 10.3   ESTIMATED POPULATIONS OF MAIN TOWNS OF SAUDI ARABIA, 1970

Riyadh	300,000
Jedda	250,000
Mecca	250,000
Taif	100,000
Damman, Dhahran al-Khobar complex	100,000
Madina	90,000
Hofuf	70,000
	1,160,000

If we assume, as we can reasonably do, that the towns (excluding the main towns) with populations of over 2,000 in 1962–3 (Fig. 10.2) have experienced the national natural rate of increase, a further 140 to 150,000 urban dwellers would be added to the total for the main cities, thus yielding a figure of between 1.30 and 1.31 million for the total urban population. Secondly, if one assumes that the natural rate of increase of the nomads has been offset by migration to the towns, the nomadic population would be 700,000. Thirdly, on the assumption that about half the natural rate of increase of the rural population is offset by migration to the towns, the rural settled population would have risen from the estimated 1.8 million in 1962–3 to about 2 million (Table 10.4).

TABLE 10.4   ESTIMATED URBAN AND RURAL POPULATIONS OF SAUDI ARABIA, 1962/63–69/70

	1962–3		1969–70	
	Numbers	*Per cent*	*Numbers*	*Per cent*
Urban	800,000	24	1,300,000	33
Nomadic	700,000	21	700,000	17
Rural settled	1,800,000	55	2,000,000	50
Total	3,300,000	100	4,000,000	100

The emphasis on infrastructure in development planning has been a leading factor in urbanization. The largest expenditure has been in the transportation sector and has been concentrated initially on linking and improving the roads in the main urban areas on the east–west axis and developing the port facilities of the terminal towns of Dammam and Jedda. The prosecution of the present road-building programme will result in the extension of good communications to the peripheral areas and in better north–south communications. In particular, the completion of the main roads between Asir, the most favoured agricultural region and the one with the highest population density, and the Jedda–Mecca–Taif–Riyadh–Dammam axis could result in the growth of urbanization in the south-west.

The oil industry has not only been the catalytic agent in the economic growth of Saudi Arabia, but has also been directly responsible for the emergence of new towns. Dhahran, Abqaiq, Ras Tannurah and many other settlements in the oil area did not exist before oil exploitation and the development of transport. The development of the four pumping stations on Tapline into the towns of Turayf, Ar'ar, Al-Qaysumah and An-Nuayriyah is an interesting example of a demographic response to oil transportation and of the sedentarization of the bedouin in the northern region of Saudi Arabia, which is regarded as one of the most nomadic parts of the country (Abdo, 1969). Sedentarization has also been conscious government policy since the creation by Ibn Saud of settlements (*hejar*) for the bedouin members of the Ikhwan.

The high rate of growth of Riyadh is a consequence of its status as the capital and administrative centre of the country, and Jedda and Taif (the summer capital) also owe part of their growth to the development of the governmental machinery. Industrialization outside the oil industry has been concentrated in the three leading cities—Riyadh, Jedda and Mecca—and Dammam is likely to benefit increasingly from industrialization, both in petrochemicals and generally when the industrial estate is set up. All major cities are characterized by a heavy emphasis on commerce and service industries which have the fastest relative growth rates (Central Department of Statistics, 1969).

The under-population of Saudi Arabia relative to its area and developmental needs is underlined by the smallness of the economically-active population. According to the 1962–3 population census, men of working age numbered only 822,000, of whom 165,000 were nomads. A negligible number of women, other than on family agricultural holdings, enter the labour force. With the likely upward trend in the natural rate of increase and the strength of traditional opposition to the employment of women, the proportion of economically active persons to total population is likely for some years to fall below the low figure of 26 per cent of the total population in 1962–3.

Saudi Arabia is not an emigrant country, nor is it a major immigrant country at present. One recent estimate puts the number of foreign workers at 150,000 with an annual increase of around 15 per cent (BNEC, 1969). The total of 150,000 is certainly an underestimate. There were 103,000 non-Saudis in the four towns of Mecca, Jedda, Madina and Taif alone in 1962–3 (Department of Statistics, 1963). It would be more reasonable to take 150,000 as the figure for 1962–3 for the whole country; at an annual increase of 15 per cent the total would rise to nearly 400,000 by 1969–70. The bulk of the foreign workers are engaged in labouring and come from other Arab countries, mainly Yemen and South Yemen. The balance are skilled and semi-skilled personnel employed as teachers (about 8,000), in government departments and in commerce and industry (about 1,000 were employed by ARAMCO in 1968) and most come from Egypt, Lebanon, Syria, Jordan (including Palestine), South Yemen and Pakistan. The unskilled labour plays an important role in the construction industry, the handling of cargo at ports and in the service industries, including domestic service; the skilled labour is vital to the development of the economy, until the educational system can train Saudis in the variety of skills needed.

The Saudi Government controls strictly the entry and employment of foreigners, both on political and socio-economic grounds, and is even stricter in granting Saudi nationality to foreigners. During the Islamic period 1381–6 (1961–2—1966–7) only 1,963 persons obtained Saudi nationality; three-quarters of them came from other Arab countries and most of the remainder from Asia: only Muslims may become Saudi citizens (Central Department of Statistics, 1967). Despite the problem created by an inadequate labour force, it is unlikely that Saudi policy will be relaxed in the future and that the Kuwaiti and Gulf states' pattern of heavy dependence on foreign labour will be repeated. An improvement in productivity should release the under-employed in the agricultural sector to meet, in part at least, the labour demands of the faster expanding industrial and commercial sectors. The gap in skilled manpower, until sufficient Saudis are trained, will probably continue to be met by the hiring of foreign consultants, the use of the services of United Nations specialized agencies and experts, and the import of individual experts and technicians on contract terms.

Conclusion

It is clear, however, that the extent to which diversification of the Saudi Arabian economy is successful and the length of time needed to place the economy on a self-sustaining basis will be governed primarily by the development of human resources, quantitatively and qualitatively. And political and social factors are very relevant. Saudi Arabia has been more fortunate than most developing countries in enjoying a high degree of political stability, which has owed much to the wisdom of its rulers and the strength of a socially cohesive religion well suited to Arabian traditions. The continuation of peaceful progress may well depend on the practicability of building a modern state on a largely theocratic basis or of a controlled transformation to a more secular and (conventionally) democratic political system.

REFERENCES

ABDO, A. S. (1969) *A Geographical Study of Transport in Saudi Arabia with Special Reference to Road Transport*, unpublished Ph.D. thesis, University of Durham, Chapters 1 and 10.

ARAMCO (1968) *The Annual Report of the Arabian American Oil Company*.

ASFOUR, E. Y. (1965) *Saudi Arabia. Long-term Projections of Supply of and Demand for Agricultural Products*, Sections 111, 3, IV, 1 and Appendix C.

BNEC COMMITTEE FOR MIDDLE EAST TRADE (1969) *The Market for Household Goods in Saudi Arabia*, a report prepared by Industrial Export Surveys for the BNEC Committee for Middle East Trade.

CENTRAL DEPARTMENT OF STATISTICS, SAUDI ARABIA (1967) *Statistical Yearbook*.

CENTRAL DEPARTMENT OF STATISTICS, SAUDI ARABIA (1969) *Estimates of Gross Domestic Product, Gross National Product and National Income of Saudi Arabia during the period 1382-3—1386-7 A.H.*

COOLEY, C. H. (1894) 'A theory of transportation', *Publication of the American Economic Association*, 9, pp. 1–148.

DEPARTMENT OF STATISTICS, SAUDI ARABIA (1963) *Survey of Population and Establishments*.

FINANCIAL TIMES (1969) 'Saudi Arabia', a survey published on 23rd June 1969.

HORNIBLOW, P. (1966) 'Health Services are free for all citizens', *Emergent Nations*, 2, pp. 23 and 24.

MALLAKH, R. (1966) 'Economic diversification is key to progress', *Emergent Nations*, 2, pp. 54–6.

MALONE, J. J. (1966) 'Saudi Arabia', *The Muslim World*, 56, pp. 290–5.

MEDAWAR, G. C. (1966) 'Agricultural expansion fulfils great hopes', *Emergent Nations*, 2, pp. 50–2 and 61.

NAVAL INTELLIGENCE DIVISION (1946) *Western Arabia and the Red Sea*, Geographical Handbook Series, Chapter 11.

PETROMIN (undated) *The General Petroleum and Mineral Organization*.

SAUDI ARABIAN MONETARY AGENCY (1964, 1965 and 1968) *Annual reports*.

SAUDI ARABIAN MONETARY AGENCY (1969) *Statistical Summary*, September–October 1969.

SHAMMA, S. (1965) 'Law and lawyers in Saudi Arabia', *The International and Comparative Law Quarterly*, 14, pp. 1034–9.

TAHER, A. H. (1966) Reprint of a lecture delivered by Dr Abdulhady Hassan Taher, Governor of Petromin, to the joint Harvard–MIT Seminar on Eastern Hemisphere petroleum on 26th April 1966, at Boston.

UNITED NATIONS (1967) *Demographic Yearbook*, Table 2, 109.

WORLD HEALTH ORGANIZATION (1963) *Report on a Health Survey of Saudi Arabia from 10th November 1962 to 31st January 1963.*

Chapter 11
The Gulf states:
petroleum and population growth
A G Hill

The five Gulf states, taken here to include the independent political units of Kuwait, Bahrain, Qatar, the Trucial States, and the Sultanate of Muscat and Oman, together form a distinctive unit within the Middle East. Part of the distinctiveness of the Gulf states is their small size both in population and area (Table 11.1); none of the units contains over one million people and only the Sultanate exceeds 84,000 sq. km. in area. These two criteria of area and population, however, understate the importance of the Gulf states both within and beyond the Middle East, for each of the five states is a considerable producer of petroleum. The oil industry and its revenues in every case entirely dominate the fiscal systems of the Gulf states and penetrate every facet of their national life. Much of the recent economic history of the Gulf region is thus concerned with the rapidity with which the traditional economic system has been swept away and replaced by modern activities consequent upon the oil industry.

TABLE 11.1   THE POPULATIONS OF THE GULF STATES

Country	Area (sq. km.)	Date	Population
Bahrain	662	1965	182,203
Kuwait	16,000	1970	733,196 P
Muscat and Oman	212,400	1969	750,000 E
Qatar	22,000	1970	130,000 P
Trucial States	83,600	1968	180,184

E = Official estimate P = Provisional census figure

Statistics shown for Kuwait exclude the Neutral Zone.

Sources: Bahrain Statistical Abstract for 1968.
Kuwait Statistical Abstract for 1971.
Muscat and Oman, British Consulate General.
Qatar into the Seventies.
Trucial States Census, 1968.

Such a change has important demographic implications. Up to 1945, the Gulf populations were both small and poor. While maritime commerce, pearl-diving and slave-trading in earlier centuries brought together a variety of racial strains in the Gulf principalities, both immigration and natural increase were almost negligible in overall importance. By contrast, the post-1945 period in the Gulf has been a period of very rapid demographic growth precipitated mostly by an influx of job-seekers from countries outside the Gulf area. In addition, much of the new-found wealth in the Gulf has been invested in health, welfare and educational facilities which, taken together, have greatly reduced mortality rates and extended the expectancy of life. Provision of such medical facilities has resulted in extremely high rates of natural increase among the citizens and the immigrant populations alike.

These general trends apply to all five Gulf states, but in detail the exact timing and the consequences of this period of rapid economic and demographic change vary considerably. Kuwait and Bahrain are the best documented examples and for this reason are dealt with at greater length. Qatar* and the Sultanate of Muscat and Oman have yet to hold their first full census of population and the recording of vital events lags proportionately behind the two north-western states.

KUWAIT

Kuwait is the most populous of the Gulf states (Fig. 11.1) with an estimated population of approximately 800,000 in 1970. Just 16,000 sq. km. in area, excluding the jointly administered Saudi–Kuwait Neutral Zone, Kuwait is a modern 'city state' with Kuwait City, the capital, containing two-thirds of the state's population. Only two other clusters of people are of note, of which the first is the town of Ahmadi, 35 km. south of Kuwait City. This town, the centre of operations for the Kuwait Oil Company, is an entirely post-1945 development. On the coast 7 km. east of Ahmadi is the second agglomeration of population outside the capital, consisting of Fahahil, a village now greatly expanded because of its closeness to three major oil jetties, and Shu'aybah, a new port with a growing stake in oil-refining and the petrochemicals industry. As a result, the pattern of Kuwait's post-oil evolution and the small size of the state territory, Kuwait's population is highly urbanized and centralized on the capital city.

In 1946 Kuwait exported oil for the first time, whereas in 1969 total production, including a half share in the Neutral Zone, totalled 141 million tons. Oil revenues to the state have mounted in step with rising oil production: revenue payments in 1968 alone amounted to $773 million. The form and pace of Kuwait's post-1945 expansion have provided the archetype for the other oil states in the lower Gulf.

* Qatar held a census early in 1970 but details are not yet available.

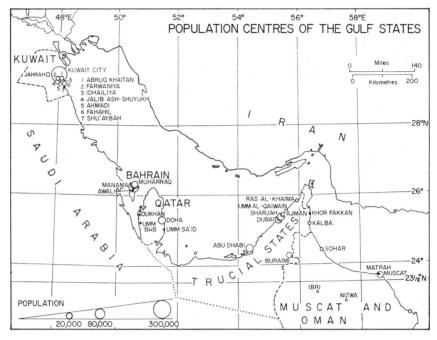

FIGURE II.I

Population growth

Until the first census of February 1957, all population statistics were merely informed guesses. Our earliest reliable source is provided by Lorimer's *Gazetteer of the Persian Gulf* published in 1908 and 1915 in two parts. Lorimer estimated Kuwait's population to be 35,000 in 1907, together with a further 13,000 nomadic *badu* commonly ranging within Kuwait's territory.

Less reliable sources, mostly established British residents, indicate that Kuwait's population grew steadily up to the 1930's, with a sudden upward surge when oil exploration began in 1935. Freeth (1956) estimated the total population at 60,000 in the 1930's, a figure expanded by the Naval Intelligence Division Handbook *Iraq and the Persian Gulf* (1944) to 70,000 for the early 1940's. Freeth quotes a figure of 100,000 for 1945, while Dickson (1956) reckoned that Kuwait contained 160,000 people in 1952.

The first census in 1957, which probably understates the numbers in Kuwait at that time, provides a total figure of 206,473. By the time of the second census in May 1961, this total had risen by 56 per cent to 321,621, with a subsequent increase of 45 per cent to 467,339 in 1965 (Table 11.2). Forward projections using arrival and departure figures and estimates of

244

TABLE 11.2   THE POPULATION OF KUWAIT, 1957–65

Census date	Kuwaitis		Non-Kuwaitis		Total	
	Total	Males	Total	Males	Both sexes	Males
February 1957	113,622	59,154	92,851	72,904	206,473	132,058
May 1961	161,909	84,461	159,712	116,246	321,621	200,707
April 1965	220,059	112,569	247,280	173,743	467,339	286,312

Source: Censuses of Population for 1967, 1961 and 1965.

natural increase point to a probable population of over 1 million by 1975 (Colin Buchanan, 1969).

While the total numbers involved are small by international standards, Kuwait's post-1945 population increase, particularly between the three censuses, represents one of the highest rates of growth in the post-war world. Even other exceptional communities such as Hong Kong, Singapore, Gibraltar, or the American Virgin Islands display lower rates of population increase than those prevailing in Kuwait. Clearly immigration is of critical significance, but numerous factors are involved in the attraction of people from throughout the Middle East area and beyond.

Immigration

At the outset, Kuwait's population was far from homogeneous. Lorimer (1908) pointed out that while the bulk of Kuwait's population was derived from eight tribes from eastern Arabia, there were also about 100 households from Najd, over 1,000 Persians, 100–200 Jews, and at least 4,000 Negroes resident in the Shaikhdom. Thus at least 16 per cent of Kuwait's population were not indigenous residents of the area in 1907.

The Kuwait Oil Company employed very few people in its pre-war activities: at the end of 1939, its labour force was only 257, consisting largely of manual workers. There was probably a small amount of immigration before 1939, but according to Dickson (1956), wartime 'was a difficult time for everyone, especially the poor of the town and in the desert, for food, clothing and medicines were almost unobtainable and great stress prevailed'. Immigration is therefore unlikely to have been very significant until after oil exporting had begun in 1946. Kuwait Oil Company's labour force grew sharply from 1,552 at the end of 1946 to 8,753 at the end of 1948. Ancillary trades and services were also growing as oil revenues flooded into the state's treasury. There was necessarily a slight delay in the disbursal of the oil money because of the lack of any modern organization equipped to take the many involved technical decisions, but the expansion of the city and its service facilities gained momentum in the 1950's. Then with the government's ambitious construction programme coupled to rising personal prosperity brought about by disbursal of public money through the land purchase scheme (Hill, 1969) the flood of immigration began.

Up to 1948, Kuwait had no formally constituted nationality code. A series of decrees and laws enacted between 1948 and 1965 gradually tightened up the distinction between citizens and immigrants. In all official publications citizens (Kuwaitis) are differentiated from alien immigrants (non-Kuwaitis) although the boundaries are slightly blurred particularly in the pre-oil period. Nevertheless, the strict nationality code allows the naturalization of a maximum of only 50 non-Kuwaitis annually even after 15 years continuous residence in the case of non-Arabs, commuted to ten years for Arabs (Amiri Decree No. 2, 1960). In the censuses, there is therefore a reasonable basis on which to distinguish citizens and later immigrants.

Non-Kuwaitis

The large-scale immigration of numerous foreigners into Kuwait is the most important demographic trend in recent years. By 1957, non-Kuwaitis constituted 45 per cent of Kuwait's total population, a proportion which rose to 53 per cent in 1965, and probably to over 55 per cent in 1970. The volume of immigration, the sources of the migrants, and the demographic attributes of the arrivals have all altered since oil-exporting first began.

An analysis of the length of residence statistics in the census volume of 1957 indicates that less than one-eighth of the immigrants enumerated in 1957 had entered Kuwait before 1947. By comparison, almost half of the 92,851 non-Kuwaitis recorded in 1957 had arrived in the previous three years. Immigrants continued to flood into Kuwait at an accelerated rate in the 1960's: by 1961, 159,712 were recorded in the census, leaping to 247,280 in the third census of 1965. Net increases in the immigrant population of 29,790, 156,478 and 50,398 were recorded in the calendar years 1966, 1967 and 1968 respectively. Clearly immigration is the factor contributing most to the expansion of the Kuwait population as a whole.

It seems that before oil exploration began in the 1930's, almost half of the foreigners in Kuwait were derived from Iran. Iraqis and Saudis each constituted about one-fifth of the immigrant population, with Omanis amounting to about a tenth of the total. In the decade 1927–37, the foreign-born population altered in origin with the arrival of proportionately more Iraqis and Omanis, and proportionately fewer Iranians and Saudis. These trends continued up to 1947 when approximately 28 per cent of the non-Kuwaitis were from Iraq, 18 per cent from Iran, 10 per cent from Oman, 8 per cent from India, and just 7 per cent from Jordan and Palestine.

In the 1957 census, the three major foreign nationality groups recorded were Iraqis, Iranians and Jordanians (including Palestinians) amounting to 28, 21 and 16 per cent of the total foreigners respectively (see Table

11.3), while Lebanese, Omanis, Indians and Pakistanis composed most of the remainder. The sudden upsurge in the proportion of Jordanians is directly related to the establishment of the state of Israel in much of former Palestine. Later figures bear out the importance of Israel's expansion on the pattern of international migration to Kuwait; by 1961, 23 per cent of Kuwait's immigrants were Jordanians or Palestinians, and by 1965 this proportion was 31 per cent.

TABLE 11.3   COMPOSITION OF THE FOREIGN-BORN POPULATION
IN KUWAIT, 1957–68

Nationality	February 1957 (per cent)	May 1961 (per cent)	April 1965 (per cent)	January 1968 (per cent)
Palestinians and Jordanians	16	23	31	27
Iraqis	28	17	10	17
Syrians	2	10[1]	7	9
Lebanese	7	10	8	6
Omanis	7	9	8	6
Egyptians	2	—[1]	4	5
Indians	4	5	5	3
Pakistanis	3	4	5	3
Iranians	21	11	12	3[2]
British	2	2	1	1
Others	8	9	9	20
Total numbers	92,851	159,712	247,280	441,971

Notes: 1. In 1961, Syrians and Egyptians were grouped together in the census under the heading of people from the 'United Arab Republic'.
2. In 1967 Iranians were apparently leaving Kuwait in considerable numbers. The reverse is probably true, for Iranians are notorious for their evasion of the entry regulations. Thus the 1968 proportion of Iranians is misleadingly low.

Sources: 1. 1957, 1961 and 1965 figures calculated from Censuses of population, tables 48, 4 and 22 respectively.
2. 1968 figures derived from 1965 Census in conjunction with arrival and departure figures for 1966 and 1967.

Another re-adjustment in the source areas of migrants, the reduction in the proportion of Iraqis, was also precipitated largely by political factors. Iraq's threat to invade Kuwait in 1961 led to the rounding up and re-patriation of many Iraqis in Kuwait. Otherwise the greater diversity of migrant sources in 1965 (Table 11.3) can be seen as a 'spread effect' where migrants travel longer and longer distances to reach the state as information about Kuwait is disseminated farther afield. Gradually the 'Gulf elements' (Iranians, Omanis, people from the Trucial States and Bahrain) have been reduced in proportion although increasing in numbers, while the proportion of 'northern area' Arabs (Jordanians, Syrians, Lebanese, Egyptians) has increased steadily. By January 1968, these latter four nationalities constituted 47 per cent of Kuwait's foreign-born population. The particularly large incursion of these nationalities in 1967 is directly related to their location in or close to the war zone with Israel.

Demographic attributes of the immigrants

While the age–sex pyramids for the non-Kuwaitis describe a classic immigrant population in a society where males are more mobile than females (Fig. 11.2), the pyramids contain an element of generalization. Each national group in Kuwait displays particular demographic characteristics which have measurably altered between 1957 and 1965. The migrant stream as a whole is apparently growing in 'maturity', gradually assuming the attributes of a settled population as growing proportions of the very young and the elderly become associated with the immigrants of working age.

Several trends can be discerned for the whole alien population. First,

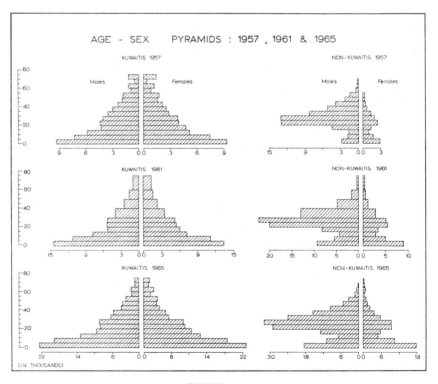

FIGURE 11.2

between 1957 and 1965, the numbers of women migrating to Kuwait rose sharply. In 1957 there were only 274 non-Kuwaiti females per thousand non-Kuwaiti males. By 1961 this figure had risen to 374, and by 1965 there were 423 females per thousand males. Associated with this increase in non-Kuwaiti women was an increase in the proportion of young children. By 1965, 15 per cent of the non-Kuwaiti population were under the age of five, compared with less than 7 per cent in 1957. Over the same period the proportion of male illiterates declined from 43 to 33 per cent, pointing to a growing sophistication in the influx of foreigners to Kuwait.

The age–sex characteristics of six major nationality groups are illustrated in Figure 11.3. Taking sex ratios first of all, the Iranians and the Omanis were the only groups not to have experienced a drop in the preponderance of males. Together with the Syrians and people from the other Gulf states, these four groups had strongly unbalanced sex ratios, with 70 per cent or over composed of males. Indians and Pakistanis, the main representatives of Asian migrants in Kuwait, had closely similar sex ratios, with 66 and 65 per cent of their 1965 populations composed of males. Most of the migrant groups from the Arab world—Jordanians, Saudis, Lebanese and Iraqis—had a male bias of between 61 and 64 per cent in their populations in 1965. In every case, the proportion of females had increased between 1957 and 1965. A fourth group—Europeans, Britons, Americans and, surprisingly, Egyptians—had almost equal sex ratios with under 55 per cent of their populations composed of males. In Kuwait, Egyptian women provide almost one-half of the female teachers in the state schools. The presence of these teachers accounts for the discordance by age in the balance between the sexes shown in Figure 11.3.

Regarding age structure, all the pyramids of national groups have a 'waisted' appearance because of the lack of adolescents of both sexes. In addition, there are very small proportions of the elderly. Both these groups have good reasons for remaining in the home country—the former for schooling, and the latter because they have passed the active age range. Most of the foreign groups have a fairly large proportion of young children, with the exception of the Iranians, the Omanis, and the people from other Gulf states. These three groups contain very high proportions of males and make frequent visits to their countries of origin. Despite the high proportion of males in the active age groups, dependency ratios have risen sharply. In 1957, adults aged 15–60 outnumbered the very young and the elderly by almost 5:1, by 1965 the ratio was 2.4:1.

It seems that demographic structure of an immigrant group in Kuwait depends largely on the type of employment a migrant can expect on arrival. Northern area Arabs, with higher levels of literacy and technical training have a higher job expectancy than the Iranians and lower Gulf peoples. Salaries are in proportion to the level of employment so that generally the educated can better afford to bring their dependants to Kuwait

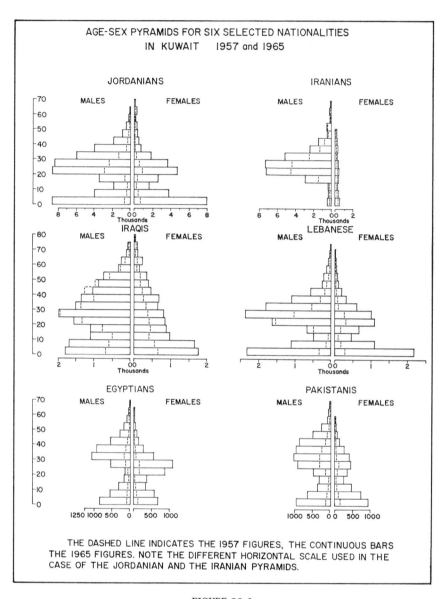

AGE-SEX PYRAMIDS FOR SIX SELECTED NATIONALITIES
IN KUWAIT 1957 and 1965

JORDANIANS

IRANIANS

IRAQIS

LEBANESE

EGYPTIANS

PAKISTANIS

THE DASHED LINE INDICATES THE 1957 FIGURES, THE CONTINUOUS BARS
THE 1965 FIGURES. NOTE THE DIFFERENT HORIZONTAL SCALE USED IN THE
CASE OF THE JORDANIAN AND THE IRANIAN PYRAMIDS.

FIGURE 11.3

and to support them in the face of high local costs of living. Two other
factors are of importance, the first of which is political. The refugee
elements in Kuwait cannot be ignored since such people are most likely
to transfer house and home to Kuwait for an extended period. Secondly,
there may be a cultural gradient in the Middle East which makes northern
area Arabs more aware of the value of Kuwait's high quality health and

educational facilities because of their greater family responsibilities. Notably the more demographically 'balanced' nationalities display a greater degree of residential stability than the strongly male populations who return to their home areas with greater frequency (Hill, 1969).

Kuwaitis

The citizen population has expanded principally by natural increase. Reliable statistics on the vital rates have only recently become available in Kuwait, but the data published indicates that the Kuwaiti population is increasing as rapidly as any group in the contemporary world. These high increase rates, approaching 4 per cent per annum, are not confined to the citizen population, for non-Kuwaitis too with their rising proportion of females, have also had access to the state's comprehensive medical services which are of paramount importance in the reduction of mortality.

Until the post-1945 period, modern health facilities were unknown in Kuwait. Conditions of ill-health prevailed despite the early attempts of the Arabian American mission to begin the practice of modern medicine in 1909, followed by the establishment of a 34-bed hospital in 1939. The first major state hospital was opened in 1949 with 100 beds followed closely by the proliferation of further specialist hospitals, clinics, operating theatres, and other treatment centres throughout the 1950's. By the mid-1960's, Kuwait had a health service with few parallels in the Middle East and which compared favourably with many European health services. The growth of these facilities is summarized in Table 11.4.

TABLE 11.4   THE GROWTH OF MEDICAL FACILITIES IN KUWAIT, 1949–67

Date	Estimated population	Total number of doctors	Persons per doctor	State hospital beds	Private hospital beds
1949	—	45	—	100	34
1953	170,000	46	3,696	611	N.A.
1957	206,000	145	1,421	1,322	N.A.
1962	402,000	462	870	2,600	N.A.
1966	506,000	606	835	3,302	384
1967	688,000	625	1,101	3,300	384

Sources: Constructed from: Statistical Abstracts, 1964–8.
Ministry of Health Reports, 1958–66.
Ministry of Health, personal communication.

At the outset, the state health facilities were freely available to all residents, although recently non-Kuwaitis have been charged a nominal sum per day spent in hospital. Thus a previously unhealthy population with appropriately high birth and death rates was exposed to free modern medical services. Clearly the most important effect of this health service was to lower mortality rates, particularly infant mortality rates. Consequently, Kuwait passed from a stage with high fluctuating birth and death rates through to a stage with still high birth rates but low death rates in a matter of 20 years.

The results of this period of rapid natural increase can be traced in the age–sex structure of the Kuwaiti population (Fig. 11.2). With a broadly triangular form, the age–sex pyramid for the Kuwaitis closely parallels the silhouette displayed by a variety of other developing countries in process of demographic expansion. In 1965, almost half of all Kuwaitis were aged under 15, and only 4.8 per cent were over age 60. The proportion under 15 has risen steadily from just 41.5 per cent of the total in 1957.

Natality and fertility

Registration of births and deaths was made compulsory in Kuwait in 1952 but until 1959 when a Statistical Section was set up within the Ministry of Health, records are scanty and unreliable. In certain instances, recourse has been made to hospital records and the municipal burial books. Births, since the majority occur in hospital, are more completely recorded than deaths.

While the registered number of births to Kuwaiti women has more than tripled between 1958 and 1966 (Table 11.5), both the crude birth rate and the general fertility ratio have also risen over the period. Proportionately more children are being born to the same number of Kuwaiti women than in all earlier years. This higher fertility is a result of a variety of factors including improved registration of births, improved health facilities, rising affluence, the young age of marriage (one-fifth of the brides in 1966 were under age of 19), the age–sex structure of the population, and a knowledge that, in an expanding economy, offspring are assured of free schooling and higher education if required.

As Table 11.5 shows, the birth rates for non-Kuwaitis are substantially below those for Kuwaitis. Nevertheless, non-Kuwaitis are reproducing rapidly as sex ratios become more balanced, and especially as the number of women in the child-bearing age group grows rapidly. Between 1957 and 1965, the proportion of married non-Kuwaitis over the age of 15 rose from 39.7 to 43.5 per cent. The higher general fertility rates of the non-Kuwaitis (Table 11.6) indicate that despite the lack of long-term settlement prospects in Kuwait (permits for work or residence, the principal means of immigration control, must be renewed annually), the foreign population makes full use of Kuwait's available medical facilities.

Births are not published by individual nationalities. General fertility rates by nationality have been derived from the 1965 census by relating the number of infants aged less than one year (divided by a factor of 0.9 to

TABLE 11.5   NATALITY IN KUWAIT, 1958–66

Year	Kuwaitis			Non-Kuwaitis		
	Births	Crude birth rate	*General fertility rate	Births	Crude birth rate	*General fertility rate
1958	4,658	37.5	231?	2,223	21.1	250?
1959	5,675	42.0	—	3,348	27.9	—
1960	6,842	46.5	—	4,774	35.1	—
1961	6,911	42.7	258	6,031	37.8	287
1962	7,921	45.2	—	7,283	40.8	—
1963	9,261	48.9	—	8,459	42.4	—
1965	11,291	51.3	268	9,764	39.4	273
1966	14,057	58.6	—	11,271	39.4	—

Source: Calculated from: (i)   Censuses of population for 1957, 1961 and 1965.
(ii) Ministry of Health Annual Reports, 1958–62 (Arabic).
(iii) Statistical Abstract, 1967.
* Related to women aged 10–40.

allow for infant mortality in the preceding year) to the females in the child-bearing age group (Table 11.6). The corrected figure for non-Kuwaiti births in the 12 months preceding the census in April 1965 is 9,354, comparing favourably with the Ministry of Health records showing 9,500 such births. This method assumes even enumeration and a uniform rate of infant mortality among the non-Kuwaitis. Despite these assumptions, the method illustrates the very high fertility of several immigrant

TABLE 11.6   CALCULATED FERTILITY RATES* BY NATIONALITY IN KUWAIT, 1965

Nationality	Calculated births	Women aged 15–44	General fertility rate
Omanis	423	1,214	348
Lebanese	1,262	3,941	320
Jordanians	4,231	13,475	314
Pakistanis	538	1,798	299
Iranians	224	775	289
Saudis	170	628	271
Syrians	633	2,372	267
Indians	457	2,293	199
Iraqis	771	4,289	180
British	91	712	128
Egyptians	391	3,235	121

Source: Calculated from 1965 Census of population, Table 23.

* Live births per 1,000 women aged 15–44.

groups—Omanis, Lebanese, Jordanians, Pakistanis, Iranians and Saudis all had fertility ratios above the figure for Kuwaitis in 1965, itself an extremely high figure. Of these groups the Jordanians are numerically the most important, contributing an estimated 13,475 births in the 12 months prior to April 1965. Overall, the fertility ratios bear out the evidence of the age–sex pyramids.

Mortality

With such fundamentally different age–sex structures, the mortality experience of Kuwaitis and non-Kuwaitis also differs greatly. The very low overall crude death rates are a reflection of the poor recording system and the peculiarly low general mortality rates of the non-Kuwaitis. Burial records were used to supplement the official mortality records, and corrected death rates are shown in Table 11.7.

TABLE 11.7 VITAL STATISTICS IN KUWAIT, 1965
(*Per thousand*)

	Crude birth rate	*Crude death rate*	*Infant mortality*	*Rate of natural increase*
Kuwaitis	51.3	9.8	49.5	41.5
Non-Kuwaitis	39.5	4.0	30.4	35.5
Total population	45.0	7.3	40.2	37.7

Sources: (i) Ministry of Health Annual Reports (Arabic).
(ii) Annual Abstract of Statistics.
(iii) Annual Reports of Kuwait Municipality (Arabic).

This table indicates the magnitude of natural increase among Kuwaitis especially, but also amongst non-Kuwaitis. With infant mortality rates reduced to European levels, natural increase is in the region of 3.5 per cent annually. At present there seems no sign of a downward trend in this rate; family limitation is unattractive to the Kuwaitis, who are eager to increase their numbers and replace the unfavourable proportion of foreigners in the state population. Non-Kuwaitis, on the other hand, see every justification in having their families in the context of Kuwait's good medical facilities. It seems that such population pressures may further accentuate the duality of life in Kuwait.

Population distribution

One aspect of the duality introduced into Kuwait by sustained immigration of foreign nationals is the differentiation of Kuwaitis and non-Kuwaitis by

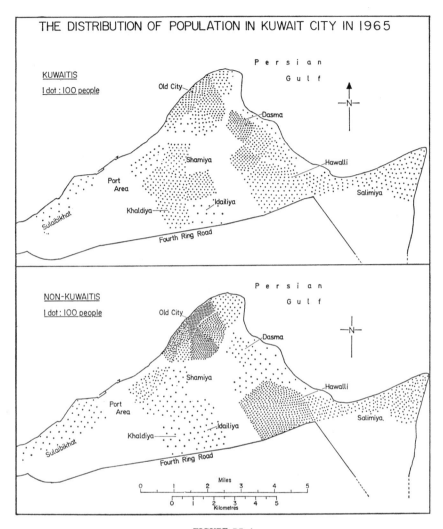

THE DISTRIBUTION OF POPULATION IN KUWAIT CITY IN 1965

KUWAITIS
1 dot : 100 people

Persian Gulf

Old City
Dasma
—N—
Shamiya
Hawalli
Port Area
Salimiya
Sulaibikhat
Khaldiya
Idailiya
Fourth Ring Road

NON-KUWAITIS
1 dot : 100 people

Persian Gulf

Old City
Dasma
—N—
Shamiya
Hawalli
Port Area
Salimiya
Khaldiya
Idailiya
Sulaibikhat
Fourth Ring Road

Miles
0   1   2   3   4   5
0   1   2   3   4   5
Kilometres

FIGURE 11.4

place of residence. Kuwait City, containing 298,701 of Kuwait's 1965 population within the fourth ring road, is the principal centre where citizens and immigrants reside in close proximity, for 56 per cent of all Kuwaitis and 71 per cent of all non-Kuwaitis resided in the capital in that year. The two groups, as Figure 11.4 illustrates, were strongly segregated by place of residence.

Two major factors are involved in the evolution of this pattern. First, non-Kuwaitis are not permitted to own land, property, or businesses in Kuwait and so must rent their accommodation from Kuwaitis. The principal areas of new housing for higher status non-Kuwaitis are in the

Hawalli and Salimiya suburbs while for lower status non-Kuwaitis the Old City provides suitable accommodation. Secondly, Kuwait City has been expanded very quickly by the purchase from individuals of land and property within the Old City by a government agency, 'Amlak al-Hukuma. Inflated prices paid by the state to individual Kuwaitis have provided the necessary capital for the building of new housing in strictly planned suburbs. Thus Kuwaitis have moved from the Old City to the new suburbs, but non-Kuwaitis, excluded from the disbursal of funds to property owners in the Old City and therefore unable to build or own new houses in the planned suburbs, have been left to fill vacancies in the Old City or to live in newer accommodation in the less closely controlled suburbs of Hawalli and Salimiya.

Outside the capital, the proportion of Kuwaitis increases in the smaller and more remote settlements. In most of the new planned suburbs, Kuwaitis constitute over 80 per cent of the inhabitants compared with 27 per cent in the Old City and just 22 per cent in Hawalli. The population of Jahrah, a town 35 km. west of the capital, consists of 74 per cent Kuwaitis, while the shanty towns of Maqwa and Warah south of the capital are over 95 per cent Kuwaiti. Clearly this duality of many settlements, especially in the capital, is likely to prove a stumbling block to the assimilation of further waves of immigrants if the present strict nationality laws remain largely unchanged.

BAHRAIN

The Amirate of Bahrain comprises a group of over 30 small islands lying some 50 km. off the east coast of Saudi Arabia. Bahrain itself is the largest island, 563.3 sq. km. in area, containing Manama, the capital city, the main port (Mina Sulman), and the oilfield in the centre of the island at Awali. Muharraq Island, 13.9 sq. km. in area, is linked to Bahrain by a causeway 2.4 km. long and has become an important suburb of Manama as well as containing the international airport. Other important islands include Sitra off Bahrain's east coast and linked to it by a bridge; Nabi Saleh, north of Sitra, which has good supplies of fresh water; and the islands of Jidda and Umm an-Nassan off the west coast of Bahrain. Together the total area of the Amirate is only 662 sq. km., slightly greater than the Isle of Man.

Despite its small size, Bahrain was one of the first Gulf states in which reserves of petroleum were discovered: exporting began in 1934. Bahrain's oil reservoirs, however, proved much smaller than those of the Kuwait oilfields and in 1969 Bahrain produced only 3.8 million tons. Thus the revenues from oil have not precipitated the period of feverish development which characterizes Kuwait's post-war experience; rather the emphasis in Bahrain has been on a more gradual period of economic and social evolution. Industrial diversification for Bahrain has been a much more pressing problem than elsewhere in the Gulf. For this reason oil-refining became a significant element in Bahrain's industrial structure at an early date. Bahrain's first oil refinery was commissioned in 1937 and was greatly expanded in capacity after the completion of the half-submarine pipeline from Dhahran to Bahrain for the processing of Saudi Arabian crude oil at the Bahrain refinery. With improved submarine pipeline facilities in use by 1952, the Bahrain refinery was considerably enlarged in 1955–6: its total crude oil run to the refinery was 84,545,000 US barrels in 1968, 66 per cent of which was derived from Saudi Arabia. At present Bahrain exports no crude oil—instead focusing on the export of refined products.

An indication of Bahrain's eagerness to further this process of economic diversification is the establishment in 1967 of a Development Bureau within the Finance Department. One of the Bureau's most successful projects is the £40 million aluminium smelter at present under construction. Ship-repairing, prawn-fishing and plastics manufacture, together with a stake in telecommunications, are among the activities of growing importance in the Bahrain economy.

Population numbers

TABLE 11.8   THE POPULATION OF BAHRAIN, 1941–65

Census date	Bahrainis		Non-Bahrainis		Total	
	Total	Males	Total	Males	Both sexes	Males
January 1941	74,040	N.A.	15,930	N.A.	89,970	48,267
March 1950	91,179	N.A.	18,471	N.A.	109,650	58,601
May 1959	118,734	59,913	24,401	17,709	143,135	77,622
February 1965	143,814	72,368	38,389	27,016	182,203	99,384

Source: Bahrain Statistical Abstract, 1967, Table 11.

Bahrain's steadier rate of economic growth has not resulted in a very rapid demographic expansion such as characterized Kuwait. Table 11.8 indicates the much smaller rate of total population increase and particularly the much lower proportion of immigrants in Bahrain when compared with Kuwait. Nevertheless, the native population is increasing at a very high rate (over 3 per cent annually between 1959 and 1965) mostly by natural means. Fifty-one per cent of the country's annual budget is devoted to the development of health, welfare and educational services, and the high standard of medical care (see below) is the primary instrument in lowering death rates as a whole.

Population distribution

In 1965, only 18 per cent of Bahrain's population were classed as rural dwellers. Underground water, particularly in the northern part of the archipelago, provides greater opportunities for agriculture than in Kuwait. Comparison of population distribution over time is complicated by changes in the status of towns and villages, but it is clear that Manama, Muharraq and suburbs have grown rapidly since the first census. In 1941, this area already concentrated 55 per cent of Bahrain's population, a figure which rose to 66 per cent in 1965, when 120,241 people lived in the capital agglomeration, the largest centre in Bahrain by a factor of twelve.

Hidd on Muharraq and Jiddhafs south-west of Manama are rapidly growing settlements as they become incorporated within the orbit of the Manama–Muharraq concentration. By 1965, these areas contained a further 7 per cent of the Amirate's population. Sitra expanded rapidly in population—from 3,926 in 1959 to 5,071 in 1965—as a result of the concentration of many of Bahrain's new industrial projects close to the nearby oil refinery and products-loading terminal. Isa Town, a new development 11 km. south-west of Manama, has a designated future population of 35,000 all of whom will be Bahrainis. The first stage, inaugurated in November 1968, provides accommodation for 15,000 people. Such a settlement may well result in the segregation of citizens in newer suburbs and immigrants in the city centre as in Kuwait. Unfortunately the censuses fail to reveal the distribution of Bahrainis and non-Bahrainis, but Bahrainis will clearly predominate in rural areas, while the immigrants will be prominent in such areas as the capital, the oil town of Awali in the centre of Bahrain island, and the industrial areas of Mina Sulman and Sitra.

Nationality

As in Kuwait, immigration to Bahrain is strictly controlled by a system of visas, together with residence and work permits which are issued by the Immigration Department of the Bahrain Government. A sponsor is required to introduce a foreigner into Bahrain as part of the labour force and it has to be shown that a Bahraini is not available for the specific type of work undertaken. Wives and children of permitted immigrants are then granted residence permits, but they may not undertake employment in Bahrain. There is no discrimination by nationality for work permits, but Bahrain relies heavily on expatriate labour in the construction industry, and in the service industries including retail trade. In the former industry Omanis and Iranians are strongly represented since they are willing to undertake heavy manual labour, while Indians and Pakistanis are important in the services sector especially retailing. A small but important pool of foreign workers is required in the oil industry which demands a high level of technical expertise; thus British and Commonwealth citizens are important in this activity.

As for the granting of nationality, Bahrain's policy is slightly more liberal than that in Kuwait. Those born in Bahrain of foreign parents are most likely to be granted Bahrain nationality. The most favoured groups for naturalization are nationals originating from Qatar, the Trucial States or Saudi Arabia. Iranians with Iranian passports are not favoured for political reasons, although those born in Bahrain are not discriminated against in any way. The total number of naturalizations has been small, totalling 432 between 1948 and 1969.

In census and other publications Bahrain citizens and foreigners are clearly distinguished, which is particularly fortunate since demographically the two groups present contrasting characteristics.

Natality, fertility and mortality

Direct statistics on natality and mortality are scarce. The age–sex statistics of the census nevertheless provide an indirect base for estimating some crude vital rates. Simplest of these is the child–woman ratio—in this instance, the number of children under five related to the number of women aged 16–50. The ratio for Bahrainis was 858 in 1959 and 852 in 1965, while that for foreigners was 425 in 1959 and 792 in 1965. Crude as these ratios are, they do indicate a very high level of fertility among the Bahraini population and a rapidly rising level of fertility among the immigrants.

Apparently natural increase in Bahrain has as yet not reached the levels attained in Kuwait. Between 1959 and 1965, the average annual increase of the Bahrainis was 36.23 per thousand, pointing to a birth rate in the region of 45 per thousand. Further calculations using the under one age groups are precluded by uneven age-recording of all children up to the age of five. Nevertheless, the 1959 census report derived a figure of 47 per thousand for the crude birth rate among Bahrainis and a crude death rate of 17.5 per thousand. Using a similar method to calculate vital rates for the year before the 1965 census results in a crude birth rate of only 32.5 per thousand, pointing to under-enumeration among the under one age group. There is no evidence in the maternity statistics of a drop in fertility as the total number of live births rose from 4,430 in 1966 to 4,875 in 1968. Neo-natal mortality also declined to rates of under 16 per thousand between 1964 and 1968, a level comparable with rates in England and Wales over the same period. About 84 per cent of all recorded births are to Bahrainis. In view of continued investment in health and welfare facilities (by 1968, there were almost 1,000 hospital beds available in Bahrain), the youthful age structure of the population and rising real levels of prosperity, there seems no reason why a continually high level of fertility should not prevail for some time.

Immigration

Bahrain's small size coupled with the limited productivity of the onshore oilfield has restricted the scale of the Amirate's economic expansion. These factors have necessitated a close control over immigration so that in 1965 there were only 38,389 foreigners in Bahrain, just one-fifth of the total population. Numbers of immigrants increased very little until the intercensal period (1959–65), when the average annual increase was over 9 per cent per annum (Table 11.8).

The post-census arrival and departure figures indicate a slight reversal of this trend between 1965 and 1968. Net emigration increased steadily from 1965, amounting to a decline in the foreign population of 9,911 from January 1965 to December 1968. This drop by almost a quarter in the foreign population can be attributed to the oil developments in the Trucial States and in Muscat and Oman which are spurring on a sizeable amount of return migration. In the years 1966, 1967 and 1968 the number of persons from Muscat and Oman declined by 1,315 and from the Trucial States by 944. Other notable drops in population numbers were registered among the Iranians (−1,045), Indians (−1,141), and British (−1,214).

TABLE 11.9   FOREIGN NATIONALS IN BAHRAIN

Nationality	May 1959		February 1965	
	Total	Males	Total	Males
Omanis	7,314	6,146	12,628	11,038
Iranians	4,203	3,188	7,223	4,495
Indians	4,043	2,698	5,383	3,208
Pakistanis	2,283	1,471	3,932	2,333
British	2,514	1,409	2,797	1,456
Saudis	1,605	1,104	1,715	1,096
Yemenis	492	467	1,582	1,541

Sources: Census of population, 1959, Table 17.
Census of population, 1965, Table 7.

In 1965, seven national groups, each with over 1,000 persons, were represented in the composition of the foreign population in Bahrain (Table 11.9). By far the most numerous group were the Omanis, followed by the composition of the foreign population in Bahrain since the first census. Principally this has involved a higher rate of immigration among Omanis compared with the once more numerous Iranian group. Indians, Pakistanis and British have all increased in numbers over the period.

The post-1965 loss of 9,911 foreigners has increased the proportion of other Arabs in Bahrain.

Population composition

Clearly the growth of the Bahraini population has been largely due to natural increase while the foreign population has increased principally by immigration. Attempts to quantify these two components are presented below but at this juncture some contrasts in the demographic structure of the two populations can be observed.

In the censuses of 1959 and 1965, age-recording of the total population was attempted for the first time. Internal and external checks testify to the completeness of overall enumeration but age-recording is erroneous in the senior age groups since birth certificates or other written proof of age are not as yet required in Bahrain.

Figure 11.5 presents the 1959 and 1965 census results graphically. The age–sex pyramid for Bahrainis suggests that this group is a nearly 'closed' population which is expanding rapidly by natural means. Overall there is a slight surplus of males (1,092 in 1959 and 922 in 1965) but this can be ascribed to errors particularly in the age groups above 31 where, in common with many Moslem countries, Bahraini women are probably under-enumerated.

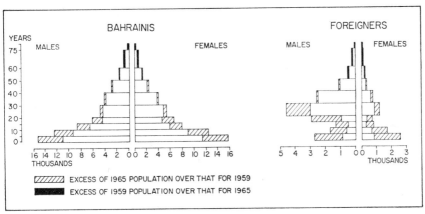

FIGURE 11.5 BAHRAIN: AGE-SEX PYRAMIDS OF BAHRAINIS AND FOREIGNERS 1959 AND 1965

In 1965, 50.5 per cent of the Bahrainis were under 16—an indication of the recent population growth. By comparison only 3.3 per cent were aged 61 and over, leaving 46.1 per cent in the economically active age groups in which just over 90 per cent of the 33,430 males were actively employed, itself a measure of Bahrain's prosperity; in contrast only 3 per cent of the females in the age group 16–60 were economically active at the time of the 1965 census, pointing to the strength of tradition in limiting the size of the workforce.

The various national groups of the immigrant population of Bahrain have different demographic characteristics, as observed for Kuwait. Unfortunately, only sex ratios are available for individual nationalities, but Table 11.9 presents the figures describing the balance between the sexes for selected nationalities. As in Kuwait, Omanis are a predominantly male group although in Bahrain Iranians display more evenly balanced sex ratios. Indians, Pakistanis, British and Americans all have a small surplus of males, while Egyptian women outnumber men because Bahrain relies heavily on Egyptians for its female teachers. Of similar importance in Bahrain's educational system are the female teachers from Jordan and Palestine.

The age–sex pyramid for non-Bahrainis serves as a general description of an immigrant population largely composed of males in the economically active age groups. In 1965, 70 per cent of the non-Bahrainis were aged 16–60 while fewer than 2 per cent were over 61. The remaining 28 per cent in the under 16 age group represent a sector of the foreign population of growing importance. Immigrants are clearly making full use of Bahrain's health service, and adding substantially to their numbers by a high birth rate. The proportion of under 16's was only 16 per cent of the total in 1959.

All the non-Bahraini males in the 16–60 age group in 1965 were economically active, compared with only 84 per cent of the Bahrainis. In addition, 63 per cent of the latter were employees, while 88 per cent of the non-Bahrainis worked as employees. Contrasts also appear in the educational status of the two groups, for in 1965 only 66 per cent of the non-Bahrainis aged 15 and over were illiterate compared with 77 per cent of the Bahrainis.

QATAR

Qatar consists of a narrow limestone peninsula 22,000 sq. km. in area. Near the west coast, a limestone ridge marks the location of the Shaikhdom's principal oilfield on which is sited the oil camp of Dukhan. Oil is pumped across the peninsula to Umm Sa'id where deeper water provides suitable conditions for tanker-loading. The village of Khawr 90 km. north of Umm Sa'id is the only other centre of importance outside the capital city of Doha. This latter centre contains three-quarters of the state's total population which was estimated at 130,000 in 1970.

The Shaikhdom produced 17 million tons of oil in 1969, yielding estimated revenues of $117.5 million. Onshore production, which began in 1949, was supplemented in 1964 by the addition of two offshore producing fields some 100 km. off Qatar's east coast. Oil still provides the backbone of the state's economy although several steps are being taken towards greater diversification. South of Dukhan at Umm Bab, a plant using nearby limestones and natural gas began production of Portland and sulphate-resistant cement in 1969 and at Umm Sa'id an ammonia and urea fertilizer plant is currently under construction. Notably only 1,343 people were employed in onshore oil production early in 1969. Qatar's development is thus following a now familiar path midway between the very rapid post-1945 growth of Kuwait and Abu Dhabi and the steadier evolution of Bahrain.

Population size and distribution

Until the results of the forthcoming census are available, exact statements about Qatar's population are impossible. Most estimates concur on a figure of 80,000 for 1969, representing a 300 per cent increase in the preceding twenty years. Until recently, little of this growth stemmed from natural increase but now, with a fully fledged medical service offering free treatment to the whole population, natural increase assumes greater significance. Over 530 hospital beds are available in Doha while four rural dispensaries (soon to be expanded) ensure that modern medicine is available throughout the Shaikhdom.

Doha has been the focus for most of the recent population growth, and reconstruction of the old city continues in conjunction with an extensive surburban development. Government compensation to Qatari property owners selling land in the city centre has totalled £3 million, providing working capital for new building in suburbs such as Rayyan 5 km. west of the capital. This phase of construction activity has provided many employment opportunities for expatriate labour but, together with the growing services sector including government and administration, has had the effect of centralizing the whole economy on Doha. The new cement and fertilizer plants outside the capital are unlikely to reverse this trend since for their operation they demand a small but technically skilled labour force which as yet the Qataris cannot themselves provide.

Thus an ambitious programme of state education has been instigated in an attempt to provide the necessary personnel to run the future economy of the Shaikhdom. In the years 1969–70, £3.2 million—11 per cent of the total budget—was spent on education. Early in 1969, almost 16,000 pupils were enrolled in Qatar's schools. Such a policy of providing free health and educational facilities to the whole population clearly involves a heavy future financial commitment as the increase rate of both the Qatari and the foreign-born populations accelerates further.

Immigration

No quantitative assessments of the numbers and origins of immigrants in Qatar are available but the same factors are involved in migration to Qatar

as to the other Gulf states. Qataris occupy the top managerial and administrative positions while immigrants constitute the bulk of the manual and
skilled technical labour force. Iranians and Omanis are prominent in the
construction industry and agriculture, while the high grade technical
positions are filled by British and other Europeans. Other northern-area
Arabs are employed in medium grade administrative and clerical roles,
and the 900 school teachers are drawn principally from Egypt and Jordan.
Overall, probably about half of Qatar's population are immigrants.

Immigration is controlled by laws of 1963 and 1964 which stipulate that
every arrival wishing to remain more than one month in Qatar must have a
residence permit. To undertake employment requires a work permit
obtainable only from the Department of Labour and Social Welfare which
constitutes a clearing house for all recruited labour. Labour Law 3 of 1962
states that a vacant position must first be offered to a Qatari and only then
to other Arabs and subsequently to other foreigners. Illegal immigration is
still considerable and in 1386 A.H. the authorities dealt with 3,746 cases
of illegal entry.

The first nationality law, published in 1961 and amended in 1963,
stated that Qataris were those people resident in Qatar before 1930.
Descendants of a Qatari father, whether born in Qatar or abroad, are also
Qataris. Nationality can only be extended to a maximum of 10 persons
annually, who must have continually resided in Qatar for 10 years in the
case of Arabs, and 15 years otherwise. Even those granted nationality are
not regarded as equal to native born Qataris 'as regards the right of working
in the public service or with regard to employment in general' until 5 years
have elapsed since the acquisition of nationality (O'Shanahun, 1968).

THE TRUCIAL STATES

The seven Shaikhdoms of Dubai, Abu Dhabi, Sharjah, Ras al-Khaimah,
Fujairah, Ajman, and Umm al-Qaiwain, known collectively as the Trucial
States, held their first census of population early in 1968. Of the 180,184
people enumerated, 58 per cent were concentrated in the two states of
Abu Dhabi and Dubai (Table 11.10). Both states are substantial oil
producers but Abu Dhabi's earlier start (production began in 1962 and
reached almost 30 million tons in 1969) has enabled the state to embark
on an ambitious programme of construction and development. Dubai's
role as the major commercial port for all seven states has ensured that the
Shaikhdom has shared in its neighbour's sudden rise in prosperity. While
not directly involved in the production of oil, the other five states have been
strongly influenced by the emergence of Dubai and Abu Dhabi as the two
principal growth points of the Trucial States. Public investment in communications and in medical and educational services is transforming the
traditional society of the area and creating a gradient of modernization

between the urban areas and the rural hinterland. Immigration is introducing strong demographic contrasts into the Trucial States: in 1968, 37 per cent of the total population were foreigners. Thus the 1968 census provides the first quantitative measure of the impact of the modern oil industry on a previously small and unsophisticated population in eastern Arabia.

TABLE 11.10   THE POPULATION OF THE TRUCIAL STATES, 1968

Area	*Total population*	*Males*	*Area*	*Total population*	*Males*
Dubai State			*Sharjah State*		
Dubai Town	57,469	34,715	Sharjah Urban Area	20,621	11,835
Other Areas	1,623	877	Western Area	2,959	1,608
			Dibba	1,010	500
	59,092	35,592	Khor Fakkan	2,280	1,168
			Eastern Area	4,610	2,443
Abu Dhabi State					
Island	22,023	18,152		31,480	17,554
Buraimi	12,898	8,585			
Desert	8,029	5,327	*Ras al-Khaimah State*		
Liwa	957	553	Urban Area	8,764	4,661
Oil Fields	2,468	2,246	Northern Area	13,276	7,279
			Central Area	1,196	619
	46,375	34,863	Southern Area	1,246	706
Fujairah State				24,482	13,265
Southern Coast	4,070	2,183			
Northern Coast	2,788	1,438	*Ajman State*		
Mountain Areas	2,866	1,576	Ajman Town	3,725	1,934
			Other Areas	520	278
	9,724	5,197		4,245	2.212
Umm al-Qaiwain State			*Total all Trucial States*		
Umm al-Qaiwain Town	2,928	1,541	(including military personnel not listed above)	180,184	111,864
Other Areas	812	438			
	3,740	1,979			

Source: Trucial States census figures, 1968.

Population distribution

By 1968 the bulk of the Trucial States population had become urban dwellers. Fifty-five per cent of the population lived in the three towns of Dubai (57,469), Sharjah (20,621) and Abu Dhabi (20,352), while the remainder were widely scattered in small towns and villages located principally along the two coasts (Fig. 11.1) with the important exception of the Buraimi oasis. This oasis in the Shaikhdom of Abu Dhabi contained a total of 12,898 people clustered mainly in the town of Al-'Ain. Only 1,153 people lived at the tanker terminal or on the onshore oilfields of Abu

Dhabi, indicating a striking parallel with developments elsewhere in the Gulf where the major concentrations of population are generally removed from the zone of oil production.

With more prolific supplies of groundwater and the relatively late start of the oil industry, almost 18 per cent of the economically active population were still engaged in agriculture and fishing. Few were true desert-dwellers. There are indications in the sex ratios of the outlying districts that internal migration to the cities is occurring. Under-enumeration of females and the shortage of information on the nationality composition of the rural areas both tend to disguise the migration which is occurring, but in two of the smaller villages of the Buraimi oasis, at Dibba, and in parts of Ajman and Ras al-Khaimah, there is a recorded surplus of females among the national population. Plainly, rising oil revenues will further accentuate this trend towards population concentration.

Most of the foreign arrivals are concentrated in the three major cities of the west coast, although 5,864 non-Abu Dhabians were recorded at Buraimi. Almost 40 per cent of all the foreigners recorded in the Trucial States in 1968 (66,193) lived in the state of Abu Dhabi. From the sex ratios, it is apparent that most of the remainder live in Dubai town where the proportion of males approaches 60 per cent of the total population. The presence of a sizeable immigrant group in parts of the Trucial States has a marked impact on population structure, where until recently out-migration was more common than in-migration. In 1965, for example, 1,105 people from the Trucial States, mostly males in the active age groups, were identified in the Kuwait population census. Since foreigners arriving in the Trucial States in the six months prior to the 1968 census were omitted from enumeration, the proportion of immigrants in the total population is likely to be higher than the census suggests. Even so, three-quarters of the population of Abu Dhabi island were not nationals of the Shaikhdom.

Population composition

Overall, the population of the Trucial States is not as youthful as in several other Gulf states (26 per cent are aged under 16) but this figure is misleading because of the variation in the structure of the national and immigrant populations. Over two-thirds of the foreign population are aged 16–40 compared with just 42 per cent of the nationals in the same age group (Table 11.11). Similarly 111,864, or 62 per cent of the total population, are males, but 51,360 of these are foreigners. The two components of the Trucial States' population plainly require separate consideration.

Of the national population, 53 per cent are males, probably because of misreporting of nationality by immigrants and by under-enumeration of females. Clear evidence of under-enumeration of infants is indicated by

TABLE 11.11   PERCENTAGE AGE STRUCTURE OF THE TRUCIAL STATES
POPULATION, 1968

Area	0–4	5–15	16–30	31–50	51 and over	Totals
Abu Dhabi State:						
Citizens	14.2	23.8	28.3	23.3	10.4	20,352
Aliens	3.7	6.4	57.6	29.8	2.5	26,023
Trucial States (excluding Abu Dhabi):						
Citizens	18.0	23.0	26.2	24.8	8.0	93,639
Aliens	14.7	14.8	41.7	24.8	4.0	40,170

Source: Calculated from: (i) The First Population Census of Abu Dhabi, 1968.
(ii) Analysis of other census figures for the Northern Trucial States, 1968.

the uneven progression of the population upwards by individual years, so that the figure of 40 per cent of the population aged under 16 is probably an understatement of the truth. Relating children 0–4 to women 16–50 yields a child–woman ratio of 598 per thousand, indicating a moderate level of fertility by Middle Eastern standards. More sophisticated methods of demographic analysis are precluded by uneven age recording.

The foreign population, 78 per cent of whom are males, display a characteristic immigrant age structure paralleled elsewhere in the Gulf. Despite the lack of females, those resident in the Trucial States have a high level of fertility, for the child–woman ratio calculated as for the indigenous population is 741. With the investment of £6 million in Dubai and £5.7 million in Abu Dhabi on new hospitals and health facilities, the mortality will decline to low levels in a short time. Thus natural increase can be expected to approach 4 per cent per annum (the current level in Kuwait) within 10 years. A closer examination of the apparently higher fertility of the immigrants in the Trucial States may then be possible as the recording of vital rates improves, but the provision of good quality health and educational facilities will influence the demographic composition of the future migrant stream.

Details of the source areas of the present immigrants are available only for Abu Dhabi, but the sources of the migrants in the six northern states are likely to be similar. In Abu Dhabi, 42 per cent of the foreigners were Iranians and a further 34 per cent stemmed from India and Pakistan. Over three-quarters of the incomers were Asians compared with the predominantly Arab influx to Kuwait. Long association with Iran coupled with the demands of the construction industry for manual labour have determined the countries of origin of the migrants. As the economy evolves, the proportion of Arabs may be expected to rise from the present figure of 15 per cent of the immigrant total. If the same proportions hold in all seven Trucial States, 51,000 of the 66,193 immigrants in 1968 can be expected to be Asians, of whom 28,000 will be Iranians.

Some idea of the demographic diversity within a single Shaikhdom can be illustrated by the example of Abu Dhabi, where 56 per cent of the state's population are foreigners comprising 23,505 males and only 2,518 females. Overall, males outnumber females by 3:1, but on Abu Dhabi island 82 per cent of the population consists of males. At Buraimi and other desert areas, Abu Dhabians were in a majority with consequent effects on the age–sex structure of these populations. On Abu Dhabi island 80 per cent and on the oilfields 88 per cent of the population were aged 16–50 compared with 59 and 63 per cent for the desert areas (including Liwa) and Buraimi. While only 9,407 non-Abu Dhabians lived outside the confines of the island, half of these were Asians (primarily Iranians and Pakistanis) living at Buraimi. Clearly the distribution of Iranians closely reflects the location of major construction projects, just as the location of most of the Europeans and Americans on the oilfields and Abu Dhabi island reflects their involvement in specialized technical tasks.

Employment and education

There is as much variation in occupation and educational status between immigrant groups such as the Iranians and the Europeans as there is between citizens of the Trucial States and new arrivals as a whole. A similar contrast is apparent between Abu Dhabi and the other six Shaikhdoms. In general, however, 43 per cent of the total Trucial States' population were economically active in 1968, of whom 18 per cent were employed in agriculture and fishing. The largest employer was the construction industry, largely centred in Abu Dhabi but employing 19,874 people overall. With 11,625 involved in government services and a further 8,590 in other services, it is plain that the tertiary sector of the Trucial States' economy outweighs all others in significance. Altogether, 49 per cent of the economically active population were involved in wholesale and retail trade, banking, transport and communications, and government and other services in 1968.

Table 11.12 illustrates the notable contrast between Abu Dhabi, Dubai and the other Trucial States in employment structure. The emergence of Dubai as a centre providing commercial, banking and transport services is apparent in comparison with the more rudimentary infrastructure currently available in Abu Dhabi. Elsewhere the traditional occupations (agriculture and fishing) are still prominent. About 46 per cent of the total labour force had never received any formal education and of the population

TABLE 11.12   TRUCIAL STATES: PERCENTAGE EMPLOYMENT IN 1968
BY STATE AND INDUSTRY

Activity	Abu Dhabi	Dubai	Other five Trucial States
Agriculture and fishing	8	7	41
Manufacturing, mining and quarrying	3	6	2
Construction	40	17	17
Oil industry	8	2	1
Wholesale and retail trade	6	19	8
Banking	1	2	0
Transport and communications	7	17	10
Government services	15	15	15
Other services	12	15	6
Total	100	100	100
Total economically active	29,284	24,014	23,715

Source: Calculated from: (i) Population Census of Abu Dhabi, 1968.
(ii) Analysis of other census figures for the Northern Trucial States, 1968.

as a whole over the age of 15, only 22 per cent were able to read and write. In Abu Dhabi, only 634 nationals had received a primary education or above, while as much as 74 per cent of the immigrants were in a similar position. Less than half of the total Trucial States' population aged 5–19 were attending school in 1968, although this figure varied from one-ninth in Fujairah to over 50 per cent in Dubai. The demographic and ethnic diversity introduced by the oil industry into the Trucial States provides a new slant on development problems in eastern Arabia.

THE SULTANATE OF MUSCAT AND OMAN

Occupying an area of approximately 212,400 sq. km. (the landward boundaries remain largely undefined), the Sultanate of Muscat and Oman is by far the largest of the five states considered in this chapter. Until 1967, the Sultanate had not joined the ranks of the oil producers of the Middle East and retained a more traditional form of economy and society than prevailed elsewhere in Arabia. In addition, the Sultan's policy of excluding all external influences coupled with the state's peripheral location have limited the intrusions of the Western world, including the gathering of accurate statistical data. Thus estimates of the Sultanate's population for 1969 vary between 500,000 and 750,000 and descriptions of the distribution and composition of this population are equally vague. A certain amount of qualitative material is available from official sources which can be used to

269

indicate trends of particular importance in this current stage of the Sultanate's demographic evolution.

Population distribution and characteristics

The economy of Muscat and Oman depended for its limited prosperity in the pre-oil period on the export of dates, together with lesser amounts of dried fish, limes, pomegranates and firewood. Most of the population were thus oasis-dwellers or nomads with the principal nodes of concentration located along the Batina coast. In the early 1960's, Muscat town contained an estimated population of 5,000, while neighbouring Matrah, administered by the same municipal body, contained a probable 14,000 inhabitants. Other minor foci were Sur and Nizwa, each with about 8,000 people. Access to groundwater supplies either on the flanks of the Jebel al Akhdar or along the coastal margin determined the distribution of most of the Sultanate's population.

Long association with Persia and particularly Baluchistan has added a considerable proportion of Iranians, Baluchis, Indians and Pakistanis to the Sultanate's population. These long-established immigrants, concentrated in Muscat–Matrah, retain their characteristic styles of dress and speech, as well as maintaining their own religions. Negroes and negroid strains are also apparent in the populations of the east coast; many are descendants of Africans imported during the slaving days of last century.

By comparison, most of the native Omanis are Arabs, speaking Arabic and practising the Ibadhi creed of Islam. Tribal affiliations to other sects of the Moslem religion also prevail.

Movement in and out of the Sultanate is strictly controlled and illegal entrants are few. Nevertheless, there are some important transfers of population to be noted. The population censuses of Bahrain and Kuwait, both held in 1965, indicate that a total of 32,148 Omanis were living abroad in these states alone. Considerable numbers of Omanis are also resident in Qatar and the Trucial States. A conservative estimate of the total number of Omanis abroad in 1965 would be 50,000. Of the number enumerated, 86.6 per cent were males, while studies in Kuwait have indicated that the 'turnover' of the Omanis is generally the highest of the alien groups in the state. These inevitably incomplete figures apparently indicate that the Omanis, before oil was being produced in their own country, were making short but frequent trips to the other Gulf states, most returning home at least once annually. Of those enumerated in Kuwait in 1965, 71.6 per cent were aged 15–39, and 70 per cent of those aged 10 and over were illiterate. Most were employees rather than of self-employed or employer status, engaged in retailing and ancillary service trades. The remittances of these Omanis abroad were an important source of finance in the Sultanate's economy.

Effects of oil

In the first year of oil production (1967), the Sultanate received royalties totalling £8 million, rising to £24 million in the subsequent year, and to an estimated £30 million in 1969. Further exploration both offshore and in the south may soon add to the Sultanate's oil reserves, but severe faulting makes a major discovery unlikely. Nevertheless, with an estimated future production of over 15 million tons from the three proven fields at Natih, Fahud and Yibal, enough money will be available to the Sultan to finance a moderate development programme.

The provision of health and educational facilities have been given high priority in all four Gulf states discussed above. Similarly, the Sultan has initiated a development programme by commissioning modern hospitals for Muscat–Matrah, Salalah, Tanam and Sur. A further six to eight hospitals are under consideration for other centres of population. These facilities will greatly add to the older established medical services provided in Muscat–Matrah, where the American Arabian Mission runs both a general hospital with four doctors and four trained nurses, and a women's hospital with one lady doctor and a trained nurse. A 19-bed charitable hospital, jointly financed by the Sultanate and the British Government, is also located in Muscat. The Sultan's armed forces and the oil companies have their own medical services.

These health facilities, taken together with the nine widely scattered health centres in the charge of doctors and the nine other rural dispensaries already in existence, will have a marked effect on the pattern of health of the Omani population. At present health standards are low and eye diseases, dysentery, malaria and tuberculosis are all endemic. Natural increase, estimated at 0.4 per cent by the United Nations, is as yet unimportant. In the future, however, both general and infant mortality rates can be expected to drop dramatically. The current infant mortality rate is probably over 100 per thousand; using the example of Kuwait, this can be expected to drop to below 50 with 15 years, giving a substantial rate of natural increase of perhaps 2 per cent per annum.

An important further addition to the population is the return migration of Omanis presently employed abroad. Should all the Omanis decide to return, this will add at least 50,000 to the total population. This return migration is desirable in view of the age–sex structure of the sample enumerated in Kuwait. Labour of all grades will be required for any development scheme and the skills the Omani migrants have acquired elsewhere will be of use in the Sultanate itself.

At present immigration of foreign nationals is strictly controlled and is restricted to specialists (e.g. European geologists or doctors, or Indian and Pakistani clerks) recruited for specific tasks. More of these specialists will be required in future but foreign nationals will not be encouraged to reside in Oman. Naturalization is only possible with the Sultan's permission which is very rarely granted. Sultanate nationality can, however, be claimed by those descended from an Omani father regardless of place of birth, a principle which may encourage descendants of Omanis residing abroad to return and claim Omani nationality. Thus sizeable population growth by natural increase and by immigration is likely in the near future.

Internal migration within Oman is currently occurring. Considerable amounts of local labour are employed both in the oilfields and at the terminal of Mina al-Fahal. From the experience of the Gulf states, it is clear that in future only minor concentrations of population can be expected to grow up either on the oilfields themselves or at the tanker terminal. Just as Kuwait City far outstrips Ahmadi, and Manama outstrips Awali, so too the growth of the Muscat–Matrah centre can be expected to outstrip the growth of all other centres in Oman.

REFERENCES

General

COLIN BUCHANAN AND PARTNERS (1969) *First Estimates of Population and Employment Growth for Kuwait: 1969–90.* Kuwait Technical Paper No. 3.
DICKSON, H. R. P. (1956) *Kuwait and her Neighbours,* London.
FREETH, Z. (1956) *Kuwait was my home,* London.
HILL, A. G. (1969) *Aspects of the Urban Development of Kuwait,* Unpublished Ph.D. thesis, University of Durham.
LORIMER, J. G. (1908) *Gazetteer of the Persian Gulf:* vol. 2, *Geographical and Statistical,* Calcutta.
NAVAL INTELLIGENCE DIVISION (1944) *Iraq and the Persian Gulf,* London.
O'SHANOHUN ASSOCIATES LTD. (1968) *Qatar 1968,* London.
O'SHANOHUN ASSOCIATES LTD. (1970) *Qatar into the Seventies,* London.

Statistical sources

GOVERNMENT OF KUWAIT:
  1957 *Census of Population* (Arabic).
  1961 *Census of Population* (Arabic).
  1965 *Census of Population* (Arabic).

1964–8 *Statistical Abstract Series* in Arabic and English, Ministry of Public Health, *Annual Reports* (1958 onwards).

GOVERNMENT OF BAHRAIN:

Third Census of Population (1959).

Fourth Census of Population (1965).

Statistical Abstract Series (1967 onwards).

TRUCIAL STATES:

Trucial States Council 1968—

(i) Trucial States Census Figures.

(ii) Analysis of other Census Figures for the Northern Trucial States.

(iii) The First Population Census of Abu Dhabi, March/April 1968.

SULTANATE OF MUSCAT AND OMAN:

A guide to the Sultanate of Muscat and Oman (n.d.).

Chapter 12
Southern Arabia: a human reservoir
W B Fisher

The south-western corner of the Arabian peninsula was, in part at least, once known as 'Arabia Felix'—fortunate Arabia. As early as the time of King Solomon, whose court was clearly impressed by the wealth displayed by a visitor from Sheba, down to Ptolemy and late Renaissance times, when cartographers such as Mercator and Ortelius still employed 'Felix', the view current was of a rich and prosperous region partly supported by a lucrative spice trade, and partly by its own intrinsic resources.

Now, isolated geographically and economically, and torn during the last ten years by political troubles, south-western Arabia must be ranked as one of the poorest areas both within the Middle East and in a world setting. Its *per capita* gross national product of about $90 is estimated at no more than a third of that of Iraq or Saudi Arabia, which have very broadly similar population numbers. There have so far been no major discoveries of oil or other mineral deposits, though a 1970 report suggests the possibility of useful copper ores; whilst closure since 1967 of the Suez route has had a disastrous effect on the economy of Aden, the chief port and probably at that time the largest town of the region. As a consequence of continuing, possibly deepening poverty over many decades, extensive migration has been a feature during the present century at least.

Politically, the area under discussion now comprises two sovereign states: the Yemen, and Southern Yemen, both of which, after a period of foreign domination, gained independence in the present century. Occupation of the Yemen by the Ottoman Turks in the sixteenth century was followed by intermittent and partial control, with phases of re-assertion and withdrawal. However, technically at least, the Yemen remained part of the Ottoman Empire until 1918 when it became an independent state ruled by an autocratic Shi'a Imam until 1962. Following a political coup and a period of civil war between radicals and traditionalist 'royalist' supporters, a dominant republican government emerged, that has gradually been recognized by most outside powers, Saudi Arabia (for long a principal supporter of the royalist faction) doing so in 1970.

Southern Yemen, formerly known as Aden Colony and Protectorate, was occupied by the British between 1843 and 1967, when as a sequel to various attempts made over several years to compose internal problems of the area by erecting expedients such as a Federation and other patterns of government, the British handed over power to local leaders and withdrew.

In its physical geography, the whole region is to be regarded as the highly imposing and convoluted south-western edge of the massive Arabian plateau. An original basement complex of Archaean rocks, sundered from the even larger massif of North and Central Africa to the west, has been disturbed by tilting and fracturing which have had the effect of producing a zone of highland that rises steeply from the Red Sea coast with only a narrow intervening coastal plain, or Tihama, to heights of over 3,500 metres. Extensive lava outpouring as a continuous capping of some higher parts has infilled relief irregularities and produced an extensive high-level plateau with steep sides, especially to the west and south. The same sequence of plateau-building is also to be seen across the Red Sea rift in the plateau of Ethiopia, which has considerable affinities in a structural sense to the Yemen.

From this imposing south-west corner, landforms gradually subside eastward to give a series of coastal ranges and plateaux that remain bold and prominent along most of the coast of Southern Yemen, but drop to a low plain at the frontier with Oman. Inland from the southern coast, the pattern continues of irregular highland ranges declining in elevation eastwards and northwards, with the Wadi Hadhramaut, which is partly erosional and partly tectonic in origin, an important feature.

The great altitude of much of Yemen induces a special climatic régime that is related to the summer rainfall maximum of East Africa and India; but effects are on a much smaller scale. Whilst almost all of the rest of the Middle East has a winter maximum of rainfall, with pronounced summer drought and heat, the Yemeni highlands have a wet summer season and a cool, fairly dry winter. But along the coastal fringe at or near sea level, the 'Middle Eastern' régime of aridity and high temperatures persist. As much as 1,000–1,200 mm. of rain normally occurs over the highest parts of the Yemen, but no more than 50–100 mm. on the peripheral lowland areas. As in the rest of the Middle East, rainfall totals can be extremely variable and capricious: since 1967 there has been prolonged drought in the Yemen, with almost total failure of the summer rains in three successive years. Annual average temperatures in the lower altitudes lie around 28–30°C, but this mean falls to 15–17°C in the uplands where in some parts frost is common during winter.

The physiographic effects produced by the combination of altitude, climatic régime and rock type are unusual and pronounced. Highly episodic rainfall on steep slopes composed in part of soft lavas, tuffs and andesites results in erosion of extensive high level valleys, some wide, some narrow and deep. Outwash of a fertile alluvial soil can thus occur. In other localities limestone of Jurassic and later ages are sometimes soil-covered, sometimes bare and karstic, and surface water may be lacking. Alkalinity of soils may

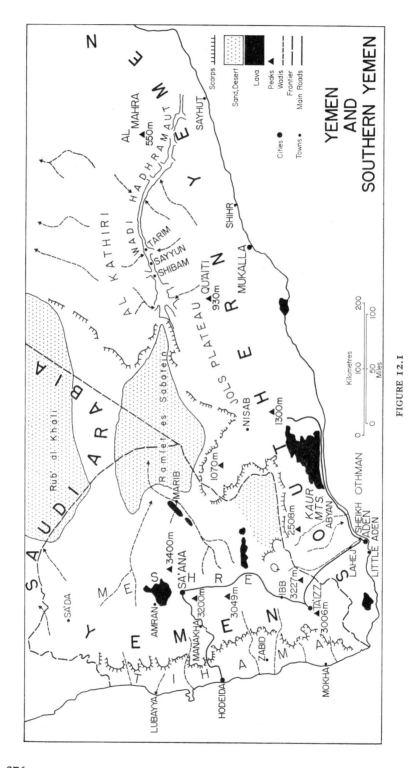

FIGURE I2.I

be a problem. Elsewhere again, exposure of highly resistant Archaean or metamorphosed series can result in skeletal soil cover only; and the base of the plateau is marked by extensive outwash of clays, sands, gravels and large detritusus. Bare expanses of lava (*harras*) also occur.

It is now necessary to discuss the two political units separately and in more detail.

THE YEMEN

Extending over some four degrees of latitude (from 13°–17°N), the Yemen does not as yet have wholly precise and demarcated frontiers, since in a few parts of the east the exact location of the political boundary is in dispute with Saudi Arabia. Various figures are given for total area: 190,000 sq. km. (Dequin), 195,000 (*Statesman's Year Book*), 195,650 (*Encyclopaedia Britannica*, 1960); and a further crucial factor in any study of the Yemen is the fact that the country has been largely closed to outside visitors since the end of Ottoman rule. The reports of Rathjens and von Wissman who visited the area in 1934 are still quoted as authoritative sources; a geological and hydrological survey was published by Geukens in 1956 on behalf of the United Nations; Rathjens has written at a later period on climate; and there have been a number of development surveys and projects undertaken after 1960 by West German, USAID, Egyptian, and Russian organizations, some of which have been published, at least in part.

The principal difficulty, so far as the present study is concerned, is that there has been no census of any kind in the Yemen, and the only demographical information comes from a number of estimates made by various observers. These estimates (of total population) are as follows:

H. Dequin, c. 1963: 4 million.
Grand Larousse, 1965: 4.5 million.
'Official Estimate', 1953: 4.5 million (source not stated), published in Europa Handbook, *The Middle East and North Africa*.
Whitaker's Almanac, 1960: 5 million.
United Nations Demographic Yearbook, 1968: 5 million.

There are a number of reservations and comments that can be made. As in many Moslem countries, seclusion of women, which is practised to a considerable extent in some parts of the Yemen, can lead to under-estimation of females. On the other hand, it is also true that seclusion is not practised among pastoral nomads, of whom there are a number in the Yemen; and also extensive temporary migration of younger males can mean that womenfolk left behind must play a greater part in normal daily activities, and tend therefore to be less secluded.

There have been no considerable minority problems in the Yemen, of the sort that have led to political action in the Lebanon, Jordan and Israel. There is not in consequence the tendency for minority groups to attempt to inflate numbers in order to achieve political advantage. Nor, with a closed, inward-looking system of rule which until 1962 at least appeared indifferent to its reputation abroad, has there been in the Yemen the feeling of national consciousness that has led at least two nations to repudiate the results of census operations as derogatory in that they produced 'too low' a figure. The Yemen until very recently has gone its own way without exercising itself as to impressions given abroad: and this included the matter of total numbers and viability. National prestige was certainly not regarded as being involved in any statement (or lack of this) as regards number of inhabitants.

It would be admissible therefore, in the light of all the foregoing points, to accept a figure of 5 million as a reasonable estimate of present numbers (1971), always bearing in mind that it is no more than a crude estimate.

One matter then emerges, which is of distinct interest. Five million is a sizeable number for a country of relatively small area, much of it mountainous, and a further substantial part arid and desertic. One may compare the adjacent country of Saudi Arabia which with enormously larger area, has possibly a similar total population; or states like the Lebanon, Jordan or Israel, with only one-half each of the Yemen's population numbers, and Syria, with only one million more (all figures as of 1969, are taken from Population Reference Bureau estimates).

This relatively sizeable grouping becomes all the more remarkable when one remembers that the Yemen has no really large towns, and certainly no large ports owing to paucity of trade—nothing comparable with Beirut, Haifa or Tel Aviv—and no oil terminals or external financial contacts like those of the Lebanon and Israel. Yet average density works out at 26 per sq. km. as compared with something like 3 per sq. km. in Saudi Arabia, and 31 in Syria, indicating a relatively numerous rural peasantry occupying relatively restricted areas that can be cultivated.

Population distribution

In the absence of any detailed information, it is perhaps most useful to attempt to relate population distribution to the varied geographical regions that make up the Yemeni habitat. From west to east, as regards geographical units, one may discern a zonal arrangement involving six distinctive zones. In the extreme west, fronting the Rea Sea, is a coastal plain, the Tihama, no more than 25–40 km. wide, and sometimes less. This is lowlying and in general sandy, with small areas of saline marsh (*sebkha*). Here and there however, silts and clays associated with stream beds, washed down from the interior highlands, occur together with non-saline

278

water. No perennial streams cross the plain, but there are a number of water courses that carry water for a time in a portion at least of their channel, and there is seepage under the porous sands and gravels. Flash discharge on a small scale can also be a favourable feature. Hence cultivation is possible in some localities, though generally high temperatures and blowing dust with scorching winds can be a major hazard. Cotton-growing has begun to develop in some localities. As well, there are a number of small ports: Hodeida, Mokha (Mocha) and Lubayya being the chief,and these, of course, add to the general population numbers in the Tihama. At the junction of the plain and interior hills there are again somewhat greater opportunities for cultivation from the alluvial outwash and water flow from the hills. Consequently the Tihama could be regarded as having rather more densely populated zones along its coastal fringe and along its eastern margin against the hills. Between is a highly difficult area inhabited chiefly by a few nomadic pastoralists.

The second of the six regions of the Yemen could be said to comprise the first foothills of the interior plateau. Relatively low altitude (under 700 m.) means that rainfall is negligible and the water-table is sometimes sunk well below the surface either because of extreme erosion of stream beds, or the prevalence of porous rock strata. Some percolation exists because of the general nature of this region, at the base of the plateau complex; but it is of a highly irregular nature, so that while man makes little use of it for cultivation, there is sufficient of an accumulation of water to provide breeding-grounds for anopheline mosquitoes, and also the water snails that are hosts to the bilharzia parasite. Because of this, malaria and parasitic diseases are still rife, and population densities are very low indeed: even the presence of water in this arid environment acts against human survival rather than fosters it.

Above the foothills, at altitudes greater than c. 750 m., is a third region, that environmentally is far more favourable: the middle slopes of the western plateau, or *serat*. This zone experiences more regular seasonal flow from streams that originate on the higher interior plateau, there are expanses of fertile soil, and seepage in the alternation of permeable and impermeable strata gives a further regular water supply. Temperatures avoid the extremes of the highest zone. Irrigated agriculture using streams and wells is therefore possible where level tracts occur or where terraces can be cut—on the sides, usually of the broader eroded wadis. Here terraced cultivation has developed on a considerable scale, with a wide range of crops and hence a relatively numerous population—the largest concentration in the entire country.

As altitude increases yet again, to levels of 1,800–2,500 m., annual rainfall becomes sufficient to allow normal rainfed agriculture. Thus on the highest plateau levels, as distinct from the hill ranges which rise even higher above the plateau surface, there is another area of active cultivation, and major population concentration. This fourth zone—the plateau high-land—is well cultivated especially on the valley floors (*qa*), and it contains most of the principal urban settlements of the country, including the capital, Sa'ana.

Eastward again, there is a more gradual descent to the inner plateau of Arabia: in geographical terms we move from the western scarp face to the interior dip slope. This dip is the Meshreq, with its highest parts adjacent to the plateau highlands deriving some benefit from surface and under-ground water flow, with, in consequence, cultivation possible in some localities. However, flow of water is distinctly less than that on the western side; and moreover, inner location behind high upland massifs leads to greatly reduced precipitation—this is characteristic of much of the Middle East—so that rainfall incidence diminishes rapidly eastwards with declin-ing altitude, with the Meshreq passing in its eastern part into the almost totally arid conditions of the Rub' al Khali.

As a consequence, population in the Meshreq is lower in numbers than that on the western slopes of the plateau, and is mostly concentrated in the higher parts closest to the plateau, or where special local advantages exist as regards water supply. At lower altitudes pastoral nomadism on a small scale is the chief occupation.

In the Meshreq especially, local water catchment by dams across narrow wadis was once practised on a large scale. As many as 80 former dams have been counted, though none are now in efficient working order. The largest, at Marib, broke down through neglect in the fifth century A.D. while others were allowed to decay or were merely abandoned, as the former Incense Route traffic declined, and commerce in spices was diverted to the sea. Now despite topographical advantages, there are hardly any dams or barrages in the Yemen, and none of a major kind; though plans are now under consideration to build a few new ones.

Various estimates have been made of the population in each of the six zones just described, and a consensus would be as follows:

	Per cent
Tihama (including coastal towns)	20
Lower western slopes	5 to 7
Higher western slopes (*serat*)	33 to 35
High plateau	30
Higher Meshreq	10
Lower Meshreq	under 2

Ethnic affinities

It would seem that the Yemeni population is far from being homogeneous as regards ethnic type. The inhabitants of the Tihama, a relatively large proportion of which are town-dwellers, show marked relationships with peoples from tropical and North-East Africa, as well as with southern Asia. Besides the seafaring contacts that have brought East Africans and some Asians, including Malays, to this part, some originally as slaves, there have been a number of migrations on a small scale of tribal units from the opposite shores of the Red Sea and Gulf of Aden: the Sudan, Eritrea, Ethiopia and Somalia. Certain of these peoples have settled in the ports, but others have established themselves as cultivators on the Tihama where their round thatched 'beehive' huts strongly indicate African rather than Arabian social affinities. As in certain other districts of coastal Arabia, the population of the Yemeni Tihama is thus extremely varied in its ethnic origins.

The inhabitants of the plateau show more clearly-defined Arabian (i.e. Semitic) affinities, with considerable similarities in racial type to the peoples of Saudi Arabia. Colour is lighter, facial appearance shows the narrower leptorrhine character, and body build is somewhat lighter. Towards the south-east there may be other non-Arabian ethnic affinities showing links to Baluchestan and the Indian sub-continent.

Demographic aspects

In the absence of any authoritative figures, one can only attempt estimations regarding population dynamics and composition. Suggestive crude birth rates most likely range from 45–50 per thousand of population; and death rates probably around 30 per thousand though both could well be higher. This last figure is distinctly higher than in most other Middle Eastern countries, and closer to those of tropical Africa. We might accept this comparison, bearing in mind the low level of production, lack of development in public amenity and infrastructure, absence of a major resource such as oil or capacity as entrepreneurs, and the extremely low reported level of productivity *per capita*. To these disadvantages must be added in the short period eight years of civil war and three consecutive years of famine due to poor rainfall.

Dequin believes the Yemeni death rate to be one of the highest in the world, which would mean a level of well over 30 per thousand; and he speaks of a rural infantile death rate (over 85 per cent of the total population are rural) of 50–80 per 100 live births. The figures for Saudi Arabia before the effects of oil exploitation suggest that crude death rates of over 30 per thousand would certainly be possible.

Public health standards are, as we have cursorily noted, below those of many other parts of the Middle East, and there have so far been very few of the improvements in sanitation and social engineering that in neighbouring regions have had such a dramatic effect upon mortality rates. Malaria is still endemic in the lower western hill areas, and when it is recalled that parts of the Lebanon and northern Palestine in the early 1940's had incidence rates of 60–96 per cent of total child population, the extent of possible occurrence in the less arid parts of the western Yemen (which in their ecology somewhat resemble the Levant uplands) will be apparent. Little if any treatment of drinking water takes place, spraying against insect vectors of disease is unknown, there are at most ten hospitals in the entire country and no more than 500 km. of surfaced road. Medical attention is scanty and, with poor communications and little opening for commercial crops, local famines are a recurrent problem. In the summer of 1970, international agencies made emergency shipments of food to relieve destitution that is thought to have affected 10 per cent of the entire population. Tuberculosis is rife in many parts. Food intake would appear to be under 2,000 calories per day: some observers have suggested an average of 1,750–1,900 calories only.

Consequently, life expectancy for Yemenis is low: under 30 years, and yet, given the high birth rate, numbers would appear to increase by 1.75 per cent to 2.25 per cent per annum.

Rural and urban

Most Yemenis live as subsistence farmers, following highly traditional methods which, however, have begun to alter in certain localities as the result of more radical governmental action since 1962. Previously, the Imam and a relatively small number of notables (some claiming descent from the original followers of Mohammed who proselytized the country during the expansion of Islam) held very large tracts as prime landlords, with leases of various kinds to small scale tenant farmers. Grazing grounds were largely in communal ownership (*dira* or *masha'a*), a feature common elsewhere in the Middle East; whilst *waqf* both, religious and private, accounted for 5–10 per cent of exploited land.

Complex rental schemes, usually in kind, operated between landlord and tenant, with various fractions of crops shared according to their nature: e.g., one-half of cereals or three-quarters of dates to the landlord, partially reflecting the contribution made by the landlord in the form of land, seed, water and implements.

Since 1962, however, the former Ruler's land has been converted to state exploitation, with workers paid fixed, sometimes cash, wages. Similarly, the power of the other landlords has tended to decline, as has also the institution of *waqf*, by which property had been dedicated to some religious or charitable object or family trust. Gradually, greater emphasis on production for sale is affecting a few commodities such as coffee, cotton, sisal and *qat* (*catha edulis*, a stimulant), which are increasingly grown for export. Nevertheless, it is still probable that no more than 10 per cent of agricultural production is offered for outside sale, the rest being for immediate subsistence. Of the land under cultivation, perhaps four-fifths is rain-fed, and the rest irrigated.

The picture is, in consequence, one of communities of peasant farmers, often tenants, or to a very small extent, paid labourers on state enterprises, relying mainly on arable land. There is, however, an element of animal husbandry, some closely associated with agricultural settlements, some on a tribal and nomadic basis, especially in the east of the country. There is the beginning of commercial exploitation for a few crops, encouraged by Russian- and Egyptian-sponsored development schemes.

Under these circumstances, some 85–90 per cent of the inhabitants of the Yemen could be considered as settled rural population, with a further 5 per cent nomadic herders, and the rest, 5 to 10 per cent, townspeople. Rural settlements tend to be tightly clustered on defensive sites or close to water supplies, with little in the way of a developed pattern or organization —morphology is strongly influenced by those two principal factors alone. Houses in the uplands may be quite strongly built of stone, and of several storeys, but on the Tihama, as has been said, isolated clusters of reed huts with a few larger rural compounds are more characteristic. On the high plateaux, stone-built huts are usual. Isolation, physical and economic, lack of amenity, and traditional ways are the chief features still of the Yemen countryside.

The towns of the Yemen are few, and generally small in size. Sa'ana, the capital, is situated on the high plateau, at an altitude of 2,500 m. and its estimated population is 110,000. Others are Ta'izz (85,000), Hodeida (50,000) and Sa'da (25,000): these four are the only ones to be described in the Saudi Arabian/US Map of 1963 as 'cities'. The rest are either very small ports, like Lubayya and Mokha (Mocha), or local market centres: Amran, Bajil, Dhamar, Ibb, Manakha, Qa'taba and Zabid. Many of the inhabitants of these towns, especially the smaller ones, are in part at least, cultivators, and so the 5 to 10 per cent of urban population given above must be considered in relation to this. However, with the recent decline of Aden as an outlet for the Yemen, the growth of Hodeida, and the beginning of development schemes, a trend to increasing urbanization is to be expected, though this is as yet apparently small.

Migration

The work of cultivation involves, in the hill areas at least, repair of terraces —a matter which would appear to be in decline, and maintenance of the irrigation systems: wells, canals, and on the lower areas, deflection of flash-flooding or seasonal flow of streams. Though these activities are highly demanding on labour, they do not involve the whole of the Yemeni farming population, since, as noted, irrigated cultivation is a minor aspect —rainfall agriculture predominates. Lack of economic development either in the countryside or the towns, with political and social isolation and a highly traditional way of life has produced much under-employment, especially in rural areas, with the classic response of widespread outward migration, both temporary and permanent.

Permanent emigration has brought Yemenis to many Arab areas of the Middle East and East Africa as sailors and increasingly as unskilled labourers; and occasionally, for the fortunate few, as merchants and entrepreneurs. Ships' crews based even on ports such as Marseilles, Cardiff and Tyneside, or the ports of Indonesia and the mainland of South-East Asia often draw recruits that originate from the Yemen, and some of these may in time come to regard themselves as a colony that does not plan ever to return to Arabia, though remittances may be sent to relatives.

More numerous, however, are temporary migrants, who now increasingly find employment in the development construction or expanding economies of other Middle Eastern states. Some temporary migrants have entered semi-permanent or long-term employment, staying outside the Yemen for years or even decades, often (though by no means always) sending remittances home and then returning. The rapid expansion of building and constructional schemes in oil-rich regions—Saudi Arabia especially—has given new openings to Yemeni emigrants who, usually without much formal education, at least initially take up unskilled occupations.

Moreover, some Yemenis move seasonally as harvesters: to the Sudan for cotton-picking, date-harvesting in lower Iraq, and a few to the myrrh and incense collection in Dhofar. Such seasonal migration is thought to involve about 200,000 Yemenis, nearly all men; whilst longer term migration means that possibly half a million Yemenis live abroad on a somewhat more permanent basis.

Of these last, a number would appear to have been abroad as exiles for political reasons, and some have returned to the Yemen after 1962. Principal countries involved in Yemeni migration are Saudi Arabia (where over 100,000 of the 3–400,000 foreign workers are thought to be from the Yemen and Southern Yemen), Ethiopia, Somalia, Libya, the Sudan, Indonesia and the Arab/Persian Gulf states. Formerly, many Yemenis found employment in Aden, but with the drastic drop in port activity there, opportunities are much less.

In addition, there is a certain amount of nomadic migration involving both the pastoralists of the Meshreq and the cultivators of the Tihama. Thesiger noted that, when rains fail, tribal units from both areas may move temporarily northwards into Saudi Arabia, and the opposite can apply when rains fail elsewhere, with temporary inward movement by non-Yemeni tribes.

Otherwise, because of the closed and secluded nature of the Yemeni state and internal difficulties since 1962, entry by foreigners has been very small indeed. Only a very few technically trained personnel were allowed entry—medicals and engineers chiefly; and in the days of the Imam these numbered well under 500. Now, there are colonies of Russian, Egyptian and West German technologists engaged on development projects, but these number under 1,500—armed forces apart.

Qat

Natural conditions in the Yemen and in Southern Yemen favour the growth of the *qat* shrub as a unique speciality—it will not flourish elsewhere. When chewed, qat leaves induce a mild narcosis and a sense of stimulus and well-being; hence *qat*-taking is a considerable social relaxation, made use of by a large proportion of the population. Qat is also addictive. Consequently, just as a number of the population in Britain regularly devote an hour or two each day to communal consumption of alcohol, so in the Yemen and Southern Yemen much time is given over to '*qat* sessions'. The leaf retains its qualities for only three days after being picked, hence it can be used only in the area where it grows—i.e. the hills of south-western Arabia —and though a few wealthy individuals outside the growing areas can afford express air freight (which does in fact occur on a very small scale), consumption tends to be limited to the Yemen and Southern Yemen.

Opinions differ strongly regarding the medical, economic and social effects of *qat* addiction, which is prevalent possibly among 70 per cent of the adult male population. Some observers see *qat* only as a mild stimulant no more harmful than moderate addiction to alcohol or even tobacco, which in a land not well furnished with amenities and luxuries provides a moderately harmless activity that for many may deaden the effects of endemic disease, reduce appetite in a territory where food is not plentiful, and at the same time is a tranquillizing social distraction.

Others, however, regard *qat*-taking is extremely harmful—as diminishing physical activity and so deleterious to the economy in that it reduces effective work and therefore general productivity. There are, it is also argued, very harmful physiological effects, on the liver especially, and regular addiction reduces mental and physical capacity. '*Qat* sessions' are mentioned by some observers as a normal feature of the afternoons—but there is the siesta habit elsewhere and also, in the west, the lunch-time alcohol session. It is, however, very seriously argued that *qat* addiction is a major element in the cycle of low production—malnutrition—low public health—low production that makes the Yemen an outstandingly poor area. Yet, on the other hand, it could be a relatively inocuous escape mechanism from the harsh economic and social conditions that stem from the geographical environment. The majority of writers, including Arabs, take the first view, but there are those who accept the second; and the former British Government in Aden followed both—it at one time totally banned *qat* as a dangerous drug, and then revoked the ban a few years later, partly, it must be added, because of the difficulty of enforcement.

If we accept the view of *qat* addiction as a social evil (and more research is obviously necessary here) then its effects on the population could be highly important, not merely because of direct effects upon the individual, but possibly (and here there has been no investigation) upon genetic and physical inheritance. Chronic alcoholism certainly affects the children of alcoholics who are demonstrably more susceptible to disease, physical disabilities and mental breakdown. Clearly, more investigation of the situation is necessary: is *qat* 'hard' or 'soft'?

THE SOUTHERN YEMEN

In its physiography, the state of the Southern Yemen exhibits considerable contrasts. From the western highlands, which are imposing in general, but more dissected and generally lower in altitude than the main Yemen plateau, heights decline eastwards. The principal area of human occupance is the narrow coastal plain, discontinuous where the interior plateau extends to the sea to give a high, closed coastline, and sometimes also broken by lava flows or craters, as at Aden City itself. Towards the east, declining altitudes mean in the main reduced rainfall; and a growing predominance of permeable calcareous rock strata result in heavily weathered karstic formations lacking surface water. This type of environment is best seen in the intricately dissected Jols region.

Human settlement tends therefore to be concentrated on or close to the coast, in the border valleys and valley benches where water and good soil are available; or in the middle portions of the Wadi Hadhramaut where sufficient water occurs at least seasonally. There is no permanent flow throughout the entire length of the Wadi, but in its middle parts, where the valley runs roughly parallel to the coastline at 150 km. inland, seepage and seasonal rainfall provide spring-fed flow that maintains itself for part of the time. There is a usable but irregular underground water-table in some localities, and in others, where the valley is narrower, *seil* (flood) cultivation can be practised. This, by no means confined to the Wadi Hadhramaut, is also a feature of parts of the coastal zone of the Red Sea and Gulf of Aden, not only in South Yemen and the Yemen, but in the eastern Sudan and Ethiopia. It involves the construction of low dams or barrages to divert seasonal floods on to particular patches of cultivable ground. By choosing differing zones of good soil in rotation on which to concentrate available water, the vagaries of rainfall can be partially mitigated; and *seil* cultivation, for long a traditional method, is now being developed on modern, more extensive lines in such areas as the Abyan district near Aden.

Besides cultivation, there is much sea-fishing from such towns as

Mukalla and Shihr, with catches even eaten by camels as well as humans. A few ridges in the extreme east where aspect in relation to monsoonal air currents is favourable offer summer pasture for nomadic pastoralists, and there is still a certain amount of frankincense collection from the small numbers of groves that remain on these hills. Some cultivation also occurs on the island of Socotra.

Politically, what is now the unitary Republic of Southern Yemen had previously experienced varied patterns of rule. The territory of Aden City, only 192 sq. km. in extent, was for long ruled directly as a British Crown Colony. The remaining territory was organized into a loose Western Protectorate, consisting of 20 semi-antonomous Arab states, and an even looser Eastern Protectorate of 23 separate states. Some of this arose from genuine ethnic and cultural differences, as for instance in the Hadhramaut, where communities such as the Mahra and Qara speak a pre-Arabic Semitic language, and show in ethnic type and culture affinities to the Indian sub-continent—some observers term them 'Veddoids'. Furthermore, following the admission of African slaves over several centuries, there is a considerable negroid element, as much as 45 per cent in places like Qishn, and the Qu'aiti and Kathiri territories. There is also some Malay and Indonesian intermixture, as many migrants have brought back wives from these areas. Other, smaller differences arose in part from distinctive ways of life as mountaineers, horsemen, pastoralists, cultivators, fishermen, traders and nomads. However, perpetuation over many years of these varied and tiny units could—and did— suggest to some outside observers a deliberate policy of 'divide and rule' or, at best, an exaggerated deference to an earlier *status quo*. Lacking the motivation of petroleum development which has operated powerfully to emphasize and facilitate separatism and delay unity in the Persian Gulf states, which have equally small populations and sometimes equally limited territories, the Aden political units were brought into a kind of unity, first as the Eastern and Western Protectorates, and then later, in the 1960's, into an overall Federation: Britain's now classic device for signifying the penultimate phase of colonial rule. Emergence of a unitary state on gaining independence seems to have substantiated the view of former divisions as minor only.

The results of acquiescence in extreme political subdivision, with varying degrees of governmental control in a territory where physical conditions are difficult and economic returns low, are seen in the statistics relating to demography. In the first place, frontiers with the Yemen to the north, and with Saudi Arabia on the north-east, were not closely demarcated, on substantially different interpretations exerted even down to the 1960's, as is shown in various maps and atlases: the US general map of Saudi Arabia, for instance, makes no attempt to show full boundaries. Moreover, with unsettled political conditions at first in the interior, and then generally within the region, census-taking became impossible. Consequently, there are official enumerations relating to the former Aden colony (excluding Perim and Kamaran islands) and a number of vaguer figures for the remaining territories. No census of the whole area has ever taken place.

Most existing figures suggest a total of 1.2 to 1.5 million inhabitants for the entire country, with 250,000 of these located in Aden territory. The city itself was estimated to have a population of 99,825 in 1965, with Sheikh Othman 29,871 and Little Aden (Al Buraqa) 9,277. The size of Mukalla, the chief port and town of the east, was estimated at 20,000.

A few statistics have appeared relating to population movement. In 1965 the Aden Government issued figures of 9,081 births and 1,929 deaths: these, if applied to the estimate of quarter million total population of Aden state give a crude birth rate of 36.3 per thousand, and a death rate of 7.7. The Population Research Bureau gives corresponding figures for 1969 as: birth rate 37 per thousand and death rate 8 per thousand, and, though this is not stated, it would therefore seem that these figures really apply, again, to the Aden region only. It is highly probable that different situations occur in the non-urbanized north and east.

The relatively low birth rate (below that of Egypt, Iraq, Jordan, Kuwait or Turkey) could be assigned to several causes: the high proportion of a sophisticated urban population in the base sample; the presence of a numerous non-Arab foreign population (chiefly British and other officials, and Indian and Pakistani merchants and technicians) many of whom were temporary short-term residents; and some non-enumeration of births and infant deaths. For 1969 an infantile death rate of 80 per thousand live births is recorded: only half of that in, e.g. Turkey.

The strikingly low death rate can be explained by some of the same factors: temporary immigrants leaving the country to retire or at the expiry of contract; a reasonably high level of public health within the Aden urban cluster; and good medical services easily to hand. However, it is much less likely that similar conditions would obtain in the less developed parts of the country, where conditions would probably be closer to those of the Yemen, with possible mortality of over 30 per thousand. From these scanty data, it would seem reasonable to infer an annual growth rate of 2.0 to 2.5 per cent which, it is estimated, could bring the total population to 1.6–1.9 million by the end of the present decade.

One important element, though possibly rather less significant than in the Yemen, is the temporary migration of South Yemenis outside the country. Traditionally, the Hadhramaut has been the major reservoir of outward migration, and the chief, though not sole, area of attraction has been the East Indies (Malaysia and Indonesia especially) where Islam is strong. This attraction is shown partly by the remarkable building styles in some parts of Southern Yemen, which show strong Eastern influences—massive, highly and intricately decorated dwellings of several storeys, quite dissimilar in style from those of Saudi Arabia or the Persian/Arab Gulf states. Many Hadhramautis found occupation as seafarers and traders, but in the climate of growing nationalist feeling within South-East Asia it is uncertain at what level this volume of traditional migration will continue, and statistics on it are lacking.

Another matter of very considerable importance is the disastrous economic consequences to Aden City following closure of the Suez Canal since 1967, and the parallel development of super-tanker fleets that are routed direct from the Persian or Arabian Gulf to Europe via the Cape of Good Hope. Aden has an important refinery which imports crude and re-sells part as bunkers to merchant ships, and the rest in various markets of East Africa and elsewhere. This trade far outweighed the rest: oil was Aden's largest import and export item. Now, with virtually no shipping using the northern Red Sea, Aden has lost some of its nodality. Further-more, withdrawal of British officials and armed forces has reduced pur-chasing power, and a number of Asian merchants have also left. All this, together with attempts to develop Hodeida, has drastically reduced general economic activity. Until the 1960's Aden acted as a general outlet for much of south-west Arabia, but with development in Asir (Saudi Arabia) and the Yemen, and the emergence of Oman as an oil state, Aden has lost much of this function, highly limited though it was.

TABLE 12.1   ACTIVITIES AT ADEN
(*in dinars*)

	1964-5	1969
Total governmental revenue	15,965,000	8,867,000
Aden port revenues	2,030,000	948,000

Source: Central Statistical Office, Aden.

Lacking major resources, facing a decline in its overseas trade, and the possibility of fewer temporary migration outlets (with the loss of remit-tances that this would entail), the state of Southern Yemen faces a difficult future. Population prospects are thus highly uncertain, but in the absence of detailed statistics, and the implied reservation that most existing ones refer to the Aden region only one can do little to carry this examination further.

REFERENCES

BETHMANN, E. W. (1960) *Yemen: on the Threshold*, Washington.
BRICE, W. C. (1966) *South-West Asia*, London.
DEQUIN, H. (1963) *Die Landwirtschaft Saudisch—Arabiens*, Frankfurt a/M.

EL ATTAR, M. S. (1965) *Le Sous-dévéloppement Economique et Social du Yemen*, Paris.

GEUKENS, J. (1956) *Geological and Hydrological Survey of Yemen*, United Nations, New York.

ISTITUTO GEOGRAFICO DE AGOSTINI (1971) *World Atlas of Agriculture*, Vol. II, Novara.

RATHJENS, C. and VON WISSMANN, H. (1934) *Landeskundliche Ergebnisse, Sudarabienreise*, Hamburg.

THESIGER, W. (1959) *Arabian Sands*.

USA DEPARTMENT OF STATE (1968) *Background Notes: South Yemen* and *Background Notes: Yemen*.

WENNER, M. W. (1967) *Modern Yemen*, Baltimore.

Chapter 13
Egypt: population and resources
A B Mountjoy

The demographic situation in the United Arab Republic (Egypt) differs in many respects from that of the other states of North Africa and the Middle East. An examination of the demographic pressures it has been experiencing during the last thirty years emphasizes the potent part that 'population' can play in a nation's affairs. Before making such an examination, the degree of reliability of the statistical data should be appraised. The first modern-type census of Egypt's population was taken in 1882 and for various reasons its results are not considered to be very reliable. From 1897 until 1947 censuses were taken decennially, and greater reliance may be placed on them. The 1957 census was not completed owing to the disturbed conditions following the Suez crisis, and the last full census was taken in 1960. A sample census was taken in 1966. There are also available publications of the former Department of Statistics, now the Central Administration for Statistics, and the Department of Public Health. As might be expected, the information collected by the decennial censuses has varied as the statistical technique has developed. Generally each successive census has demanded more information and has been more complete than its predecessor. Unfortunately this means that comparison of figures in certain categories is not possible over any length of time, e.g. 'personal occupation' first appeared in the 1917 census, 'number of wives' in 1927, 'place of birth' in 1937 and questions on fertility in 1947.

To a great extent such shortcomings reflect the great difficulties involved in attempting to carry out an accurate census of a population mostly illiterate and not particularly well disposed to such enumeration. In the early censuses there was no doubt a good deal of guess work and inaccuracy and the earlier ones are thought to be undercounts. In general the age group figures in each census are unreliable, since the mass of the population is genuinely ignorant on the subject. Once a birth is registered (and in the country districts many are not) the whole matter is forgotten and the figures recorded in the censuses represent guesses at the ages of individuals rather than accurate facts. Owing to the Moslem lunar calendar moving eleven days forward each year and the consequent variation in the dates of the religious festivals, it is practically impossible for the census to be taken on the same day each time. This has to be overcome by adjusting all figures to a set day (1st July). It should be noted that the census is a *de facto* one and thus it is essential that it should be carried out when conditions are normal.

It will be seen that numerous sources of error and unreliability are apparent in the data, but no statistical exercise of such magnitude and scope can be perfect, and it is clear that each census is more accurate than its predecessor and has produced more information. Far more than heads are now counted; indeed the Egyptian Government defined the last full census as 'the process of collecting, compiling and publishing demographic, economic and social data pertaining at a specified time to all persons in a country'. Much information on economic activity, educational status, duration of present marriage, size of households, number of rooms, etc., was included in addition to age, sex, religion, place of birth, marital status (including number of wives), etc. Egypt has the longest experience of census-taking in the region and her last full census was a sophisticated operation of reasonable reliability.

Size and distribution of population

The official estimate of Egypt's population in 1967 was 30,907,000 and the net annual increase to this total was of the order of 770,000 (Central Agency, 1968). These are remarkably high figures when set against the geographical circumstances of the Republic: a desert state of which less than 4 per cent is habitable. The overriding problem that faces the Egyptian people and their government is that of pressure of population upon limited resources: a situation different from most of the other countries of North Africa and the Middle East. The immediate social, economic and political problems that receive day-to-day publicity are usually manifestations of this crucial situation which has worsened since the Second World War. The situation has influenced and shaped government policy, particularly in the social and economic spheres.

Whereas the total area of Egypt is 1,002,000 sq. km., the cultivated and settled area, consisting of the valley and delta of the River Nile, various oases in the Western Desert and a number of mining towns along the Red Sea coast, amounts only to about 35,500 sq. km. Some 99 per cent of the total population live in these areas. This limited distribution of the population means that the country's overall density figure (30 per sq. km.) is almost meaningless and, in fact, could give a totally erroneous impression of the demographic situation. Density of population per habitable square kilometre has much more significance, and in 1967 it was as high as 843.

The Nile Valley from the Sudanese frontier down to Cairo comprises Upper Egypt, while the Delta, from Cairo to the sea, is known as Lower Egypt. Some 35 per cent of the population is to be found in Upper Egypt and 64 per cent in Lower Egypt. The last 30 years have seen a significant change in these proportions, for the corresponding figures in 1937 were 40 per cent and 57 per cent. Egypt's habitable area is divided administratively into 25 governorates. Four of these are sparsely populated border areas (Red Sea, Sinai, Matruh and New Valley), with a total estimated population of 344,000 in 1966, and five are urban areas, all in Lower Egypt (Cairo, Alexandria, Port Said, Ismailiya, Suez). Of the remaining governorates eight are in Lower Egypt and eight in Upper Egypt. The five urban governorates in 1966 accommodated 22.5 per cent of the population. Cairo, the capital with over 4 million population (and the largest city in Africa), now accounts for 13.6 per cent of the total population and in size far surpasses all other Egyptian cities (Table 13.1).

TABLE 13.1 DENSITY OF POPULATION IN EGYPT, BY GOVERNORATES, 1966

Governorate	Total population	Area (sq. km.)	Density per sq. km.	Density per sq. mile
Cairo	4,219,853	214	15,046	39,120
Alexandria	1,801,056	290	6,210	16,146
Port Said	282,977	829	341	887
Suez	344,789	307	1,123	2,920
Ismailiya	264,098	397	616	1,602
Beheira	1,978,889	4,592	431	1,120
Damietta	431,596	599	720	1,872
Kafr el Sheikh	1,118,495	3,492	321	834
Gharbiya	1,901,117	1,995	953	2,478
Daqahliya	2,285,332	3,462	660	1,716
Sharqiya	2,107,971	4,701	448	1,164
Minufiya	1,458,048	1,514	963	2,503
Qalyubiya	1,211,764	944	1,283	3,335
Giza	1,650,381	1,078	1,531	3,980
Faiyum	935,281	1,792	522	1,357
Beni-Suef	927,910	1,313	706	1,625
Minya	1,705,602	2,274	750	1,950
Asyut	1,418,164	1,553	913	2,373
Sohag	1,689,397	1,540	1,097	2,852
Qena	1,470,812	1,811	812	2,111
Aswan	520,567	882	590	1,534
Red Sea	37,818	—	—	—
New Valley	59,385	—	—	—
Matruh	123,707	—	—	—
Sinai	130,849	—	—	—

Source: Derived from *Statistical Handbook, United Arab Republic*, Cairo, 1968.

Over most of the country population density is very high: almost every governorate records more than 600 per sq. km. Only those with extensive areas of unreclaimed desert and lagoon (Kafr el Sheikh, Sharqiya, Faiyum) record less. Several rural governorates have densities of about, or over,

800 per sq. km.: these include Gharbiya, Minya, Asyut, Sohag, Qena. Such rural population densities resemble those to be found in the great delta areas of South-East Asia.

Composition

Information on the age and sex composition of the Egyptian population is better than for most developing countries. Indeed, in many developing countries age and sex data are either not available or only just becoming available as a result of a first enumeration. Egypt's longer history of census-taking also helps to reduce errors although some inaccuracy is inevitable where, as in rural areas particularly, births and deaths are not always registered. Furthermore, in a country where birth certificates are not issued, as the years pass age may not be remembered with certainty and the rural census figures show a bunching in the tens, especially noticeable in the higher age groups. Generally under-enumeration prevails and corrections are applied to the raw data to present a more accurate picture (El-Badry, 1955). The age and sex pyramid (Fig. 13.1) is compiled from adjusted figures and it reveals the broad-based pyramid typifying the common post-war experience of most developing countries.

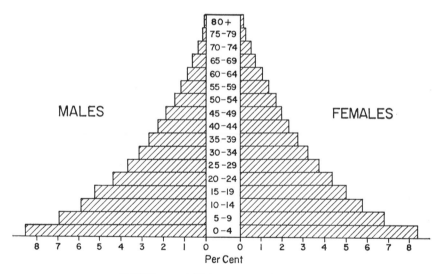

FIGURE 13.1 AGE-SEX PYRAMID OF EGYPT

The 'juvenility' of the population is very apparent: some 43 per cent of the population are under 15 years of age, well over half the population are under 20 years (cf. 38 and 48 per cent respectively in 1947), and more than two-thirds of the population are under 30 years of age. This implies a population of high fecundity—43 per cent of females are of child-bearing age (15–44 years) compared with 38 per cent in England and Wales in 1961. The sharply tapering shape of the pyramid also suggests a relatively poor expectation of life. Life expectancy at birth in 1960 was about 52 years for males and 54 years for females compared with 36 years and 42 years respectively in 1937 (cf. England and Wales 68 and 74 years in 1964).

About half the Egyptian population lives in rural areas without health bureaux and it is in these areas that there is under-registration of births and deaths. This becomes clear when comparison is made between rural areas with and without health bureaux. These rural health bureaux are being extended over the country. Each serves 10–15,000 population and offers medical and nursing facilities, a clinic, child and maternity welfare services. Recent work estimates that under-registration of births in rural areas without health bureaux has been diminishing in recent years and since 1956 the relative deficiency is of the order of 9 per cent and over the whole country under-recording of births is about 5 per cent. Similarly there is considerable under-registration of deaths in rural areas without health bureaux and the degree of under-reporting may be as high as 22 per cent. Thus, reported crude birth and crude death rates are under-counts probably by about 2 per thousand and 3 per thousand respectively (El-Badry, 1965).

A closer examination of the statistics suggests that a majority of under-reported deaths are infant deaths, for infant mortality rates of all other urban areas are lower than those of Cairo, and of rural areas lower still. Since medical, clinical and hospital facilities are probably more adequately available in Cairo than anywhere else in the republic (except in Alexandria), such a situation leads to the conclusion that infant mortality is reasonably accurately reported in Cairo and is under-reported in increasing proportion in other urban areas, rural areas with health bureaux and rural areas without health bureaux. During the last thirty years the spread of medical aid and hygiene has helped to reduce the recorded infant mortality rate from 162 to 119 per thousand live births.

Fertility

Unadjusted crude birth and crude death rates are plotted in Figure 13.2 and serve to indicate recent trends. The Egyptian population is highly fertile and since, as we shall see, external migration is negligible, the rapid growth of the population is almost entirely due to the excess of births over deaths. The graph demonstrates that whereas increasing medical care and spread of hygiene since the Second World War have brought about substantial reductions in the crude death rate, the crude birth rate has shown little variation throughout this century and is still substantially above 40 per thousand. The graph makes it clear that the growing rate of

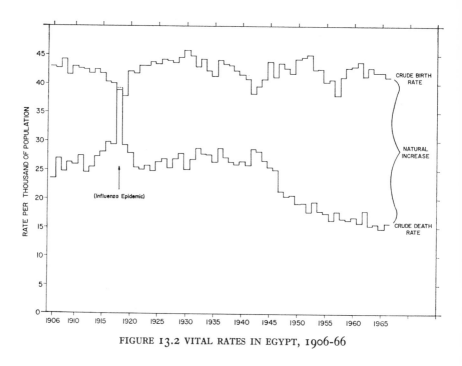

FIGURE 13.2 VITAL RATES IN EGYPT, 1906-66

increase of population results not from a higher birth rate, but from a diminishing death rate.

There are many causes contributing to the high fertility of the Egyptian people. One frequently cited arises from the poverty, overcrowding and lack of amusements in the rural areas. However, the spread of radio and television in recent years has had only marginal effects upon the birth rate. As in other Moslem states, marriage is almost universal, but child marriage is now scarce, although the age of first marriage is generally low. Polygamy, permitted by the Moslem religion, is a further contributive factor but not of major importance. Over recent years there has been a small increase in polygamous households, although they still represent only 4 per cent of the total households (cf. 3 per cent in 1937). The ratio of married Moslem women to married Moslem men in 1960 was 1,029 to 1,000 (1,035 in 1937).

The fashion for large families continues, partly as an old age security measure and for economic reasons—for in a cotton-growing country children can earn money for the household at an early age. Egyptian women are proud of their fertility (as the men are of their potency) and in a land where divorce is not a difficult procedure, bearing children tends to make the wife's position more secure. Furthermore, the desire for sons usually means that the wife continues to bear children until enough sons have been born. Divorce, much more frequent than polygamy, is diminishing.

In 1943 the number of divorces in Cairo was equal to 44 per cent of the number of marriages; in 1952 for the whole country it was 30 per cent, and by 1966 it had dropped to 21 per cent.

A comparison of the estimated fertility rates in Arab countries for 1965 shows the age group 20–24 years in Egypt as being the most fertile age group. In all other Arab states it is the 25–29 year group that shows maximum fertility (Cairo Demographic Centre, 1969). Owing to substantial non-reporting of births and deaths in the rural areas it is not easy to calculate accurate age specific birth rates nor to determine a reliable net reproduction rate for Egypt. El-Badry has made calculations based upon statistics for Cairo and Alexandria (as being the most reliable available) and arrives at a net reproduction rate as high as 2.3 in 1960 (El-Badry, 1965).

Migration

External migration plays a very small part in recent Egyptian demographic history. Few Egyptians leave their country for good, and the numbers of foreigners entering and residing in Egypt is small. The number of foreigners rose from a little over 100,000 at the beginning of this century to 225,000 in 1927 and thereafter decreased. In 1960, 143,000 were recorded. Since 1952, with the passing of successive measures of nationalization and the confiscation of property and assets, the numbers of Greeks, Syrians, Italians and Lebanese, formerly an important element in Egypt's commercial middle class, have undoubtedly dwindled still further. Except for study and pleasure, few Egyptians leave their country and they nearly always return. There are probably fewer than 100,000 Egyptian nationals now living abroad, and many of these are in a new category of professional persons, especially teachers, now employed by, or seconded to, other Arab countries. Thus migration, whether 'in' or 'out', has negligible effect upon the rate of growth of the population which therefore is almost entirely by natural increase.

Within Egypt, a pattern of migration noted in earlier censuses seems to persist. That is, a substantial movement of population—mainly males—from the crowded poor governorates of Upper Egypt (Aswan, Qena, Sohag and Asyut) to urban centres, mainly of Lower Egypt. By 1960 the percentage of migrants from these governorates registered in the urban governorates was 76, 54, 74 and 72 respectively. Cairo and Alexandria were the main magnets: for example, up to 1960 two-thirds of the net out-migration from Aswan governorate was to Cairo and Alexandria. During this century the spread of debilitating intestinal worm diseases associated with the perennial irrigation has lowered the working capacity of the bulk of the fellahin to the north, and the more active labourers from the schistosomiasis-free southern governorates readily find employment at the ports and wherever manual labour is required. A new feature that has become evident in recent years and is indicated by the 1960 census (which records governorate of birth) is that women are increasingly taking part in this out-migration from Upper Egypt. Previously most of the out-movement was of males alone; the more recent figures indicate an increase in the migration of families. The four named governorates show a mean of 13 per cent of females born in them enumerated in other governorates in 1960; in 1947 this proportion was only 7 per cent.

These internal migrations may be related to the economic conditions in these four governorates, among the most densely peopled in Egypt although still relying heavily upon the age-old system of basin irrigation. Under this system, Nile floodwaters are directed on to the land, stand for about forty days and are then drained off. Crops are then sown in the rich silt-covered soil. These are the only crops possible, for after harvest the land remains sunbaked and parched for the rest of the year. Farther north, canal irrigation in the dry season using the waters stored in the dams to the south permits more than one crop a year: thus in any one year the crop area here considerably exceeds the area of farm land. Thus in the four most southerly governorates the density of population per sq. km. of crop area is formidably high, attaining as much as 700 per sq. km. in the mid-sixties. In Lower Egypt (except for Qalyubiya and Minufiya, adjacent to Cairo and where industry is expanding) density per sq. km. of crop area averages about 400 persons. In the south of Egypt there are relatively few non-agricultural opportunities of employment and here is to be found some of the worst poverty in the Republic. On the other hand, the Delta governorates (except for Qalyubiya and Minufiya) have a very low out-migration, partly because there is relatively less pressure upon the land, especially bearing in mind the enlarged crop area associated with perennial irrigation, but also because a greater and growing variety of non-agricultural work is available. The two governorates of Qalyubiya and Minufiya, lying just north of Cairo, record a higher rate of out-migration than for the rest of Lower Egypt. Their contiguity to Cairo is a principal factor in bringing this about. At the 1960 census over 70 per cent of both male and female migrants from these two governorates went to the urban governorates, principally Cairo. The rapid growth of the capital city since the Second World War is mainly due to in-migration. In 1965, some two-fifths of its inhabitants were born elsewhere.

With the exceptions of Giza and Aswan, in-movement to rural governorates is very small. Most of the movements into Giza governorate have been to the town of Giza across the river from Cairo and now a rapidly expanding suburb. In 1960, 22 per cent of the population of Giza governorate were born outside that governorate. Substantial in-migration to Aswan governorate may seem paradoxical in view of the high out-migration, but this is explained by the presence of many constructional works including the High Dam, the growth of factories relying on cheap hydro-electric power from the dam and expansion of the iron ore mines, all offering employment. Large numbers move in from the neighbouring governorate of Qena for, as has been noted, the long-established preference persists for the Nubians of Aswan to move to the towns of Lower Egypt for employment.

Population growth

The current rate of growth of Egypt's population, estimated at about 2.64 per cent per annum is very high (Cairo Demographic Centre, 1969). This is surpassed in a number of other developing countries where rates of over 3 per cent are quoted, but their geographical circumstances are different. Egypt is a desert state with limited agricultural land and even greater limitations upon the expansion of that land. This is why the relentlessly mounting rate of increase to Egypt's population over the last half-century has become so serious to the Egyptian people and their governments.

The first reasonably reliable census, taken in 1897, recorded a total population of 9,700,000. The census of 1966 recorded a total of 30,139,000 —an increase of over 200 per cent in 70 years. The rate of increase has not been uniform, as the logarithmic graph (Fig. 13.3) shows. There occurred a high rate of increase in the early years of this century as perennial irrigation was introduced and more farm land became available. There followed a uniform rate of growth of about 1.2 per cent per annum until the Second World War. Since the war the maintenance of a high birth rate coupled with a diminishing death rate has pushed the annual rate of increase almost to 2.7 per cent. This means that the annual increment to the Egyptian population is now of the order of nearly 800,000 and if this rate remains unaltered the present population will double its numbers during the next twenty-five years.

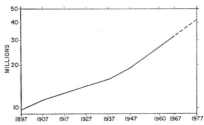

FIGURE 13.3 SEMI-LOGARITHMIC GRAPH OF EGYPT'S POPULATION GROWTH 1897-1977

There is still much scope for a further reduction of the crude death rate. The recorded levels of about 16 per thousand (actual rates are probably about 19 per thousand of the population) are still some way above the crude death rates of the developed countries (as well as many developing countries where rates below 10 per thousand are now being recorded). If the crude birth rate stays at or near its current level of 42 per thousand (actual rates are probably about 44 per thousand) and the crude death rate continues to drop towards the 10 per thousand level, then a rate of increase of over 3 per cent per annum is likely within a very few years. This would mean the addition of over a million new mouths each year. This situation is not merely possible but seems probable, for there is no early prospect of any sharp diminution of the crude birth rate that would be necessary to counteract effects of the medical revolution upon crude death rates. Forecasting future totals of Egypt's population has been a chastening experience for demographers over the last thirty years, for almost all have been under-estimates. An extrapolation in 1952 based upon the 1937–47 rate of population increase indicated a population of 33 million by 1977 (Mountjoy, 1952a)—a total probably attained by 1970. In 1959 the *Yearbook of the UAR* published an estimate that the 1977 total population would be about 34.8 million, a total now likely to be reached in 1971–2. The current rate of increase suggests 42 million by 1977 (Fig. 13.3). This is in close accord with the 'high' projection published in the *Tables of Basic Statistics, UAR, in 1963* which estimates a population of 45.7 million by 1980. Since the annual rate of increase is likely to become still greater, it seems probable that even this 'high' projection may be an under-estimate.

Egypt is still principally an agricultural country, despite considerable efforts at diversifying her economy in recent years. The relationship between the population at successive census years and the cultivated and crops areas is demonstrated in Table 13.2. It will be seen that whereas the population more than doubled (219 per cent) during the period 1897–1960, the area of farm land increased by only 26 per cent and the crop area by 52 per cent. This mounting pressure upon agricultural land, the country's basic resource, has been withstood by many efforts to increase productivity from existing acres. There has been an intensification of the farming

TABLE 13.2 POPULATION, CULTIVATED AREA AND CROP AREA OF EGYPT, 1897–1960

Year	Total population	% increase per decade	Cultivated area (feddans)	Crop area (feddans)
1897	9,715,000	—	4,099,070	6,871,700
1907	11,287,359	16.2	5,357,640	7,624,620
1917	12,750,918	13.0	5,307,534	7,724,980
1927	14,217,864	11.5	5,529,756	8,606,340
1937	15,932,694	12.1	5,333,330	8,362,340
1947	19,021,840	19.8	5,797,600	9,138,570
1960	26,062,000	30.5	6,100,000	10,367,730

1 feddan = 1.038 acres.

Areas are the mean of five years centred on every fifth year.

economy, improvement in agricultural techniques (including wholesale reliance on the practical science of the irrigation engineers), the greater use of artificial fertilizers, the introduction of new crops and new strains of existing crops and, at the same time, the expansion of non-agricultural occupations to help pay for the necessary extra imports of foodstuffs. During the past thirty years the yield of wheat per feddan has risen by 27 per cent and that of maize by 33 per cent, but cotton yields have scarcely increased. Yields of all crops in Egypt are high, thanks to the intensive methods of farming, and the scope for increasing the yield per area would seem to be limited.

One further indication of growing pressure of population upon the land may be gleaned from the figures of land ownership and crop area per head (Tables 13.3 and 13.4). In recent years changes have been brought about by land reform, but this in itself does not produce additional land but redistributes what there is. If we examine the average holding per owner we find that the amount has dwindled steadily from 5.7 feddans in 1900 to 2.01 feddans in 1965. Similarly the crop area per head of population, standing at 0.7 feddans in 1900, by 1965 had dwindled to 0.36 feddans. The number of landless peasantry, who earn a precarious livelihood as agricultural labourers, and their families now number more than 4 million.

Urbanization

As in most developing countries, the post-war period has seen a marked and increasing expansion in urbanization. Pressure of population upon limited agricultural resources on the one hand and government support for industrialization on the other has inevitably speeded a movement from the country to the towns (Fig. 13.4). Reference has already been made to inter-governorate migrations and the foremost position of Cairo and Alexandria as recipients of most of the rural migrants. The urban population of Egypt is officially designated as that found within the five urban governorates, the capitals of the 16 rural governorates and the district capitals of the border governorates. In 1966 their combined populations totalled 12,384,500, or 41 per cent of the total population. In 1960 they accounted for 37 per cent of the total population, whereas in 1897 the urban population was put at 14.5 per cent and comprised about 1,400,000 persons. Thus the urban population of Egypt has increased nearly eight-fold during the last 70 years while the total population has trebled (Abou El-Ezz, 1959).

The overwhelming importance and growth of Cairo and Alexandria are made clear from a closer examination of the figures. These are the two largest cities of the African continent, being of 'million' rank. There are only four 'million' cities in the whole of Africa: Johannesburg and Casa-

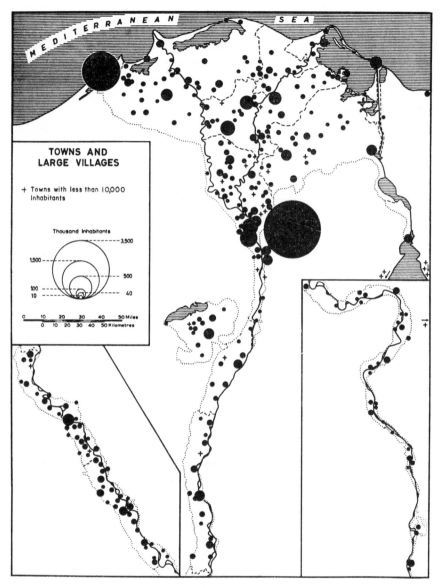

FIGURE 13.4

blanca are the other two. Cairo and Alexandria dwarf all other cities in Egypt, and as capital and chief port, the centres of administration and the location of the majority of industry they have an attractive power far in excess of the Canal Zone and country towns. With their 1966 populations of 4,220,000 and 1,801,000 respectively, they include a half of Egypt's urban dwellers and account for 20 per cent of the total population. Cairo

302

has more than trebled its total population during the last 30 years and it seems very likely that by 1971 or 1972 she will be numbered among the 14 or 15 world cities each with over 5 million inhabitants (Mountjoy, 1968). In 1966 nearly two-fifths of Cairo's population and one-third of Alexandria's population had been born elsewhere.

Cairo is thought by many to have become too big, too congested and too vulnerable in time of war. It has grown at the expense of medium-sized towns which are still few in number and, even in the heavily populated Delta, more widely dispersed than such towns in Britain. They generally have a very limited industrial base and serve mainly as market towns and centres of local administration (Sadek, 1961). In recent years the Egyptian Government has pursued a policy aimed at the wider dissemination of industrial plants: a few have become located in Upper Egypt, in the Delta towns, and especial emphasis was being placed upon the Canal Zone towns before that zone became a scene of conflict in 1967. Such policies may reduce the flow of migrants to the two great cities, but so far such reduction has only been marginal.

Social and economic effects

Despite great industrial expansion during the last decade, the UAR is still basically an agricultural country (national income in 1963: agriculture 28 per cent, industry 23 per cent). The country's geographical circumstances coupled with the tardiness of past governments in grappling with the population problem at an early stage has led to the current very serious situation whereby mounting excess of births over deaths has reduced or even nullified many of the measures designed to relieve them.

Population pressure is Egypt's overriding problem; it was a contributive factor in bringing the revolutionary government into power. It has shaped social and economic policy and has had repercussions upon political affairs. Land reform, the construction of the Aswan High Dam, desert reclamation as part of the drive to expand the area of farm land, vast investment in a number of large industrial establishments are all part and parcel of the 'modernization of Egypt' pursued by the revolutionary government in order to raise productivity in all sectors of the economy, to reduce the gap between rich and poor, and to restore a sense of dignity and cohesiveness to a nation humiliated and demoralized after centuries of oppression. These measures have involved tremendous capital investment (much of it borrowed) and have yet to show a full economic return. One measure that helps to indicate economic progress (although it has many imperfections) is a comparison of real *per capita* income over a given period. In a Memorandum of 1959 it was estimated that there had been no increase in the real *per capita* income between 1913 and 1957 (National Planning Committee, 1959); in fact, during this period national income increased by 65 per cent (at 1954 prices) but the population increased by about 100 per cent.

The first decade after the Second World War was a very critical one in Egypt's history. The post-war population explosion had begun but the increasing poverty of the masses made little impact upon the ruling class, most of whom were large landowners. They profited by the growing pressure of population on the land in terms of soaring rents and land prices and diminishing costs of agricultural labour. This situation did not change overnight when the revolutionary government took power in 1952. The old ruling class was stripped of land, power and privilege, but necessarily the introduction of a new order took time. Moreover, the new government (of amateur status) found itself struggling against a rate of population increase which had been rising inexorably from 1.9 per cent in 1947 to 2.6 per cent in 1965. From the beginning the new government found itself devoting nearly all its energies to providing land and work for increasing numbers and to re-distributing the national income more equitably in order to reduce poverty and distress. The 'medical revolution' which improves health and lowers crude death rates is especially effective in reducing infant mortality rates. Children thus saved in infancy are likely to live out an appreciable lifetime, and far more female children will reach child-bearing age. The expectation of life is increased. Thus the proportion of both young and old increase in populations that demonstrate rapid expansion and this has economic as well as social significance. The large number of children of low or negligible productivity and the smaller but significant proportion of old folk together have to be supported by the productivity of the remaining adult population. The proportion of children to the population as a whole has increased steadily. In 1947, 26 per cent of the population were under 10 years of age; in 1965 the proportion was 31 per cent. If we take the proportion of the population in the working age group (15–59 years) we find it has diminished from 56 per cent in 1947 to 52 per cent in 1965. Thus the dependency ratio has increased.

Young and old in a society are capital-absorbing rather than capital-creating, and with populations of great juvenility immense capital investment becomes necessary to provide basic housing, health and education services and this absorbs capital urgently needed in other more immediately productive sectors of the economy. Despite substantial efforts the education services in Egypt have not yet succeeded in coping with the great population increases. The fight against illiteracy makes slow progress; the proportion of the population of 10 years and over who were illiterate only declined from 74 per cent in 1947 to 69 per cent in 1960, while their number actually increased from 10.4 millions to 12.5 millions. Although schooling is normally compulsory between the ages of 6 and 12 years, in 1961–2 only 63 per cent and in 1965–5 71 per cent attended school.

Education is regarded as a principal factor in ultimately reducing birth rates. Clear correlations exist between levels of education and fertility levels: generally fertility decreases with education. Thus in the urban governorates it has been calculated on the 1960 statistics that for every 100 children ever born to illiterates there will be 82 children born to elementary certificate holders, 63 children born to those with secondary school certificates and 53 children to university graduates (Rizk, 1962). In addition, the greater the spread of education, especially that of a technical character, the greater the potential productivity of the nation. A hard and prolonged battle is being fought on the education front and tremendous investment is being required. It is recognized that in the development of education lies the whole future of the nation: its character and its numbers.

Land reform

Deployment of scarce resources in developing countries is now carefully planned in order to make the most of the limited capital and other resources available, to avoid wasteful duplication and to correlate growth in the various sectors of the economy to unite into an harmonious whole. However, in the UAR it was not until 1960 that a first comprehensive Five Year Plan became introduced and implemented. For most of the preceding eight years the revolutionary government had been struggling in an *ad hoc* fashion with the difficulties of the situation it had inherited. Pressure of population on the land exacerbated by the distorted pattern of land ownership, whereby two-thirds of the farmland of Egypt was owned by only 6 per cent of the landowners (Table 13.3), speedily led the new government to pass a Land Reform Act which took away land held in excess of 200 feddans (300 in certain cases) and to redistribute it among the peasantry. Subsequent legislation further reduced the maximum permitted holding by a family to 100 feddans. The land ownership pattern has changed drastically and in 1965 two-thirds of the farmland was shared between 98 per cent of land owners in plots of 5 feddans or less. In all, by 1964 773,000 feddans had been redistributed to some 267,000 new owners. Thus, including families, nearly 1.5 million had benefited. By 1968 a total of nearly one million feddans had been expropriated and the redistribution continues.

Co-operative societies have been successfully established to fulfill earlier functions of the landlord as a provider of finance, seeds, fertilizer and marketing. Further measures safeguarded the position of tenant farmers (about 4 million) and regulated their rents, generally reducing them. These measures improved living conditions by increasing the income of approximately 5 million individuals by £E80 millions. Since the inception of these measures agricultural output has risen thanks to incentives, to better farming supported by the co-operative system, to the provision of agricultural credit, the new ownership policies and new techniques, and better

TABLE 13:3   DISTRIBUTION OF LAND OWNERSHIP IN THE UAR, 1952 AND 1965

Size of holding (feddans)	1952 (before the Promulgation of the 1952 Land Reform Law)				1965			
	Land owners (thousands)	Area owned (thousand feddans)	Percentage Land owners	Percentage Area owned	Land owners (thousands)	Area owned (thousand feddans)	Percentage Land owners	Percentage Area owned
Under 5	2,642	2,122	94.3	35.4	3,033	3,693	94.5	57.1
5–10	79	526	2.8	8.8	78	614	2.4	9.5
10–20	47	638	1.7	10.7	61	527	1.9	8.2
20–50	22	654	0.8	10.9	29	815	0.9	12.6
50–100	6	430	0.2	7.2	6	392	0.2	6.1
100–200	3	437	0.1	7.3	4	421	0.1	6.5
Over 200	2	1,177	0.1	19.7	—	—	—	—
Total	2,801	5,984	100%	100%	3,211	6,462	100%	100%

Source: Statistical Handbook, United Arab Republic, Cairo, 1968.

seeds and stock emanating from newly set up agricultural research stations (Saab, 1967).

To retain perspective it must be noted that the total amount of land redistributed amounts to no more than 12 per cent of Egypt's farm land and still leaves many hundreds of thousands of peasant families landless. With the recent growing expansion of the population, even if all farm land were redistributed in small peasant holdings, there would still be landless peasantry. Thus the Egyptian Government has supported its land reform programme with other measures designed to increase the area of farmland as well as its productivity. The two principal steps have been the building of the High Dam at Aswan, and the initiation of a considerable programme of desert and marsh reclamation and rehabilitation of marginal land.

The vast Aswan High Dam has been built about 5 km. south of the old Aswan Dam to make available even more of the Nile water for Egyptian agriculture. Also by its immense storage capacity it removes for ever the fear of water shortage or excessive flooding, both of which could cause disaster in such a heavily populated agricultural land. Before the High Dam was completed, in an average year nearly 45 per cent of the Nile flood flowed into the Mediterranean unutilized. However, there are great annual fluctuations in the Nile discharge: in a low year every drop might be required by agriculture, and if two low years came in succession the existing dams at Aswan and Jebel Aulia (in the Sudan) might have no water to store and there could be disaster. The Aswan High Dam has twenty-five times the capacity of the old Aswan dam. It will take some years to fill and when in full use will allow of such control that no excess water need flow to waste in the Mediterranean—in fact, already there is no longer a flood season in Egypt.

From the agricultural point of view, the water from the High Dam will permit the conversion of 700,000 feddans from basin to perennial irrigation (making possible more than one crop a year over this area); it will give a guaranteed water supply to 1.2 million feddans of newly reclaimed farm land and allow a rice crop of up to one million feddans to be grown each year (rice is greedy for water but is a major export crop). An immense amount of hydro-electric power will be generated at the dam—six times the total energy previously consumed in Egypt. This will benefit and facilitate the expansion of industry and release at least two million tons of fuel oil for export.

The extension of farm land

The area of farm land increased by only 300,000 feddans in the 40 years from 1907, thus falling well behind the increase in population. Moreover, out of the total of 5,797,000 feddans in 1947 up to 20 per cent suffered from salinity, alkalinity, inadequacy of irrigation and drainage facilities.

To cope with the extreme pressure of population a programme of expanding and improving the cultivable area was quickly put in hand by the revolutionary government. Suitable land for reclamation on the desert edges beside the Delta, and areas of marsh and lagoon nearer the Mediterranean had slowly been improved, but all such work was restricted by lack of a guaranteed water supply, for the waters stored in the two big dams had become fully utilized. Thus major efforts in the Delta and contiguous desert areas were retarded until waters of the High Dam became available from 1971.

Nevertheless, all that could be done was done and under the first Five Year Plan (1960–64) 400,000 feddans were reclaimed or improved in the Nile valley and 80,000 feddans of desert were reclaimed. The various land reclamation projects are shown in Figure 13.5: two of particular note are the desert-reclaiming schemes in Tahrir (Liberation) Province and the New Valley. Tahrir was a new province announced by the revolutionary government soon after it attained power. It extends along the western edge of the Delta, midway between Cairo and Alexandria, and falls into southern and northern sectors. The southern sector consists of sandy soil and depends for irrigation on the Nile and underground sources. The poverty of the soil has slowed down development here and the target of 75,000 feddans by 1965 was not quite attained.

The northern sector is of loamy calcareous soils and depends entirely upon the Nile water for irrigation. By 1968 some 62,000 feddans had been reclaimed and emphasis was being placed on growing high value crops such as grapes, citrus fruits, plums and dates. As the land becomes productive, so carefully planned new settlements are established. Family holdings are of 2 to 5 feddans and in the new villages houses, schools, medical and veterinary clinics, a market, mosque and premises for co-operatives are built. So far taming the desert has proved slow and expensive: the resettled population by 1968 numbered only 25,000.

The New Valley scheme is associated with the oasis depressions in the Western Desert, well away from the Nile valley. The major oases are Kharga, Dakhla, Farafra and Bahariya. Within and around them are large expanses of level land having soils amenable to cultivation. Drilling down to 3,000 ft. has discovered good water of artesian character from the underlying Nubian sandstone. Since agricultural development here depends entirely upon the provision of subterranean water, much work is now being done assessing the water available, its source and rate of natural replacement. Geological, soil and topographical surveys are being undertaken. Successful pilot projects have been launched in Kharga and Dakhla oases initially covering 21,000 feddans. New tarmac roads have been constructed between newly sited villages, and health and social services have been provided. In all, by 1965 39,000 feddans had been reclaimed in these oases.

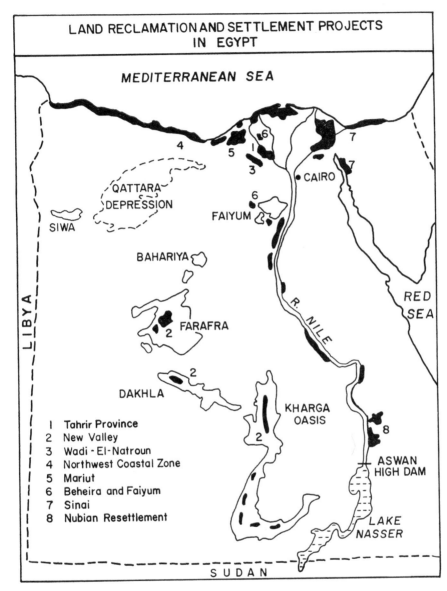

LAND RECLAMATION AND SETTLEMENT PROJECTS
IN EGYPT

MEDITERRANEAN SEA

QATTARA
DEPRESSION

SIWA

BAHARIYA

FARAFRA

DAKHLA

LIBYA

CAIRO

FAIYUM

R. NILE

KHARGA
OASIS

RED
SEA

ASWAN
HIGH DAM

LAKE
NASSER

1 Tahrir Province
2 New Valley
3 Wadi - El-Natroun
4 Northwest Coastal Zone
5 Mariut
6 Beheira and Faiyum
7 Sinai
8 Nubian Resettlement

SUDAN

FIGURE 13.5

The other areas where active reclamation has been proceeding are
shown on Figure 13.5. By 1967 over 700,000 feddans of land had been
reclaimed (but not all was in full agricultural production), more than a
third of it from the desert. It is not possible to advance more than the
vaguest estimates of the total area of new farmland these schemes may
ultimately yield. Only a part of them depends upon the waters of the

Aswan High Dam; the scope of the rest depends mainly upon well and artesian irrigation and these resources are yet imperfectly known. The potential area of all these schemes has been put at about 6 million feddans, almost the equal of the present cultivated area (6,300,000). It is unlikely, however, that anything like this total will ever become viable farm land.

What is clear from the foregoing is that the revolutionary government is making striking advances in expanding agriculture in Egypt in terms of more land, more water and more support (in education and services) to the farmer. The relentlessly increasing rate of population growth, however, is overtaking these measures. It is now admitted that when the Aswan High Dam is in full operation and all the new land it is planned to irrigate is in production (possibly by 1975, but this is unlikely), even then the total crop area per head of population will be worse than it is today (Table 13.4). Large successful developments in the desert reclamation schemes might ease this situation, but it seems that at best the current ratio can only be held and not improved. The long term view therefore is sombre, for population expansion will not stop when all the planned land and water is utilized. Even if birth control and family-planning measures become widely adopted in Egypt, owing to the age structure of the population there will be a considerable time lag before any reduction in the rate of population increase becomes effective.

TABLE 13.4   CROP AREA PER HEAD IN EGYPT, 1947–75

Year	Population	Crop area (feddans)	Crop area per head (feddans)
1947	19,022,000	9,138,000	0.47
1960	26,062,000	10,368,000	0.40
1965	29,390,000	10,500,000	0.36
1975	35,000,000	12,500,000	0.35 (est.)

Industrial development

As a consequence of pressure of population upon the land the post-war period (and especially since 1952) has witnessed considerable efforts to change the occupational structure of the working population; to facilitate a shift from agriculture to manufacturing industry and service activities. Protective measures to aid and foster industrial development in Egypt were applied from 1930 but the haphazard unco-ordinated developments of the following 20 years made but a minor contribution to the national income and to reducing the serious population pressure (Mountjoy 1952b). After the revolutionary government had found its feet considerable capital investment was made in infrastructure, particularly transport, and this provided a useful base for the introduction of the two Five Year Plans in 1960 and 1965 (Mountjoy, 1966). During the decade 1960–69 successful advances were made. Today Egypt is the second industrial country of Africa, following only the Republic of South Africa. Loans and grants from the World Bank and mainly Eastern Bloc sources and lesser investment by the West have brought into being or expanded many capital-intensive plants including cement, iron and steel, oil production and refining, fertilizer production. To the old-established agriculture-based industries of milling, sugar-refining and cotton textiles have been added scores of new consumer goods and service industries: light and heavy engineering, electrical engineering, vehicle assembly, radio, television, refrigerator manufacturing and so on. The war with Israel has diverted capital from the general economy but has also led to the establishment of many plants producing military equipment previously imported, and the training of large numbers in engineering and technological occupations. The mines and oil wells of Sinai have been denied to Egypt by Israel's occupation, but great success has attended the oil-prospecting in the Western Desert and, at 12 million tons, more oil is now produced annually than when the Sinai fields were Egyptian. Above all, the vast potential of the Aswan High Dam hydro-electric power is becoming realized from 1969.

Industrial expansion is now well under way, and a growing body of 'technocrats' is coming into being to sustain its momentum. By 1966 industrial production had expanded more than two and a half times since 1951 (Index 1950–51 = 100, 1965–6 = 265), and industry's share of the national income from a mere 10 per cent twenty years ago is now of the order of 25 per cent. In recent years investment in industry has been three times as great as investment in agriculture and the 'industry and construction' labour force has trebled (to 1,200,000) in the last twenty years. However, in view of the vast increase in population this labour expansion is modest, although it must be remembered that as industry expands it increasingly requires growth in ancillary and service activities. Nevertheless agriculture still provides employment for over half the occupied population.

The need to pay for increasing imports of food (750,000 tons in 1950, 2,000,000 tons in 1963) has helped to stimulate exports. In the ten years 1959–68, exports increased from £E166,000,000 to £E279,000,000. Not only have the traditional agricultural exports been increased (cotton, rice, onions) but potatoes and fruit now appear on the list. Manufactured goods such as cotton yarn and fabric (£E2 million in 1956) accounted for £E58 million in 1968, and with recent discoveries in the Western Desert oil and oil products may soon bring in £E30–60 million per annum. Even so, the value of imports surpasses that of exports by at least £E100 million each year and the loss of Suez Canal revenue and tourist receipts has been serious; tourism is now being fostered again. It is likely that the food imports of the future will increase rather than lessen and the expansion of exports to include more manufactured goods will be necessary: here quality and competitiveness assume importance if foreign markets are to be found.

How far pressures of population have pushed the revolutionary government into the creation of a national socialist state it is difficult to say. It is certainly true that the policies of the government have become more left-wing radical over the years. When it came into power in 1952 it was determined to break the power of the 2,000 or so 'land barons' and free the mass of the population from its feudal mentality, yet its early measures were moderate, far more moderate than had the revolution been a rising of the peasantry and working classes rather than of the middle class. The need for the provision of more employment, for retaining wealth in the country and distributing it more equitably led to a series of measures of Egyptianization and the removal of foreigners from businesses, sequestration of businesses and properties, limitation of share-holding, the pegging of directors' salaries and so on. Tighter and tighter has become the government's grip on the economy in the name of economic planning. With the demographic situation as it is, there is little margin for waste, for ill-advised or unco-ordinated investments. Thus the position has now been reached where all the means of production are under the direct control of the government, both in the public and the private sectors of the economy. In these measures the mass of the population is solidly in support of its government, for they have seen the face of their country changed dramatically since 1952. They have received great benefits: better housing, health, schools, the modest wherewithal to buy simple consumer goods. The visitor to Egypt today who knew it in the past is struck by these changes and by the enthusiasm and seriousness with which the villagers order their affairs in their co-operatives. To Western eyes these people may still have very little, but to those who have had nothing a little is a lot.

Conclusion

The population problem of Egypt is serious and is likely to become even more severe during the next decades. By 1985 it is estimated that the expectation of life at birth for males will be 55.5 years and for females 58.8 years: an increase of about nine years upon the 1965–70 figures (Cairo Demographic Centre, 1969). The slow acceptance of family-planning methods by the masses suggests that no marked diminution of the high birth rate is likely and this, related to the larger numbers entering the reproductive years, means even greater accretions to the population. Estimates by the Central Agency for Public Mobilization and Statistics of expected population in 1985 give a lower limit of 39 million and an upper limit of 52.5 million. The upper limit seems more realistic, and to support such numbers all the potential new farm land must be successfully utilized (especially that in the New Valley) in order to maintain the existing low levels of living. Beyond 1985 the situation looks even more serious, for little new land or water is likely to remain unexploited and population expansion will not suddenly cease.

The revolutionary government is open to censure in that vital years have been passing and the real problem of reducing fertility has been given secondary attention in favour of more positive and spectacular economic measures. Determined attempts to further birth control all over the country only began in 1965. Birth rates must be lowered to match the notable drop in death rates. Much will also depend upon success in reducing fertility through later age of marriage and attempting to make fashionable smaller families. The time lag must be remembered; such actions now cannot hope to have much effect for the next 15–20 years owing to the age structure of the present population. The low level of literacy among the masses is likely to retard successful acceptance of birth control policies for some time. The first eighteen years under the revolutionary government have seen much done in the fields of social and economic development but real advances in the standard of living have been held back by unabated increase of population. Little has yet been done to face this problem: the time remaining to grapple with it may be all too short. Disaster has been postponed, not removed.

REFERENCES

ABOU-EL-EZZ, M. S. (1959) 'Some aspects of migration in Cairo', *Bulletin de la Société de Géographie d'Egypte*, 32, pp. 121–41.

CAIRO DEMOGRAPHIC CENTRE (1969) *Demographic Measures for Arab Countries of North Africa and South-West Asia.*

CENTRAL AGENCY FOR PUBLIC MOBILIZATION AND STATISTICS (1968) *Statistical Handbook, UAR, 1952–67.*

CENTRAL AGENCY FOR PUBLIC MOBILIZATION AND STATISTICS (1963) *Handbook of Basic Statistics, UAR, 1962.*

EL-BADRY, M. A. (1955) 'Some Demographic Measurements for Egypt based on the stability of Census Age distributions', *Millbank Quarterly*, 33, pp. 268–305.

EL-BADRY, M. A. (1965) 'Trends in the components of population growth in the Arab countries of the Middle East', *Demography*, 2, pp. 140–86.

MOUNTJOY, A. B. (1952a) 'Egypt's Population Problem', *Transactions of the Institute of British Geographers*, 18, pp. 121–35.

MOUNTJOY, A. B. (1952b) 'The Development of Industry in Egypt', *Economic Geography*, 28, pp. 212–28.

MOUNTJOY, A. B. (1968) 'Million Cities: Urbanization and the Developing Countries', *Geography*, 53, pp. 365–74.

MOUNTJOY, A. B. (1971) *Industrialization and Under-developed Countries* (London), Chapter 9.

NATIONAL PLANNING COMMITTEE (1969), *Memorandum No. 121*, Cairo.

RIZK, H. (1962) 'Social and Psychological factors affecting Fertility in UAR', *Symposium on Family Planning*, Cairo.

SAAB, G. S. (1967) *The Egyptian Agrarian Reform, 1952–62*, London.

SADEK, D. (1961) 'Medium-sized towns in the Urban pattern of Modern Egypt', *Bulletin de la Société de Géographie d'Egypte*, 34, pp. 111–24.

Chapter 14
Libya: economic development and demographic responses
R G Hartley

That part of the Mediterranean littoral which is now Libya was little more than a geographical expression before the genesis of the modern state in 1951. It was a sprawling and amorphous entity, acting as an east–west routeway and as a zone of transition between the Mediterranean north and the continental Sahara. Its disturbed history of foreign domination, small population of one million people, and scantiness of known resources in the 1,759,540 sq. km. of territory had retarded development, and human activity remained closely in subjection to the vagaries of the environment.

On this background of direct and pervasive influence by geographical factors, has been superimposed a veneer of economic benefits afforded by petroleum exploitation. In the ten years since Libya first exported oil in 1961, the country has become one of the world's five largest producers and exporters.

The effect of the growing oil sector on the rest of the economy has been fundamental and diffuse. In particular it gave rise to a stream of revenues accruing to the government in the form of valuable foreign exchange, 70 per cent of which is earmarked by law for development and modernization projects. Between 1963 and 1969 the concession-holding companies have paid over £L800 million to the government as royalties, taxes and other charges levied on petroleum production and export. Average *per capita* incomes rose at least tenfold in the ten years preceding 1970—the estimated annual income of £400 a person in 1970 is the highest in Africa. The corollary of this recent economic upsurge has been a significant adjustment in the country's social, political and cultural structure, and at a pace experienced by few developing countries. Libya's two population censuses since independence, in 1954 (Ministry of National Economy, 1959) and 1964 (Ministry of Economy and Trade, 1966), reflect only two still pictures of this rapidly changing situation, but they bring into sharp focus many fundamental development issues. At the same time, the two censuses provide an historical perspective of Libya's process of transition from one economic and demographic equilibrium to another.

Stages of growth and duality in the Libyan economy

Certain geographic characteristics remained fundamentally significant in the region's history while others were peculiar to a particular era. In essence, Libya was composed of three separate and distinct regions*— Tripolitania in the north-west, Cyrenaica in the east, and the Fezzan in the south—each having more in common with neighbouring countries than with each other. A few Berber-speaking areas in the west indicate a now reduced but once important ethnic affinity with the Maghreb; and commercially eastern Libya had traditional ties with Egypt. North-west Libya was first colonized by the Phoenicians and the north-east by the Greeks, while the southern interior was linked more with West Africa. Neither the permeation of the country with a common Arabic culture and Moslem faith between the sixth and thirteenth centuries, nor the imposition of the Roman and Turkish Empires in the first and sixteenth centuries respectively, succeeded in checking the separate evolution of the three regions.

Throughout Libya's varied early history, though, was the existence of an urban–rural dichotomy. Despite the decline in urban population from an estimated 200,000 persons in the Roman era to 50,000 in Turkish times (Jusatz, 1967), the economic functions of the towns remained constant. The towns continued to serve as the loci of foreign settlement, as central places for a very circumscribed hinterland, and as break-in-bulk points both for trans-Saharan trade and agricultural exports. The rural areas remained backward, with peasant agriculture near the coast, and nomadic tribes inland; generally they were free from urban dominance.

Colonization schemes initiated by the Italians during their occupation of Libya (1911–43) set in motion a chain reaction of economic and social responses whilst the Libyans themselves had been unable to mobilize their own resources to benefit from the increasing demand for North African products. The Italians invested $150 million (IBRD, 1960), a sum far in excess of any previous injection of capital. It was particularly important because it helped to bridge the gap between the unequal economic growth rates of town and country. The extension of the agricultural area by land reclamation, long-term investments in water conservation, farm buildings and equipment, and the construction of necessary social amenities combined to benefit the rural area (Falchi, 1939).

The Italian occupation also caused a geographical and occupational redistribution of the population. The expropriation and colonization of 15 per cent of the total productive land in northern Libya by 140,000 Italian peasant workers caused a significant displacement of the indigenous

---

* In 1963 Libya abandoned its federal administrative structure, and the original three provinces of Tripolitania, Cyrenaica and the Fezzan were subdivided into ten Muqatta (Regions). The old provincial names are used in this chapter for ease of reference.

population (Pan, 1949); 40,000 Libyans are estimated to have migrated to neighbouring countries, and 30,000 to the towns of Tripoli and Benghazi during 1911–40. In part, this large out-migration relieved the rural areas of a slowly increasing population on a static resource base. As such, external human pressures permanently achieved what the environment had been forcing upon the indigenous population for some time.

The removal of Italian troops in 1943 and the suspension of the colonization schemes in 1940 created new problems of demographic response despite the stabilizing influence of the British and French administrations. There was a paradoxical situation of urban demands for employment while unemployment of the indigenous population rose, a reflection both of the type of employment opportunities and the supply of labour available. The return of Libyans who had emigrated during the Italian occupation intensified the urban unemployment and aggravated the growing social disorder. However, educational advances based on foreign aid and the introduction of some provincial autonomy helped to prepare the Libyans for independence in 1951.

Just as the political decision to form an independent Libya was initiated in the United Nations, so the post-independence period of economic growth depended primarily on external aid. At first, aid was in the form of grants and loans (Lockwood, 1957), for Libya became virtually a development laboratory for the under-developed lands. From 1956 onwards, though, expenditure by companies searching for oil provided the bulk of the country's revenue. However, it was only in the early 1960's that Libya's economy began to undergo the spectacular phase of its transformation. By 1968 the value of petroleum exports alone had become about £L670 million: equal to three times the value of imports, which in themselves were one hundred times greater than domestic exports excluding oil.

However, the large inflow of foreign revenue also created problems. Significantly, it initiated a demand for domestic trade and services which could not be met by local factors of production. One of the most disturbing features of this development has been the growth of tertiary services (like administration, commerce, building and the army) at the expense of primary activities, without any appreciable growth in the secondary sector. By expanding development projects the government injected vast quantities of purchasing power into the income stream thereby intensifying the problem. Although some accumulation of foreign assets has been achieved, a good deal has been spent locally, mainly in the urban areas, resulting in spiralling wages, price rises of 10 per cent per annum (Economist Intelligence Unit, 1965) and inflation (Economic Research, 1961).

Before the advent of petroleum, agriculture was the largest productive sector in the economy, employing 70 per cent of the labour force and contributing 30 per cent of the gross domestic product. Its contribution has now declined to no more than 4 per cent, but efforts have been made by the government to expand agricultural output. In the First Plan between 1963–8, for instance, £L50 million was spent on agricultural development and this will be increased threefold in the Second Plan ending in 1974. Much of this expenditure is in the form of agricultural credit, price support and the subsidization of farm machinery and fertilizers. Agricultural production seems to have responded to this stimulus, growing at an average annual rate of 4–5 per cent during the 1960's. Together with the estimated decline in agricultural employment by 1 per cent a year, labour productivity has risen significantly. But scarcity of rainfall, shortage of water and soils impoverished by centuries of neglect have set physical limitations to the expansion of agricultural production. As such, the 3.8 million hectares of agricultural land (2 per cent of the country's total area), much of it meadow and pasture, has remained almost constant in the last ten years. With the squeeze of high costs of production and the rapidly growing domestic demand, agricultural exports have now vanished. It was estimated that by 1970 the value of agricultural production equalled imports for the first time.

Against this background of foreign influence which has shaped and exploited the country's development on a national scale, local problems and conditions have influenced the rate and nature of change. Four factors have been identified as particularly significant (Higgins, 1959). First, the Libyans themselves have lacked the capacity to direct and finance their own economic development. Second, Libya faces a problem of incentive, for climatic and political fluctuations have continually encouraged the Libyans to take the short-term view. Third, the manpower problem has emerged as a serious restraint on continued non-inflationary economic growth. Finally, there is the problem of scale; in a country of 1,759,540 sq. km., the scattering of one and a half million persons presents grave difficulties of production and supply. Oil benefits did not provide an easy or complete solution to these problems.

To some degree, the exploitation of oil did refocus attention within the country itself, for the quasi-concentration of oil resources around the Gulf of Sirte is situated in the zone between the three provinces. Yet the geographical locus of economic development became increasingly compact, as manpower, families and institutions were drawn into an urban framework. Possibly more than most forms of external stimulus, the oil industry has had little direct contact with the traditional economy. The industry's labour requirements are small (12,000 persons in 1967), and even the oil exploitation takes place geographically outside the traditional economy. Not only did the urban nuclei of Tripoli and Benghazi become the administrative centres of the oil industry, but more important, they became the receiving centres for the indirect benefits from oil revenues. As trade, transport and service activities grew in conjunction with imports, it was inevitable that the towns would become the foci of the modern sector being the major ports and domestic markets. With the difficulty of extending the agricultural or habitable area, these trends continued to widen the gulf between the developing and stagnant sectors of the economy.

Distribution and density of population

Libya's process of adjustment from one socio-economic system to a new equilibrium is taking place within well-defined and reasonably stable geographical boundaries. Within the critical, quantitative limits set by the physical environment, however, the controls on Libya's population distribution are more a complex of physical and human determinants, and are more emphatically qualitative.

The two outstanding features of Libya's population distribution are its marked coastal concentration and its small absolute size. About three-quarters of the 1,840,000 persons (1970 estimate) live within 20 miles of the sea (Figs. 14.1 and 14.2). On a provincial basis the proportions of the total population remained relatively stable between 1936 and 1964. Tripolitania, with only 14 per cent of the total area, contained 62 per cent of the total population in 1964. The respective proportions for Cyrenaica were 50 per cent and 33 per cent, and for the Fezzan 36 per cent and 5 per cent. Despite the doubling of Libya's population between 1936 and 1964, the average density remained under one person per sq. km.

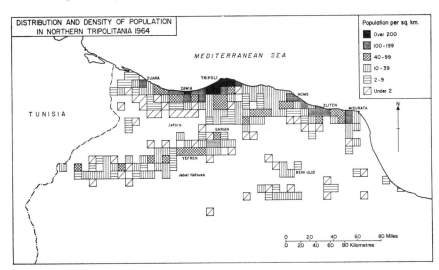

FIGURE 14.1

The country consists of a mosaic of discontinuous and better watered, settled territory, scattered in wide expanses of arid and semi-arid land. Nevertheless, three physiographic zones of population concentration can

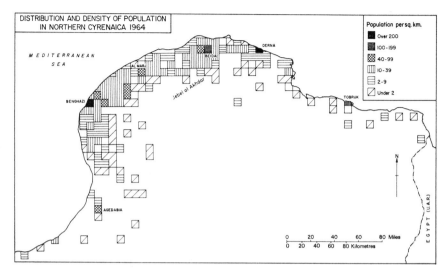

FIGURE 14.2

be identified. The coastal area, particularly in Tripolitania, contained about 55 per cent of the total population in 1964. The two inland hill areas in northern Libya known as the Jebel Nefousa and Jebel al Akhdar supported about 20 per cent, while the interior oases to the south of the Jebels and in the Fezzan accounted for about 8 per cent of the total population. The remaining 17 per cent were classified as nomadic and semi-nomadic persons in the 1964 population census. While small groups of true nomads migrate within well defined territories throughout the country, the bulk of the 300,000 semi-nomads undertake seasonal migrations from the sedentary areas, particularly from the two northern Jebel zones.

Increasing temperature extremes to the south make the Tripolitanian coast and the Jebel al Akhdar the most favoured physical environments for optimum working and living conditions. Thus, mean annual temperature ranges of 14°C on the coast increase by 4°C only 40 miles inland, and may reach 25°C in interior regions (Doxiadis Associates, 1964).

However, it is the indirect influences of the physical environment which set more specific limits to Libya's ecumene. The presence or absence of water is the critical factor in Libyan agricultural production, and hence in influencing the distribution of three-quarters of the population.

The principal agricultural products—barley and olives—seldom produce reliable and profitable yields in locations where the average rainfall is less than 200 mm. per annum (Stewart, J. H., 1958). Levels of agricultural technology have developed little in extending the cultivated area beyond these limits, while constant overgrazing prevents the growth of perennial forage grasses in the zone 150–200 mm.

Bounded by the 150 mm. isohyet, the Tripolitanian agricultural zone covers about 24,600 sq. km., 8 per cent of the provincial area. Except for a small wedge of better watered territory near Sirte, this land comprises a coastal strip averaging 30 km. in width, with a 100 km. wide bulge in the central section and a tongue extending west along the Jebel Nefousa.

Rather than varying in a straight-line linear ratio with rainfall, Tripolitania's rural population density increases in a geometric or 'exponential' rate as rainfall increases. This indicates in general how productivity is controlled by rainfall and to some extent how population density responds to that productivity.

The presence of groundwater tends to reinforce the concentration of the rural population in the higher rainfall zones by dictating local variations in the intensity of production and determining the potential for agricultural expansion. The bulk of the 105,000 hectares of irrigated land in northern Tripolitania (Lalevic, 1967) depends on groundwater accumulating in the Tertiary and Quaternary sediments of the inland and coastal plain, known as the Jefara, which have given rise to two water-tables (Hill, 1960). The Phreatic water-table around Tripoli is accessible to the Libyans using traditional *dalu* (leather bucket) irrigation techniques. The high density of wells in the *saniya* (Arab garden oases) supported about 100,000 persons in 1958. A deeper Quaternary aquifer situated within 48 km. of Tripoli was exploited by the Italians using diesel and electric pumps, enabling large-scale commercial farms to expand southwards into previously unoccupied territory.

In the vast pre-desert and desert areas of Tripolitania receiving less than 150 mm. rainfall per annum, there are numerous pockets of agriculture and population concentration. These scattered areas, limited in extent, depend essentially on controlled perennial irrigation from wells and springs, and uncontrolled flood irrigation known as 'wadi culture' (Stewart, J. H., 1958). Situated mainly on the dip-slope of the Jebel Nefousa, these methods of water utilization support approximately 100,000 persons (Fig. 14.4).

Cyrenaica displays the same three physiographic elements that influence Tripolitania's rural population distribution—coast, Jebel and inland desert —though with differences in scale, location and structure. The abutment of the Jebel al Akhdar against the northern coast wedges a coastal plain around Benghazi in the west, but only a thin coastal strip in the north and east. From the coast the Jebel rises in two tiers to a crest of 800 m. near Beida. The two scarp faces form a regular arcuate boundary to the dissected limestone massif, though an intervening terrace between the two tiers occurs near Al Marj (Fig. 14.5).

In contrast to the Tripolitanian tendency for rural population density to increase geometrically with increasing rainfall, Cyrenaica has a linear progression. Part of the reason lies in the smaller total population and the larger areas of rainfall zones, and part in the structure of the Jebel. Rapid percolation of rainwater, caused by the absence of impermeable rock strata, has limited the development of irrigation, while fracturing has dissected the high limestone massif, prohibiting animal movement across the region. Thus, more than half of Cyrenaica's rural population lives in rainfall zones receiving less than 300 mm.—almost twice the proportion that occurs in Tripolitania. Much of this land occurs on the southern slopes of the Jebel al Akhdar, dip-slope wadis providing patches for seasonal harvesting and an economic dependency on pastoralism. The

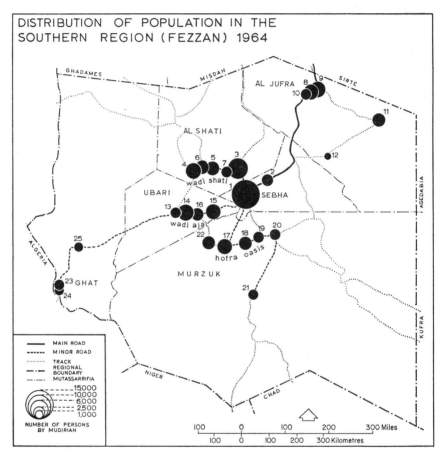

FIGURE 14.3   DISTRIBUTION OF POPULATION IN THE SOUTHERN REGION
(FEZZAN) OF LIBYA, 1964

The numbers refer to the following administrative districts:

1. Sebha Town; 2. Al Gedid and Buanis; 3. Brak; 4. Idri; 5. Bergin; 6. Al Hassawna; 7. Al Maguartia; 8. Hon; 9. Waddan; 10. Socna; 11. Zella; 12. Al Fugha; 13. Ubari; 14. Garifa; 15. Bint Bayyah; 16. Oragen; 17. Murzuk; 18. Traghen; 19. Um al Araneb; 20. Zuila; 21. Gatrum; 22. Wadi Atbah; 23. Ghat; 24. Al Berket; 25. Ouinat.

absence of perennial river flows or large catchment areas makes the Jebel unfavourable for extensive wadi culture.

The Fezzan is the least densely populated of Libya's three provinces, containing an estimated 86,000 persons in 1966 in an area of about one million sq. km. Extremes of climate have set distinct limits to human habitation, many areas receiving no rain for several consecutive years. Irrigation water is the main determinant of agriculture and hence population distribution, for pastoralism is of small importance.

Until recently, agriculture was limited to oases where water-tables lay near the surface. Three parallel wadis—Al Shati, Ajal and Hofra—developed as the main concentrations of population (Fig. 14.3). The extent of population distribution depended on the traditional techniques of irrigation, while density of occupance was influenced by the degree of land fragmentation. New techniques of exploiting deeper artesian water, particularly in Wadi Hofra, have partly extended the Fezzanese ecumene. However, difficult drainage, high water-tables, over-exploitation and intense evaporation have caused much potentially fertile land in the oases to become saline. It has been estimated that the area under cultivation has been reduced by 50 per cent since 1900 (Whiting Associates International, 1967).

Within the Libyan agricultural zone defined by rainfall and irrigation potential, two distinct patterns of occupance are set on a similar background of physical conditions indicating the force of non-physical determinants. One is a traditional system of agriculture reflecting a 'natural' response to the physical environment, with a haphazard evolution; the other is a planned and predetermined agricultural system.

Although many of the traditional farms have grazing rights, particularly in Tripolitania (Bottomley, 1964), their economic viability is primarily determined by the size and location of irrigated patches in the coastal *saniya*. Physical, economic and social factors have combined to produce small, fragmented holdings. High population densities, varying from 3 to 10 persons per hectare, reflect not only the inherent fertility of the coastal area, but also the subsistence nature of the traditional agricultural system. Over-exploitation of water for irrigation has caused sea water infiltration in many of the coastal *saniya* (Hill, 1960).

In contrast, two types of modern commercial undertakings were established by the Italians in the 1930's. The 'concession' farms were private commercial enterprises developed on some of the best land in northern Libya and directed to dry land tree cultivation of olives and almonds. These farms covered approximately 127,000 hectares in 1958, giving a population density of about 1 person per hectare; less than one-quarter of the density of most of the *saniya* oases. The 'demographic' holdings were established at the end of the Italian period of occupation as a political move and with no thought of strict financial return in the short term (Fisher,

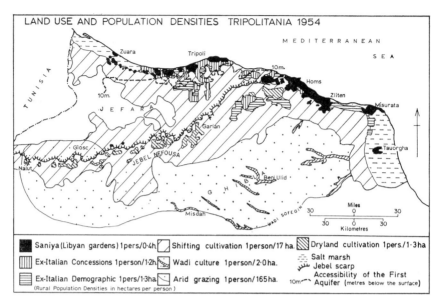

FIGURE 14.4

1953). Situated on slightly marginal land in the steppe zones of the eastern Jefara and Jebel Nefousa, the holdings were initially geared at self-sufficiency. About 90,000 Libyans occupied the 103,000 hectares in 1958 (Fig. 14.4). Following an agreement with Italy, the Libyan Agricultural Bank began to grant long-term loans to nationals to enable them to purchase farms previously owned by Italians. Nearly 1,700 such loans were made in 1959–60 with a total value of more than £L2 million. In co-operation with the Ministry of Agriculture, 2,000 long term loans valued at £L3 million have also been made to improve existing farms and to help establish new ones.

In Cyrenaica and the Fezzan, human elements are weakening the tendency for population to concentrate in the higher rainfall zones. Pastoralism, associated with the Bedouin tribes, has thrived in areas outside the dissected and thickly wooded high plateaux of the Jebel al Akhdar (Fig. 14.5). Inevitably this form of land use has supported population densities lower than the potential of the land, though it has been argued that pastoralism is well suited to the physical environment (Evans-Pritchard, 1949). The growth of planned settlement in Cyrenaica, thought of initially by the Jews (Gregory, 1909), partially implemented by the Italians, and developed by the Libyans (Buru, 1965), is also cutting across the 'grains' imposed by the physical environment. The National Agricultural Settlement Authority, for instance, has been particularly active in the Jebel al Akhdar, attempting to settle semi-nomads by establishing new farms, reclaiming land, drilling wells and planting fruit trees.

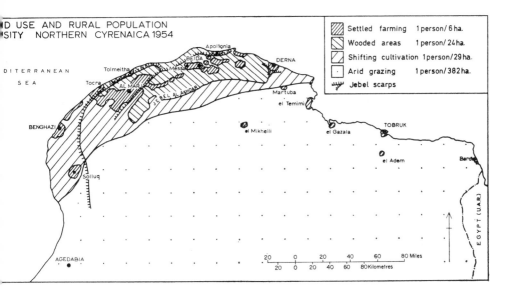

FIGURE 14.5

Within the well-defined limits set by the physical environment, there-fore, the fine balance between determining factors and population distribu-tion has been disturbed, though not in equal degrees in each province. Occupation by foreigners and economic wealth from oil revenues have strengthened the influences of the non-physical environment. The sum of these forces, or controls, has been to produce two tendencies: one is the inertia of the present geographical limit of population distribution, itself a product of physical and human determinants interacting in a complex temporal framework, and the other tendency is the growth of population around urban nuclei.

Urbanization

As the main line of penetration of a modern economic sector into a tradi-tional socio-economic system, the Libyan towns are achieving a dominance out of proportion to the size of the country's total population. Over one-fifth of its total population is contained in the two cities with over 100,000 inhabitants, Tripoli and Benghazi.

The pace of Libyan urbanization shows no signs of slackening and the major towns are beginning to dominate most forms of political and economic life. Between 1954 and 1966, the percentage of the total popula-tion living in settlements of more than 20,000 inhabitants increased from 18 to 25. Four-fifths of the increase in urban populations occurred in the two major cities of Tripoli and Benghazi.

About one-half of the total population lived in settlements containing more than 500 inhabitants; yet the total number of settlements above this size showed remarkably little increase since 1954. Thus, while the overall pace of urbanization has increased rapidly, the process of settlement multiplication has gained little momentum.

Although it is convenient to regard Libya's population as distributed in a series of discrete and isolated clusters, it must be realized that this settlement concept is artificial. In Cyrenaica and the Fezzan, settlements are distinct and well-defined, but in Tripolitania dense rural settlement along the coast precludes accurate sub-division of urban units (Ministry of National Economy, 1959); 39 settlements containing over 2,000 inhabitants have been identified (Ministry of Planning and Development, 1966).

The distribution of these Libyan settlements by size suggests a regularity similar to a linear pattern on a double logarithmic graph (Fig. 14.6). The degree of regularity between the size and rank of towns—expressed formally as the 'rank-size rule' (Stewart, C. T., 1958)—helps to generalize about Libya's settlements. The distribution seems to follow the theory that rank-size distributions conform more closely to a theoretical S-shape than to a linear log-normal distribution (Zipf, 1949). The irregularities of Libya's pattern appear similar to the primate settlement-size distributions identified by Berry, 1961; log-normally distributed lesser settlement sizes (up to 9,000 persons in the case of Libya) are followed by a gap because settlements of intermediate size are absent (9,000 to 20,000 persons), and then by a rapid cumulation to a dual peak (Tripoli and Benghazi). On a provincial basis, true primacy dominates the settlement-size distributions, including the Fezzan.

Since post-war reconstruction, federation and Cyrenaican oil finds, Benghazi has grown to rival Tripoli as a major urban centre. In contrast to the major towns, rank-sizes of medium-sized towns have remained similar since 1917 (Agostini, 1922–3), tending to confirm other empirical evidence that a slightly concave settlement distribution is common below the primate city. The stability of the Libyan rank-size settlement distribution over space and time suggests that it might be viewed as a steady-state phenomenon. This condition has been defined as one of entropy, in which the distribution is affected by a myriad of small random forces (Simon, 1955). Contrary empirical evidence indicating that entropy is associated with log-normal city-size distributions and not with well developed primacy has also been produced (Berry, 1961). Neither theoretical nor empirical evidence would appear to explain Libya's peculiar settlement pattern.

Libya's urban structure does not appear to be a function of the level of economic development, industrialization or urbanization. To some extent, Libya's urban structure is similar to other countries which are smaller than average (in terms of ecumene), have a short history of urbanization and are economically and politically simple. Thus, the settled area support-

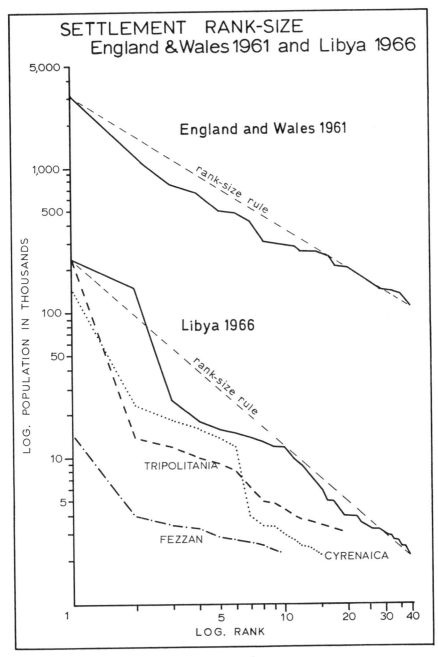

FIGURE 14.6

ing about four-fifths of the population is small (about 50,000 sq. km.); rapid urbanization is essentially a post-war phenomenon; and there has been the impact of a few strong forces, particularly the superimposition of a commercial export sector on a peasant agricultural system. While the type and degree of this duality has changed since 1917, essentially the towns have remained orientated outside Libya. As such, the grafting of Libyan 'primate' cities on top of a lower log-normal distribution of settlements emphasizes the nature rather than the level of the country's economic development.

Size and spacing of settlements

The distribution of urban centres in Tripolitania is similar to the distribution of the rural population. Tripoli dominates the central coastal zone and is flanked by the medium-size towns of Suk el Giuma and Zawia (Fig. 14.1). While the greatest amount of urban growth has taken place in and around Tripoli, six settlements have recently evolved independently of the established pattern. Cyrenaica, in contrast, has a more regular pattern, the larger towns being evenly spaced along the coast and the Jebel al Akhdar (Fig. 14.2). There is also less gradation of settlement sizes than in Tripolitania. New settlements since 1954 have tended to cluster around Beida, the new town constructed as capital, and Benghazi.

The spacing of Libyan settlements tends to form a pattern that is empirically valid, though at a level different from other countries. Towns of a given size are more widely spaced where rural population density is low, farming is extensive, agricultural production is low, and where the town itself has a low proportion of workers in manufacturing activities (King, 1961). The wider spacing of Cyrenaican settlements vis-à-vis Tripolitanian settlements (37 and 24 km. from their nearest neighbour respectively) may be partly attributed to the nature of the region's agriculture.

However, the question of Libya's settlement spacing is particularly complex because of the contact between the modern and traditional economies. By 1970, for instance, imports of agricultural produce, mainly through Tripoli and Benghazi, equalled the £L30 million of food which was produced in the country itself. As such, the equilibrium of functional dependency between towns and villages has become disturbed. In effect, the largest urban centres have become source areas for agricultural produce, thereby usurping some of the trading functions of the small settlements.

The relationship between the size and economic function of Libyan settlements appeared to differ from empirical evidence (Stewart, C. T., 1958). The range of urban functions, whether specialized, dual or varied, was more closely associated with the location than with the particular size of settlements. Cyrenaican middle-sized towns indicated a specialization of economic functions, while duality predominated in the equivalent

Tripolitanian towns, indicating the different stages of urban growth which Libyan regions are experiencing. Stewart maintained that 'in pre-industrial subsistence economies, villages are orientated to the countryside and the agricultural population; the towns face one another only'. In contrast, increasing contact between urban and rural areas appeared to be taking place in Libya. Thus, in Tripolitanian towns at least, the process of erosion of the traditional Libyan economy was reflected in the dual economic functions of their urban structures.

Two contrasting processes have influenced Libya's urban structure. First, both the pattern and hierarchy are being preserved. Historical inertia and water supply have dictated the coastal and Jebel concentrations in both Tripolitania and Cyrenaica, although local determinants have influenced particular regional distributions. On a national scale, some limit must exist to the number of settlements and towns that a population of one and a half million inhabitants can support. Despite the traumatic economic changes, notably few new settlements were created between 1954 and 1966, suggesting that the settlement pattern has reached an optimum state. Continued government expenditure on schools, hospitals and houses on the basis of the present distribution of population will tend to preserve the existing settlement pattern.

The sizes of Libyan settlements, however, have been more susceptible to change. Benghazi now rivals Tripoli as a major growth point. The new town at Beida has been established in a hitherto lightly urbanized area, while Sebha, the main Fezzanese urban centre, has grown rapidly since the construction of the 1,126 km. Fezzan Road from the main coastal highway.

Internal migration

During the period of rapid urban growth, migration was the significant mechanism of demographic change, and a stimulus to reactions in other demographic and economic conditions. Despite the disruptive forces and regional inequalities which it initially provoked, internal migration acted as an instrument of cultural diffusion and social integration. As such, migration was a necessary element of normal demographic and economic adjustment to a new equilibrium.

In view of the small total population, the scale of Libyan migration was particularly significant. In 1964 over 600,000 persons in Libya, nearly 40 per cent of the total population, had changed residence during their lifetime. Over half of this group was composed of nomads and semi-nomads involved in some form of seasonal movement and shifting cultivation. A further 175,000 Libyans, 12 per cent of the total citizen population born in Libya, were enumerated in a major administrative region other than their region of birth, over half being enumerated in Tripoli and

Benghazi. Of the remainder, 37,000 were Libyan citizens born abroad and 49,000 were foreigners living in Libya; two-thirds of this group were also resident in the two major urban centres.

Each province displayed a distinct pattern of net migration both within and between the three provinces (Fig. 14.7). On the basis of place of birth and residence in 1964, Tripolitania showed a net loss to Cyrenaica of about 31,000 persons, and a net gain of about 3,000 from the Fezzan. Within the province the bulk of the net movements were from the interior regions to Tripoli, the only region showing a net increase.

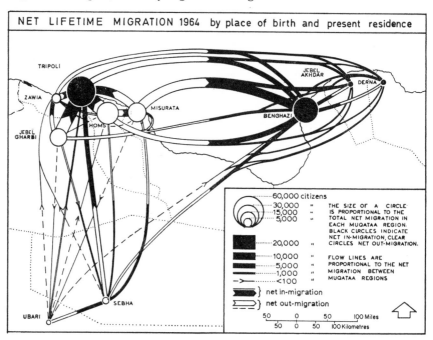

FIGURE 14.7

Apart from the net gain of 31,000 persons from Tripolitania, Cyrenaica experienced a net gain of 4,000 persons from the Fezzan. Most of the growth through migration was concentrated in Benghazi. The majority of Benghazi's immigrants came from Tripolitania, particularly from Misurata, although some internal migration also took place from the Jebel al Akhdar and Derna regions.

The Fezzan showed a net loss in both Sebha and Ubari and in the migrations to the two northern provinces despite some net gain from the Jebel regions in Tripolitania. However, the largest volume of migration was internal, from Ubari and Sebha Muqataa.

Three-quarters of the migrants originated in Tripolitania, most from the coastal region east of Tripoli. Declining water-tables combined with ease of transport to Tripoli are likely factors causing the out-migration of 62,000 persons, forming 20 per cent of the 1964 population of Homs and Zliten.

Half of Tripolitania's in-migrants were concentrated in Tripoli; most had originated in the surrounding regions of Zawia, Jebel Gharbi, Homs and Misurata. Oil exploitation in the Sirte lowlands in part caused an influx of outsiders to Sirte, Al Jufra, Agedabia and Benghazi Districts. However, as many of the migrants originated in the surrounding semi-arid areas they may have been mostly semi-nomadic persons.

Cyrenaica had a high level and rate of in-migration accounting for 36 per cent of the national total. Like Tripoli, Benghazi contained the bulk of the provincial total, though the other towns of Derna, Tobruk and Beida also received many migrants. In contrast to Tripolitania, the smaller towns received migrants mainly from local areas.

Determinants of differential urban migration

While certain common trends are apparent in the nature of the migrations to and from Tripoli and Benghazi, the volume and direction of migration has produced different scales of urban growth. Thus, Tripoli had three times as many in- and out-migrants as Benghazi and five times as many foreigners. Four factors have influenced this pattern:

(a) Both Tripoli and Benghazi have experienced different stages of development. Tripoli was the first capital, had a large resident Italian community, and was the initial centre for oil and government administration. In contrast, Benghazi suffered internal strife during the Italian occupation of the 1930's, never supported a large foreign community, and endured much wartime destruction. Post-war reconstruction, particularly of the port, was delayed by lack of capital and the uncertainty concerning the future of the Eastern province. Drastic changes occurred only after administrative decentralization and Cyrenaican oil finds. The location of offices, repair shops and warehouses attracted an inflow of capital and people, which in turn stimulated consumer-orientated industries and service activities.

(b) Tripoli has a central geographical location in relation to its fertile hinterland which comprises the country's largest population concentration. Thus, Tripoli offers optimal transfer costs, for no agricultural region is able to monopolize primary production so as to create a supply-centred industry. Moreover, Tripoli has developed as the transport node for the whole province; in 1966, 10 or more buses per day served areas containing three-quarters of the provincial population. Benghazi, in contrast, has no fertile or densely populated hinterland; it is situated on the western extremity of Cyrenaica's 1,000 km. coast-

line, and its port has had to compete with the natural harbour at Tobruk.
(c) The size, function and distribution of other settlements in the two
northern provinces has undoubtedly influenced the growth of the two
principal cities. While no Tripolitanian town rivalled Tripoli in size or
variety of functions, the isolated urban centres of Derna and Tobruk
have remained separate and important urban units. The recent expansion
of Beida may further offset the concentration of Cyrenaican urban
population in the principal city.
(d) Finally, the amount and type of migration to Tripoli and Benghazi is
as much a product of the urban attractions as the 'push' factors in rural
areas. The 'snowballing' process or urbanization in Tripoli has diver-
sified its employment opportunities, compared to the relative specialization in Benghazi. Moreover, visits to Tripoli by agricultural workers and
military conscripts since the 1920's have given the city a longer history
of contact with its rural and urban hinterland than has Benghazi with its
surrounding territory.

Of the myriad of situations and choices facing potential migrants, two
would seem to be of particular relevance in Libya. First, the contrast
between the two urban centres of Tripoli and Benghazi and the rest of the
country is so marked that the choice of destinations for potential migrants
is clear-cut. No other town in Libya provides a similar gamut of employment, educational and medical facilities. Thus, rural to urban movement
has developed as the significant migration pattern. Stepped migration does
not appear to have been of great importance in Libya, although lifetime
migration statistics may cloak past movements. Significantly, the stagnation
of middle-sized towns suggests that Tripoli and Benghazi have absorbed
migrants from both rural and local urban areas.

Second, the choices of changing residence would still seem to depend
primarily on the nature of the rural environment. As distance was not a
major determinant of migration size or direction on a national scale, and as
Tripoli and Benghazi were the dominant attractions for potential migrants,
'push' factors in rural areas would seem to be the significant determinant
of Libya's migration patterns.

The characteristics of the migration streams appear to have varied in
time. There has been a recent growth in the proportion of young children
in the major urban centres. This has occurred despite the high proportion
of single men in the productive age groups, particularly in Benghazi. A
decrease in urban infant mortality may in part have caused an expansion
of natural increase in the major cities. However, the growth of *bidonvilles*
(shanty towns) with poor sanitary and medical facilities would suggest that
infant mortality has not changed radically. An equalization of the sex ratio
of Tripoli-bound migrants would suggest that certain migration streams
increasingly have a family structure.

The consequences of migration to Libyan cities are two-fold. In the long term, migration will allow Libya's traditional economic system to be eroded, both by enlarging the modern economic sector and by removing the core labour force on which the traditional economic system depends. Increasing inter-provincial migrations should also tend to weaken the provincial distinctiveness which is so characteristic of Libya. As such, the current migration trends will in the long term act as a force for cultural diffusion and possibly social integration.

In the short term, however, the redistribution of the economically active population has produced both social and economic disruption. Neither the migrants themselves, nor the communities at the origins or destinations have been able to cope with the speed or volume of migration. In rural areas, release of pressure on meagre resources has been offset by the lack of a youthful labour force. In the cities, pressure on urban housing has, in part, created the *bidonvilles*, while the educational, medical and transport facilities have been stretched to their present limits. Yet there has been little immediate benefit from the new source of urban labour, and there is a danger that serious urban unemployment and under-employment will increase. The causes and results of these problems form a key element in the change of the Libyan economic and demographic systems.

Manpower resources

The Libyan economy is confronted simultaneously with two persistent, yet seemingly diverse manpower problems; shortage of persons with critical skills in the modernizing sector, and surplus of labour in the traditional sector. Both problems are intimately related, having their roots in the changes which are inherent in the process of economic development. Both are related to the structure and distribution of the population; and paradoxically, the shortage of persons with critical skills is one of the contributing causes of the surplus of people without jobs (Harbison, 1962).

The current labour problems are new only in degree. Before the expanded economic opportunities afforded by oil, economic development was curtailed as much by the quality of the labour force as by the inadequacies of the material resources. As the tempo of modernization quickened, the problems of the labour force were aggravated. The situation of job shortages and surplus of workers in the early 1950's was replaced by a shortage of workers, in both quality and quantity, during the 1960's.

Changes in the nature of Libyan manpower problems were initially stimulated by the type of economic development in Libya. Recently, however, the structure and pattern of the population itself has determined the scale of labour force growth. The actual workforce of 424,000 persons (1967) is now approaching the potential supply of labour of working age, thereby setting limits to future economic growth.

According to the 1964 population census, the economically active population numbered approximately 373,000 persons comprising less than one-quarter of the total population, a situation similar to other North African countries. The increase of 35,000 economically active persons between 1954 and 1964 represented only 7 per cent of the total increase in population. The consequent ratio of active to inactive persons in the population rose from 1.8 in 1954 to 2.0 in 1964. This large and increasing ratio of 'dependency' is influenced by the demographic and educational structure of the population.

In Libya, as in most countries, the males are primarily responsible for economic livelihood. Crude activity rates for males were similar to other North African countries, but were generally below those of more developed countries. In contrast, the crude activity rates for Libyan females were among the lowest in the world. This had the overall effect of lowering the 1964 rates for both sexes to a level 40 per cent below the 1962 world average.

Apart from a certain amount of under-enumeration (Nair, 1967) and variable classification of economically active females, the initial effects of rapid urbanization have also been partly responsible for the small number of women in full-time employment. The decline in traditional activities where women play an important role, particularly agriculture and handicrafts, has been influenced by the increase in incomes and the necessity for a period of adjustment in urban settings. There is also a social reluctance to let women work outside the family sphere, especially when earnings have increased sufficiently without women having to work. Two other elements have exaggerated this inclination; one is the inability of women to meet the requirements of urban jobs (the high percentage of female aliens in urban employment is testimony to this situation). The other contributory factor has been the relatively sluggish development of activities in which women are more readily accepted, especially light manufacturing and certain commercial and service activities.

The Libyan age structure also inhibits the supply of labour. The citizen population has a progressive age structure, its pyramid having a broad base and a rapidly tapering top with increasing age. It is an age structure with a large potential for growth, with 44 per cent of the population under 15 years of age in 1964. The heavy load of dependants, together with the relative and absolute deficiency of adult manpower that is inherent in such an age structure, adds to the handicap of low labour productivity and increases the difficulties of social advancement.

Education

The strict government control of immigration, particularly of foreign workers, imposes severe strains on the Libyan educational system. As all professional, technical and other skilled manpower must have the necessary school and university education at the appropriate level, the output of the educational system inevitably sets limits beyond which the supply of these categories cannot be stretched.

Total school attendance increased from about 50,000 pupils in 1954 to 190,000 in 1964 (Auble, July 1965) when the school population accounted for one-quarter of the total economically inactive persons. The loss of such a large proportion of Libyan youth from work which was low in productivity created two problems. First, there was the need for a stop-gap of trained and qualified persons. The 40,000 Italians and 10,000 Jews provided a valuable productive workforce in the pre-independence period. Their depletion was only partly reinforced by an influx of British and American skilled persons and by other Middle Eastern semi-skilled labour since independence. Secondly, before oil revenues, Libya found it cheaper to provide employment rather than schooling. The long-term implications are that the high cost of the present educational system, detracting as it does from more immediately productive investments, will be offset by the cost of not training the population in subjects relevant to the country's problems. Up to 1963, however, a poor economic return was being obtained from the resources employed; for instance, an intake of 50,000 children to grade 1 primary schools was matched by an output of only 400 secondary school leavers.

The conflict of short-term losses, both financial and of manpower, versus long-term returns on educational outlays, has produced significant adaptations in the economy. The shift in the pattern of early employment has necessarily raised the level of skill throughout the economically active population; in theory, the young age groups are an efficient route for introducing new skills into a country with a youthful age structure. In Libya, limited intake capacity in secondary schools, together with the large numbers of drop-outs and failures, produce an inadequate output from the educational system.

Types of economic activity

While the demographic characteristics of the population limit both the potential and actual supply of the labour force, the precise sectoral changes in the economy have been largely a product of the type of economic growth. In turn, the sectoral changes have been partly responsible for the recent geographical and occupational redistribution of the population.

Omitting the dominating influence of the mining activities over gross domestic product, agriculture's proportion of total product had fallen from 25 per cent to 15 per cent between 1958 and 1964 (and has since tumbled to no more than 4 per cent). But the decrease in young and aged agricultural workers and the investment of government capital in the industry had the effect of doubling both *per capita* (of those economically active) and total product value during the same period. In view of the small amount of agricultural credit made available by Libyan banks, £L8 million during 1957–64 (Ministry of Economy and Trade, 1966b), it is likely that a significant under-employed element was removed from the agricultural sector. Agricultural activities accounted for about a third of the 424,000 total employment in the late 1960's.

Mining activities produced half of the total domestic product in 1964 and formed the fastest growing industrial sector. In terms of employment opportunities, however, their stimulus was small. From a total of 400 workers in 1954, a peak of 12,000 persons had been reached by 1964. *Per capita* products of the economically active males were eighty times that of agriculture, even though half the Libyan employees were classified as unskilled labourers in 1964 (Ministry of Economy and Trade, 1966c). A recent revival of exploration outside the Sirte basin may create new employment demands.

Despite an increase in employment and a doubling of their domestic product value between 1958 and 1964, manufacturing activities suffered a decreasing share of the total product excluding mining activities. But in contrast to tertiary activities, mining and manufacturing activities are not completely dominated by the two major cities, the mining being concentrated in the Sirte basin, and the manufacturing being prominent in smaller towns, particularly Misurata (Blake, 1968). About 8 per cent of the total labour force are engaged in manufacturing activities.

The revenues from oil exports were brought to bear most significantly in the tertiary sector of the economy. Tertiary activities accounted for 70 per cent of the domestic product (excluding mining) and nearly half of the economically active males in the late 1960's. The external sources of income made possible a high level of imports which provided the basis of most profits earned in wholesale and retail trading, personal services, commerce and banking. It also provided the bulk of the government revenue, creating a big demand for offices, houses and transport facilities. Both construction and transportation activities increased their value of domestic product five times in six years, and their share of employed persons three times in the ten years preceding 1964. Construction workers now account for 11 per cent of the total labour force. However, the service sector showed the largest domestic product value, particularly the government services, followed by wholesale, retail, storage and trade.

Outside the agricultural sector, over half of the economically active citizens in 1964 were concentrated in Tripoli and Benghazi. To a certain extent Tripoli had lost its overall dominance in the early 1960's, having controlled nearly two-thirds of the 1956 labour force in activities other than agriculture. Not only had Benghazi emerged as a major centre of tertiary activities by 1964, but most Libyan regions contained a growing modern economic sector, particularly in the towns.

Modern and traditional economic sectors

On the basis of workers' economic status, three groups of economic activities delineated the modern and traditional economic sectors. First, economically active citizens classified as 'workers on own account' and 'unpaid family workers' were essentially traditional economic groups. Both groups reflected small-scale production and unpaid labour (in terms of wages or salaries). Agriculture and commercial activities had 80 per cent and 76 per cent respectively of their labour force classified in this traditional sector. Second, the modern economic sector contained a large proportion of wage-paid labour, typical of the 'employers' and 'employees' economic status groups. Mining, construction, public utilities and service activities showed not less than 95 per cent of their labour forces in the modern economic sector defined thus. Finally, a group of activities contained elements of both the modern and traditional sectors, both transport and manufacturing activities containing only two-thirds of their workforce in the modern sector.

Defined as 'employers' and 'employees' combined, Libya's modern economic sector increased its proportion of the total male workforce from 33 to 52 per cent between 1954 and 1964. Expressed regionally, those Muqataa contained more than half their labour force in the modern sector in 1964 were, in decreasing order of significance, Tripoli, Benghazi, Sebha, Derna and Tobruk. The regions with the smallest proportions were the Tripolitanian Muqataa of Homs, Misurata and Jebel Gharbi. Zawia and Ubari were slightly below the national average.

As with the economy as a whole, oil revenues have indirectly provided the financial basis for industrial changes in the urban centres, particularly in Tripoli and Benghazi. Increased income, large capital resources, a favourable balance of payments, improved social conditions, and more efficient communications have produced a sense of security and optimism, and an efflorescence of tertiary activities. Most of the factors determining the concentration of the modern economic sector in urban centres have been highlighted. Some expansion of industry had taken place before the benefits of oil wealth, a partial infrastructure had been established, and, as the origin of public and private revenues, the cities of Tripoli and Benghazi became the optimum location for both demand and supply requirements. However, four economic factors may combine to restrict further economic growth:

(a) The role of the government sector has become increasingly dominant as a source of both income and employment. Despite the administrative decentralization and growth of Beida and Sebha, Tripoli still has nearly one-third and Benghazi one-sixth of the total Libyan employees involved in service activities. Moreover, both Tripoli and Benghazi have over one-quarter of their economically active citizens involved in government services.

(b) The importance of trade and service employment (and the 'get-rich-quick' attitude of the entrepreneurs) based on the reliance on imports, has offset real progress in the use of local resources. Increased demands and rising prices will further attract people to the service trades, particularly in the urban centres of Tripoli and Benghazi. Imports are beginning to supplant rather than supplement local production.

(c) The shortness of Libya's rapid economic development span still causes a lack of confidence in long-term investment by private entrepreneurs. High capital accumulation has taken place in the form of hoarding (particularly assets in foreign banks and some durable goods) as well as along traditional lines (for instance, real estate and short-term commercial ventures). These effects have stimulated land speculation, inflation and rising land prices. Particularly affected are the low income brackets in urban areas (comprising about 40 per cent of Tripoli's population in 1966) thereby stimulating the growth of shanty-towns.

(d) Localization of economic functions in Tripoli and Benghazi is in part a mark of the economic development typical of the modern sector. Concentration of resources provides a compact market, enables economies of scale to be utilized, and attracts specialists and specialized industries. Nevertheless, further division of the urban industrial structure may be detrimental to future growth; specialization should not inhibit interdependence of sectors, while concentration of resources and employment should not offset growth elsewhere.

The recent growth of the economy has initiated new manpower demands but restraints imposed by actual and potential sources of labour supply are now taking effect. In the long run, the surplus potential, particularly in agriculture and traditional female economic activities, will help to meet the demands of the modern economic sector. In the short run, however, acute shortage of skilled personnel may damage the sustained economic expansion which has typified the post-oil export phase in Libya.

The continued accretion of the population in Tripoli and Benghazi has been a demographic adjustment to the location of economic opportunities. So great has been the process of industrial linkage and inertia, that the urban disadvantages of rising labour, rental and import costs have been offset. A vicious circle of concentrated economic growth is taking place. Just as the Libyan economy increases its tertiary bias, so the growth of consumer-orientated economic activities and consuming power becomes urban biased. The forces of the market have thus partly determined both the distribution and industrial structure of the population.

Significantly, however, the structure, distribution and growth of the Libyan population itself has set quantitative and qualitative limitations to the nature of the economic growth. Adaptations in the occupational structure and distribution of the population have been demographic responses to the new economic demands. Nevertheless, the accumulation of the total stock of human resources will dictate the level and rate of future economic growth.

Population growth

After Kuwait, Libya's annual rate of population increase between 1954 and 1964 was the fastest in the Middle East and North Africa. According to a comparison of the two population censuses, the rate of growth of 3.6 per cent per annum was impressively high, but the actual volume of increase was small in relation to neighbouring countries. Despite a rate of growth nearly twice as large as Algeria's, Libya's annual increment was only one-quarter as great. Even so, at current rates of growth Libya would double its population in twenty years.

The demographic transition of high population growth which Libya is now experiencing appears to demonstrate the classic situation of reduced mortality and maintained high fertility. However, this idealized sequence and direction of change is only partially applicable to the Libyan demographic transition because the timing and content of the modernization process has itself changed. Consequently, the key demographic variables of fertility, mortality and migration are responding to a set of proximate causes which contain new elements, occur in new combinations, and have a pace never experienced before.

Patterns of fertility

As yet Libya does not have a complete system of birth and death registration, but two sample surveys undertaken in 1950 and 1963 give some precision to the pattern of fertility in the country. The 1950 sample of 3,000 settled and semi-nomadic tribesmen near Zawia indicated gross live birth rates of 56 and 64 per thousand respectively (El Shanawany, 1951). Although high, these rates compared with other North African estimates for the same period. A demographic analysis of Benghazi City in 1964 (Divo, 1964) showed a crude birth rate of 54 per thousand, indicating the relative stability of the birth rate since Libyan independence.

The two sample surveys also suggested that similar fertility patterns prevailed in both urban and rural areas. The association between urban life and low fertility has been observed so frequently, however, that urbanization has been seriously suggested as a means to control population growth. In addition, an entire theory concerning the 'changing functions of the family' has been formulated to explain the decline in fertility associated with urbanization (Abu-Lughod, 1963). It is, therefore, particularly significant that in Libya urban and rural fertility patterns remained similar during the period of rapid economic change.

It would seem that there were few inducements to women to practise some form of birth control. Even the rapid increase in female education from 5,000 in 1965 to 40,000 in 1967 failed to erode the traditional fertility attitudes. This was no doubt caused by the large increase in primary education for girls aged under 10 years, rather than for women of child-bearing ages. Nor did the increase in female employment in the modern economic sector appear to deter women from increased pregnancy. In fact, generous family allowances may actually have encouraged an increase in fertility levels. Whatever the precise causes, the alternative benefits of decreased cost and inconvenience to pregnant and child-bearing women had little attraction to either urban or rural citizens between 1954 and 1964.

Patterns of mortality

The maintenance of a high, stable birth rate during 1954–64 implies that the large rate of population growth was due either to significant net immigration or to a marked decline in mortality. The low level of official net immigration—14,000 persons between 1957 and 1964 (Ministry of Economy and Trade, 1966b)—suggests that a decline in mortality was the proximate cause of the population growth.

Published mortality statistics indicate a drop from 42 to 5 deaths per thousand between 1953 and 1965; a feasible but highly unlikely situation. It is certain that the general Libyan mortality rate did not remain stable during the period of rapid economic change. Fluctuations caused by droughts and epidemics were matched by better nutrition, improved obstetrical care, and prevention, control or cure of certain diseases. Evidence from a variety of sources would suggest that crude death rates decreased from about 35 to 20 per thousand between 1954 and 1964, and that the urban death rates appeared to have been below the rural rates in both 1954 and 1964, although the amount of change was greater in rural areas.

Health experts in Libya emphasize that an infant mortality rate of 300 per thousand live births was probable in 1965. Indeed, Libyan statistics for 1959 indicated a rate of 400 per thousand live births (Föllmer, 1960). With such an infant mortality rate, the birth rate could hardly have prevented the population from declining, even with very low mortality in other age groups. There thus appears to have been some decline in infant mortality between 1952 and 1965. While there was little difference in urban and rural conditions in 1954, urban rates were substantially below rural rates in 1964.

At present, infant mortality is highest among babies delivered at home, particularly in rural areas, and 98 per cent of the Libyan births are still delivered at home. Infections due to unclean obstetric practices and to the ignorance of domestic midwives account for the large number of still-births and significant maternal and perinatal mortality.

While respiratory infections during the first six months of life are responsible for the bulk of the infant mortality, thereafter deaths are due mostly to intestinal causes. Excessive breast feeding with no supplementary feeding causes malnutrition before weaning, usually between 1–2 years of age (Jusatz, 1967). Indigestible food partly explains the inadequate weight increase of infants, their protein deficiency, and their reduced resistance against disease.

Disease occurrence and distribution

In the late nineteenth century, high urban population densities and poor sanitary and medical facilities made the towns as vulnerable to the quarantinable diseases as the rural areas. Improved hygiene by the Italians helped to remove the threat of plague, typhus, smallpox and cholera, although the large scale of the country, the long distances between individual settlements and the difficulty of communication discouraged the rapid spread of epidemics. However, two types of disease still impair healthy environmental conditions.

'Nestling epidemic' diseases, prevalent in an area independent of the occupants, are transmitted to man by insects, water and foodstuffs. The Tripolitanian coast around Tripoli and Tauorgha, Benghazi and the Fezzanese oases have been the main potential and actual centres of malaria outbreaks, though the rate of infection is small. Bilharziasis, however, is a more serious epidemic disease greatly dependent on physical environmental conditions.

Conditioned by the cultures of various communities are diseases associated with low standards of hygiene. Bacterial eye diseases and trachoma are widespread in the desert oases where high summer temperatures and stagnant water encourage infected flies to proliferate.

Much is being done to eradicate these diseases. A malaria eradication programme was launched in 1958, while mobile units carry out the fight against bilharziasis and trachoma, directed by the Epidemiology Centre for Trachoma. Teachers are being trained in the use of hygiene, and maternal and child centres are being built in most large concentrations of population. Despite the inevitable localization of specialized medical facilities in Tripoli and Benghazi, the Libyan government has succeeded in establishing a wide distribution of scarce medical resources. Nevertheless, many diseases which are capable of being controlled are still rampant, particularly tuberculosis, measles, whooping cough, amoebiasis and enteritis. Two broad types of disease and sickness have a particular bearing on Libya's population and economic growth. First, diseases responsible for

341

the high infant mortality are key elements in the potential growth. Second, many diseases still intensify sickness, remove people from the labour force and lessen their ability to concentrate on work. Undoubtedly, the quality of health in the Libyan population is as significant for further economic growth as the total numbers of the population.

Natural increase

Most experienced statisticians and planners in Libya feel that the inter-censal annual growth rate of 3.6 per cent is too high. Three possible explanations for this exceedingly high rate of increase have been suggested (Auble, May 1965). First, it is possible that the 1954 population census was an under-enumeration, it being the first census of its kind conducted in the country (apart from two Italian surveys undertaken in 1931 and 1936). Second, increased internal migration, impending elections, and regional grants based on population may have caused an overcount in the 1964 census. Finally, some illegal immigration between 1954 and 1965 is likely to have occurred. In the past, many Libyans are known to have emigrated to Algeria, Tunisia, Chad, Niger and Egypt, particularly during the Italian colonization in the 1930's, and their return in recent years has been stimulated by the expansion of urban occupational opportunities.

In order to check these uncertainties and to suggest the probable rate and amount of recent population growth, certain assumptions must be made. If the birth rate estimate of 45 per thousand is accurate (and there is no evidence to suggest it was less), an infant mortality of 300 per thousand and a net immigration of 34,000 between 1954 and 1964, would give a probable death rate of 20 per thousand. Such fertility, mortality and migration assumptions, verified by the available empirical evidence, suggest that the probable intercensal natural increase was approximately 2.8 per cent per annum.

A shift in the relative importance of migration and natural increase in Libya's urban growth is indicated by the contrasting situations in Tripoli and Benghazi. Over one-half of Tripoli's growth during the ten year intercensal period was composed of natural increase, compared with only one-third in Benghazi. Improvements in Tripoli's sanitary and medical facilities developed quicker than in Benghazi, while a move towards family migration to Tripoli has been identified. The phenomenon of increasing proportions of urban growth being composed of natural increase has also been noticed in Egyptian cities (Abu-Lughod, 1963).

Population projections

Even if the Libyan population increased at the intercensal rate of 3.6 per cent per annum, the annual increment would only be 70,000 persons—

small in relation to Egypt's 700,000 annual increment. However, a Libyan population double its present size in the next 25 years, and certainly 2 million by 1974, has serious economic, social, political and geographical implications.

Despite the small size of the population relative to other developing countries, the pressure of increasing demands on existing economic resources and social infrastructure will be serious. Already there is a great demand for houses, schools, hospitals and other non-productive but vital facilities. These pressures will be selective depending on the structure of the future population. If the current fertility and mortality patterns are maintained, by 1974 over 50 per cent of the population will be composed of children under 15 years of age. The number of families can be expected to increase at 3.2 per cent per annum, the number of potential mothers at 2.3 per cent, and the number of old people at about 1.0 per cent. Even if the current rate of increase is not maintained, those presently alive will present a new demographic pattern in the near future. Thus, those persons aged 5–19 years in 1964 will provide nearly half a million potential persons for the labour force by 1984. This would form a 58 per cent increase over the age group 25 to 39 years in 1964. The actual work force in 1984 will be determined partly by the sectoral demands of the economy (particularly the participation of women) and partly by the delay of entry into the workforce imposed by the educational system.

Regionally, the pattern of population distribution will reflect continued urbanization. Geometric projections of the population indicate that Tripoli and Benghazi together will comprise over 26 per cent of the total population in 1972, compared with 24 per cent in 1964. Even if internal migration becomes less of a determining factor in urban growth, their continued increase and dominance will be assured through natural increase.

The choice for Libya in the next ten to twenty years is between very rapid and moderately rapid growth in population. Government control of further immigration may lessen the present increase through net immigration. Mortality rates appear to have been reduced from 35 to 20 per thousand persons between 1954 and 1964. A continued reduction is likely considering the expansion of medical facilities, the increase in education for women, better nutrition and personal hygiene, government housing schemes and improved sanitary conditions.

No analogous reduction in fertility seems to have occurred among Libyans, either in rural or urban areas. Yet a reduction in fertility would make the process of modernization more rapid and more certain. It would accelerate the growth in real incomes, provide more effectively the possibility of productive employment for all adults who need jobs, and make the attainment of universal education easier; it would also have the immediate effect of providing the women of Libya with some relief from constant pregnancy, parturition and infant care.

Conclusion

Evidence of Libya's recent past suggests that the country is experiencing an intermediate stage in the process of demographic transition. This stage is characterized by a geographical and occupational redistribution of the population, preceding and accompanying the increased population growth caused by mortality decline. The cause of this increased population mobility is primarily economic, although the precise form is also determined by Libya's physical, social and cultural environments. The characteristics of this stage of transition are related to a marked dichotomy between urban and rural areas. Although the initial difference between the two areas was economic, the transformation of a modern economic sector permeates the country's social, cultural and hence demographic structure. The consequent duality in the socio-economic characteristics of the population forms both the means by which further erosion of the traditional economic system takes place, and also an incipient stage for further demographic transition.

Libya's demographic and economic evolutions indicate similar stages, though different rates of change for the two transitions. Thus, the major deviation from the model of demographic transition appears to be in the time lag between economic growth and the resultant demographic response. Libya's stage of economic development indicates the characteristics of the take-off, where urban growth and non-agricultural occupations are beginning to dominate the nation's economic structure. Yet the country's demographic conditions are not those of the transition proper, appearing characteristic of the early stage of transition.

Despite the rapidity of the economic transformation, Libya's pattern of development cannot be dismissed merely as a unique or exceptional case. Many of the Libyan deviations from the normal process of economic–demographic evolution bear a systematic relation to each other and to the historic and cultural context of their appearance. Part of the reason lies in the nature of the economic growth itself and part in the country's geographical anatomy.

The growth of a modern economic sector associated with tertiary economic activities gave a forced boost to urban growth and a development unrelated to the indigenous economy. As such, the country's economic transition may not have reached such a mature stage as take-off.

Geographical conditions have also combined to set quantitative and qualitative limits on the direction and rate of population and economic change. Of particular significance have been the large scale of the country, its location as a zone of transition, the small absolute size of its population, its meagre resource base apart from petroleum, the strength of the Moslem culture, and the low level of indigenous technology. This amalgam of conditions has produced national distinctiveness within a wider context of association with other rapidly developing countries.

The basis for further demographic and economic changes has been laid. Just as the preconditions for sustained economic growth have been achieved, so the decline in mortality, initiated by economic development, marks the incipient stage of the demographic transition. Yet it seems implausible that the country can sustain its high fertility, despite the breathing spell afforded by economic growth. Since the economic advantages of a reduction in fertility are cumulative, the ultimate benefits are greater, the sooner it occurs. However, the decline in fertility depends on the alteration of long-established customs and institutions; economic growth by itself, even if allowed by the population structure, cannot guarantee the consequent decline in population growth. As such, economic growth remains a necessary but insufficient condition for Libya's continued rapid pace of modernization.

REFERENCES

ABU-LUGHOD, J. (1963) 'Urban–Rural differences as a function of the demographic transition: Egyptian data and an analytical model', *American Journal of Sociology*, 69, pp. 476–90.

AGOSTINI, E. DI (1922–3) *Le popolazioni della Tripolitania, Notizie etniche e storiche*, Governo della Tripolitania, Tripoli; and *La popolazione della Cirenaica*, Governo della Cirenaica, Benghazi.

AUBLE, A. (May 1965) 'Technical problems in forecasting the population of Libya', *Statistical Paper No. 7*, Ministry of Planning and Development, Tripoli.

AUBLE, A. (July 1965) 'Student enrolment data through 1964–5', *Statistical Paper No. 8*, Ministry of Planning and Development, Tripoli.

BERRY, B. J. L. (1961) 'City size distributions and economic development', *Economic Development and Cultural Change*, 9, pp. 573–88.

BLAKE, G. H. (1968) *Misurata: a market town in Tripolitania*, Research Paper No. 9, Department of Geography, University of Durham.

BOTTOMLEY, A. (1964) 'Economic growth in a semi-nomadic herding community', *Economia Internazionale*, 17, Genoa.

BURU, M. (1965) *El Marj Plain: A Geographical Study*, unpublished Ph.D. thesis, University of Durham.

DIVO INSTITUT (1964) *City of Benghazi School Equipment Program until 1974*, I, Frankfurt.

DOXIADIS ASSOCIATES (1964) *Housing in Libya*, I, Tripoli.

ECONOMIC RESEARCH DEPARTMENT OF THE NATIONAL BANK OF LIBYA (March 1961) *Inflation in Libya*, Tripoli.

ECONOMIST INTELLIGENCE UNIT (February 1965) *The Price Control Systems in Libya: A Critical Analysis*, Tripoli.

EL SHANAWANY, M. R. (1951) *The Organization of the Vital Statistics of Libya*, The United Nations, Tripoli.

EVANS-PRITCHARD, E. E. (1949) *The Sanusi of Cyrenaica*, Oxford.

FALCHI, N. (1939) 'Le peuplement rural des provinces libyennes', *Le Travail Agricole International Review*, 2, Rome.

FISHER, W. B. (1953) 'Problems of modern Libya', *Geographical Journal*, 114, pp. 183–99.

FÖLLMER, V. W. (1960) 'Die Sanglings—und Kindersterblichkeit und ihre Ursachen in einen Entwicklungsland', *Deutsche Medizinische Wochenschrift*, 45.

GREGORY, J. W. (1909) *Report of the work of the Commission sent out by the Jewish Territorial Organisation—for the purpose of a Jewish Settlement in Cyrenaica*, London.

HARBISON, F. H. (1962) 'Human resource development planning in modernizing economics', *International Labour Review*, 85.

HARTLEY, R. G. (1968) *Recent Population Changes in Libya: Economic Relationships and Geographical Patterns*, unpublished Ph.D. thesis, University of Durham.

HIGGINS, B. (1959) *Economic Development: problems, principles and policies*, New York.

HILL, R. W. (1960a) *Agriculture and Irrigation on the Tripolitanian Jefara*, unpublished Ph.D. thesis, University of Durham.

HILL, R. W. (1960b) 'Underground water resources of the Jefara Plain', in *Field Studies in Libya*, eds. S. G. Willimott and J. I. Clarke, Department of Geography, University of Durham.

INTERNATIONAL BANK FOR RECONSTRUCTION AND DEVELOPMENT IBRD (1960) *The Economic Development of Libya*, Baltimore.

JUSATZ, H. J. ed. (1967) *Libyen–Libya*, Berlin.

KING, L. J. (1961) 'A multivariate analysis of the spacing of urban settlements in the United States', *Annals of the Association of American Geographers*, 51, pp. 222–33.

KROELLER, E. H. (August 1960) *Food Balance Sheet for Libya, 1959*, Ministry of National Economy, Tripoli.

LALEVIC, D. (1967) *A Study of Libyan Agriculture and its Present Situation*, Ministry of Planning and Development, Tripoli.

LOCKWOOD, A. N. (1957) 'Libya—building a desert economy', *International Conciliation*, 512.

MINISTRY OF ECONOMY AND TRADE, LIBYA (1966a) *General Population Census, 1964*, Tripoli.

MINISTRY OF ECONOMY AND TRADE, LIBYA (1966b) *Statistical Abstract, 1965*, Tripoli.

346

MINISTRY OF ECONOMY AND TRADE, LIBYA (1966c) *Employment in the Petroleum Mining Industry, 1964,* Tripoli.

MINISTRY OF NATIONAL ECONOMY, LIBYA (1959) *General Population Census, 1954,* Tripoli.

MINISTRY OF PLANNING AND DEVELOPMENT, LIBYA (1966) *Inventory Reports of Planning Consultants,* Tripoli.

NAIR, A. N. K. (1964) *A Survey of Requirements of Professional, Technical and Skilled Manpower in Libya, 1964–9,* Ministry of Labour and Social Affairs, Tripoli.

NAIR, A. N. K. (1967) *Libya's Manpower Resources and Educational and Training Needs, 1964–71,* Ministry of Labour and Social Affairs, Tripoli.

PAN, C. L. (1949) 'The Population of Libya', *Population Studies,* 3, p. 1.

SIMON, H. A. (1955) 'On a class of skew distribution functions', *Biometrika,* 42, pp. 425–40.

STEWART, C. T., JR. (1958) 'The size and spacing of cities', *Geographical Review,* 48, pp. 222–45.

STEWART, J. H. (1958) *Land and Water Resources in Tripolitania,* US Operation Mission to Libya, Tripoli.

WHITING ASSOCIATES INTERNATIONAL (1967) *Fezzan Inventory Report,* Tripoli.

ZIPF, G. K. (1949) *Human behaviour and the principle of least effort,* Cambridge.

Chapter 15
Tunisia: population patterns, pressures and policies
J I Clarke

Individuality and disequilibrium

A small country, measuring only 164,000 sq. km., Tunisia contrasts
markedly in size with its two neighbours, Algeria and Libya, yet it has a
distinctive personality, attributable partly to its extensive plains and the
profound influence of Mediterranean conditions, both climatic and
human, making it less harsh than its neighbours, and partly to a strong
sense of nationality which dates back to the Hafsite dynasty beginning in
A.D. 1236. In other words, the Tunisian republic, unlike so many new
African states, is not merely a reflection of European boundaries and
administration but has real national identity. Although the evolution of a
stable society was blunted by the duel between the Turks and Spaniards in
the Mediterranean during the sixteenth century and then by Turkish
misrule, piracy and internal anarchy among warring nomadic groups,
Tunisia reveals long traditions of sedentary and urban life, especially
along the coastal zone. In addition, its culture has evolved in response to
successive invasions and colonizations, especially by Romans, Arabs,
Turks and French, all of whom have left deep traces. A sort of ante-room
for the Maghreb, Tunisia has often been the first recipient of new ideas
and cultures.

The most lasting cultural impact has been that of the medieval Arab
invasions, and today nearly all of the 4.8 million people (1969 estimate)
are Arabic-speakers and Moslems, and Arabic has given Tunisia a homogeneity and unity lacking in Algeria and Morocco, where Berber communities are much larger. The most profound external impact in recent
times was during the period of the French protectorate (1881–1956), but
the impact has been more economic, demographic and geographic than
cultural. Despite European decolonization since political independence,
Tunisia is experiencing rapid population growth, a fact which is causing
some concern owing to relatively high population density (29 per sq. km.)
and modest natural resources. Unlike its neighbours, Tunisia has only small
oilfields to assist economic take-off. The Tunisian economy therefore

remains closely linked to France, in spite of efforts to reduce its colonial character.

The present rapidity of population growth results mainly from a substantial decline in mortality, initiated during the later years of the French protectorate and continued since independence through an active public health programme. One Tunisian answer to the problem of a general disequilibrium between population growth and economic growth has been the introduction of a family-planning programme along with a variety of social measures to encourage a rise in the status of women—a major innovation in the Arab World, but which has had so far only limited demographic results. The increase in the rate of population growth to 2.8 per cent per annum is contrary to the government's hopes and expectations, but it is evident that government policies are having considerable influence upon this rate of growth.

Tunisia is also illustrative of the prevalence of regional disequilibrium in developing countries; disequilibrium which arises partly from natural conditions and partly from the work of man. Tunisia exhibits a marked climatic and biogeographic zonation from Mediterranean conditions in the north through steppe conditions in the centre to desert in the south, a zonation only modified by mountains and a double maritime façade. Average annual rainfall diminishes from more than 1,500 mm. in the north–west to less than 100 mm. in the south, while annual variability increases in the same direction. Accordingly, traditional modes of life varied from sedentary cultivation in the north and east through various forms of semi-nomadism in the centre and south-east to almost 'pure' nomadism in the south-west. One result of European rule was the intensification of regional disequilibrium through the economic advancement of the moister northern and maritime regions and the near neglect of the less favoured semi-arid and arid regions in the centre and south. European rural colonization was largely confined to regions with a Mediterranean or maritime climate, where modern mechanized agriculture evolved in vivid contrast with the pastoral nomadism and traditional forms of sedentary cultivation which prevailed in the drier zones. Within the more developed, colonized zones the principal urban centres expanded under European impetus and presence, four-fifths of the Europeans being town-dwellers. The external orientation of the economy toward Europe stimulated the growth of the ports of Tunis, Sousse, Sfax and Bizerta. Tunis, the capital and primate city, has been particularly attractive to migrants and contains a growing proportion of the total population, despite the departure of large numbers of European residents in the years immediately following Tunisian independence (1956). Certainly, one of the major problems facing the Tunisian Government is that of regional disequilibrium, but there is evidence that it is well aware of the problem.

Population data

Although the quantity of demographic data for Tunisia does not rival that of neighbouring Algeria, it is much greater than for most other countries of the Middle East and North Africa and is sufficient to provide a real basis for demographic analysis.

The first census held in 1886 applied only to the French population. Another was held in 1891, and in 1896 a census enumerated the whole European population, but succeeding quinquennial censuses were not extended to the Tunisian population until 1921. However, the censuses of 1921, 1926, 1931 and 1936 were far from satisfactory, often relying on tax lists instead of questionnaires, and the only modern censuses are those of 1946, 1956 and 1966 which throw considerable light on the last decade of the French protectorate and the first decade since independence. Although the quality and quantity of data have greatly improved from census to census, there is still under-enumeration probably amounting to 4–5 per cent (Secrétariat, 1968).

Vital registration dates from 1886 for Europeans and from 1908 for Tunisians, but few accurate data are available for the Tunisian population before 1957, except for Tunis. In general, registration of births is much fuller than that of deaths, although registration of female births is less frequent than that of male births, and there is a dearth of information on births according to nationality, age of mother, etc., and on deaths by age group. Registration of marriages and much other registration has improved immensely in recent years, but the summary character of much of the published data makes detailed demographic analysis difficult. The results of a sample survey of 27,000 households held in 1968 provide invaluable additional indications of vital rates throughout Tunisia (Vallin and Paulet, 1969).

Population growth during the French protectorate

Estimates of the total population of Tunisia at the beginning of the French protectorate in 1881 are of the order of 1–2 millions, but no great reliance can be placed upon them (Ganiage, 1959). In 1844 an Ottoman census gave a total of 950,000 and in 1868 there was an official estimate of 1,007,200. Ganiage (1966) has recently estimated the population of 1860–61 to be 1,070,000–1,100,000 on the basis of his analysis of tax-payers, and it is probable that the total at the beginning of the protectorate was not substantially higher than this. At that time there were about 30,000 Jews in Tunisia, of whom half were living in Tunis and the remainder in ports, in the island of Djerba and in towns of the interior (Ganiage, 1959). Tunis also contained over 10,000 Europeans, mostly Maltese and Italians along with small Greek and French communities, and many of whom, particularly the Maltese, were extremely poor (Ganiage, 1960). Tunis had about 80–90,000 inhabitants, including about 60,000 Moslems, 15,000 Jews and 10,000 Christians, and the only other town with more than 10,000 inhabitants was the holy city of Kairouan, forbidden to all but the faithful and containing hardly 20,000 people. Bizerta, Sousse and Sfax were small ports, little bigger than places like Mahdia and Monastir (Ganiage, 1959).

Before the advent of the French the demographic régime was 'primitive', with birth and death rates high and the natural increase of population low. Islam, the backbone of society, stressed the advantages of large families, celibacy was almost unknown and sterility a common motive for repudiation of a wife and divorce. The superiority of the male sex, emphasized by the Koran, meant the degradation of women as drudges, recluses and bearers of children. Naturally, women aged quickly and this was a primary cause of polygamy, especially successive polygamy, in which a man discarded a wife and took another. It must also be said that although an abundance of children motivated family pride, they were essential to offset the fearfully high mortality rates.

TABLE 15.1   EVOLUTION OF POPULATION OF TUNISIA, 1921–66
(*in thousands*)

Census	Tunisian population			Foreign population			Total
	Moslems	Jews	Total	Moslems	Europeans	Total	
1921	1,826	48	1,874	63	157	220	2,094
1926	1,865	53	1,918	67	175	242	2,160
1931	2,087	55	2,142	72	196	268	2,410
1936	2,266	59	2,325	70	213	283	2,608
1946	2,833	71	2,904	87	240	327	3,231
1956	3,544	58	3,602	86	255	341	3,943
1966	—	—	4,463	—	—	70	4,533

Source: République Tunisienne, Secrétariat d'Etat au Plan et à L'Economie Nationale, *Bulletin Mensuelle de Statistique*, Nov.–Dec. 1966, no. 143–4, p. 1.

Forty years after the beginning of the French protectorate the 1921 census produced a total of 2,094,000 persons (Table 15.1), including some 157,000 Europeans, of whom the majority were Italians (Table 15.2). Under the stimulus of improved economic conditions and declining mortality resulting from a reduction in epidemics, the Moslem population grew rapidly and nearly doubled between 1921 and 1956, when it totalled a little over 3.5 million. Its fertility was not appreciably influenced by European presence, largely because the traditional pattern of large families persisted, sustained by Islam. It is true that the position of women improved a little and that polygamy declined, but the influence of religion remained strong.

TABLE 15.2   EVOLUTION OF EUROPEAN POPULATION OF TUNISIA, 1881–1968

Year	French	Italian	Maltese	Others	Total
1881	708	11,206	7,000	—	—
1886	3,500	16,763	9,000	—	—
1891	9,973	21,016	11,706	—	—
1896	16,207	55,572	10,249	—	—
1901	24,201	71,600	12,056	3,244	111,101
1906	34,610	81,156	10,330	2,799	128,895
1911	46,044	88,082	11,300	3,050	148,476
1921	54,476	84,799	13,520	3,320	156,115
1926	71,020	89,216	8,396	4,649	173,281
1931	91,427	91,178	8,643	4,045	195,293
1936	108,068	94,289	7,279	3,569	213,205
1946	143,977	84,935	6,459	4,178	239,549
1956	180,450	66,909	7,793		255,152
1961 (est.)	65,000	40,000	5,000		110,000
1968 (est.)	25,000	12,000	1,000	4,000	42,000

Source: L. Chevalier, 'Le Problème Démographique Nord-Africain', Institut National d'Etudes Démographiques, *Cahier no. 6*, Paris, 1947, p. 22, and later censuses and estimates.

Unfortunately, illiteracy, poverty, malnutrition and bad housing also persisted, so that the great bulk of the population were living in unsatisfactory conditions (Sebag, 1951). To give only two examples: in 1937–8 it was shown that 67 per cent of the population had less than an adequate calorie intake (Burnet, 1939), while in 1946 some 61.7 per cent of the families living in the 33 towns with more than 5,000 inhabitants occupied overcrowded accommodation (*L'Annuaire*, 1947).

The Tunisian Jewish population rose from 48,400 in 1921 to 71,500 in 1946, of whom about 60 per cent lived in greater Tunis, but by 1956 their numbers had fallen to about their pre-war size owing to departures for Israel.

During most of the period of the protectorate Tunisia was attractive to Moslems of other North African countries, including substantial numbers of Libyans (Clarke, 1959), Algerians and Moroccans who came as miners, watchkeepers or to fulfil some other particular occupation for which their countrymen were known (Marty, 1948).

Although established as a protectorate by the Treaty of Bardo in 1881, Tunisia was more closely integrated into the French empire and became a 'colonie de peuplement', an outlet for French inventiveness and speculation. The protectorate lasted 75 years and in that time the number of Europeans living in Tunisia rose from about 19,000 in 1881 to 255,000 in

1956 (Table 15.2), through immigration and rather higher natural increase than pertained in Europe at the time. Although by 1956 they were still only a small minority of 7 per cent of the total population, the Europeans had an immense influence upon the economy and the human geography of the country. In 1956 only 16 per cent of the Europeans lived in rural areas, and although they numbered less than 2 per cent of the Tunisian rural population they possessed nearly 2 million acres of land, one-twelfth of the productive area and about one-fifth of the cultivated area including much of the best land in the more humid northern zone. There were many rural scenes reminiscent of southern France and Italy, for vines, olives, citrus fruits and grain were the basic grops, with market gardening around Tunis. Colonists successfully penetrated the steppes only along the eastern coastal zone where a small number established the splendid and vast olive plantations in the hinterland of Sfax. Some 84 per cent of all the Europeans were living in towns, especially the ports and in particular Tunis and its suburbs which contained more than half of all the European residents in the country.

The Europeans were a mixed bag. The French included a small minority of 'grosse bourgeoisie' who were mostly agricultural but had other interests, while the majority were middle class administrators, professional men, shopkeepers, traders and farmers. There was also a substantial French working class, especially in garages, on the railways or in industries such as at the Ferryville (now Menzel Bourguiba) arsenal south of Bizerta. The proportion of workers among the Italian population was higher, although there were many Italian farmers in the north-eastern part of the country. The Maltese community included many in commerce or trade in Tunis as well as some farmers in the Cap Bon peninsula. In addition, there were small communities of Spaniards and Greeks, mostly in the ports.

Italians greatly outnumbered French at the beginning of the protectorate (Table 15.2) and formed the majority of the immigrants during the principal phase of European immigration between 1881 and 1921, so that by the latter year they numbered nearly 85,000 in comparison with 54,000 French. Their numbers, however, were seen as a political threat to French control, and so they were stabilized by (a) naturalization, which was accorded to Italians, Maltese and Tunisian Jews after the First World War; (b) the effect of the law of 23rd December 1923 regulating the statute of foreigners; (c) limitations on Italian immigration; and (d) the expulsion and departure of a number of Italians during and after the Second World War. Consequently, by 1956 there were fewer people of Italian nationality in the country than at the beginning of the century, whereas the number of persons of French nationality grew nearly eight times and comprised many people of Italian and Maltese origin. On the other hand, some Maltese retained both French and British nationality.

Decolonization

The colonial-type economy was to some extent advantageous to the Tunisians in that it introduced European capital and integrated Tunisia into the world economy, but it had the great disadvantage that many of the products of the Tunisian soil brought only indirect benefit to Tunisians; phosphates and iron ore were obvious examples. The exported and invariably untreated raw materials became grist for the nationalist mill. Further justification for the nationalist cause—if any were needed—was found in the reduction of the powers of the Bey and his regional administrators, the *caïds*, by the French Resident-General and his *contrôleurs-civils*. It was strange that a liberal republic should wish to protect a Beylical autocracy, but the Bey became a puppet to sign decrees; any opposition, such as that by Moncef Bey, led to deposition and exile. In fact, far from being a protectorate, the French administration directly controlled most aspects of Tunisian life. The social impact of Europeans was less, and they formed a nation within a nation. The bulk of the Tunisian population remained true to Islam and to the customs of the Moslem way of life, but many urban Tunisians were deeply impregnated by French culture, spoke fluent French and adopted Western dress and customs.

Inevitably, independence brought decolonization. Net emigration of Europeans began slowly from 1954 during the political disturbances preceding independence, and then increased markedly until 1961, and has since steadily diminished, except in 1964 when the farms of colonists were expropriated and nationalized (Table 15.3). Net annual out-migration has ranged from about 20,000 to 55,000, and the cumulative total between 1956 and 1966 exceeded 350,000, a large sum for a small population. It is difficult, however, to calculate either the precise rates of departure or the numbers of foreigners present in the country, as published data of the entry and departure of persons according to nationality are complicated by the many foreign tourists, Europeans working in technical or cultural co-operation or for foreign companies, as well as those foreigners who come and go annually because they have property or money in Tunisia. Moreover, the various embassies in Tunis can provide only the numbers of nationals registered with them, and have no information on numbers resident.

Despite statistical inadequacies, it is evident that the departure of Europeans from Tunisia was less abrupt than from Algeria, although many French *fonctionnaires* left hurriedly after independence. In general, the Italians and Maltese left more gradually. By 1968 the number of Europeans in the country had diminished to 42,000 or less than one per cent of the total population, of whom only about 24,000 were long-term residents—less than one-tenth of the total in 1956. Probably nine-tenths of the long-term residents lived in or around Tunis, and most of the

TABLE 15.3   NET MIGRATION BY NATIONALITY, TUNISIA 1956–66

Year	Totals	French	Italian	British	Libyan	Algerian	Tunisian (including Jews)	Others
1956	—	−31,723	−5,130	—	—	—	−9,468	—
1957	−48,581	−35,065	−5,424	−513	−573	−403	−6,826	+223
1958	−32,801	−28,150	−3,838	−281	−1,173	+2,423	−2,177	+395
1959	−26,383	−16,179	−6,374	−419	−1,685	−439	−1,738	+451
1960	−27,925	−13,165	−8,693	−154	−2,422	−93	−2,618	−780
1961	−54,957	−29,631	−11,341	−474	−6,518	−279	−6,626	−88
1962	−31,331	−5,356	−7,323	−269	−7,913	−2,284	−8,949	+763
1963	−22,141	−2,943	−3,363	+34	−4,580	−4,457	−6,958	+126
1964	−30,071	−5,637	−5,732	+23	−7,087	−2,508	−10,245	+1,115
1965	−27,922	−3,105	−2,966	−69	−8,237	−2,567	−11,411	+433
1966	−18,790	+752	−1,063	−17	−5,774	−1,480	−12,637	+1,429

Sources: Annuaire Statistique de la Tunisie, vol. 13, 1961–2, p. 32 and vol. 15, 1964–5, p. 34, and *L'Economie de la Tunisie en Chiffres,* 1966, pp. 12–13.

remainder were in Sousse or Sfax. The European rural population has departed entirely. The French population numbered about 25,000, half of whom were old residents including a high proportion of retired persons— former customs officials, *gendarmes* and ex-soldiers—and a small number of employed persons, in commerce, banks, travel agencies, etc., but generally at lower echelons. The other half were temporary residents, particularly people in the *Co-opération technique et culturelle.* In addition, there were about 1,000 Algerian Moslems of French nationality living in Tunisia; about 170,000 Algerian refugees who found political asylum in Tunisia during the War of Independence (1954–62) returned to Algeria after its independence in 1962.

The Italian population of Tunisia in 1968 amounted to 12–13,000 of whom about 10,000 were old residents and the remainder temporary residents. Many of the old residents were still employed in industry, commerce and artisanal activities, while the temporary residents were mostly employed by Italian constructional or oil companies. Many of the people of Italian origin who had acquired French nationality during their residence in Tunisia have departed to live in France.

Most of the old Maltese population became French citizens of Tunisia, especially after the law of 1923, and many have now also emigrated to France. Even among those who retained dual nationality, many have opted to go to France because few Maltese living in Tunisia spoke any English. Most of those with British passports have no longer any family or financial ties with Malta, and now the Commonwealth Immigrants Act impedes emigration to Britain. Today about 1,000 Maltese remain, most of whom are old, and about 120 people are paid relief each month by the British Embassy. It looks as if the Maltese community, once a lively element in the life of Tunisia, will soon die out.

The Tunisian Jewish population, which numbered 57,800 in 1956 had fallen to 5,000 in 1965, and since then many more have left, especially since the 1967 Arab–Israeli war. The old Jewish *hara* in Tunis has been demolished and the Jewish community has almost disappeared.

The Libyan population of Tunisia has also dwindled. The 1956 census enumerated 18,500 Libyans, a smaller number than during the interwar years and probably smaller than reality, because many Libyans found it advantageous to call themselves Tunisians when in Tunisia. Most were Tripolitanians who came to Tunisia decades ago (Clarke, 1959), escaping from the Italian fascist régime in Libya and finding Tunisia a richer country where work could be obtained in the phosphate mines of the Gafsa region or as farm workers. Since the abrupt emergence of the Libyan oil industry the migration stream has been reversed, Tripolitanians living in Tunisia being anxious to return to Libya. At the same time many Tunisians are also seeking employment in Libya where there is a labour shortage. Others have gone to work or to study in France or overseas. Unfortunately, the migration data of Tunisians (Table 15.3) make no distinction between Moslems and Jews.

The obvious result of the emigration of foreign nationals from Tunisia has been to produce a more homogeneous population. Indeed, it is more homogeneous now than at any time during this century, and so the vital rates of the Moslem population will largely determine population growth.

Population growth since 1956

In these circumstances the government's attitudes to public health and to family-planning are of great significance. Unfortunately, the Tunisian Government has made inaccurate assumptions as to the relative movements of fertility and mortality.

In the *Perspective Décennale de Développement* (*1962–71*), prepared to enable Tunisia to embark upon a period of planned economic development, it was assumed that the actual rate of growth of the Moslem population was 2.2 per cent per annum. This was certainly a conservative estimate, for the natural increase rate for 1962 was probably nearer 2.6 per cent. However, more serious is the fact that the *Perspective Décennale* was based upon the hypothesis that there would be a progressive decline of the population growth rate during the ten-year period; it assumed an average annual increase rate of 1.9 per cent between 1961 and 1966 and only 1.7 per cent between 1966 and 1971. On this basis the total Tunisian Moslem population would have increased from 3.9 millions in 1961 to 4.7 millions in 1971, at an average annual rate of 1.8 per cent. It was expected that improved social and economic conditions and rising *per capita* incomes would effect this considerable reduction in natural increase. Obviously, the *Perspective Décennale* was unduly optimistic about a decline in the rate of population growth. In assuming that fertility would decline more rapidly than mortality, it was arguing that Tunisian experience would run contrary to that of all other developing countries. In fact, Tunisia is at the moment a fairly typical example of the many developing countries whose demographic growth is mostly determined by rapid mortality decline accompanied by much less change in fertility. Instead of declining, natural increase rose until 1966 when it was probably 2.8, although since then it may have declined to 2.6 in 1968 (Lapham, 1970) owing to a recent downturn in the crude birth rate. However, the present population size does not differ greatly from projections based on constant fertility made by Seklani (1961) in 1960, and by the Service Tunisien des Statistiques in 1964, both projections envisaging a much higher population for 1971 than forecast in the *Perspective Décennale*. Unfortunately, it is impossible to calculate the present rate of natural increase from published registration data, because there is substantial under-registration of both births and deaths as well as late registration. Birth under-registration may be about 12 per cent, while death under-registration may be as high as 50 per cent. The differences between the numbers of births and deaths registered each year, 130–160,000, are therefore exaggerated.

TABLE 15.4 EVOLUTION OF MORTALITY IN TUNISIA, 1946–66

Year	Crude death rate (per thousand)		Infant mortality rate (per thousand)		Expectation of life at birth (years)	
	Tunisia	Tunis	Tunisia	Tunis	Tunisia	Tunis
1946	26.0	23.0	—	202.0	37	38
1951	23.0	19.4	—	178.0	41	43
1956	20.0	20.3	170	189.7	43	48
1960	18.0	15.3	—	90.6	53	56
1966	17.0	—	116	75.0	55	—

Source: M. Seklani, 1967–8, vol. 1, pp. 240–1, and *L'Enquête Nationale Démographique Tunisienne*.

In a detailed study of mortality in Tunisia, Seklani (1967–8) calculated that between 1946 and 1965 the crude death rate declined from 26.0 per thousand to 15.0 (see Table 15.4). He pointed out that in 1946 mortality conditions in Tunisia were comparable with those of Sweden in 1820, France in 1850 and Spain in 1910; by 1956 they were comparable with Sweden in 1872, France in 1895 and Spain in 1930; and by 1966 they were probably similar to those of France in 1930. The national demographic survey held in 1968 revealed a death rate nearer 17 per thousand, but the scale of decline is still great. The general decline in mortality is closely linked with the considerable improvement of medicine and public hygiene in Tunisia, the first phase of which drew to a close in the late 1950's and saw a massive reduction in a number of endemic or epidemic infectious diseases, such as smallpox, typhus, typhoid fever and malaria. A second phase which began in the late 1940's has been primarily concerned with social maladies such as tuberculosis and infant mortality. The latter declined spectacularly from about 220 per thousand in 1946 to about 120 per thousand in 1966, and this is rapidly broadening the base of the population pyramid (see Fig. 15.1): in 1966, 46.3 per cent of the population were aged under 15 compared with 42.6 per cent in 1956 and 41.7 per cent in 1946. Moreover, in 1966 over one-third (33.7 per cent) were under 10 years and well over a half (54.7 per cent) under 20 years, the median age being 16.8 years. Declining mortality is therefore instrumental in producing a younger population.

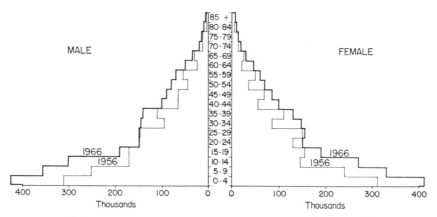

FIGURE 15.1 AGE-SEX PYRAMIDS OF TUNISIA, 1956 AND 1966

Mortality decline mainly results from improved medical and public health facilities. Before the First World War Tunisia had only two or three main hospitals, concentrated in Tunis; by 1965 there were 16, with a scattered distribution, and 33 hospital beds per 10,000 inhabitants. In 1966 there were 666 doctors, one for every 6,800 inhabitants, a fairly high level for a developing country. As medicine has been 'socialized' and made much more available to the Tunisian population, the number of sick persons treated has constantly risen. Tunisians now feel much freer to visit hospitals, and this is posing great difficulties to the hospital system, affecting its efficiency. The cost of this progress is increasing and will continue to do so; Seklani (1967–8) has demonstrated that the part of the national budget allocated to public health doubled between 1946 and 1966, and the expenditure per inhabitant rose four times. Its effect was to reduce mortality by about 40 per cent and increase the average life expectancy by about 33 per cent. Admittedly, these are not adequate indices of the improved health of the nation, but they are indicative of a radical change in mortality conditions.

Mortality is rather lower in the capital than in the country as a whole, but not substantially so, partly because medical facilities in Tunisia are not as unevenly distributed as in some developing countries and partly because living conditions for inhabitants of the *bidonvilles* of Tunis are very poor. Bchir (1967) notes that the infant mortality rate of Tunis is higher than in wealthy suburbs like Carthage, healthy hill towns like Zaghouan or towns with more socially homogeneous populations like Sousse.

In contrast with the decline in mortality, there has been much less change in fertility. In 1956 the average size of the completed Tunisian family was about 5.6 children. Seklani (1966) calculated a general fertility rate of 191 per thousand for 1960, a gross reproduction rate of 3.32 and a net reproduction rate of 2.37. Little variation was found in fertility according to the socio-economic category of the father, and any differential fertility was probably linked more with the age at marriage of the mother and with the duration of the marriage than with social class. During the first decade after independence there appears to have been no marked change in birth rates, but in 1967–8 they may have declined sharply. If Lapham's estimates (1970) of under-enumeration and under-registration of births prove correct, the crude birth rates fell from 47–50 per thousand during the early 1960's to 43–44 in 1967–8; according to the registration data there was a fall from 42–46 to about 38. Lapham points out, however, that this significant change in birth rates may result from structural factors causing temporary fluctuations, rather than from a true decline in fertility.

A variety of factors may be adduced in relation to this change in birth rates. There has been, for example, a reduction in the proportion of women of reproductive age, from 49.3 per cent in 1946 to 46.2 per cent in 1956 to 43.1 per cent in 1966. This has resulted from a shortage of women aged 20–29 in 1966, owing to lower fertility and/or higher mortality during the Second World War (Picouet, 1969), along with a broadening of the base of the population pyramid (Fig. 15.1) through declining mortality. However, the increased survival of children will mean a great rise in the potential number of parents during the 1970's.

TABLE 15.5   PERCENTAGES OF WOMEN MARRIED, TUNISIA, 1956–66

Age group	Percentage of women married		Change
	1956	*1966*	
15–19	39.8	18.5	−21.3
20–24	76.8	71.1	−5.7
25–29	89.1	88.5	−0.6
30–34	90.6	92.4	+1.8
35–39	88.0	91.8	+3.8
40–44	82.9	87.9	+5.0
45–49	72.2	81.8	+9.6
50–54	62.3	70.4	+8.1

Source: Lapham, 1970, p. 249.

According to Lapham (1970), the most significant factor affecting the recent reduction in birth rates is the later marriage of women (Table 15.5). In particular, there has been a great reduction in the proportion of women married aged 15–19: from 39.8 per cent in 1956 to 18.5 per cent in 1966. This reduction, which also occurs to a lesser extent in the age group 20–29, is seen throughout Tunisia but percentages of women married age 15–19 are much lower in the more urbanized northern and central governorates than in the rural southern ones (Lapham, 1970). Later marriage is no doubt an indication of the success of the Bourguiba régime in raising the status of women. Remarkable social advances were made early after independence by the introduction in August 1956 of the 'Personal Status Code', which replaced Koranic law with a single legal system for all Tunisians. Polygamy was prohibited, divorce modified and the minimum age of marriage postponed to 17 for women and 20 for men. Women were given the vote, and the veil was condemned as a 'dust rag'. Increased education and employment of women also helped in the process of modernization of Tunisian womanhood: the number of girls attending primary school rose from 64,549 in 1956–7 to 277,553 in 1966–7, which represented more than half of all girls of primary school age. In 1966–7 there were also 8,046 girls taking medium and professional education and 18,829 receiving secondary education. In addition, there has also been a substantial increase in the numbers of women employed in industry, commerce and administration. Indeed, by 1966 they amounted to one-fifth of the total non-agricultural labour force.

A third factor influencing birth rates has been the increase in birth control and direct measures to reduce family size. The traditional pro-natalist régime, supported by the French, was modified. In 1960 a decree limited family allowances to four children only, and in the following year the import and sale of contraceptives were permitted. In 1962, the government, aware that economic development was being impeded by population growth, began consultations with the Ford Foundation with a view to implementing a family-planning programme as a means of checking the rate of population growth. With technical assistance from the Population Council (of New York) and a grant from the Ford Foundation, Tunisia became in 1964 the first African or Arab country to undertake a national family-planning programme (Brown and Daly, 1968; Daly, 1966; Daly, 1969). The President, the government, the Destourian Socialist Party and latterly the medical profession, gave support and publicity to the programme and, moreover, surveys indicated that a high proportion of Tunisian couples wanted family-planning information and services although few knew how to limit family size (Morsa, 1966). By 1968 it was hoped that 120,000 women would be using intra-uterine contraception, which would reduce the birth rate by 8–10 per cent. In addition, a law passed in 1965 legalized abortion for women aged 30 or more with five or more living children. Sterilization is also permissible by law, and many female sterilizations are performed.

The family-planning programme has not proceeded anywhere near as rapidly as its organizers would have wished (Vallin and Lapham, 1969). In the four years between June 1964 and May 1968 only 42,460 first insertions of intra-uterine devices (IUD's) were made, about one-third of the original aim. There were many rejections and by June 1969 only 39,000 women, or 5.4 per cent of the total number of women aged 20–44, were protected by any form of contraception (Lapham, 1970). Among these women is a high proportion aged 30 or more with numerous children, as well as a high proportion of wives of working-class men (Seklani, 1967).

The limited early success of family planning has been attributed partly to female disillusionment over IUD's, especially after coercion was exercised in some rural areas, and partly to President Bourguiba's change of heart on the desirability of family-planning, publicized in a television speech on 12th August 1966. By comparing the raw results of the 1956 and 1966 censuses, he stated that the rate of population increase was 'around 2.2 or 2.3 per cent'—well below the real rate and rate of natural increase. He felt that this was a reasonable rate of growth and praised marriage and the family and admonished celibates for shirking their social responsibilities, but said that 'every family should be satisfied with four children'.

Despite difficulties, the family-planning programme survived, and a new one was launched in January 1968, largely financed by the Ford Foundation and USAID, with the emphasis on 'the pill'. At least most people in Tunisia have been made aware of the availability of family-planning services and these are by no means confined to the cities, but even if the present programme is successful it is not likely to have a dramatic effect upon population growth (Vallin, 1968). Much greater effort is necessary, especially in view of the problems of economic growth. For example, the four-year plan 1965–8 only foresaw a 2.8 per cent annual increase in agricultural production, an increase almost entirely absorbed by population growth, which also impedes the necessary investments in industrialization. Even a 5 per cent annual increase in the national income is insufficient to provide these investments. Nevertheless, in spite of difficulties, particularly widespread calamitous floods, Tunisia has demonstrated quite impressive economic growth, and this is visible in many parts of Tunisia.

Pattern of population distribution

The pattern of population distribution in Tunisia (Fig. 15.2) has responded to a variety of physical and human influences. Most evident are the contrasts between the more populous coastal zone and the less populous interior and between the more populous north and the less populous south, so maritime influence and climatic conditions have certainly been important. In addition, the momentum of past distributions is observable, high densities being found especially where there are long traditions of sedentary and urban life (Despois, 1937; Despois, 1961; Lalue and Marthelot, 1962; Attia, 1969). With these considerations in mind, four broad distributional zones may be described: the coastal, tellian, steppe and desert zones.

Some 54 per cent of the total population of Tunisia live on about 16 per

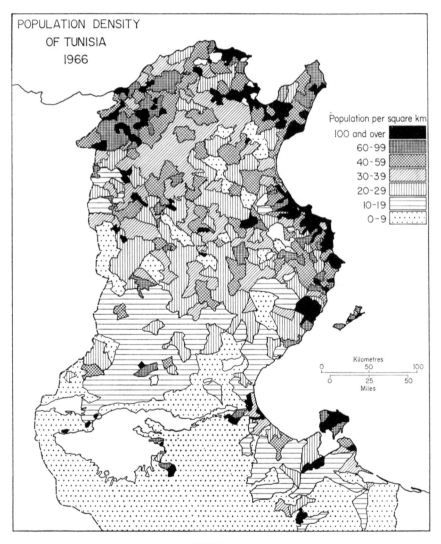

FIGURE 15.2

cent of its area in a narrow, discontinuous coastal zone stretching from the vicinity of Bizerta in the north to the Gabès region and the island of Djerba in the south including the region of Tunis, the Cap Bon peninsula, the Sahel of Sousse and the Sfaxian region. Much of this zone exhibits great continuity of urban and sedentary cultivating populations since Punic and Roman times, especially in the Sahel of Sousse where the inhabitants of large villages have practised Mediterranean polyculture, based on the olive, along with artisanal activities. And on the island of Djerba dry cultivation of tree crops, particularly olives, has enabled a cohesive Berber civilization to evolve, although the high densities on the island also reflect the periodic emigration of Djerbians, especially as grocers (Clarke, 1957), as well as their artisanal and commercial expertise and the recent growth of tourism. During this century European colonization also caused localized high densities particularly in and around the four main port-cities: Tunis, Bizerta, Sousse and Sfax. Indeed, in 1960 this coastal zone contained 14 of the 18 localities with 20,000 inhabitants or more, and it also accounts for two-thirds of the national income (Attia, 1969; Aydalot, 1966).

Within the coastal zone special mention must be made of the north-east region, including the three governorates of Bizerta, Tunis and Nabeul, where densities generally exceed 80 per sq. km. and are over 300 per sq. km. in the region of Tunis. Although comprising only 6 per cent of the area of the country, these three governorates contain 32 per cent of the total population and provide over 50 per cent of the national income (Attia, 1969). The north-east is the main growth pole of Tunisia and during the period 1926–66 its proportion of the total population rose from 22 per cent to 32 per cent and the proportion of its population living in communes rose from 20 to 40 per cent. A drift to the north-east is a basic characteristic of Tunisia, and the government's task in attempting to offset this process is no easy one.

The second zone of population distribution is the tell of northern Tunisia, where annual rainfall exceeds 400 mm., rising to over 1,500 mm. in the north-west. A distinction occurs between on the one hand those mountain massifs which have been traditionally occupied and often densely peopled, such as Kroumirie, and on the other the plains of the middle Medjerda valley and the plateaux of the high tell which were extensively cultivated for cereals especially by European colonists. Modernization, and particularly mechanization of agriculture, has frequently brought about an impoverishment of the peasantry and a flight to Tunis (Poncet, 1959). It also had an adverse effect upon the many summer transhumants from central and south Tunisia who have had the habit of escaping from summer drought by moving into the tell looking for pastures for their flocks and work for themselves as harvesters (Clarke, 1955). The tellian zone has therefore a patchy population distribution, and it is also feebly urbanized, there being only three towns with more than 10,000 inhabitants

—Beja, Le Kef and Jendouba—although there are a number of smaller regional and mining centres.

South of the tell is the steppe zone, which may be roughly delimited by the 400 and 150 mm. isohyets. In general, the steppe zone is relatively sparsely peopled with densities descending below 30 per sq. km. in parts, but the low steppes in the east are less sparsely peopled than the drier, less developed high steppes in the west. While on the low steppes there has been widespread development of plantations and sedentarization of nomads, and Kairouan grew from 34,000 to 45,000 in the period 1956–66, on the high steppes pastoral nomadism still prevails, associated with shifting cultivation of cereals and the collection of esparto grass. In recent years, however, a paper pulp factory has been established at Kasserine and has stimulated rapid growth of that small settlement. Unfortunately, many of the towns in the steppe zone are merely used as stepping stones by migrants who are eventually attracted by larger towns.

Tunisia's desert sector lies south of the 150 mm. isohyet and is a spearhead into the Sahara. Covering about 56 per cent of the country it contains only 12 per cent of the population, so that densities are very low. The majority of the people are localized in (a) oases, like those of Gafsa, the Djerid and the Nefzaoua, (b) the peninsula of Zarzis, where olive plantations are extensive, (c) the mountain villages of the Monts des Ksours, long occupied by sedentary and semi-nomadic peoples many of whom live in underground dwellings, (d) the phosphate mining centres in the region of Gafsa. Elsewhere sparse population distribution is associated with pastoralism. The economy of the desert zone is strongly supplemented by revenues from migration of various types (Clarke, 1957); unfortunately, although many migrants leave, with the intention by making a seasonal or temporary move they often settle in the cities of the north. Consequently, there is a constant drain; in 1926 the south contained 17.5 per cent of Tunisia's population, but by 1966 only 12.7 per cent lived there. The government is trying to arrest some of this flow, but the problem is the choice of optimum growth poles in the south—it is unlikely, for example, that the new chemical works at Ghannush north of Gabès will either employ a large labour force or attract other industries (Aydalot, 1966).

Urbanization

Tunisia has experienced several phases of well-developed urban life, and many towns can vaunt Phoenician and Roman remains as well as large Arab *medinas*. Towns have long been strongholds of religious life, and sheltered behind their ramparts, town-dwellers followed a different way of life from that of rural populations; foreign commerce, fishing and artisanal industries were notable, but some towns evolved more as a result of political strategy than economic considerations. Under the French, however, the linking of the economy with Europe meant the growth of ports, especially Tunis, Sfax, Sousse and Bizerta. Although Tunis already had 80–90,000 people when the French took over the country in 1881, by 1956 it contained about five times that number, and between 1921 and 1956 Sfax, Sousse and Bizerta all more than doubled in size (Table 15.7). As the numbers of European residents increased, new rectilinear quarters were built in juxtaposition to the old Arab medinas, whose winding alleys and confused plans often gave a false impression of disorder. Never to blend, these contrasting urban elements were symptomatic of the super-imposition of European culture. As the protectorate proceeded, the main towns were to gain new elements—European suburbs and Arab *bidon-villes*, the spacious residential areas of the former contrasting vividly with the congested squalor of the latter. In general, there was a fairly close correlation between the rate of urban growth and the size of the European community (Clarke, 1952), of whom in 1946 about 141,000 or 60 per cent lived in Tunis and its suburbs and 15 per cent in four other coastal towns: Ferryville (now Menzel Bourguiba), Bizerta, Sfax and Sousse. These were the main poles of attraction, the small towns of the interior and those of the Sahel and the south growing only slowly. Rural–urban migrants included a wide variety of people, from overpopulated mountain massifs and islands of refuge (Djerba and the Kerkena Islands), the Sahel and desert oases, from areas extensively colonized by Europeans, and from nomadic tribes badly affected by drought or bad harvests—most were fleeing from poverty, hoping for employment in the towns.

By 1956 the population living in communes had risen to 1,250,000 or 32.5 per cent of the total population, although the communes contained only 28.6 per cent of the Tunisian population. Unfortunately, this commune definition of urban population does not always coincide with the urban way of life, and in some cases it gives a much reduced impression of the urban population (Ledjri, 1969). Moreover, intercensal comparisons are bedevilled by changes in the number of communes; in 1956 there were 75, but in 1966 there were 133. Consequently, the population living in communes in 1966, which amounted to 1,820,000 or 40.1 per cent of the total population is not usefully compared with that of 1956. This period is also bedevilled for purposes of analysis of urban growth by the European exodus, so that it is appropriate to consider locality size data for 1956 and 1966 (Table 15.6). Between these two censuses the number of people living in localities with 5,000 inhabitants or more rose by over half a million from 30.8 to 37.0 per cent of the total population, and the number of such localities rose from 49 to 83; so despite difficulties of data and the European exodus it is evident that there has been continued urbanization.

The patterns of town growth during the intercensal period 1956–66 (Table 15.7 and Fig. 15.3) reveal some of the changes which have taken

TABLE 15.6   URBAN SIZE CATEGORIES IN TUNISIA, 1956–66

Size category	Number of towns		Population		Percentage of total population	
	1956	*1966*	*1956*	*1966*	*1956*	*1966*
100,000 and over	1	1	410,000	468,997	10.8	10.3
50,000–99,999	1	3	65,635	180,341	1.7	4.0
25,000–49,999	6	10	214,018	332,761	5.7	7.3
10,000–24,999	24	26	362,646	389,249	9.6	8.6
5,000–9,999	17	43	114,629	306,665	3.0	6.8
Total	49	83	1,166,928	1,678,013	30.8	37.0

TABLE 15.7   GROWTH OF TOWNS IN TUNISIA, 1921–66

	Population (in thousands)							Percentage increase 1956–66	Males per 1,000 females 1966
	1921	*1926*	*1931*	*1936*	*1946*	*1956*	*1966*		
Tunis	171.7	186.0	202.4	219.6	364.6	410.0	469.0	14.4	1,150
Sfax	27.9	27.7	40.0	43.3	54.6	65.6	70.5	7.5	1,020
Sousse	19.8	21.3	25.3	28.5	36.6	48.2	58.2	20.7	1,092
Bizerta	19.1	20.6	23.2	28.5	39.3	44.7	51.7	15.7	1,035
Kairouan	19.4	19.4	21.5	23.0	32.3	34.0	46.2	35.9	1,103
Le Bardo	—	—	0.8	1.0	7.1	16.0	40.7	154.4	1,029
Nabeul	7.0	7.8	8.5	9.1	11.0	14.0	34.1	143.6	1,041
Menzel Bourguiba	4.3	4.5	6.1	6.3	29.3	34.7	33.8	−2.6	1,057
Gafsa	6.4	7.8	11.8	11.3	11.3	24.3	32.4	33.3	1,199
Gabès	16.9	15.1	15.6	18.6	22.5	24.4	32.3	32.4	1,098
La Goulette	5.6	7.4	9.3	10.9	14.9	26.3	31.8	20.9	1,068
M'Saken	16.0	16.6	18.5	20.1	21.8	26.1	28.1	7.7	1,079
Béja	9.1	10.5	11.6	13.3	22.2	22.7	28.1	23.8	938
Hammam-Lif	2.3	2.8	4.9	6.7	19.2	22.0	25.1	14.1	1,010
Le Kef	7.4	7.4	8.5	8.9	11.2	14.7	23.2	57.8	1,098
Ariana	—	—	5.1	5.5	9.7	16.3	22.0	35.0	1,091
Moknine	11.7	12.2	13.2	14.2	15.7	17.7	20.4	15.3	962
Monastir	8.7	8.3	9.4	10.6	8.7	12.6	20.4	61.1	1,133
Kalaa Kebira	10.8	11.8	13.7	15.0	14.3	16.7	18.8	12.6	927
La Manouba	—	—	—	—	7.4	14.8	18.7	26.4	1,114
Mateur	6.4	7.1	7.8	7.4	12.7	14.6	16.9	29.5	1,049
Radès	2.6	3.3	4.0	4.5	11.1	13.2	16.8	27.3	1,046
El Marsa	—	—	5.1	5.7	6.1	14.2	16.3	14.8	1,060
Mahdia	—	—	8.6	8.5	9.2	10.8	15.9	47.2	1,048
Jemmal	—	—	8.3	8.2	9.2	11.2	15.0	33.4	991
Jendouba	—	—	—	—	—	8.0	14.8	60.0	1,118
Kelibia	—	—	—	—	—	11.8	14.0	18.6	1,049
Tozeur	11.1	11.1	11.6	11.7	12.5	11.8	13.9	17.8	1,023
Ksar Hellal	—	—	—	—	—	12.2	13.9	13.9	991
Menzel Temine	—	—	6.3	7.8	8.6	11.3	13.1	15.9	1,088
Metlaoui	—	—	—	—	—	7.1	12.8	80.3	1,130
Hammamet	—	—	—	—	—	7.1	12.5	76.1	1,113
Ksour Essaf	—	—	9.9	10.0	9.9	11.3	12.3	8.8	898
Hammam Sousse	—	—	—	—	—	9.4	11.9	26.6	978
Zarzis	—	—	7.1	7.5	9.2	10.8	11.7	8.3	978
Ben Arous	—	—	—	—	—	—	11.6		1,091
Houmt Souk	—	—	—	—	—	4.2	10.9	159.5	1,154
Redeyef	—	—	—	—	—	11.8	10.5	−11.0	1,056
Nefta	12.8	13.3	13.0	13.6	14.2	14.6	10.4	−28.8	951
Ras Jebel	—	—	—	—	—	10.0	10.2	2.0	945

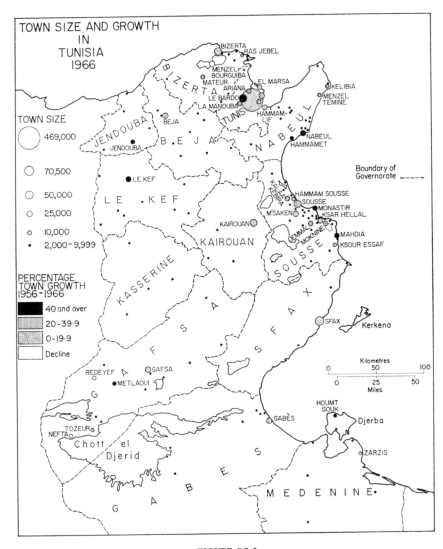

TOWN SIZE AND GROWTH IN TUNISIA 1966

TOWN SIZE

- 469,000
- 70,500
- 50,000
- 25,000
- 10,000
- 2,000 - 9,999

PERCENTAGE TOWN GROWTH 1956-1966
- 40 and over
- 20 - 39·9
- 0 - 19·9
- Decline

Boundary of Governorate _____

Kilometres
0   50   100
0   25   50
Miles

FIGURE 15.3

place in Tunisia since independence. Owing to the departure of Europeans, the four main towns (Tunis, Sfax, Sousse and Bizerta), some of the former European suburbs of Tunis (e.g. Hammam-Lif, El Marsa) and a few towns in the north-east (e.g. Kelibia, Menzel Temine) grew modestly, and Menzel Bourguiba even declined slightly. Two other towns which declined are in the remote south-west—the oasis of Nefta and the phosphate mining centre of Redeyef—and the oasis of Tozeur grew little, because of out-migration. Moderate growth occurred in many of the old towns of the Sahel (M'Saken, Moknine, Kalaa Kebira, Ksar Hellal, Ksour Essaf), but

367

Monastir and Mahdia are obvious exceptions. Like Nabeul, Hammamet, Gabès and Houmt Souk, these two towns have grown rapidly, largely because they have become important seaside resorts attracting many foreign visitors; though they have other functions—Mahdia is a fishing port and Nabeul an artisanal centre, especially for pottery. Kairouan also benefits from tourism, but like several other regional centres (Gafsa, Gabès, Béja, Le Kef, Jendouba), it has been stimulated by the regional policy of the Tunisian Government.

This policy has not arrested the growth of the capital, which increased by 59,000 between 1956 and 1966, and some of its suburbs expanded quickly, especially Le Bardo but also La Goulette, Ariana, La Manouba and Radès. By 1966 Greater Tunis attained 667,000 inhabitants or 14.7 per cent of the total population, nearly half of all the population of places with 10,000 inhabitants or more in Tunisia. In spite of the European exodus, Greater Tunis grew by 227,000 inhabitants during the period 1946–66, and still shows strong polarity and urban primacy (Fig. 15.4). For example, it contains about four-fifths of all the manufacturing industry in the country.

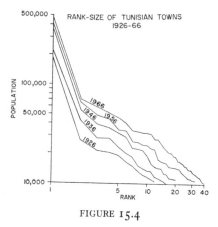

FIGURE 15.4

Some indication of the effects of this growth may be seen in the unbalanced sex ratios of the capital (Table 15.7); in 1966 the city had an excess of 32,600 males and the agglomeration an excess of 38,100, a reflection of the preponderance of male migrants. On the other hand, like many other Arab countries Tunisia has a preponderance of males—owing to female under-enumeration, relatively high female infant and child mortality, and the low proportion of old people—and the only Tunisian towns with 10,000 inhabitants or more where females are preponderant are Ras Jebel, Zarzis and Nefta and a number of old towns in the Sahel: M'Saken, Moknine, Kalaa Kebira, Jemmal, Ksar Hellal, Ksour Essaf and Hammam Sousse.

Conclusion

Like many other developing countries, Tunisia is suffering from disequilibrium between rapid population growth and modest economic
growth, disequilibrium between expanding regions and declining regions,
and disequilibrium between the polarity of a large primate city and the
rest of the country.

Unlike many other states in the Arab world, Tunisia has only a small oil
industry, and its economy depends on variety rather than specialization.
With lands stretching over several types of climate, its agriculture is
diverse, although it still retains the influence of colonialism, being oriented
towards the production and export of crops like olive oil, wine, dates and
citrus fruits. Decolonization and the re-distribution of land among
Tunisians have posed problems, as has the settlement of pastoralists on
subdivided *habous* land (endowed to Islamic foundations), but many were
overcome during the Three-Year Plan, 1962–4. Progress has also been
made in the development of processing industries, especially of phosphates,
iron ore and lead, which were in colonial times mainly exported crude.
Oil is also refined, at Bizerta. With government investment and encourage-
ment, especially during the Four-Year Plan, 1965–8, industrial expansion
has occurred, but industries still account for only a small proportion of
national income and are mostly located at ports. One other important
sector of development is the tourist industry, although in the days of
package-deal holidays there are complaints that Tunisia has to suffer too
many European tourists for too little return. Once again, it encourages the
growth of the coastal zone.

In Tunisia the modern sector of the economy is especially localized in
the coastal zone, but being a small country with good internal communications and a strong government encouraging social change and regional
development the impact of modernity is more widespread. Indeed,
Tunisia is more 'transitional' than 'traditional', though it would be untrue
to suggest that it is undergoing an economic revolution. Its *per capita* gross
national product is only $200, and chronic unemployment and under-
employment are still rife. Moreover, the country is greatly dependent upon
foreign aid to finance its development schemes.

To encourage the rise in standards of living the Tunisian Government
has wisely adopted a family-planning programme. Its attitude has been
rather ambivalent, but in view of the opposing forces of modernism and
tradition, the conflicting advice of East and West and the current debate
on the interrelations between population growth and economic growth,
this ambivalence is not surprising. Nevertheless, Tunisia has demonstrated
remarkable leadership among Moslem countries in this matter.

REFERENCES

ANNUAIRE STATISTIQUE DE LA TUNISIE, Tunis, since 1946.

ARDANT, G. (1961) *La Tunisie d'aujourd'hui et de demain. Une expérience de développement économique*, Paris.

ATTIA, H. (1969) 'La répartition géographique de la population tunisienne à partir du recensement de 1966', *Revue Tunisienne de Sciences Sociales*, 17–18, pp. 505–24.

AYDALOT, P. (1966) 'La structuration de l'espace économique tunisien', *Revue Tunisienne de Sciences Sociales*, 5 pp. 65–93.

BCHIR, M. (1966) *La Mortalité Infantile en Tunisie*, Tunis (thèse de doctorat).

BCHIR, M. (1967) 'Données récentes sur la structure de la mortalité infantile en Tunisie; résultats d'enquêtes', *Revue Tunisienne de Sciences Sociales*, 10, pp. 43–72.

BOU HASNA (1938) 'Observations sur le mouvement démographique des populations musulmanes en Tunisie', *La France Méditerranée et Africaine*, fasc. 3, pp. 102–12.

BROWN, G. F. and DALY, A. (1968) 'The Tunisian family-planning program', in J. C. Caldwell and C. Okonjo (eds.), *The Population of Tropical Africa*, pp. 419–23.

BURNET, E. (1939) 'Enquête sur l'alimentation en Tunisie', *Archives de l'Institut Pasteur*, 28, pp. 407–578.

CHEVALIER, L. (1947) *Le Problème Démographique Nord-Africain*, Institut National d'Etudes Démographiques, Cahier No. 6.

CLARKE, J. I. (1952a) 'The population of Tunisia', *Economic Geography*, 28, pp. 364–71.

CLARKE, J. I. (1952b) 'Des problèmes du nomadisme estival vers le nord de la Tunisie', *Bulletin de L'Association de Géographes Français*, No. 228, pp. 134–41.

CLARKE, J. I. (1955) 'Summer nomadism in Tunisia', *Economic Geography*, 31, pp. 157–67.

CLARKE, J. I. (1957) 'Emigration from southern Tunisia', *Geography*, 42, pp. 96–104.

CLARKE, J. I. (1959) 'Some observations on Libyans in Tunisia', *Cahiers de Tunisie*, Nos. 21–22, pp. 89–100.

CLARKE, J. I. (1969) 'Population policies and dynamics in Tunisia', *The Journal of Developing Areas*, 4, pp. 45–58.

DALY, A. (1966) 'Tunisia' in B. Berelson *et al.* (eds.), *Family-Planning and Population Programs*, Chicago, pp. 151–61.

DALY, A. (1969) 'Le programme de planning familial en Tunisie', *Revue Tunisienne de Sciences Sociales*, 17–18, pp. 307–20.

DESPOIS, J. (1937) 'Signification historique d'une carte de la densité de la population en Tunisie', *Congrès International de la Population*, Paris, 4, pp. 15–22.

DESPOIS, J. (1961) *La Tunisie. Ses Régions*, Paris.

GANIAGE, J. (1959) *Les Origines du Protectorat Français en Tunisie (1861–81)*, Paris.

GANIAGE, J. (1960) *La Population Européenne de Tunis au milieu du XIXe siècle. Etude Démographique*, Publications de la Faculté des Lettres, Université de Tunis.

GANIAGE, J. (1966) 'La population de la Tunisie vers 1860. Essai d'évaluation d'après les régistres fiscaux', *Population*, 21, pp. 857–86.

LALUE, R. and MARTHELOT, P. (1962) 'La répartition de la population tunisienne', *Annales, Economies, Sociétés, Civilisations*, 2, pp. 283–301.

LAPHAM, R. J. (1970) 'Family-planning and fertility in Tunisia', *Demography*, 7, pp. 241–53.

LEDJRI, M. N. (1969) 'Le recensement général de la population (mai 1966)', *Revue Tunisienne de Sciences Sociales*, 17–18, pp. 127–70.

MARTY, R. (1948) 'A Tunis: éléments allogènes et activités professionelles', *IBLA*, pp. 154–88.

MORSA, J. (1966) 'The Tunisia Survey: a preliminary analysis', in B. Berelson *et al.* (eds.), *Family-Planning and Population Programs*, Chicago, pp. 581–93.

PICOUET, M. (1969) 'Etude de la structure par âge de la population tunisienne à partir de l'examen des pyramides d'âges', *Revue Tunisienne de Sciences Sociales*, 17–18, pp. 177–213.

PICOUET, M. (1970) *Description et Analyse Rapide des Migrations Intérieures en Tunisie*, Tunis.

PONCET, J. (1959) 'L'évolution géographique du peuplement tunisien à l'époque récente', *Annales de Géographie*, 58, pp. 247–53.

SEBAG, P. (1951) *La Tunisie*, Paris.

SECRETARIAT D'ETAT AU PLAN ET A L'ECONOMIE NATIONALE (1968) *Recensement Général de la Population et des Logements, 3 Mai 1966: Population par Age, Sexe, et Etat Matrimonial*, Tunis.

SEKLANI, M. (1961) 'La population de la Tunisie. Situation actuelle et évolution probable jusqu'en 1986', *Population*, 16, pp. 473–504.

SEKLANI, M. (1966) 'Les sources et les données fondamentales de la démographie tunisienne', *Revue Tunisienne de Sciences Sociales*, 5, pp. 7–51.

SEKLANI, M. (1967) 'La famille tunisienne au seuil de la contraception. Etat actuel et transition possible', *Revue Tunisienne de Sciences Sociales*, 11, pp. 53–74.

SEKLANI, M. (1967-8) *La Mortalité et le Coût de la Santé Publique en Tunisie*, 2 vols., Université de Tunis.

VALLIN, J. (1968) 'Planning familial et perspective de population en Tunisie 1966–75', *Revue Tunisienne de Sciences Sociales*, 12, pp. 71–88.

VALLIN, J. and LAPHAM, R. (1969) 'Place du planning familial dans l'évolution récente de la natalité en Tunisie', *Revue Tunisienne de Sciences Sociales*, 17–18, pp. 379–413.

VALLIN, J. and PAULET, G. (1969) 'Quelques aspects de l'enquête nationale démographique tunisienne', *Revue Tunisienne de Sciences Sociales*, 17–18, pp. 227–48.

Chapter 16
Algeria: changes in population distribution, 1954-66
K Sutton

For a country with a declared intent to pursue a policy of planned economic development, as in the case of Algeria with its First Plan of Development (1967-9), a basic necessity is a set of reliable socio-economic statistics. The violence and chaos preceding and following Algerian independence in July 1962 involved much population movement within the country as well as an exodus of French colonists from it, and consequently the need for a fresh census was urgent. The previous proper census had been in November 1954, though a limited one was carried out in 1960 by the French authorities, but this had amounted to little more than a simple enumeration with many gaps and inaccuracies resulting from the then prevailing state of war.

This chapter aims to present the results of the 1966 census which have been processed and made available by the Algerian authorities so far, and to suggest factors in the analysis of regional variation in population change in the intercensal period 1954–66.

The 1966 census

One of the first tasks of the *Commissariat National au Recensement de la Population* (CNRP) was to establish the wider objectives of the proposed census. From Autumn 1964 representatives of various ministries and other interested bodies, including the *Institut de Géographie* of the University of Algiers, were invited to meetings of the CNRP to indicate the kind of information they were seeking and to collaborate in the preparation of the census questionnaires (Prenant, 1967). Spring 1965 saw an experimental trial census in two communes: Rouiba in the eastern suburbs of Algiers, and Messâad in the mountains of the Ouled Naïl in the Saharan Atlas chain. Difficulties of poorly defined census units and of dispersed settlement were found in the latter, and the reluctance of military authorities to have barracks enumerated were encountered in Rouïba.

The proper census operation of 1966 involved immense organizational problems for a newly independent country. The seriousness of the exercise had to be imparted to the general public. Enumerators had to be recruited from the literate section of the population, largely coming from the school and student bodies with teachers and other local intelligentsia acting in a supervisory capacity. Consequently, the census enumeration of Northern Algeria took place during a week of the school spring vacation focusing on the reference date of 4th April 1966. For the two Saharan departments of Saoura and Oasis, 1st January 1966 had earlier been taken as the reference date. The fact that the work was carried out within the space of one week gave this census a considerable advantage over that of 1954 which had lasted a month.

Two questionnaires were completed for each household, one covering the inhabitants, the other the building. Each individual gave information on his sex, age, place of residence (both on the census date and on the date of independence) family relationships between members of the household, matrimonial status, mother tongue, education and main occupation. For the building, details were sought concerning the number of rooms, their degree of occupation, condition of the fabric and provision of basic services. Later criticisms have centred on the exacting nature of the questionnaire in view of the inability of the illiterate majority of the population to reply directly, and on the difficulties of comprehension for self-subsistence peasant agriculturalists of the notion of professional activity—farming was often conceived of as a way of life rather than work. Also the lack of a question on residence in 1954 does not allow any direct analysis of inter-censal population movement.

A third problem, along with the mobilization of personnel and the preparation of the questionnaire, was the division of the country into census districts prior to the census operation. With the help of aerial photography these districts were delimited on maps and plans so that each contained about 500 people, which formed the unit for each enumerator. These districts varied in size and were often found to contain a much larger population than previously supposed with attendant difficulties and pressures for the enumerator concerned. One result of this carto-graphic operation was that there now exists a collection of nearly 25,000 sketch maps and plans which are more up-to-date than the existing set of topographical sheets left over from the French days (Bahri, 1968a).

The mass of results is still in the process of being analysed at a centre in Oran where an IBM 360 computer has aided calculations. After a 2 per cent sample to give provisional estimates, a full enumeration was published exactly a year after the census, giving population totals by administrative divisions. More detailed socio-economic statistics have so far been limited to the results of a 10 per cent sample extracted from the full census. In fact, to get comparable degrees of precision this overall 10 per cent sample was made up of a 5 per cent sample for the departments of Alger, Constantine and Sétif, a 10 per cent sample for Annaba, Aurès, El-Asnam, Médéa, Mostaganem and Oasis, and a 20 per cent one for Saida, Saoura, Tiaret and Tlemcen. Unfortunately for the geographer, this was not 10 per cent of the population of each commune but was instead the total population of 10 per cent of the communes of the departments. Hence the socio-economic data published so far are only applicable, within inherent sampling errors, on the level of the fifteen departments and no results can be given for smaller units, such as arrondissements and communes, of more value for judging spatial variations. This limitation of the 1966 census will become apparent in the course of this chapter.

Eventually an exhaustive processing of the results is anticipated giving full details at a commune level. This prospect has prompted the CNRP to plan for the production of an Economic and Demographic Atlas of Algeria, and discussion has commenced with French authorities on the application of automatic cartography methods to such a project (Bulletin de Liaison, 1968).

The Algerian population in 1966 and its distribution

The total registered population at the 1966 census date was 12,101,994. This was made up of 11,293,792 residents who were present at their home address at the date of reference; 483,053 residents who had been absent at the date of reference for under six months but were still in Algeria; 268,868 residents who were absent abroad though in regular communication with the original household through correspondence or cash remittances; and 56,281 *comptée à part*, people who for reason of work, health, education or imprisonment lived in a community rather than in a family household. Consequently, if one excludes the 268,868 emigrants the total residential population was 11,833,126 persons to which must be added the personnel of the armed forces excluded from the count, an estimated 80,000. Undoubtedly this system of categories must have given some scope for both double enumeration and the exclusion of individuals (CNRP, 1967e).

The population growth represented by these results compared with the 1954 and 1960 censuses can be seen from Table 16.1. The 1856 census was the first to include both Moslem as well as European sectors of the population, though only for those territories then under French administration which by 1861 included roughly Northern Algeria and parts of the Saharan territories. In addition to the territorial incompleteness of the early censuses, Bahri considers that all enumerations prior to 1966 tended to under-estimate the native or Moslem population save perhaps that of 1948 which was close enough to wartime issuing of ration-cards to allow both greater precision and a check (Bahri, 1968a).

For comparative purposes the CNRP is going back to the last full census of 1954 in order to calculate rates of increase and of urbanization, as the 1960 census incurred gaps in coverage and is not considered to have been of sufficient accuracy. Thus the 1966 registered population represents an increase of 2,572,268 on the 1954 population total. To directly translate

TABLE 16.1   ALGERIAN CENSUS TOTALS, 1856–1966

Census year	Moslems	Non-Moslems	Total*
1856	2,307,300	180,300	2,496,100
1861	2,732,900	220,800	2,966,800
1866	2,652,100	251,900	2,921,200
1872	2,125,100	279,700	2,416,200
1876	2,462,900	344,700	2,867,600
1881	2,842,500	412,400	3,310,400
1886	3,287,200	464,800	3,817,300
1891	3,577,100	530,900	4,124,700
1896	3,781,100	578,500	4,429,400
1901	4,089,200	633,800	4,739,300
1906	4,477,800	680,300	5,231,800
1911	4,740,500	752,000	5,563,800
1921	4,923,200	791,400	5,804,300
1926	5,150,800	833,400	6,066,400
1931	5,588,300	881,600	6,553,500
1936	6,201,100	946,000	7,234,700
1948	7,679,100	922,300	8,681,800
1954	8,449,300	984,000	9,529,700
1960	9,760,000	1,093,000	10,853,000
1966	—	—	12,101,994

* Includes small population living in communities rather than family households.
Sources: Good, 1961; Tiano, 1967, CNRP 1967 e.

this 25.5 per cent increase into an average annual growth rate of a little over 2 per cent is rather misleading as a considerable population movement took place during the 1954–66 period. At least nine-tenths of the European minority, i.e. the 984,000 non-Moslems of the 1954 census, departed in an exodus from Algeria, mainly in independence year, 1962. To a small extent the flight of the Europeans at independence was countered by an influx of about 200,000 emigrants returning from Tunisia and Morocco.

Longer term population movement, involved in the emigration of workers to France and elsewhere, will be dealt with later: 268,868 of them are included in the 1966 census though estimates of the total number involved vary from 500,000 to 700,000. Thus as a basis for calculating population growth, Prenant considers it better to take only the non-French (sometimes called Moslem) population (Prenant, 1967). He estimates a 1954–66 increase of 3,355,000 or 39.3 per cent which gives an annual rate of increase of 3.2 per cent, a much higher and more realistic figure on which to base population projections. This would give a projected population of around 13,725,000 in 1970, or, if one excludes emigrants absent overseas, a residential population of 13,547,726 (CNRP, 1967a). Similarly a residential population of 15,979,910 has been projected for 1975.

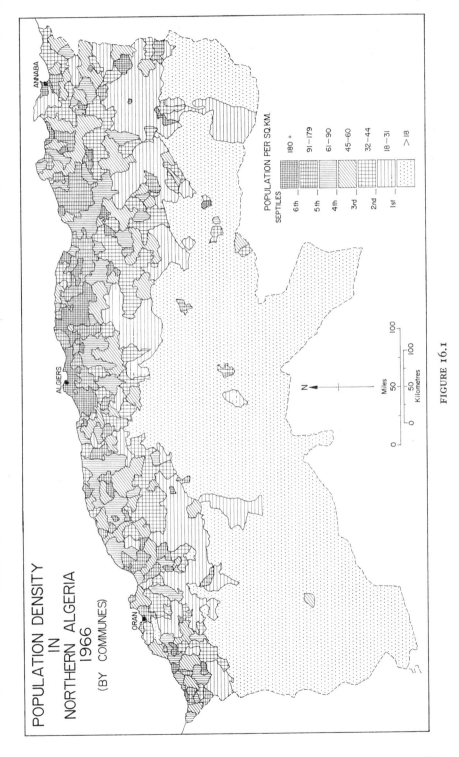

POPULATION DENSITY
IN
NORTHERN ALGERIA
1966
(BY COMMUNES)

POPULATION PER SQ. KM.
SEPTILES

6th   180 +
5th   91–179
4th   61–90
3rd   45–60
2nd   32–44
1st   18–31
       > 18

ANNABA

ALGIERS

ORAN

N

Miles
0   50   100
0   50   100
Kilometres

FIGURE 16.1

The regional variations of population density as mapped from the 1966 census (Fig. 16.1) show in general terms the continuing pattern of concentration in the coastal or Tell cities and plains. Absolute totals and densities are given by departments in Table 16.10, but Figure 16.1 uses commune data allowing a more sophisticated picture and interpretation of this Tell–Sahara decline in population densities. Generally the coastal strip has above 50 inhabitants per sq. km. ranging up to a peak of just above 40,000 per sq. km. in the first and second arrondissements of the city of Algiers which include the pre-French *casbah*. More continuous extents of high density settlement are found in the Mitidja plain and Sahel behind Algiers with the arrondissements of Blida (218 per sq. km.), Alger Sahel (359) and Dar el Beida (183). Similarly the traditional high densities of the Grande Kabylie have prevailed with an overall figure of 138 persons per sq. km. for the department of Tizi Ouzou reflecting in this case high rural densities as well as urban settlements. Indeed a belt of high density, essentially rural population, extends eastwards through the Petite Kabylie to the borders of the Collo Massif representing in part a cultural 'island' within the coastal Tell mountains, traditionally an area of Berber settlement which attracted less interest and hence less disturbance from the French colonists. High densities are found in arrondissements such as Djidjelli (112 per sq. km.), Bejaïa (139), Bougaa (98) and Sidi Aid (109). Significantly, this Grande Kabylie–Petite Kabylie region will stand out again as a distinctive unit when population evolution is considered.

Less extensive areas of high population density are found around coastal cities and often their associated small coastal plains. The communes of Annaba and the adjacent plain of Annaba, together with Skikda, provide instances in eastern Algeria. Farther west Mostaganem and the communes of the lower Chelif trough contribute to an average density of 155 per sq. km. for the arrondissement of Mostaganem. A similar spread around Oran is limited by the Sebkha d'Oran which separates off the specialist viticultural communes of the arrondissements of Aïn Témouchent (65 per sq. km.). Coastal Tell mountains again provide the physical setting of fairly high density settlement of the western frontier arrondissement of Ghazaouet (119 per sq. km.). Population densities drop sharply inland with peaks around urban centres such as Mascara, Tlemcen, El Asnam, Sétif and Constantine. Even farther south those few communes which show above 50 per sq. km. are really only reflecting the presence within their area of a town, often a regional administrative and service centre such as Saïda, Tiaret, Bou-Saada, Batna and Biskra. Generally the communes of the high plains, steppes, and Saharan Atlas show sparse population densities, arrondissements such as Frenda (14 per sq. km.), Aïn Oussera (11) and Bou Saada (11) being representative. Relative density as a population parameter loses its meaning in the Sahara departments, where high density oases contrast with almost total absence of population in vast areas, and seasonal nomadism adds a further difficulty to the study of distribution.

An interesting refinement to the pattern of population distribution has been its recalculation to fit some of the 'homogeneous zones of physical geography' which have been established for the CNRP. Seventeen 'homogeneous zones', as set out in Table 16.2, further emphasize the north–south gradient of population densities.

TABLE 16.2 EXAMPLES OF POPULATION DENSITIES BY 'HOMOGENEOUS ZONES OF PHYSICAL GEOGRAPHY', 1966

Homogeneous zone	Area (sq. km.)	Population	Density per sq. km.
Littoral zone	1,415	1,944,054	1,374
Low littoral plain	8,600	897,715	104
Low interior plain	6,300	826,437	131
Tell Basin	7,690	713,736	93
High plain of 'annual cropping'	24,425	1,162,985	48
High steppe plain	44,810	474,969	11
Saharan Atlas and Piedmonts	150,520	767,785	5

Source: Bardinet, 1967.

Socio-economic composition

The census age structure of the Algerian population gives the typical broad-based pyramid associated with developing countries reflecting a high natality, youthfulness and growth potential (Fig. 16.2). The percentage of people who can only state a 'presumed' often approximate age (i.e. cannot produce a birth certificate issued by the *Etat-Civil*) increases with age and is greater on the female side of the pyramid. Consequently, if the age distribution were to be plotted by single years, the graph would show marked heaping at the round numbers for ages given to the enumerators. Another inaccuracy stems from the under-registration of females, so that males form 50.2 per cent of the total despite the effects of war and male-dominated emigration overseas. Indeed something of a gap might have been expected on the male side of the pyramid from reports of losses during the independence war, 1954–61, but the slight excess in the 20 to 49 years age group of 1,949,300 females to 1,867,200 males would hardly seem to support this. Nevertheless, the losses and suffering during the liberation struggle were considerable and the economic and settlement dislocations, which are considered later, had lasting effects.

The extreme youthfulness of the Algerian population would appear to be increasing if the 1966 figures are compared with those for the 1954 Moslem section of the population (Table 16.3). The increasing dependency burden on the working age groups, many of whom are in fact unemployed

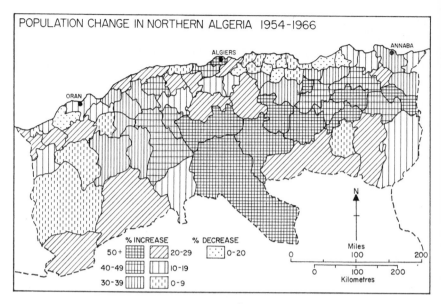

POPULATION CHANGE IN NORTHERN ALGERIA 1954-1966

FIGURE 16.2

TABLE 16.3   PERCENTAGE AGE GROUPS IN ALGERIA

Age group	Algeria		France 1965
	1954 (Moslems only)	1966	
0–19	53	56	34
20–59	42	37	49
60 and over	5	7	17

Source: CNRP, 1967 c.

or under-employed, of the 47 per cent of Algerians who are under 15 years of age is evident as are the problems of extending educational facilities to cover all children.

One factor behind this high birth rate and extreme youthfulness is the continued high marriage rate. High nuptiality was remarked upon by Good for the 1948 and 1954 censuses and, although the 1966 sample census does not allow comparable rates to be calculated yet, 54.4 per cent of the male population and 55.3 per cent of the female population of 10 years of age and above were married (Good, 1961; CNRP, 1967c). According to Tiano, 60 per cent of the Algerian women are married before the age of 19, compared with 4 per cent in France (Tiano, 1967).

One major change in the composition of the Algerian population, which has been given statistical confirmation by the 1966 census, is the exodus of the majority of the European colonists. As many of those French people who stayed have taken out Algerian citizenship, the total of 68,400 French nationals recorded in the 1966 census will include many who have arrived since 1962 to work in the new Republic or as technical assistance personnel in the French aid programmes. It should be stated that a higher total of 92,086 French nationals was recorded for 31st March 1965 by the French *Journal Official* (Revue de Presse, 1965), including 28,683 technical assistance personnel and their families, 20,683 in industry, 8,199 in the French services and 6,275 employees in the tertiary sector. Both sources show similar regional distributions with, according to the 1966 figures, 32,000, or nearly half, residing in the Algiers department. Oran department with 16,200 was the only other large concentration, followed by Annaba department with 3,600, and Oasis department with 3,000 (CNRP, 1967–8, Vol. I). The impact of this massive departure of the French will be discussed more fully later. One result is that Moroccan rather than French nationals composed the largest non-Algerian group in the population, totalling 99,300 of which 72,000 were in the single department of Oran. Other nationalities totalled 28,800.

TABLE 16.4   LANGUAGE COMPOSITION OF ALGERIAN POPULATION

	Number	*Per cent*
Arabic	9,734,100	81.5
Berber	2,267,300	17.9
French	77,600	0.4
Others	23,000	0.2
Total	12,102,000	100.0

Source: CNRP, 1967 c.

These resident French nationals would obviously form the bulk of the 77,600 people with French as their declared mother tongue (Table 16.4). The significant minority of Berber speakers is markedly concentrated in the Kabylie and other areas of eastern Algeria, particularly the more mountainous regions. Compared with the national average of 17.9 per cent, Berber speakers form 44.5 per cent of the department of Aurès, 40.8 per cent of Sétif, and 81.8 per cent of Tizi–Ouzou, the heart of the Grande Kabylie (CNRP, 1967–8, Vol. I).

The marked decline in French as the mother tongue, although it is still in frequent use in business and academic life, is accompanied by a state policy of arabization which, with the help of Arabic-speaking teachers from Middle Eastern countries, is gradually converting the secondary school curriculum to one taught in Arabic. The year 1972, the tenth anniversary of independence, is considered as the date for an even greater degree of arabization in the country's higher education and commercial life.

Several of these aspects of the composition of Algeria's population are indices of under-development and nowhere is this so apparent as in the employment statistics available from the sample analysis of the 1966 census. The total active population amounted to 2,832,200, or 23.4 per cent of the total population. This figure does not include the 1,200,000 women who declared themselves as housewives but who undoubtedly in the agricultural sector participated to some extent in farm activities. A higher economically active population was recorded in 1954 totalling 3,200,000 of which 1,100,000 were women. Allowing for data deficiencies and problems of definition, the departure of the European workforce and the increased youthfulness of the Algerian population would appear to have resulted in a relatively smaller section of the population being economically active and supporting the rest. To obtain the *real* active population (Table 16.5) one has to deduct those working and living abroad, about 234,100, and those younger workers still to find their first employment, another 262,900 persons, so leaving a total of 2,335,200 individuals.

TABLE 16.5   REAL ACTIVE ALGERIAN POPULATION, 1966

Children 6–14 years of age in employment	72,500
Individuals above 15 years of age in employment	1,652,400
Individuals above 15 years of age unemployed or under-employed, having previously been employed	610,300
	2,335,200

Source: CNRP   1967 c.

These statistics indicate a total of 873,200 unemployed in 1966 or 34 per cent of the active population (excluding those working abroad). This unemployment is more apparent (and probably more often declared) in the town than in the country, and Tiano quotes a figure of 64 per cent unemployed in the towns (Tiano, 1968). Whatever the true figure, unemployment is an incomplete parameter without some estimation of under-employment, which is particularly severe in rural areas where agriculture is often seasonal. Tiano, in comparing the number of work-days necessary for Algerian agriculture with the number available from the adult working population in rural areas, concludes that Algerian agriculture has an index of under-employment of 68.5 per cent. An earlier employment enquiry by Bourdieu published in 1963 gave an under-employment index of 32 per cent for wage-earners and 37.5 per cent for non-wage-earners. A report for the *Caisse Centrale de Mutualité Sociale Agricole* in 1960 indicated that 50 per cent of the workers were employed for fewer than

100 days a year and a further 15 per cent for between 100 and 260 days (Tiano, 1967; Bourdieu *et al.*, 1963). This under-employment is a further obstacle to economic development by hindering the possibility of local capital accumulation.

Of the large numbers of unemployed recorded in 1966, 610,300 had previously worked, the majority (426,400 or 69.9 per cent) in the economic sector comprising agriculture, forestry, hunting and fishing. This large number of unemployed agriculturalists, together with the fact that the total number of employed in agriculture represented a drop of about 300,000 persons compared with the 1954 census, reflects the size of the rural exodus and shows, as Bahri has suggested, the effect of regroupment on the rural economy (Bahri, 1968b). The next most important former activities of the 1966 unemployed were building and public works (8.2 per cent) and government services (6.0) (CNRP, 1967–8, Vol. II).

TABLE 16.6 REAL ACTIVE POPULATION OF ALGERIA BY BRANCH OF ECONOMIC ACTIVITY, 1966

Branch of activity	Algerians	Foreigners
Agriculture, forestry, hunting and fishing	1,300,000	7,300
Extractive industries	23,600	3,000
Manufacturing industries	159,900	7,900
Building and public works	121,100	2,600
Electricity, gas and water services	11,700	700
Commerce, banking and insurance	149,500	7,000
Transport, warehousing and communications	87,900	3,300
Government and other services	372,400	28,000
Others and not declared	109,100	5,700
Total	2,335,200	65,500

Source: CNRP, 1967 c.

Of that part of the active population in employment 55.6 per cent were in the agriculture, forestry and fishing sector and 16.0 per cent in government and other services (Table 16.6). Manufacturing industry, of which the largest branches are food processing, textiles, clothing and shoe manufacturing and mechanical industries, accounted for merely 6.8 per cent and only rose significantly above this average in the departments of Algiers (15.6 per cent), Oran (9.3) and Tlemcen (10.3). An interesting employment contrast is provided by the foreign element of the real active population, mainly French and Moroccans. The part of foreign technical assistance is reflected by the greater emphasis on the manufacturing and service branches of economic activity.

A final aspect of Algeria's socio-economic composition which can be appreciated from the 1966 census is the degree of schooling in the country.

TABLE 16.7   SCHOOL LEVEL ACHIEVED BY PERSONS AGED 10 YEARS AND OVER
IN ALGERIA, APRIL 1966

	Number	*Per cent*
Have not attended school	5,894,900	74.1
Primary school	1,272,800	16.0
Koranic school	378,100	4.7
Secondary school	301,400	3.8
Higher education	25,800	0.3
Not classed above and not declared	87,400	1.1
Total	7,960,400	100.0

Source: CNRP, 1967 c.

Illiteracy remains high, acting as a brake on economic development. Of just under 8 million individuals of 10 years of age and above, 74.6 per cent were illiterate, 5.5 per cent read only Arabic, 10.6 per cent read Arabic and French, 8.9 per cent only French, and 0.4 per cent read other languages. Few of those who had attended school had reached higher educational levels than primary and koranic schools (Table 16.7). As a quarter of the national budget is devoted to education, much recent progress has been made, even since the 1966 census. The number of pupils in the public primary education sector increased from 777,636 in 1962–3 to 1,461,776 in 1967–8. With a small addition of pupils in private schools this represented 47.6 per cent of the children of school age (i.e. 6 to 14 years old). For girls the figure was only 36.5 per cent, compared with 58.5 per cent for boys (Remili, 1969). Full schooling is planned for 1980 and looks possible in view of the progress made for the start of the 1969–70 school session when the Algerian school population reached 2 million, 400,000 of them starting school for the first time (Revue de Presse, 1969b). The number of university students has reached nearly 10,000.

Natural increase

In countries such as Algeria the absolute totals produced by censuses are of greater interest because intercensal estimates of population growth based on vital rates of natural increase are very unreliable indeed, particularly on a regional scale. From 1901, births, marriages, divorces and deaths were registered by local officials. In January 1954 the system of individual vital registration certificates was to have been extended, having already been in force for non-Moslem Algerians since 1935, but the disturbances of the War of Independence prevented the system from working effectively, except in the urban communes. Official statistics of cause of death began to be collected only at the beginning of 1956 (Good, 1961). The continued problem through incompleteness of registration would seem to be reflect in the 1966 sample census by the age structure of the population, in that only 5,597,200 of the total of 12,102,000 people could present an age certificate, the rest being recorded by 'presumed' age. This 'presumed' age section increases with age, but even of those children less than one year old 40 per cent had still to be listed under 'presumed' age (CNRP, 1967–8, Vol. II). An attempt was made to calculate birth rates from the 1966 sample census for each department. Varying from 44 to 58 per thousand, they averaged about 50 per thousand for Algeria as a whole. Child–woman ratios were also calculated, again by departments, but there was little correlation, which must make the use of such results rather doubtful. Consequently there is a tendency to rely on urban data for figures of vital rates, especially for mortality rates, as a higher level of registration is achieved in cities. A recent study by Seklani testifies to this, as does Good's earlier study (Seklani, 1969; Good, 1961). An alternative is to postulate using the evidence of the 1966 census; thus Prenant has recorded 'an average annual growth rate of 32 per thousand compatible with a birth rate slightly above 50 per thousand and a death rate of 20 per thousand' (Prenant, 1967).

This birth rate of around 50 per thousand is also quoted, though from different sources, by Tiano and Seklani (Tiano, 1967; Seklani, 1969). It represents a continuation of the high birth rates calculated by Good for the 30 main urban centres, which had shown a fairly steady rise from 44.6 per thousand in 1947 to 52.4 per thousand in 1959 with a peak of 56.5 per thousand in 1958. She reported that 'the birth rate appears still unduly high, and the demographers of the Central Statistical Service do not accept it' (Good, 1961). However a later study by the Central Statistical Service revealed an increase of 33 per cent in the number of births between 1960 and 1963 in 54 urban centres. Again uniqueness was invoked in that the number of births in 1963 was considered higher than normal, being the first year of peace with postponed marriages taking place and the temporary separation of many couples being ended (Les Mouvements . . ., 1963). The results of the 1966 census certainly seem to have confirmed the general applicability of these high birth rate figures.

Mortality rates suffer the same uncertainties, with registration being even lower. Based on data from 30 urban communes, they showed a pronounced fall from 27.4 per thousand in 1947 to 16.7 per thousand in 1955. On a revised population base for 1959, the mortality rate was down to 20.7 per thousand (Good, 1961). This level was postulated from the 1966 census although an analysis for the Greater Algiers region only gives an extremely low rate of 10.1 per thousand, recording respectable life expectancies of 61.6 years for men, and 64.3 years for women (Analyse Démographique, 1968). Seklani quotes this as an urban death rate in comparison with a higher rural one of 18.0 per thousand. All of this would seem to indicate a recent trend towards a lower death rate and certainly this seems to have been the case for infant mortality: Good's urban figures fluctuate between 191 per thousand live births for 1947 and 165 per thousand for 1959. By 1965 for Greater Algiers infant mortality is recorded as down to 92 per thousand, still leaving much scope for improvement.

Allowing for the many uncertainties expressed about the above figures, a continuing high natural rate of population increase of about 3 per cent per annum seems inevitable for Algeria. This has prompted recent calls for a massive programme of family-planning to maintain the employment situation in the medium term and to solidify the efforts at economic development in the long term. A sample attitude survey of 2,140 Algerian couples in 1966 showed approval in principle for birth-control from 51 per cent of men and 50 per cent of women in urban areas, and 30 per cent of men and 36 per cent of women in rural areas (Boukhobza and Von Allmen, 1969). At the request of the Ministry of Health, the religious position was reviewed by the *Conseil Supérieur Islamique*, which was far from enthusiastic, though agreeing to family limitation in cases of necessity (Commission Interministérielle, 1968). Although this gave scope for varied interpretation, the government's policy seems likely to be that of a recent speech by President Boumedienne: 'With regard to what is called "galloping demography", we are not supporters of false solutions such as birth-control. We consider that that is equivalent to suppressing the difficulties instead of seeking adequate solutions to them' (Revue de Presse, 1969a).

Internal migration

The 1966 census has added further data to a growing body of information on migration both within Algeria and between it and other countries, usually in search of better job opportunities. National aspects of migration are reviewed here; regional variations will be considered later in the chapter.

As a gauge of internal migration the 1966 census is of limited use, because place of birth data were not collected as the answers were thought likely to have been of doubtful validity. Such imperfections in the knowledge and memories of many individuals were perhaps indicated by the high number of 'presumed' ages given. Instead of birthplace, the census sought details of place of residence on 1st July 1962, a memorable date as it was Independence Day. Allowing for obvious problems resulting from the temporary displacement of population during the war, the results are interesting. During less than four years 9.5 per cent of the population involved of 10,216,400 had migrated outside their 1962 arrondissement of residence (CNRP, 1967–8, Vol. I), although in addition to this absolute movement of 960,558 there would have been localized rural–urban movement within the same arrondissement. Of the basic 9.5 per cent, 3.7 per cent had moved from another department and 2.8 per cent had moved from another country, presumably indicative of emigrants returned from France or wartime refugees from Tunisia and Morocco. The receiving departments are those with low percentages of people still living in them, such as Algiers (79.4 per cent), Annaba (84.4) and Oran (85.9), and the departments of departure are those with high percentages: El Asnam (96.8), Tiaret (96.7) and Mostaganem (95.6).

Rural exodus accounts for much of this internal population movement. Estimates of the scale of this exodus vary; Tiano evaluated it at 110–120,000 a year (Tiano, 1967), while Cote has suggested a figure of 170,000 a year for the intercensal period (Cote, 1968b). Certainly the War of Independence played a considerable part in disturbing traditional rural societies and, through the concentration of population in centres, together with the related clearance of 'free-fire zones', the French army's anti-guerrilla strategy stimulated much of this movement.

The result has been a quickening of the rate of urbanization. The CNRP calculated from the census that the country's urban network consisted of:

Urban— 65 communes—33.0 per cent of Algerian population
Semi-urban— 29   ,,   — 5.6 ,, ,,   ,,   ,,
Semi-rural— 29   ,,   — 4.7 ,, ,,   ,,   ,,
Rural—553   ,,   —56.7 ,, ,,   ,,   ,,

The urban and semi-urban categories included 4,699,200 or 38 per cent of the total legal population (CNRP, 1967d). When comparison is made with earlier urban levels—26.9 per cent of the Algerian population were urban in 1954—it is seen that Algeria has a faster rate of urban growth than the rest of the Maghreb (Cote, 1968b). Allowing for the departure of about 900,000 French colonists, the bulk of whom were town-dwellers, the rural–urban movement assumes even vaster proportions. Contrastingly, the rural Algerian population has been calculated as having increased only 19 per cent during the intercensal period 1954–66, less than the rate of the natural increase (Prenant, 1967).

This considerable rural–urban movement was undoubtedly stimulated by the regroupment policies adopted by the French army during the War of Independence. The organized concentration or cantonment of the native population was nothing new in French colonial policy in Algeria and can be likened to similar approaches adopted elsewhere in the face of revolutionary guerrilla warfare. The first regroupments date from 1955 in the Aurès region where the revolt had commenced in November 1954. At first the displacements were linked with the setting up of *zones interdites* or 'free-fire zones' and up to 1957 many peasants were simply chased off their lands. In 1958 it became a systematic policy with the deliberate regrouping of the poor, scattered hamlets and the movement of the inhabitants of more isolated mountain villages to centres where there could be supervised more easily, which often meant to the military camps themselves. With the construction of fortified defences on the eastern and western frontiers towards the end of 1958, further methodical clearing operations affected large sectors of countryside. In November 1959 this military policy came under the supervision of a newly-created *Inspection Générale des Regroupements* in an attempt to turn the process into a policy of social and economic development for rural areas (Lesne, 1962). By now the dimensions of the policy were being realized, although official figures and estimates vary considerably. The *Inspection Générale des Regroupements* officially totalled 1,958,302 people in regroupment centres on 1st April 1961 (Cornaton, 1967), but its early 1960 estimates had given 2,157,000 (Etude monographique, 1960). As many regroupment centres can be found which were not listed in the official documents, Cornaton considers that a more realistic figure for 1961, the year when hostilities ceased, would be 2,350,000, 26 per cent of the total Moslem population or one in three of the rural population. If those who sought refuge in already existing towns and villages are added, Cornaton has estimated that 3,525,000 people or 50 per cent of the rural population were affected by the military activities (Cornaton, 1967). Undoubtedly, this formed one of the most brutal population displacements in history.

This regroupment policy had a detrimental effect on agricultural and pastoral activities. The excessive distance from the former cultivated lands was worsened by military curfews, or the absolute restriction of free-fire zones. Only rarely was extra arable land available adjacent to the new centre. Occupational surveys of individual centres have consequently shown low percentages in agriculture and a great increase in declared unemployment. Regroupment was especially hard on southern nomadic and semi-nomadic people, of whom nearly 400,000 were regrouped in tent encampments in the departments of Tiaret, Saïda, Oran, Médéa, Batna and Annaba. No official documentation remains about the Sahara but the existence of important centres of regroupment near El Oued, Touggourt and Bechar is known. Obviously their old nomadic way of life now became impossible and it has been estimated that Algerian nomads lost 90 per cent of their flocks (Cornaton, 1967).

Perhaps more serious than economic difficulties were the sociological and psychological effects of this uprooting of rural communities. Suddenly they were exposed to new attitudes and new values. The viewpoint of employment providing a monetary salary replaced the subsistence attitudes of peasant agriculture. There was a lessening of community feeling and of peasant loyalty to his land. Women, deprived of the privacy of courtyards and of the absence of men away working in the fields, now had to lead even more cloistered lives and adopt the veil. It all amounted to a 'kind of emigration on the spot, with regroupment making the "depeasantized" peasant an exile on his own land, *un émigré chez lui*' (Bourdieu and Sayad, 1964). Nevertheless the new, though limited, range of foodstuffs, clothes and other consumer goods altered peasant values, and certain sanitary, medical, and educational facilities had now been experienced. The attraction of a traditional peasant life in a rural mountain *ghourbi* or *mechta* could never be quite the same after the trauma of regroupment.

The spatial effect of these changed values is expressed in the permanency of many of these regroupments after their initial cause, the pre-independence hostilities, had ceased. Tiano considered that probably half a million people moved on to the towns when the regroupment centres were progressively abandoned during 1962–3 (Tiano, 1967). While such a movement to the towns probably took place, recent studies have refuted the idea of abandonment. In the last year before departing, the French authorities had encouraged some movement back and met with some success in the Kabylie and Ouarsenis mountain areas. However, local uprisings against the new Republic in 1963 resulted again in some areas being cleared of their population. Despite such contradictory trends, studies in the western Mitidja have shown that of the 50 centres containing about 35,000 people, 30 centres still remained at the end of 1966 accommodating nearly 20,000 people (Claude, 1966). Unfortunately, statistics for a national picture are not available but Cornaton's study adds further evidence of the permanency of the centres. In the poor eastern arrondissement of Collo, the 46 centres which in 1961 housed 85,358 people, still contained 62,556 in 1965. In the economically better-off arrondissement of Aïn Témouchent near Oran, the same period saw an increase in the population of its 28 centres from 30,093 to 35,295. Some of the peasants were still near enough to their land to work it, others had found alternative employment. Intermediate situations of static population in regroupment centres were found in other areas (Cornaton, 1967). The long-term effects on the Algerian settlement pattern of this temporary military expediency seem established; its regional effect on patterns of population change is discussed later.

As Cornaton observes, using an expression of Germaine Tillion, this mass of regrouped people have been abandoned 'in the middle of the ford'. They have been uprooted from their environment, both geographical and sociological, without being given the means to put down new roots where they have been dumped. No longer peasants, they are not yet townfolk (Cornaton, 1967). Yet the regroupment centres could play a part in future rural development in Algeria along the lines of 'village-centres' or 'king villages' adopted in other countries, concentrating certain functions and institutions and so acting as a brake on rural exodus. Indeed, de Planhol has seen this as aiding economic development (Planhol, 1961), but so far Cornaton sees the centres as dead-weights adding to the already high unemployment levels. If the movement of population involved in regroupment had been spread over half a century this judgment might have been different.

External migration

As well as considerable internal movement, Algeria has recently experienced much longer distance migration abroad, mainly to France, seeking both work and refuge. Of the European colonial population of approximately 1,100,000 persons in 1960 (Norbye, 1969), it is reckoned that at least nine-tenths departed from Algeria, mainly in independence year, 1962. Forming the vast bulk of the skilled *cadre* and, together with perhaps 500,000 French troops, accounting for much of the local consumer market, their departure virtually meant the collapse of the country's economy. The Gross Domestic Product has been calculated as having fallen by 28 per cent between 1959 and 1963 and, in view of the investments of the Constantine Plan, an even greater fall would be registered if GDP statistics were available for 1961–2. To take just one consumer indicator, the output of beer fell drastically from 1.27 million hectolitres in 1961 to 0.20 million in 1963 (Norbye, 1969).

To some extent an outlet for the increased unemployment created by this slump was already in existence—temporary migration to France. From the first departures in 1905 this movement has swollen to a level of considerable economic importance both to France and Algeria. The constant rapid growth from 1946 slowed down after 1964 when both French limitation on entry and Algerian worries on the loss of relatively skilled personnel started to have an effect. Obviously total estimates vary and have to take into account gains through births in France and losses through naturalization to French citizenship, but there are probably 700,000 Algerians living in France and other countries of Europe. Only 268,868 of these were recorded as 'residents absent abroad' in the 1966 census. Another recent trend has been that individual emigration is being replaced progressively by family emigration, with the number of Algerian families in France growing from 7,000 to 40,000 between 1954 and 1966. In terms of employed emigrants they show a marked concentration in 'Industrial France', with the Paris region having 41 per cent of employed Algerians, Rhône–Alpes 16 per cent, Provence–Côte d'Azur–Corsica 10 per cent and Nord 8 per cent (Battesti, 1967).

As well as siphoning off some of Algeria's unemployed surplus, these emigrants are of vital importance as a source of revenue in that they represent perhaps 20 per cent of the country's total employed, and at significantly higher wage levels. It has been estimated that they send back home about 30 per cent of their earnings as remittances. Tiano considered that this amounted to 650 million dinars a year in 1966–7; other 1967–8 estimates are of 800 million and of 900 million (Maghreb Digest, 1967;

TABLE 16.8   NUMBER OF ALGERIAN EMIGRANTS IN FRANCE, 1912–67

1912	—	5,000	1936	—	85,000
1915	—	80,000	1946	—	50,000
1919	—	10,000	1950	—	154,000
1925	—	90,000	1955	—	290,000
1930	—	65,000	1960	—	347,000

1962	—	410,000
1963	—	461,000
1964	—	505,000
1965	—	496,000
1966	—	537,000
1967	—	580,000

Source: Cote, 1968 a.

Tiano, 1967; Cote, 1968a). As this represents more than the export revenue of wine or citrus fruits, it can be appreciated how such remittances keep many communities indeed whole regions going. Apart from such obvious economic benefits, overseas emigration is, for the time being, of vital importance in slightly easing the unemployment problem within Algeria. Even the earlier French Constantine Plan with optimistic projections for employment growth still had a shortfall which, it proposed, would be accommodated by emigration to France. For the future though, this large emigrant community in Europe could provide qualified technicians and capital for Algeria's planned industrialization.

Regional aspects of population change, 1954–66

Population movement, both internal and external, is just one of the factors to be considered in looking at the interesting regional patterns of 1954–66 population change revealed by the 1966 census (Fig. 16.3). With the exception of the arrondissements around Algiers, El Asnam (Chélif Valley) and Sétif, rapid population growth has not been in those areas with high initial population densities and the Mediterranean to Sahara gradient of

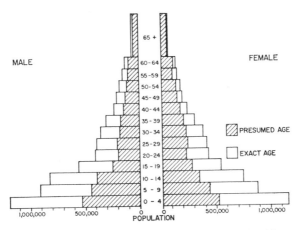

FIGURE 16.3 AGE-SEX PYRAMID OF ALGERIA, 1966

Figure 16.1 stands in sharp contrast to this more complex pattern of regional variation in population change. Compared with an overall national population increase of about 29 per cent during the period 1954–66, most of the northern coastal Tell showed a distinctively slower rate of growth. Indeed population decreases were recorded in the Grande and Petite Kabylie coastal mountain areas with losses of up to 19 per cent of the 1954 total recorded in Sidi Aïch arrondissement and 18 per cent in El Milia. Three of the seven arrondissements of the Tizi Ouzou department recorded population declines and another three only managed much lower than average growth. Further low growth rates were also recorded in the western Tell around Oran, with a 2 per cent decrease in Aïn Témouchent, and in arrondissements bordering on the Moroccan frontier. By contrast, there is an east–west belt of arrondissements with high growth rates lying, in general terms, between the northern Tell Atlas and the southern Saharan Atlas ranges. With the exception of the western parts, increases of 40 per cent and more have been recorded in much of the High Plains and Steppes, the Hodna Mountains and the northern parts of the Aurès Mountains, mostly areas of low population density. If continued, rates of increase such as those of Aïn Oussera (85 per cent), Batna (74), and Aïn M'Lila (60) would double the population of these areas in less than twenty years. The highest rates of increase of all were recorded in the Saharan departments, where Ghardaïa and Djanet arrondissements increased 83 and 81 per cent respectively.

Obviously some of these generalizations can be refined if population change is examined on a commune level. Cote has looked at the 251 communes of the Constantine region of eastern Algeria (Cote, 1968c). Here the slowly increasing or declining populations of the northern Tell and the Petite Kabylie contrast with the increases registered by communes around Annaba and its small but rich plain. The southern slopes of the Tell Atlas combine with communes of the Hautes Plaines Constantinoises into a fairly homogeneous zone of high increases. Remarkably high increases are registered in the Hodna basin while the Aurès Mountains show a complex pattern, with communes in the north-west of the massif and on its northern piedmont showing increases and those in the east and south stagnating or declining. The Nememcha Mountains also are only slowly increasing in population except for the communes of Bir El Ater with the recently developed Jebel Onk phosphate workings. Similar population stagnation afflicts the adjacent Saharan piedmont. Thus Cote's examination of population changes by communes for the Constantine region tends to confirm the generalization made on Figure 16.3 on an arrondissement level of presentation.

If the more rapid rates of growth for Algiers, Annaba and Constantine were to be expected, it is more difficult to explain the total complexity of regional variation revealed by the 1966 statistics. Fertility, mortality and internal and external migration are all involved and it is unlikely that any one single factor is dominant nationally in influencing the regional variation, although on a local scale the paramount importance of low birth rates, new industrial development, wartime disruption and the departure of the Europeans could be invoked. Regional demographic variation aside, the direct movement of population between 1954 and 1966 is a product of many 'push' and 'pull' factors, which have regional disparities. The relative importance of these are discussed in this last section of the chapter.

The inadequacies of the socio-economic sample survey section of the 1966 census have already been described and these prevented the use of reliable birth and death rates at a geographically meaningful level, namely arrondissements. A few of the migration factors, or attempted indices of them, were examined by arrondissements for Northern Algeria and their correlations with population change between 1954 and 1966 tested by regression analysis. Indices thus tested were (a) population density 1954, (b) population density 1966, (c) percentage agglomerated 1966 (an attempted urbanization index), (d) French as a percentage of the total population in 1960, (e) percentage of Moslem population regrouped in 1960, (f) percentage of population absent abroad according to the 1966 census, and (g) percentage of population absent elsewhere in Algeria. Low correlations, significant at the 99 per cent level, were established for the index of population regroupment ($r = -0.397$) and for the index of population absent abroad ($r = -0.3335$). As just two of a collection of 'push' and 'pull' factors involved in population movement, these low correlations hint at the possibilities of further research. Several of the factors which would need quantifying at least at the level of the 76 arrondissements of Northern Algeria can be tentatively discussed, and some of their effects on regional variation in population change postulated.

Population regroupment, as an indicator of the trauma of the Algerian War on the country's population, can be examined regionally (Fig. 16.4). Although the visual and statistical correlations are far from complete, areas of high wartime disturbance, as expressed by regroupment, are often areas of low population increase. The east–west belt of rapid population increase would seem to fit in with a belt of arrondissements generally with less than 25 per cent of the 1960 Moslem population regrouped. Contrastingly, several areas of high regroupment can also be picked out on the population change map as areas of low increase or decline: Grande and Petite Kabylie, the eastern Aurès Mountains, and particularly western Oranais which had extensive free-fire zones up against the electrified barrier of the Moroccan frontier during the war. The effect of regroupment in terms of social breakdown of traditional rural society has been established (Bourdieu and Sayad, 1964) and, together with numerous local examples of the permanency of the centres (Claude, 1966), this represents a fairly widespread rejection of a return to pre-war hamlets and villages. For

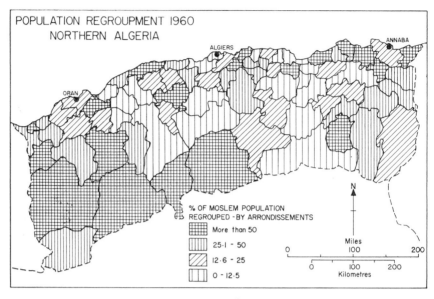

POPULATION REGROUPMENT 1960
NORTHERN ALGERIA

ANNABA

ALGIERS

ORAN

% OF MOSLEM POPULATION
REGROUPED - BY ARRONDISSEMENTS

More than 50

25·1 - 50

12·6 - 25

0 - 12·5

N

Miles
0   100   200

0   100   200
Kilometres

FIGURE 16.4

many the regroupment centre must have meant one step, perhaps the decisive step, in a drift to the towns, rather than a temporary refuge during hostilities. Where the centres were established in agriculturally more favoured areas, such as along the southern fringes of the Mitidja plain or the northern piedmont of the Aurès Mountains, the ability of the former home areas, often in the over-populated mountain massifs physically damaged by war and drastically depleted of their stocks of sheep and goats, to attract back their original inhabitants was very much lessened. When it is remembered that regroupment statistics can only be regarded as an incomplete indicator of wartime movement involving half the Algerian rural population, its part in explaining the regional aspects of this particular intercensal map of population change cannot be overstressed.

A second factor which, if not displaying such marked regional differences, would seem of considerable importance both in explaining the 1954–66 patterns and particularly in predicting future developments, is the regional disparity in the rate of natural increase. Rural–urban disparities of birth rates, the effect of military losses and of out-migration in warping the age and sex structure, lower urban rates of infant mortality, can all be postulated as showing meaningful variations if examined on an arrondissement level. The inadequacies of the 1966 sample census and the present incompleteness of birth and death registration, especially in rural areas, limit any explanative attempts using this variable, and prevent accurate regional projections of natural increase.

Although important, demographic differences could not have accounted for such great regional variations indicated on Figure 16.3. A third group of factors covering the relative economic development or attractiveness of different parts of Algeria must be held to account for much variation. Such factors would prompt much internal migration of people and even act as an impetus to migration overseas. A rather complex influence has been the departure of nearly a million French colonists and their families on independence. Measured as a percentage of the population of each arrondissement in 1960 they shared a high correlation with both the 1954 population densities (r = 0.5194) and the 1966 densities (r = 0.5262). As they provided the bulk of the consumer market their exodus meant severe economic difficulties for local producers and manufacturers particularly in and around Algiers, Oran, Constantine and Annaba. Indeed in population terms it can be doubted if the towns and surrounding areas of Oran, Aïn Témouchent, Mascara and Ghazaouet have yet recovered from this loss. In Oran and Mostaganem departments European settlement was fairly high in arrondissements other than those containing the main town, and formed 14 per cent or more of the 1960 population of four out of the five arrondissements composing the Oran department. However the European exodus also stimulated movement in by Algerians to occupy their jobs, their farms, and even their homes. Even if, in view of the drastic drop in employment in the secondary and tertiary sectors, the actual new vacancies were not all that numerous, the likelihood of urban employment was an attractive force. Similarly, the new self-management farms taking over from the abandoned and expropriated European estates offered job opportunities at government-established minimum wages. This has been seen as a factor maintaining the population of regroupment centres around the Mitidja plain, population which had been moved from surrounding mountain areas (Claude, 1966).

More recently, internal movement must have been stimulated by new job opportunities created by Algeria's economic development, particularly at development poles such as Algiers, Arzew with its gas liquefaction plant and petrochemicals industry, and Annaba with its iron and steel complex which was opened in 1969. Further points of attraction include Skikda, the terminal for new oil and gas pipelines under construction, Jebel Onk with its phosphate mining and Ouenza with its iron ore exploitation. The continued development of the Saharan oil and gas fields can be seen as partly behind the 50 per cent intercensal growth of the population of the Oasis department, the second fastest growing department. Compared with the scale of the unemployment problem to be tackled, Algeria's industrialization programme so far has not provided many jobs, but as a factor in attracting prospective labour to certain localities it must be playing a considerable part in population movement. In a limited way the polarization effects of such economic development are now beginning to be counteracted by government efforts to stimulate development in neglected areas such as the Aurès and the Grande Kabylie (Europe France Outremer, 1969). Regional three-year plans include textiles, shoe manufacturing, artisanal development and rural electrification.

Most of this recent economic development has been in established urban centres, and so continued rural–urban drift is a fourth component in explaining regional variation in population change. Definitions of 'urbanized population' vary and the 1966 census figures of 'agglomerated population', namely those living in centres of at least 100 buildings, distant from each other by less than 200 metres, clearly overstate the position (Table 16.10). Prenant considered that between 1954 and 1966, despite the departure of some 800,000 European townsfolk, Algeria's urban population grew by a third to attain the figure of 3,700,000 inhabitants, nearly a third of the total population. Excluding the Europeans, the number of urbanized Algerians has doubled (Prenant, 1968). The most noteworthy expanding towns are frequently also the economic growth poles mentioned earlier. Thus Algiers grew from 449,929 in 1954 to 897,352 in 1966 and, if its suburban ring of communes is included, it now forms a metropolis of 1,106,990. Substantial increases were also shown by Blida and other towns of the Algiers Mitidja and coastal Sahel regions. As second city, Oran has not had the attraction of the capital and its slower growth from 274,772 to 325,481 (metropolitan area in 1966, 366,509) probably reflects its greater difficulty in overcoming the effects of the exodus of French colonists; Oran lost about 180,000 compared with Algiers' loss of 315,000. Indeed of the 41 towns with 20,000 or more inhabitants in 1966, Oran was the fourth slowest in terms of increase since 1954. Centres of rapid urban growth were Constantine, Batna, Sétif, Médéa and Tizi Ouzou, while lower rates of growth were registered at Annaba and Sidi Bel Abbès, again places where the effect of European departures can be invoked (CNRP, 1967a; Prenant, 1967).

A fifth factor in considering regional population change is partly connected with the attractiveness of certain economically growing and urbanizing regions, namely the 'push' forces implicit in regional discrepancies of out-migration, be it movement abroad or internally within Algeria. The 1966 census provided data which although underestimating the scale of movement, certainly abroad, do allow some idea of the major source areas of such movement. The data are of registered population absent both abroad and elsewhere in Algeria. For the first category the emigrant had to be in touch with his former home by letter or remittance payment; for the second, the migrant should have left his home less than six months previous to the date of census. In the absence of other more satisfactory migration data, Figure 16.5 essentially shows this recent movement. Eastern Algeria stands out as a major source region, including the Aurès Mountains, the Hautes Plaines Constantinoises, the Petite Kabylie, and particularly the Grande Kabylie where high movement abroad renders such out-migration an important factor in the stagnating and even declining population of the Tizi Ouzou department and sur-rounding arrondissements. In absolute terms Algiers and Oran are large source areas though of course they also form major reception areas. Locally out-migration is also significant in the El Asnam-Tenès area and up against the Moroccan frontier around Ghazaouet and Tlemcen. Con-versely low migration from some of the central arrondissements, particu-larly in the department of Médéa, can be postulated as a factor behind the extremely high rates of 1954–66 population increase there.

As observed earlier, the census recorded only 268,868 migrants out of an estimated 700,000 Algerians living abroad. If the census results are extrapolated to the higher figure, emigrants are found to total 16.9 per cent of the total population of the department of Tizi Ouzou, 14.5 per cent of Sétif and 7.5 per cent of Constantine (Cote, 1968a). The full results in Table 16.10 show the considerable regional variation of this movement abroad, primarily of workers, and together with the probably greater internal movement it reflects both the economic opportunities offered by Algeria's various regions, and people's evaluations of them. As a conse-quence many localities must have come to depend largely on remittance payments from these emigrant workers to form the basis of their money economy. A study of the Petite Kabylie, where emigrant workers formed 4.5 per cent of the total population of Collo arrondissement, 10 per cent of Djidjelli, and 20 per cent of El Milia, considered that the average remit-tance per emigrant per month was 130 francs (about £10). It was estimated that about 5 milliards old francs a year were being sent back into the area, that is about £4 million, to help support a population of 60,000 families (Seklani, 1965). Thus although initially reflecting economic inadequacies of the home region, out-migration might later be an impor-

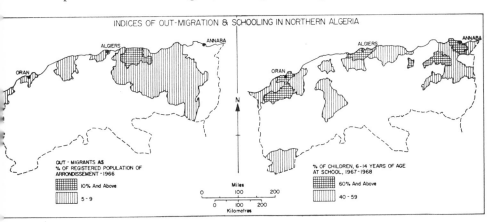

FIGURE 16.5

397

TABLE 16.9   PROVISION OF ELECTRICITY AND GAS IN ALGERIA, 1966

	No. of dwellings	*With electricity and gas*	*With electricity only*	*With gas only*
Department centres	365,500	213,200	82,200	12,900
Arrondissement centres	234,500	90,300	39,900	25,300
Commune centres	263,500	68,300	36,700	30,400
Other agglomerated settlements	229,300	20,100	15,200	24,700
Scattered dwellings	685,000	5,700	11,600	24,000
Total	1,777,800	397,600	185,600	117,300

Source: Bahri, 1968 b.

tant source of income for a region and be a means of transmitting the 'spread effects' from an economically faster-growing area.

A fairly broad factor prompting population movement is the better social infrastructure (in terms of medical and educational facilities) available in certain regions, usually the more advanced and urbanized areas. This is particularly the case in the regional variation in schooling (Fig. 16.5). Reasonably high figures of above 60 per cent of the children between 6 and 14 years of age going to school in 1967–8 were only achieved in arrondissements containing major cities like Sétif, Sidi Bel Abbès and Tlemcen as well as the four largest cities. Other high rates were found in the vicinity of these cities and in the Grande Kabylie region (CNRP, 1969). Perhaps this last instance reflects education as a 'push' as well as a 'pull' factor, in that education can lead to an increased emigration of those educated as they cannot find employment appropriate to their increased status in their home locality.

For the future, the expansion of education has a high priority in Algeria, and the statistics employed in Figure 16.5 must have been considerably modified by the fact that 400,000 children started school for the first time in Autumn 1969, bringing the Algerian school population up to 2 million (Revue de Presse, 1969b). For the time being, however, the illiteracy rates revealed by the 1966 sample census must still represent a considerable economic drawback for many departments: Médéa 86 per cent, illiterate, Saïda 85 per cent and Tiaret 84 per cent (see Table 16.10). Medically the same departments figure among the least endowed parts of Algeria, Saida having 3 doctors per 100,000 inhabitants, Sétif 4, Médéa and Aurès 5 each, in comparison with Algiers 28 and Oran 20. Obviously indicators such as these are very much an expression of degrees of urbanization, and this is especially noticeable in some of the statistics of housing standards from the sample census (Table 16.9).

TABLE 16.10 REGIONAL ASPECTS OF THE ALGERIAN POPULATION

Departments	I Population,* 1954	II Population, 1966	III Density of population,* 1966 (per sq. km.)	IV Per cent growth,* 1954–66	V Per cent agglomer- ated,*† 1966	VI Total French population 1960
Alger	1,077,257	1,648,168	523	52	87	400,213
Annaba	729,872	949,989	37	30	50	67,921
Aurès (Batna)	561,208	765,052	22	36	44	8,505
Constantine	1,209,057	1,513,068	76	25	45	77,698
El Asnam	627,417	789,583	62	26	32	21,701
Médéa	631,057	870,163	16	37	28	11,822
Mostaganem	607,512	778,863	69	28	36	48,296
Oasis	332,462	505,553	0.4	50	69	N.D.
Oran	857,311	958,366	57	11	84	294,912
Saïda	190,285	236,950	4	24	39	8,525
Saoura	155,073	211,474	0.28	37	72	N.D.
Sétif	935,316	1,237,927	73	32	45	20,298
Tiaret	267,110	361,962	14	35	39	14,192
Tizi Ouzou	800,892	830,758	138	3	56	9,990
Tlemcen	371,956	444,118	55	19	63	23,837
	9,353,785	12,101,994		29	54	1,007,910

* 'Population municipale' or registered population minus the 'population comptée à part' namely people who for reasons of work, health, education or imprisonment live in a community rather than in a family household.

† Agglomeration of at least 100 buildings, distant from each other by less than 200 m.—*not* to be equated with 'urban' population.

N.D. = No data.

VII Per cent of population born before 1–7–62 still living in the same arrondisse- ment in 1966	VIII Per cent absent abroad, 1966 (extra- polated figures)	IX Per cent under 15 years of age, 1966	X Socialist (autogestion) sector as per cent of total agricultural area, 1967	XI Agriculture as per cent of total employment, 1966	XII Per cent of children 6–14 years of age attending school, 1967–8	XIII Per cent of illiteracy, 1966	XIV Number of doctors per 100,000 inhabitants, 31–12–65
79.4	2.6	47.1	66.9	30.5	83.2	55.9	28
84.4	2.3	49.3	14.5	60.2	49.2	77.0	14
93.4	5.4	49.0	4.4	70.3	34.7	79.2	5
93.5	7.5	47.6	16.7	54.2	46.0	75.3	10
96.8	3.9	48.0	19.8	72.5	31.5	83.5	5
95.0	1.8	47.6	2.9	78.4	25.9	86.0	5
95.6	3.9	48.2	37.2	68.4	37.5	77.8	11
92.3	1.7	45.0	0.0	49.5	48.0	77.5	10
85.9	2.3	47.0	48.5	37.9	66.7	63.7	20
93.4	0.9	47.0	44.8	75.6	33.5	85.1	3
91.5	1.6	44.2	0.0	68.0	61.9	80.4	10
92.9	14.5	47.4	13.6	57.7	39.8	80.1	4
96.7	1.0	48.2	19.4	68.0	34.6	83.9	9
91.0	16.9	41.9	8.0	49.7	50.1	75.3	7
93.6	6.5	47.1	28.0	44.9	50.0	73.3	11
90.5	5.8	47.2	5.4	55.6	—	74.6	12

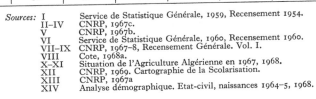

Sources:	I	Service de Statistique Générale, 1959, Recensement 1954.
	II–IV	CNRP, 1967c.
	V	CNRP, 1967b.
	VI	Service de Statistique Générale, 1960, Recensement 1960.
	VII–IX	CNRP, 1967–8, Recensement Générale. Vol. I.
	VIII	Cote, 1968a.
	X–XI	Situation de l'Agriculture Algérienne en 1967, 1968.
	XII	CNRP, 1969. Cartographie de la Scolarisation.
	XIII	CNRP, 1967a
	XIV	Analyse démographique. Etat-civil, naissances 1964–5, 1968.

Conclusion

Many of the factors suggested as influencing regional population change would seem to favour movement to the coastal Tell region with its cities, developing industries and richer, more advanced agriculture. Social infrastructure, urbanization and economic development in particular promote cumulative causation type of growth in areas which already have the higher population densities. However, Figure 16.3 of 1954–66 population change reflected a much more complex pattern of regional variation. In the absence of adequate regional data on natural increase and migration, largely the fault of a poorly constructed sampling frame for the analysis of the 1966 census results, many of the reasons behind this complexity can only be postulated. Within these limitations, the population geography of Algeria can be seen to reflect the continued importance of the trauma of independence, particularly the departure of European colonists and disruptions caused by the regroupment policy. Thus the 1966 census, although a necessary statistical basis of a planned economy, still reflects the effects of the War of Independence and the departure of the French. Such factors, while having explanative importance, limit its predictive possibilities for regional population projections.

Furthermore, the Algerian economy up to 1966 was still recovering from the chaos and stagnation of one of the harshest decolonizations to follow the granting of independence. An indication of recovery and of economic growth came in 1967 when the Gross Domestic Product grew by 11 per cent. Similar growth in 1968 suggested the possible achievement of a steady rate of growth (Farrell, 1969). The growing oil industry was making its hoped-for contribution; in expanding its oil production 10 per cent, the Algerian national economy automatically would grow by 2 per cent. All three years 1966–8 saw increases in oil production above this 10 per cent level. In view of this take-off in the Algerian economy the desirability of a new census in the early 1970's would seem imperative. Only then could genuinely post-independence trends be analysed without the 'noise' engendered by the numerous unhappy events of the 1954–66 period. The results of a fresh census would form a much more realistic basis for the country's planning than those shown by the 1966 census.

ACKNOWLEDGMENTS

The author would like to acknowledge the kind provision of grants towards visits to Algeria in 1967 by the Twentieth International Geographical Congress Fund and in 1968 by the Central Research Fund of the University of London. Much valuable advice was given by Messieurs C. Bardinet, A.-M. Bahri, J. Nash and others of various departments of the Sous-Direction des Statistiques, Algiers, whom the author would like to thank along with the *documentalistes* of the Sous-Direction's Documentation Centre.

REFERENCES

ANALYSE DÉMOGRAPHIQUE. ETAT-CIVIL, NAISSANCES, 1964–5 (1968), Sous-Direction des Statistiques, Algiers.

BAHRI, A.-M. (1968a) 'Le Recensement algérien de 1966', *Revue Algérienne des Sciences Juridiques, Economiques et Politiques*, 5 (2), pp. 415–27.

BAHRI, A.-M. (1968b) 'L'Activité et l'habitat à travers le recensement algérien de 1966', *Revue Algérienne des Sciences Juridiques Economiques et Politiques*, 5 (3), pp. 779–85.

BARDINET, C. (1967) 'Densités de population en Algérie au recensement de 1966', *Annales Algériennes de Géographie*, 4, pp. 1–20.

BATTESTI, L.-M. (1967) 'Les travailleurs algériens dans l'économie française depuis le 1er. juillet 1962', *L'Information Géographique*, 31 (4), pp. 159–68.

BOUKHOBZA, M. and VON ALLMEN, M. (1969) 'L'enquête socio-démographique algérienne: quelques résultats et problématique sociologique', *Revue Tunisienne de Sciences Sociales*, 17–18, pp. 293–306.

BOURDIEU, P., DARBEL, A., RIVET, J.-P., SEIBEL, C. (1963) *Travail et travailleurs en Algerie*, Paris.

BOURDIEU, P. and SAYAD, A. (1964) *Le Déracinement. La crise de l'agriculture traditionnelle en Algerie*, Paris.

BULLETIN DE LIAISON. CARTOGRAPHIE ET STATISTIQUE (1968), 2, Algiers

CLAUDE, P. (1966) 'L'évolution des Centres de Regroupement de la Mitidja occidentale', *Annales Algériennes de Géographie*, 2, pp. 120–46.

CNRP (COMMISSARIAT NATIONAL AU RECENSEMENT DE LA POPULATION) (1967a) *Données Rapides sur la Population Algérienne*, Algiers.

CNRP (1967b) *Recensement de la population agglomerée secondaire et éparse des 15 départements algériens*.

CNRP (1967c) *Recensement Général de la Population et de l'Habitat, 1966. Données Abrégées. Résultats du Sondage*, Algiers.

CNRP (1967d) *Algérie du Nord. Etude du Réseau Urbain. Esquisse de Tableaux par Région de dominance des villes*. Service de Cartographie—Urbanisme.

CNRP (1967e) *Recensement Général de la Population et de l'Habitat, 1966. Situation de Résidence par Commune*, Algiers.

CNRP (1967–8) *Recensement Général de la Population et de l'Habitat, 1966*.

Vol. I—Démographie générale, instruction, exploitation par sondage.

Vol. II—Caractéristiques sociaux économiques de la population.

Vol. III and IV—Données démographiques complémentaires. Données sur l'habitat.

CNRP (1969) *Cartographie de la Scolarisation*. Service de Cartographie—Urbanisme.

COMMISSION INTERMINISTERIELLE POUR L'ELABORATION D'UNE POLITIQUE DE LA NATALITE (1968) *'La Position du Conseil Supérieur Islamique sur le Planning Familial'*—Document, 23rd April 1968.

CORNATON, M. (1967) *Les Regroupements de la Décolonisation en Algérie'*, Paris.

COTE, M. (1968a) 'L'émigration Algérienne à l'étranger', *Annales Algériennes de Géographie'*, 5, pp. 152–54.

COTE, M. (1968b) 'L'urbanisation dans les trois pays du Maghreb', *Annales Algériennes de Géographie*, 5, p. 158.

COTE, M. (1968c) 'L'évolution démographique du Constantinois (1954–66)', *Revue Tunisienne de Sciences Sociales*, 15, pp. 237–42.

DERBAL, Z. (1969) *Bibliographie sur la Démographie en Algérie*, Algiers, Sous-Direction des Statistiques.

ETUDE MONOGRAPHIQUE SUR QUELQUES REGROUPEMENTS (1960) Statistique Générale (Sous-Direction des Statistiques), Algiers.

EUROPE FRANCE OUTREMER (1969) 471, 'Le programme spécial de développement de la Kabylie', and 'Le programme de développement des Aurès', pp. 50–53, Paris.

FARRELL, R. E. (1969) 'L'Economie algérienne après sept années d'indépendence', *Problèmes économiques*, 116, pp. 15–20, Documentation Française, Paris.

GOOD, D. (1961) 'Notes on the Demography of Algeria', *Population Index*, 27 (1), pp. 3–32.

LESNE, M. (1962) 'Une expérience de déplacement de population; les centres de regroupement en Algérie', *Annales de Géographie*, 71, pp. 567–603.

MAGHREB DIGEST (1967) 'Second General Assembly of the Algerian Brotherhood in Europe', 5 (4), pp. 72–4, Los Angeles.

MOUVEMENTS (LES) NATURELS ENREGISTRÉS DANS LA POPULATION ALGÉRIENNE EN 1963, Sous-Direction des Statistiques, Algiers.

NORBYE, O. (1969) 'The Economy of Algeria', in Robson, P. and Lury, D. A., *The Economies of Africa*, London.

PLANHOL, X. DE (1961) *Nouveaux villages algérois*, Paris.

PRENANT, A. (1967) 'Premières données sur le recensement de la population de l'Algérie (1966)', *Bulletin de l'Association de Géographes Francais*, 357–8, pp. 53–68

PRENANT, A. (1968) 'Rapports villes-campagnes dans le Maghreb; l'exemple de l'Algérie', *Revue Tunisienne de Sciences Sociales*, 15, pp. 191–216.

REMILI, A. (1969) 'Démographie et scolarisation en Algerie', *Revue Tunisienne des Sciences Sociales*, 17–18, pp. 633–58.

REVUE DE PRESSE (1965) 98, September–October, Algiers.

REVUE DE PRESSE (1969a) 'L'Anniversaire du 19 juin', 136, June–July, Algiers.

REVUE DE PRESSE (1969b) 'La Rentrée scolaire', 138, October, Algiers.

SEKLANI, M. (1965) 'Petite Kabylie: aspects démographiques et problèmes d'emploi', *Revue Tunisienne de Sciences Sociales*, 3, pp. 147–58.

SEKLANI, M. (1969) 'Croissance démographique comparée des pays du Maghreb 1950–90', *Revue Tunisienne des Sciences Sociales*, 17–18, pp. 29–52.

SERVICE DE STATISTIQUE GENERALE (1959) Résultats statistiques du recensement de la population du 31 octobre 1954, Algiers.

SERVICE DE STATISTIQUE GENERALE (1960) Premiers résultats du recensement de population de 1960. Résultats définitifs.

SITUATION DE L'AGRICULTURE ALGÉRIENNE EN 1967 (1968) *Statistique Agricole*, 7, December 1968. Ministère de l'Agriculture et de la Réforme Agraire, Algiers.

TIANO, A. (1967) *Le Maghreb entre les Mythes*, Paris.

TIANO, A. (1968) *Le Développement économique du Maghreb*, Paris.

Chapter 17
Morocco: urbanization and concentration of population
G H Blake

Morocco was estimated to have a total population of 14,264,000 in the middle of 1969, thus ranking third in the Arab world after the UAR and Sudan, and seventh in Africa. Many of the characteristics of the population of Morocco are typical of the countries discussed in previous chapters, including a high rate of increase. The degree of urbanization, about 30 per cent, is by no means exceptional, but the rapid growth of a few large towns and the appearance of a large number of small towns are features of particular interest, as is the exodus of the large number of Europeans and Jews in the last twenty years. Only Algeria has witnessed the emigration of more Europeans, and no other Middle Eastern or North African country has seen the departure of more Jews than Morocco.

Morocco is dominated by the highest and most rugged ranges of the Atlas system and these give the country its characteristic geographical personality, forming an effective divide between the favoured plains and plateaux of the north and west, and the semi-arid Saharan regions to the south and east. The High and Middle Atlas mountains in particular act as a kind of water tower, their western slopes catching rainfall from south-westerly and westerly air masses from the Atlantic. Most of the major rivers in Morocco flow west to the Atlantic, and several of these have dams to create large modern irrigation schemes. Groundwater resources, soils and rainfall are also more conducive to settlement in western Morocco than elsewhere, and only a small proportion of the population inhabit the oases south and west of the mountains. Thus the population of Morocco is unevenly distributed between a populous, urbanized zone, and a vast sparsely populated zone, in much the same way as in other parts of the Middle East and North Africa.

Census data

On the face of it Morocco has more census data available than most developing countries. Prior to independence in 1956 Morocco was divided into three Zones: an International Zone around Tangier, a Spanish Zone in the north, and a larger French Zone in the south. In 1956 these territories were united to form the Kingdom of Morocco, though Spain has retained the northern towns of Melilla and Ceuta. In the French Zone no fewer than six censuses of population were conducted before 1956, but their results are unfortunately of rather limited value. In 1921, 1926 and 1931 crude techniques were employed, and in certain parts of the country not yet under effective French control rough estimates were made which generally resulted in underestimates. The 1936 census was the first to cover the whole French Zone, but house counts and a multiplier were often substituted for head counts. The results were again inaccurate whether they were in fact an overall overestimate (Stewart, 1964) or an underestimate of the rural population (Noin, 1962). The first post-war census of 1947 was by means of a count of ration cards, resulting in overestimates of 2 per cent of the country districts and 7 per cent in the towns (Breil, 1947). The last French census of 1951–2 was more reliable than its predecessors although Jews and Europeans were counted in 1951 and Moslems in 1952. A population pyramid was actually constructed based on a sample of the Moslem population, revealing that nearly one-third of the population were under 10 years of age.

In the Spanish Zone, the authorities were demographically less assiduous than the French, having attempted population estimates in 1930 and 1940, both of which were very inaccurate, and a census in 1950. In the International Zone estimates of population were made from time to time but no census was ever carried out. It is therefore a complicated and sometimes frustrating exercise to compare population statistics for the three zones before independence with those of the Kingdom of Morocco today. The only census to cover the whole country at one time and using the same methods of enumeration throughout was conducted in 1960, and this still provides the only accurate basis for population studies and projections in Morocco. The 1960 enumerations of urban populations which included the majority of Morocco's Europeans and Jews can be regarded as quite accurate. Enumerations of rural populations are probably less reliable though still far more useful than in any previous census. At the time of writing (1969), two out of four promised volumes of the 1960 census have yet to appear.

A new census was carried out in 1970 with the assistance of UN experts. The preliminary results of this census may be available by the end of 1971 and should provide data with which accurate demographic studies can at last be made concerning one of the most critical periods of Morocco's social and economic evolution. Meanwhile it is possible to outline in general terms some of the characteristics of the population of the country.

405

Composition

The 1960 census classified the population of Morocco in three major groups (Table 17.1). 'Foreigners' included French (175,000), Spanish

TABLE 17.1   COMPOSITION OF POPULATION OF MOROCCO, 1960

	Number	*Per cent*
Moroccan Moslems	11,067,929	95.2
Moroccan Jews	162,420	1.4
Foreigners	395,883	3.4
Total	11,626,232	100.0

(92,800) and Algerians (93,000) as well as a number of other nationalities, and cannot therefore be equated with the 'Europeans' of earlier censuses. Although less than 5 per cent of the population were non-Moslems in 1960 their importance in the life of the country was still considerable, and had been at its greatest only a few years before (Fig. 17.1). Since 1935 the Moslem population had increased by 68 per cent and foreigners by 49 per cent, but the number of Jews had already fallen by 12 per cent. The years since 1960 have seen the Moslem population continue to increase at rates variously estimated between 2.8 and 3.3 per cent per annum, while the number of foreigners has fallen to 170,000 (1967). The estimated number of Jews remaining in Morocco was 53,000 in November 1967 (Maghreb, Etudes et documents, 1968).

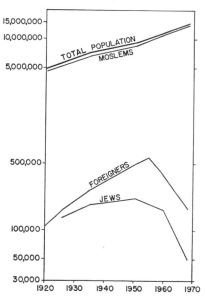

FIGURE 17.1 SEMI-LOGARITHMIC GRAPH OF POPULATION GROWTH IN MOROCCO, 1952 AND 1960

Moroccan Moslems

The first of the three great Arab invasions of North Africa occurred during the seventh century. At that time Berbers were established chiefly as sedentary farmers throughout the better watered parts of the Maghreb, particularly in the lowland areas. Their origins are obscure, but Berbers were identified as such from very early times by Phoenicians, Romans and others in spite of the apparent existence of several physical types among them. The first Arab–Islamic conquerors were not numerous and their impact on the Berbers was probably quite limited in Morocco, but in the eleventh and twelfth centuries two further waves of Arab invaders broke on the Maghreb whose influence has been profound. The Arabs brought Islam and the Arab language and the widespread practice of nomadism while in lowland regions both north and south of the Atlas Mountains their presence resulted in the emergence of an Arabo-Berber ethnic mixture whose language was Arabic but with cultural affinities with both groups. In the mountains of Morocco, from the Rif in the north to the Anti-Atlas in the south, Berber blood and language and cultural traditions survived, although in time most Berbers were converted to Islam. Today there are three chief dialects of Berber in the country, all largely confined to the highlands. About 80 per cent of the population speak Arabic, 10 per cent Berber and 10 per cent are bilingual (Martin, 1964).

For statistical and administrative purposes no distinction is made between Arabs and Arabo–Berbers, both groups being classified together as Moroccan Moslems, a desirable arrangement in view of the erstwhile tensions between them. In addition, other minor groups are also classified as Moroccan Moslems, notably the negroid elements who came to Morocco originally as slaves, servants or soldiers from the sixteenth century onward and who are now found particularly in the oases of southern Morocco where they are often referred to as *haratin*.

In 1952 the Moroccan population was predominantly rural, only 22.5 per cent living in towns of over 5,000 inhabitants. By 1960 the proportion had risen to 26.3 per cent, whereas in the same year 95 per cent of the Jews and 87 per cent of the foreigners in Morocco were urban dwellers. Thus a high proportion of the rural population of Morocco has traditionally consisted of Moslems, and since the exodus of Jews and Europeans this proportion has increased. Even so, the proportion of the Moslem population living in towns had risen to 29.2 per cent in 1967 as a result of both natural increase and rural–urban migration, and Moslems now constitute an increasingly large proportion of the total urban population.

The overall view of the Moslem population presented in the 1960 census almost epitomizes the demographic problems of the developing world. The natural rate of increase was high at about 3 per cent per annum, resulting in a population one-third of which was under 10 years of age, significantly more than in 1952 (Fig. 17.2). Associated in part with this youthful age structure was the moderate proportion (39 per cent) of the Moslem population classified as 'active', i.e. employed or seeking employment; in the towns, 28 per cent were active compared with 43 per cent in rural areas. Predictably, the level of activity was a great deal higher among males (50 per cent) than females (28 per cent), specially in the towns. So, too, a large proportion of the 16 per cent literates in the Moslem population were males. The participation of Moslems in various branches

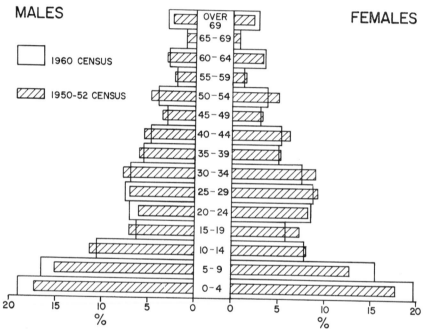

FIGURE 17.2 AGE-SEX PYRAMIDS OF MOROCCAN MOSLEM POPULATION, 1952 AND 1960

TABLE 17.2 PERCENTAGE OF MOSLEM URBAN AND RURAL POPULATIONS IN VARIOUS BRANCHES OF ACTIVITY, MOROCCO, 1960

	Urban population	*Rural population*
Agriculture, forestry, fishing	4.5	86.4
Industries, crafts, mining	25.4	3.3
Services, commerce	45.1	4.9
Not defined	4.5	1.9
Unemployed	20.5	3.5
	100.0	100.0

Source: Census, 1960, Vol. II, p. 202.

of activity is also revealing (Table 17.2). The high proportion of unemployed in the towns speaks for itself, when at the same time a growth
rate of 3 per cent means approximately 120,000 more jobs to find each
year.

Moroccan Jews

In the early 1950's when the Jewish population of Morocco was larger
than at any time in its history, there were more Jews in Morocco than in
Algeria and Tunisia combined. The origins of Morocco's Jews can be
traced to several periods of history, but when Jewish communities first
became established in Morocco is less certain. A few Jews almost certainly
came with Phoenicians from Tyre and Sidon from the eighth century B.C.
(Chouraqui, 1965), while others probably reached Morocco after the fall
of the First Temple in Jerusalem in 586 B.C. After the destruction of
Palestine by the Romans in A.D. 70 and the failure of the Jewish revolt in
Cyrenaica shortly afterwards, Jews arrived in the Maghreb in larger numbers. Several centuries later small groups of Jews from Arabia and Egypt
moved into the Maghreb in the wake of the conquering Arab armies, and
established themselves chiefly in the towns as traders and craftsmen
(Despois, 1964). The most important influx of Jews, however, occurred
following their expulsion from Spain during the fifteenth, sixteenth and
seventeenth centuries, several thousand settling in the towns of northern
Morocco, especially Tangier, Tetuan, Fès, Rabat and Salé. Most were
traders or skilled artisans and some were highly educated.

Most of these influxes of Jews involved quite small numbers, and in the
context of two and a half thousand years of Moroccan history they are
numerically insignificant. It therefore seems certain that the number of
Jews in Morocco increased more through the conversion of Berbers than
through immigration, chiefly in the years before the Islamic invasions. This
fact explains the existence of several very small and ancient Jewish communities in southern Morocco and elsewhere. According to M. Eisenbeth
(1952), the surnames of North African Jews may be taken as evidence of
the importance of indigenous elements, half of them being of Arabo–
Berber origin, one-sixth Spanish, Portuguese or Italian, and one-eighth
Hebrew–Aramaic (Despois, 1964). If anything, the proportion of Arabo–
Berber names was higher in Morocco than for North Africa as a whole.

The number of Moroccan Jews grew rapidly between 1921 and 1952,
though apparent growth rates of 4.8 per cent and 5.4 per cent for the intercensal periods 1921–6 and 1931–6 in the French Zone cannot be taken
seriously. The Jewish population for the whole of Morocco has been
estimated as 185,000 in 1935, 218,000 in 1952 and 162,000 in 1960
(Census, 1960). Allowing for a net annual emigration of about 20,000 Jews
from 1948 until 1962 (Chouraqui, 1965), the average annual increase of the

Jewish population in this period was apparently 3.3 per cent. In fact, it was undoubtedly lower, although the rate of increase was still rather higher among Jews than Moslems.

The emigration of Jews from Morocco began in 1948 largely as a result of the formation of the state of Israel. The exodus continued gradually until the peaks of 1955 and 1956 when 25–30,000 left each year, partly because of the emigration of many French who had tended to protect and favour the Jews to a degree which irritated the Moslems. From 1957 to 1961 Jews were forbidden to leave Morocco, but emigration began again in 1961 when the right of departure was restored. By 1965 a further 100,000 Jews may have left Morocco, reducing the community to some 70,000 (Noin, 1965). Today only 53,000 remain, less than half of one per cent of the total population.

The distribution of Jews at the 1960 census still largely reflected patterns characteristic of the period prior to 1948. Indeed, apart from Casablanca, the location of Jewish communities in 1960 had not changed radically since the nineteenth century. Nearly 95 per cent were urban dwellers, the few thousand rural Jews being scattered in three dozen or so small centres notably in the Upper Sous and the oases of the Draa, Dades and Tafilalt. On the other hand, 80 per cent of all Jews were to be found in the nine largest towns, 45 per cent of them in Casablanca alone. Besides the communities in the large towns on the one hand and rural villages on the other, another 15 per cent of the Jewish community were located in small- and medium-sized towns. In some of these towns even in 1960 Jews still represented a significant proportion of the total population, 27 per cent in Erfoud for example, 23 per cent in Midelt and 20 per cent in Demnat (Le Coz, 1961). It is of particular interest that in all the main centres along the ancient Saharan trade route through Erfoud, Midelt, and Sefrou to Fès, the Jews represented between 15 and 25 per cent of the population. Today they have almost entirely disappeared from these centres, their ancient *mellahs* now being occupied by Moslems.

The occupational structure of the Jews in 1960 showed 42 per cent as labourers and artisans and almost exactly the same proportion engaged in commerce of one kind and another, a higher proportion that in 1952 (Census, 1960). One reason for their increased involvement in commerce was that many Jews migrated in the first place from inland towns where they were frequently engaged in craft industries, to the large urban centres of Casablanca and Rabat-Salé. Besides affording greater security the existence of relatively large Jewish communities in these towns provided strong attractions to their co-religionists. At the same time, the high level of literacy among the Jews (57 per cent in 1960) was an obvious advantage in the adoption of life in the large towns.

The only Jewish communities of any size remaining in Morocco today are in Casablanca and Rabat-Salé. In addition, there are a few hundred in

Marrakesh, Fès, Meknès and Tangier. Elsewhere there are practically no Jews left in Morocco.

Foreigners

Seen in the context of centuries of migrations, the rise and fall of Morocco's European population has been swift but spectacular in its nature and consequences.

French and Spanish activity began in earnest in Morocco in 1904 when a Spanish sphere of influence was defined in the north and a larger French sphere of influence was defined in the south, with an International Zone around Tangier. When the French Protectorate was formally established in 1912 there were already a few thousand Europeans in Morocco, including French, Spanish and Italians. A large influx of French occurred immediately following the Protectorate treaty in 1912 and again at the end of the First World War. By 1936 there were 191,000 Europeans in the French Zone, over 70 per cent of whom were French citizens. After the Second World War the French population once again increased rapidly, chiefly by immigration, so that by 1955, the year before independence, there were 350,000 Frenchmen out of an estimated total of 460,000 Europeans in the French Zones (United Nations, 1956). On the eve of independence 5.4 per cent of the population of French Morocco were classified as foreigners. Algerians were the largest group after the French, most of them refugees from the Algerian War who began arriving in large numbers in eastern Morocco after 1954. With the independence of Algeria in 1962 many of them returned home and few remain today.

The European population of the Spanish Zone grew more gradually than in the French Zone, from 48,000 in 1930 to approximately 87,000 in 1955. This nevertheless represented 8.4 per cent of the total population of the Spanish Zone. All but a few hundred were Spanish citizens. Rural colonization was not encouraged in the Spanish Zone, nor were physical conditions much incentive, so that most Europeans were in six coastal towns—Larache, Assilah, Ceuta, Tetuan, Al-Hoceïma and Nador, with some farms around Ceuta, Tetuan and Larache. In the International Zone, more than a quarter of the total population of 170,000 were Europeans in 1956. Among them were a few farmers, but the vast majority lived in Tangier itself. More than half the Europeans in the International Zone were Spanish.

In contrast with the Spanish and International Zones, European rural settlement was vigorously promoted in French Morocco, where a number of relatively flat and well watered regions near the coast were conquered and secured in the early years of the Protectorate. By 1953 European holdings amounted to approximately one million hectares, distributed

411

among nearly 6,000 farmers, slightly more than one per cent of the rural population, but responsible for about one-quarter of the gross value of all crops (Stewart, 1964), the chief areas of settlement being the Triffa, Saïs, Rharb, Chaouïa, Tadla, Haouz and Sous plains. In the years immediately following Moroccan independence, about 25,000 Europeans emigrated annually until 1961 when the numbers dropped sharply. Some of the greatest losses occurred in rural areas and from the small inland towns, but decolonization in Morocco was extremely slow compared with Algeria. The 1960 census still showed 7.6 per cent of the active French population to be engaged in agriculture, and although figures are not available, a handful of European farmers remained in 1968.

At the time of independence there were altogether 590,000 Europeans in the three Zones of Morocco, 4.6 per cent of the total population, but by 1967, only 170,000 'foreigners' remained, 1.2 per cent of the total population. Most of these are engaged in private industry and commerce, in the liberal professions, or as technical experts. The proportion of foreigners concentrated in Casablanca and Rabat-Salé is now higher than at any time —well over 60 per cent, while the proportion of Europeans who are French has fallen.

Distribution and density

In June 1960, 70.7 per cent of the population of Morocco were rural dwellers, and 29.3 per cent lived in urban centres of over 2,500 inhabitants. As a consequence of the continued high levels of rural–urban migration and natural increase, the urban population has undoubtedly increased since 1960, possibly to between 32.5 per cent and 33.5 per cent of the total population. The percentage in towns of over 5,000 inhabitants increased from 26.3 per cent in 1960 to 29.9 per cent in 1967 (Division du Plan, 1968).

Comments in this section are largely based on the findings of the 1960 census together with the *Atlas du Maroc* (1963). Although some details will have changed, the general pattern illustrated in Figure 17.3 is substantially the same as ten years ago. As in many of the countries discussed in this volume, the population of Morocco displays a basic disequilibrium between a relatively populous half, with many towns and an average density of over 50 persons per sq. km., and a sparsely populated half with no towns to speak of and in which the average density is barely 5 persons per sq. km. This situation has existed for centuries as a result of environmental influences but in recent years economic development has occurred in the half already favoured by environment, emphasizing the imbalance.

The rural population can be considered in three zones—Arid Morocco,

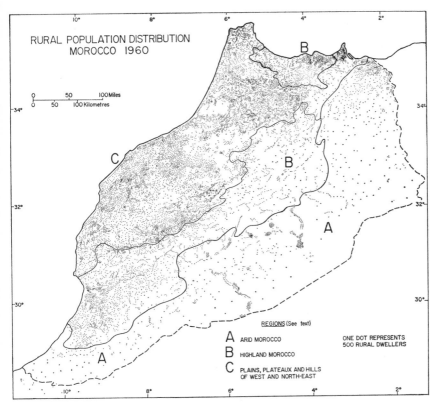

FIGURE 17.3

Highland Morocco, and the plains, plateaux and hills of west and north-east Morocco.

Arid Morocco embraces the whole pre-Saharan region in the south, and a dry eastern region which includes the Moulouya valley and the mining settlements around Oujda. This vast region supports no more than 6 per cent of the rural population, yet it covers about one-third of the country. In the east, rainfall is generally less than 200 mm. per annum, while in the south it is frequently below 100 mm. The eastern region in particular is very sparsely populated with perhaps one per cent of the rural population, most of them nomads. In the pre-Saharan region a number of remarkable oases are supported by watercourses from the Atlas range, containing the renowned fortress-like *ksour*, some of the largest villages in Morocco. In the oases along the Dades, Draa, Rheriss, Ziz, Guir and Todra valleys densities can be over 100 per sq. km., and locally in some oases well over 1,000 per sq. km. Altogether pre-Saharan Morocco supports some 5 per cent of the rural population, but probably less than one per cent of the whole of Arid Morocco is cultivated.

413

Highland Morocco represents about one-third of Morocco and supports about one-third of the rural population. The Anti-Atlas and the west and central High Atlas Mountains, referred to by the French as 'Le Pays Chleuh', support about 15 per cent of the rural population of Morocco. The western Anti-Atlas in particular are a reminder that strong disharmonies exist in Morocco between environment and population densities. In this region, where there is a shortage of both water and cultivable land, densities are commonly 50 and sometimes 70 persons per sq. km. with the result that a great deal of temporary and permanent migration to the towns occurs in response to pressure on the land. The Chleuh region is one of the oldest settled areas of sedentary cultivation in Morocco, already densely populated when the present economic revolution began.

In contrast, the whole of the eastern High Atlas and the Middle Atlas is a sparsely populated area containing only 9 per cent of the rural population, and with average densities around 20 to 25 persons per sq. km. Agriculture is less well developed, and pastoralism, often involving elaborate transhumance, is extremely important both on account of history and physical limitations. Permanent settlement is found up to 2,300 metres. The Rif Mountains of northern Morocco, although quite small in area, support another 9 per cent of the rural population. Densities vary greatly from commune to commune, some being as low as 15 per sq. km. and others over 150, depending largely upon local variations of soil and rainfall. Again, notably in the eastern Rif, densities are often surprisingly high partly on account of the importance of temporary migration.

The remaining one-third of Morocco, comprising the plains, plateaux and hills of the west and north-east, embraces about 60 per cent of the rural population. These two areas are generally below 500 m. in height, soils are deeper and more fertile than elsewhere, and besides higher and more reliable quantities of rainfall a number of large rivers sustain extensive irrigation schemes, with the result that more than half the surface area is cultivated. Western Morocco also supports by far the highest densities of livestock.

Although its share of the rural population is no more than 3 per cent, the north-east includes the peninsula of Nador-Melilla where intensive cultivation utilizing abundant water supplies from the basalt massif, fishing and iron-mining enable densities of 100–150 persons per sq. km. Eastwards along the coast the plain of Triffa supports densities of around 60 per sq. km., due to a large modern irrigation scheme originally colonized by the French.

The rural populations of western Morocco are both economically and numerically of great importance, and amount to 57 per cent of the nation's rural dwellers on about one-third of its surface area. The bulk of these are found in four important sub-regions:

(1) The Mid-Atlantic plains (15 per cent of Morocco's rural population),

lying between Casablanca and the Oued Tennsift to the south, are a semi-arid area of fertile soils devoted above all to pastoralism and vegetable and cereal cultivation. In the Doukkala and Abda plains densities are commonly 50 per sq. km. and pressure on land has resulted in persistent rural–urban migration, chiefly to Casablanca.

(2) In the Sebou basin (14 per cent of Morocco's rural population) densities vary considerably. In the Saïs plains large-scale modern farming is practised chiefly for the production of cereals and vines, but densities are not above 60 per sq. km. In the older settled Rharb plains good soils and irrigation can support densities of over 100 per sq. km. locally.

(3) The interior plains at the foot of the Atlas Mountains together account for about 11 per cent of the rural population. The Tadla and Haouz regions are both irrigated and very densely populated.

(4) The Sous basin (4 per cent of Morocco's rural population) has densities of 45 per sq. km. in spite of low rainfall, poor sources of groundwater, and generally sandy soils. This surprisingly large population is supported partly by temporary migrations to Europe and other parts of Morocco.

Several areas of low population density, below 15 per sq. km., can be distinguished in western Morocco, particularly the plateaux and massifs which lie between the well peopled Atlantic plains and the interior plains— Zemmour, Rehamna, and parts of the Phosphate Plateau. The sandy, forested Marmora region is also very sparsely populated.

The great majority of the 117 urban centres with over 2,500 inhabitants listed in the 1960 census were located in the west (Fig. 17.4). The only large town in Highland or Arid Morocco is Oujda, and these regions contained only 12 per cent of the urban population. Within western Morocco itself there is a remarkable concentration of population in a zone no more than 160 km. in length and 50 km. wide, running from Knitra to Casablanca. This small region embraces about one-fifth of the population of Morocco.

Urbanization

The urban scene in Morocco at the beginning of this century was very different from that of today. Only 8 or 9 per cent of the population were urban dwellers, living in two dozen or so centres of which Fès, the largest, numbered rather fewer than 100,000 and Marrakech perhaps 50,000. Unlike other countries of North Africa, most of the important towns were situated inland on the lowlands of the north and west. Since the Middle Ages, Moroccan trade had been chiefly along routes from south to north, and very little external trade had been carried on by sea except via Tangier (Montagne, 1951). Some Moroccan kings had even discouraged seaborne trade for fear of foreign influences, and the Atlantic coast offered few natural harbours affording protection from the common heavy surf or swell. Thus in 1900 the ports at Essaouira (then called Mogador), Safi, Casablanca, and Rabat-Salé were small and their trade extremely light.

It is evident from Table 17.3 that urbanization is proceeding at an accelerating rate. From 1900 to 1936 the urban population increased at 3.3 per cent per annum; from 1936 to 1952 at 4 per cent, rising to 4.8 per cent between 1952 and 1960. The present annual rate of increase is 5.1 per cent which is high even for a developing country (Noin, 1968). Another remarkable feature is the number of small towns. In 1960, there were 47 with fewer than 5,000 inhabitants and a further 25 between 5,000 and 10,000. In fact, if certain settlements with fewer than 2,500 inhabitants yet with genuine urban functions were included, the number would be far higher. Since 1960 small urban centres have appeared at the rate of four or five per annum.

TABLE 17.3   URBAN GROWTH IN MOROCCO, 1900–69

Year	Number of towns	Percentage of total population
1900	27	8–9
1920	40	11
1936	56	16
1952	92	26
1960	117	29.3
1969	155 (est.)	33 (est.)

Source: D. Noin (1968) *et al.*

The creation of a number of towns fulfilling entirely new and specialized functions was predictable following the advent of European administration and the gradual diversification of an exclusively agricultural economy. Thus a dozen or so mining towns sprang up largely in connection with the extraction of phosphates, coal and iron, while along the Mediterranean coast and in the Atlas Mountains a number of small tourist resorts were founded by the Spanish and French. Much more numerous were a series of small market towns, sometimes also fulfilling administrative functions, established particularly in the regions of modern agriculture and European colonization. A few of these towns grew out of centres already in existence, but many were new, and their functions were generally well defined either because of deliberate planning or economic necessity. However, after the Second World War a number of settlements achieving urban status have been quite unplanned and their economic basis is not at all clear. Since 1956 even more have appeared. Some, like Bouznika on the road between Casablanca and Rabat, offer roadside services; others are little more than tiny dormitory towns for industries along the Knitra–Casablanca axis. It is also significant that a number of small towns have arisen in regions of strong emigration, suggesting that some centres are commonly used, if not actually created, in a process of stepped migration to the big cities (Division du Plan, 1968). In these, high levels of unemployment are experienced.

At the other end of the urban hierarchy there are ten large towns, five with 100,000–200,000 inhabitants (Tetuan, Safi, Knitra, Oujda, Tangier), four with 200,000–500,000 (Meknès, Fès, Marrakech, Rabat-Salé) and, in a category by itself, Casablanca with 1.2 million inhabitants in 1968. The growth of these towns has been an outstanding feature of the years since 1936 when there were only three towns with over 100,000 inhabitants in Morocco. In contrast with the situation seventy years ago, six of the largest towns are now situated on or near the coast. Although Meknès, Fès and Marrakech still rank among the top ten their rates of growth since 1952 have tended to be lower than other large towns, with the exception of Tangier which lost many Europeans through emigration before 1960.

In 1960, 37 towns fell into the 10,000–100,000 bracket, but only three of these had populations exceeding 50,000. The Spanish towns of Melilla (80,000) and Ceuta (73,000) were also in this category in 1960 (Spanish Information Service, 1962). In other words, Morocco's urban hierarchy featured a large number of small towns, ten large towns including an obvious primate city in Casablanca, and relatively few towns of medium size. It seems certain that the census of 1970 will reveal a structure basically similar to this, though with considerably more small and very small towns. What may well have changed is the proportion of the total urban population contained in each bracket. In 1960 69.6 per cent of the urban population was to be found in the ten largest towns, 26.8 per cent in the 5,000–100,000 range, and 3.6 per cent in towns with less than 5,000 inhabitants. Casablanca itself accounted for one-third of Morocco's urban population. Estimates made in 1967, however, suggest that the ten largest towns contained 67 per cent of the urban population, and Casablanca 28 per cent, with a correspondingly higher share in both small and medium-sized towns. These figures could owe something to the government's strenuous efforts to decentralize industries, but this may be wishful thinking.

The rapid urbanization of Morocco can be explained in the first place by the high rate of natural increase of the urban Moslem population. It has been mentioned that the urban population increased by 4.8 per cent per annum from 1952 to 1960 and that today the rate has risen to 5 per cent. With high birth rates of 45–50 per thousand and death rates declining to 18.7 per thousand in 1960, the population as a whole has maintained rates of increase from 2.8 per cent to 3 per cent per annum during the period since 1952. The urban population, however, has registered higher rates of natural increase largely because of lower death rates. Thus in 1962 the urban death rate was 14.8 per thousand and the rate of increase was put at 3.2 per cent (Noin, 1968). It is therefore reasonable to attribute approxi-

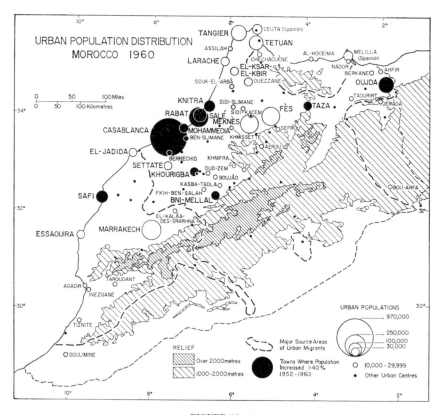

FIGURE 17.4

mately two-thirds of the overall increase in urban dwellers during the last
two decades to natural increase rather than migration, although much of
the high natural increase rate is attributable to recent migrants in the
reproductive age groups. During the intercensal period 1952–60 nearly
one-third of all towns with over 10,000 inhabitants grew at rates approximately in accordance with natural increase. Some of these, it is true, lost
Europeans and Jews during the period and might otherwise have achieved
increases above normal. Marrakech and Fès among others actually registered growth rates below the national rate of increase, and have been
described as 'declining cities' as a result (Awad, 1964).

Any increase in the number of urban dwellers not accounted for by
natural increase is largely the product of migration from rural areas.
While migrants have contributed about one-third of the national increase
in the urban population, their importance varies from town to town.
Since the natural rate of increase is comparable in all urban centres in
Morocco, the fastest growing towns are those receiving the greatest number of migrants (Fig. 17.4). Not all these are rural migrants; the 'declining

cities' referred to above undoubtedly lost Moslem citizens to other towns, as well as Jews and Europeans overseas.

Rural-urban migration

Rural–urban migration was stimulated in Morocco during the early years of the Protectorate by the familiar myth of wealth in the towns established by the Christians, as well as by four famines in 1913, 1921, 1928 and 1937, but it was only in 1936 that the movement was fully appreciated when the census revealed that 25,000 migrants were reaching the towns each year, 60 per cent of the annual increase of the rural population. The level of migration subsequently rose to about 30,000 per annum and remained at this level until 1952, but by 1960 it had risen to 45–50,000. Numbers have risen again since 1960, possibly to as many as 80,000 per annum according to official estimates. However, in spite of the sharp increase in absolute numbers, these figures actually represent a declining proportion of the annual increase of the rural population. Rural–urban migration today only absorbs about one-third of the annual increase in rural areas compared with two-thirds in 1936, so that in Morocco as a whole it is misleading to think of a 'rural exodus' except in a few notable areas.

Two groups of towns have attracted the lion's share of rural emigrants in Morocco. By far the most important are the coastal towns of the mid-Atlantic zone including Casablanca, Mohammedia, Rabat-Salé and Knitra, which received more than half of all migrants between 1952 and 1960, one-third settling in Casablanca. Indeed from 1936 to 1952 Casablanca, Rabat-Salé, and Knitra also took in more migrants than any other Moroccan city except Meknès, and the signs are that the trend continued in 1969. The reasons for the massive influx into these towns are not difficult to find. All enjoy the advantages of centrality and good access to the most populous and productive hinterland in Morocco. The French built a fine artificial harbour at Casablanca to facilitate export of minerals and vegetables, and made Rabat their capital city thus generating a large services sector. Besides these positive advantages, creating a relatively large demand for labour, the Casablanca–Knitra region also happens to be the most obvious focal point for migrants from parts of southern Morocco which have poor resources and an established tradition of temporary migration. The number of migrants to these towns, hardly surprisingly, has far exceeded the number of jobs available and a high proportion remain unemployed or under-employed. In spite of this, the majority who reach the towns remain there permanently. Housing has also been unable to keep pace with the population growth in these towns and Casablanca, Rabat-Salé, Knitra and Mohammedia possess the most extensive *bidonvilles* in Morocco. Those around Casablanca are incomparably the largest, accommodating over 150,000 persons, but on the other hand a much higher proportion of the inhabitants of Knitra and Mohammedia live in *bidon-villes*. Casablanca still receives some 25,000 migrants each year.

The second group of towns receiving large numbers of rural migrants comprises two dozen or so centres with over 10,000 inhabitants in various parts of Morocco, all of which have enjoyed a measure of economic prosperity for a variety of reasons. They include for example Oujda, capital of eastern Morocco, the mining towns of Khouribga and Jerada, the sardine port of Safi and several important regional centres such as Bni Mellal, Khmissètte and Meknès. Together these towns have probably absorbed over a quarter of the rural migrants in recent years. The rest can be assumed to have gone to a large number of small towns. As a rule, small towns attract predominantly local countrymen and the larger towns migrants from greater distances. Mining towns in particular make surprisingly little use of local labour, as has been shown in some excellent studies on the subject (Trystram, 1957; Prothero, 1965). Thus the mines of the north-east (iron, lead, coal) rely on large numbers of Chleuhs from south-west Morocco, and the manganese mines of the High Atlas are worked almost entirely by migrants from the eastern Rif in northern Morocco.

Figure 17.4 indicates the major source areas of rural migrants at the present time, embracing the following six regions:

(1) The oases of Arid Morocco, including the Draa valley, the Tafilalt and Figuig in the east.
(2) The Sous basin and some neighbouring parts of the High and Anti-Atlas.
(3) The Atlantic plains of Doukkala and Chaouïa south and south-west of Casablanca.
(4) The high interior plains of Tadla and Srarhna.
(5) The Rif Mountains and the Pre-Rif to the south.
(6) The High Plateau of eastern Morocco.

It is interesting that these six regions, whose importance is generally recognized by all writers on the subject, correspond fairly closely with major source areas identified on the basis of the 1952 census by Petit and Castet-Barou (1956). Their method was to assume a uniform rate of population growth throughout Morocco and to calculate a theoretical increase for each administrative unit for the period 1936–52, any shortfall being attributed to emigration. In spite of its obvious methodological weaknesses, their work broadly confirmed a familiar pattern; two-thirds of rural migrants were from regions south of Casablanca. So, too, Montagne (1951) studying migrants in certain large towns concluded that 40 per cent were from southern Morocco, 53 per cent from the Atlantic plains (which he took to include parts of the Sebou basin), and 7 per cent from elsewhere. More recent enquiries agree with Montagne to a very large extent, though migrants from northern Morocco are undoubtedly more numerous than fifteen or twenty years ago (Buy, 1966). In terms of absolute numbers and their impact on the towns, the densely populated Atlantic plains and the Sous basin can be assumed to yield a high proportion of rural migrants. However their social and economic importance in the source regions tends to be greater where populations are less dense. In some areas of the south, for example, four-fifths of the adult male population may be away in the cities, and their remittances are indispensable to the maintenance of subsistence levels.

The most fundamental cause of rural–urban migration in Morocco is the poverty and population pressure in the regions from which most of the migrants are drawn. The migration of southerners in particular may well be the same movement in modern guise which has in every epoch, drawn tribesmen of the south northwards in search of better land and a new life (Montagne, 1951). In recent times the movement took the form of complex patterns of temporary migration, including that of masons, miners, artisans and shopkeepers with their families to the towns of the Atlantic coast, and the migration of farm workers to the Tadla and Chaouïa plains and elsewhere. Locally, but not everywhere, temporary migration has today given way to permanent migration as the population has increased and pressure on land has become more acute. The plains of Doukkala and Chaouïa are two areas where population pressure is the prime cause of migration; the same may be said of the Tadla and Srarhna regions.

Against this background of a harsh environment and rising population may be set a host of contributory factors in the process of rural–urban migration. Two of these are worth stressing. First, the fact that 32.9 per cent of families living by agriculture in Morocco own no land of their own, and 41.3 per cent own less than two hectares provides sufficient reason for many, not only in the south, to leave the land (Noin, 1968). Secondly, for those fortunate enough to find work in the towns the rewards are a real attraction. A mineworker, for example, can earn in a month what he might have scraped together in twelve as a peasant farmer, and for thousands of country dwellers this offers a bright alternative to irregular harvests.

Overseas migration must be mentioned briefly. Fewer Moroccans now find work overseas than in Spanish and French times, but the number of countries involved has increased. The Ministry of Labour has signed labour conventions with West Germany, Belgium, France and Libya, whereby Morocco provides an agreed number of workers, contracted for a year at a time. Most of these are unskilled, among them many miners and agricultural labourers. In 1968 there were 14,000 Moroccans in these countries, and in addition about the same number in countries with whom no formal arrangement exists, including Holland, Spain and Gibraltar. Moroccans overseas are not numerically important, but according to the Bank of Morocco their remittances in 1966 exceeded for the first time

Moroccan payment of expatriate civil servants and technical assistance personnel.

Conclusion

During the next decade the population of Morocco will almost certainly increase more rapidly than at present. One forecast is that in the early 1970's the death rate will fall below 15 per thousand and the birth rate will rise to over 50 per thousand. Meanwhile fertility rates (the average number of live births per woman of child-bearing age was 6.7 in 1962) are not likely to decline significantly. The result could be a natural increase rate of 3.5 per cent, among the world's highest. The economic implications of such an increase are obvious. With an increasing proportion of the community in the non-productive age groups, more of current output must go to current consumption, leaving less for investment. Additional public expenditure will be required on health and education, while accelerating urbanization will create an urgent need for more housing. Over half a million children will leave school each year, about one-third of whom will be actively seeking employment, while in certain rural areas man–land ratios will reach critical levels. In other words 'it will be very difficult to maintain present economic standards, let alone achieve the sort of growth needed to provide self-sustaining take-off' (International Bank, 1966).

Largely as a result of the recommendations of the International Bank, in 1966 the Moroccan Government invited the Ford Foundation to implement a family-planning campaign. But in spite of an inquiry conducted among urban women indicating that a surprisingly high proportion were favourably disposed to the idea of contraception, the campaign has had disappointing results so far. Only a few thousand women have sought advice and the number has not increased from year to year. Possibly more centres are needed, or a more vigorous propaganda campaign, but whatever the reason, it seems clear that family-planning is not going to make a significant contribution to solving Morocco's economic problems for a very long time indeed.

REFERENCES

AWAD, H. (1964) 'Morocco's expanding towns', *Geographical Journal*, 130, pp. 49–64.

BREIL, J. (1947) 'Quelques aspects de la situation démographique au Maroc', *Bulletin Economique et Social du Maroc*, No. 35, 133–47.

BUY, J. (1966) 'Bidonville et ensemble moderne: approche sociologique de deux populations de Casablanca', *Bulletin Economique et Social du Maroc*, No. 101–102, pp. 71–121.

CHOURAQUI, A. (1965) *Les Juifs de L'Afrique du Nord entre L'Orient et L'Occident.*

COMITE NATIONAL DE GEOGRAPHIE DU MAROC (1963) *Atlas du Maroc*, Rabat.

DESPOIS, J. (1964) *L'Afrique du Nord*, Paris.

DIVISION DU PLAN ET DES STATISTIQUES, RABAT (1968) *Situation Economique, 1967.*

EISENBETH, M. (1952) *Les Juifs de L'Afrique du Nord*, Algiers.

INTERNATIONAL BANK (1966) *The Economic Development of Morocco*, Baltimore.

LE COZ, J. (1961) 'Premiers résultats du recensement démographique de 1960', *Notes Marocaines*, No. 15, pp. 31–5.

MAGHREB (1968) 'Les Juifs d'Afrique du Nord. Leur situation et leurs problèmes en 1968', *Maghreb, Etudes et Documents*, No. 27, pp. 24–36.

MARTIN, J. et al. (1964) *Géographie du Maroc*, Paris.

MONTAGNE, R. (ed.) (1951) *Naissance du Prolétariat Marocain*, Paris.

NOIN, D. (1962) 'La population du Maroc', *L'Information Géographique*, 26, pp. 1–12.

NOIN, D. (1965) 'La population du Maroc en 1965', *Revue de Géographie du Maroc*, 11, pp. 99–101.

NOIN, D. (1968) 'L'urbanisation du Maroc', *L'Information Géographique*, 32, pp. 69–81.

PETIT, J. C. et CASTET-BAROU, R. (1956) 'Contribution à l'étude des mouvements de la population marocaine musulmane et de l'exode rural', *Bulletin Economique et Social du Maroc*, No. 68, pp. 421–58.

PROTHERO, R. M. (1965) *Migrants and Malaria*, London.

SERVICE CENTRAL DES STATISTIQUES, RABAT (1965) *Résultats du Recensement de 1960*, Vols. I et II.

SPANISH INFORMATION SERVICE (1962) *Spain*, Madrid.

STEWART, C. F. (1964) *The Economy of Morocco*, Cambridge, Mass.

TRYSTRAM, J. P. (1957) *L'Ouvrier Mineur au Maroc*, Paris.

UNITED NATIONS (1956) *Demographic Yearbook.*

Index

Abbasid Empire, 97, 102, 108, 112
Achaeans, 161
administrative towns, 56, 86, 116, 227, 238, 302, 303, 378, 416
age composition or structure, 17, 20, 21, 58–60, *59*, 70, 73, *74*, 99, 127, 140, 154,
    188, 198, 209–11, *210*, 224–5, 229, 236, 248–51, *250*, 252, 254, 259, *261*,
    262, 266–8, 270, 271, 291, 292, *294*, 294–5, 304, 310, 313, 332, 334, 343,
    358, 368, 374, 379–80, 385, *391*, 394, 398–9, 405, *408*
agriculture, 26, 28, 37, 46, 49, 51, 52, 53, 56, 59, 60, 61–2, 65–6, 68, 74, 75,
    79–81, 82, 88, 92, 94, 99, 101, 104, 106, 110–15, 116, 125, 134–5, 137–40,
    140–1, 145, 148–9, 156–8, 161, 164, 168–9, 171, 173, 174, 175, 179, 180, 193,
    198, 203–5, 206, 207, 216–18, 226, 229, 230, 232–3, 235, 258, 268, 279–80,
    282–3, 286–7, 298, 300–1, 303, 305, 307–10, 311, 316, 317–18, 320–5, 328,
    331, 334, 335–6, 337, 349, 353, 361, 363–4, 369, 382, 383, 388, 400, 408,
    411–12, 413–15, 421
agricultural land, abandonment of, 42, 78, 111, 114, 149, 323
    extension of, 48, 65–6, 84, 135–6, 138, 139–40, 171, 299, 300–1, 303, 307–10,
    309, 312–13, 316, 318, 321
Ahmedis, 191
Alawi Moslems, 22, 141–2
altitudinal zonation, 22, 278–80
ancient cities, 28, 84
Arabic, 57–8, 72, 99, 101, 104, 107, 108, 142, 270, 348, 381–2, 384, 407
Arabs, 22, 71, 72, 82, 99, 105–6, 141, 146, 161, 183, 187, 188, 190–1, 193, 196,
    206, 212, 246, 264, 267, 270
    Arab conquests, 99, 104, 107, 348, 407, 409
    Arab–Israeli conflict, 108, 159, 182–3, 185, 198–200, 203, 205–6, 212, 215,
    247–8, 291, 303, 311, 355
    Arab World, 17, 145, 182, 185, 224, 249, 349, 369, 404
Armenian Catholics, 107, 149, *151*
Armenian Orthodox, *see* Gregorians
Armenians, 22, 42, 58, 71, 72, 100, 107, 141–2, 149, 163, 170, 175
Assyrians, 22, 71, 72, 100, 107, 141, 170
Azeri, 72

Bahais, 72, 191
Bakhtiari, 72, 82

424